In Memory of

Antonio Paños (aged 40), Pascual Picapeu (aged 37), Mariano Ortega (aged 11), Pascual Vicente (aged 66), Tomasa Sevilla (aged 31), Antonio Lapiedra (aged 32), Francisco Fuertes (aged 60), María Sanz (aged 28), María Josefa Fray (aged 52), Francisco Alfayer (aged 38), Juan Pedradas (aged 64), Manuel Candao (aged 56), Tomasa Ibáñez (aged 50), Celestina Jordán (aged 23), José Fuertes (aged 38), Pablo Fernández (aged 58), José Fuentes (aged 28), Manuel Castillo (aged 60), Juana Alfayed (aged 50), Javiera Navarro (aged 32), Antonio Pedrejas (aged 36), Simona Jordán (aged 54), Joaquina Fuertes (aged 19), María Pena (aged 67) and all the other forgotten victims of the Peninsular War. *Requiescant in Pacem.*

PENINSULA
EYEWITNESS

PENINSULAR EYEWITNESSES

THE EXPERIENCE OF WAR
IN SPAIN AND PORTUGAL
1808-1813

CHARLES ESDAILE

Pen & Sword
MILITARY

First published in Great Britain in 2008 by
Pen & Sword Military
an imprint of
Pen & Sword Books Ltd
47 Church Street
Barnsley
South Yorkshire
S70 2AS

ISBN: 978 1 84415 191 2

Typeset in Ehrhardt by Pen & Sword Books Ltd

Printed and bound in England by CPI UK

Pen & Sword Books Ltd incorporates the imprints of:
Pen & Sword Aviation, Pen & Sword Maritime, Pen & Sword Military,
Wharncliffe Local History, Pen & Sword Select, Pen & Sword Military Classics,
Leo Cooper, Remember When, Seaforth Publishing and Frontline Publishing.

For a complete list of Pen & Sword titles please contact:
Pen & Sword Books Limited
47 Church Street, Barnsley, South Yorkshire, S70 2AS, England
E-mail: enquiries@pen-and-sword.co.uk
Website: www.pen-and-sword.co.uk

Contents

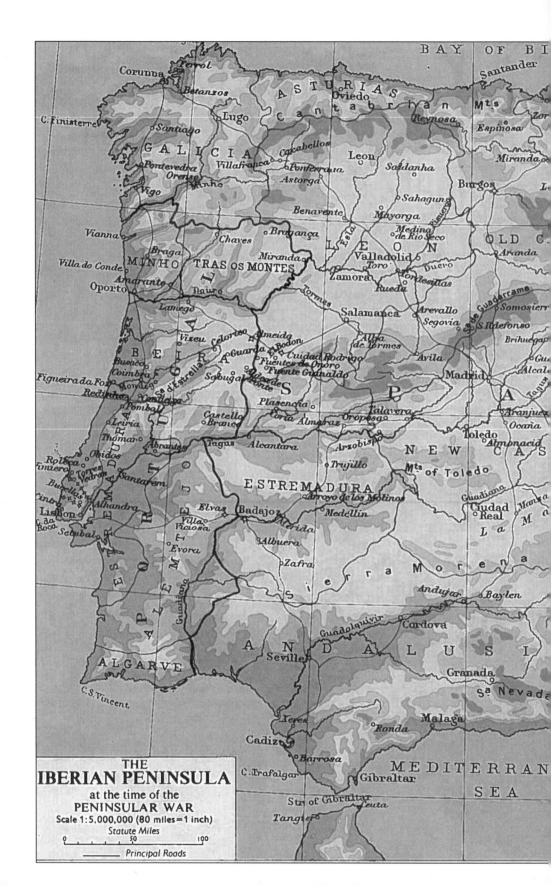

BAY OF BI

Santander

Corunna
Ferrol
Betanzos
ASTURIAS
Oviedo
Cantabrian Mts
Reynosa
Espinosa
Zor

C. Finisterre
Santiago
Lugo
GALICIA
Cacabellos
Leon
Saldanha
Miranda

Pontevedra
Orense
Villafranca
Ponferrada
Astorga
Burgos
L

Vigo
Minho
Benavente
Sahagun

Mayorga
Medina
de Rio Seco
OLD C.

Vianna
Chaves
Bragança
LEON
Valladolid
Aranda

Braga
Miranda
Toro
Ducro

Villa do Conde
MINHO
TRAS OS MONTES
Zamora
Rueda
Tordesillas

Amarante
Douro
Tormes
Salamanca
Arevallo
Segovia
de Guadarrama
Somosierr

Oporto
Laviego
Vizeu
Celorico
Almeida
Bodon
Alba
de Tormes
Avila
S.Ildefonso
Brihuega

Figueira da Foz
Busaco
Coimbra
BEIRA
Guarda
Ciudad Rodrigo
Fuentes de Onoro
Fuente Guinaldo
Madrid
Gu
Alcal

Redinha
Mondego
Sobugal
Plasencia
Oropesa
Talavera
Aranjuez
Ocaña

Pombal
Leiria
Castello
Branco
Corta Almaraz
Arzobis
Toledo
Almpnacid

Thomar
Abrantes
Tagus
Alcantara
NEW
CAS

Rolica
Vimiero
Obidos
Torres Vedras
Santarem
Trujillo
Mts of Toledo

Burellos
Cintra
Alhandra
ESTREMADURA
Arroyo de los Molinos
Guadiana
Ciudad Real
Manza
M
La

Lisbon
C. da Roca
Setubal
Elvas
Badajoz
Villa Viciosa
Evora
Medellin
Merida
Albuera

Zafra
Sierra Morena
Andujar
Baylen

ALGARVE
Guadiana
Cordova
Sevilla
ANDALUSI

C.S. Vincent
Guadalquivir
Granada
Sa Nevada

Jerez
Ronda
Malaga

Cadiz
Barrosa
C. Trafalgar
Gibraltar
MEDITERRAN

THE
IBERIAN PENINSULA
at the time of the
PENINSULAR WAR
Scale 1:5,000,000 (80 miles=1 inch)
Statute Miles
0   50   100
Principal Roads

Str. of Gibraltar
Ceuta
SEA
Tangier

Preface

Sitting in Madrid's Parque del Retiro on a warm summer morning one feels a long way from the horrors of war: the sun is shining, the flowers are in bloom, the trees are a mass of green, and there is little to be heard but the song of the birds. Some 200 years ago, however, the scene would have been a very different one. A few yards to the north of where I am sitting now would have stood the bastions and palisades of the great earthen citadel which Napoleon threw up to ensure his control of the Spanish capital, while all around me would have stretched a scene of devastation. At the beginning of the Peninsular War, the Retiro had been the gardens of the royal palace and as such had been characterised by beautiful avenues, extravagant fountains and a complex system of lakes and canals. Within a few years, however, all that had gone. As an English officer brought to Madrid in 1812 remembered, 'The gardens . . . were entirely neglected: the *jets d'eau* no longer acted, and the basins . . . were entirely empty. The gardens were strewed with fragments of sculpture and mutilated statues, that of Narcissus alone remaining perfect, because it was out of the immediate reach of the destroyers. In short, the whole edifice presented the appearance of the devastations of the Goths and Vandals rather than the visit of the encouragers and protectors of the arts as the French style themselves.'[1] Two hundred years on, with Spain on the brink of her celebrations of the bicentenary of the uprising against Napoleon, it is important that such memories are not forgotten. What occurred in the Iberian Peninsula between 1808 and 1814 was the most devastating struggle to have been witnessed in Europe since the Thirty Years' War. Out of a total population of no more than 16,000,000, at least 500,000 people died and possibly many more. Add to that the military losses – those of the French alone may have amounted to as many as 500,000 men – and one is confronted by a tragedy of epic proportions. What is more it is an experience whose scars continue to mark Spain, in particular, to this day: the bitter political divisions that make the country such a troubled place are in some ways as surely the legacy of the Peninsular War as the marks of Napoleon's cannon balls that pepper the landmark triumphal arch known as the Puerto de Alcalá.

Spain and Portugal's struggle against Napoleon, then, is still very much a live issue. But what does this particular book have to offer the reader? Over the past twenty-five years or more, I have written about the Peninsular War in many guises. I have studied its historiography, its campaigns and its diplomacy; I have looked at the impact it had on Spanish society and politics; I have sought to place it in the wider context of both the Napoleonic Wars and the history of Spain; I have analysed the armies which took part on either side and the irregular combatants who gave the English language the word 'guerrilla'; and now I am even beginning to think about its archaeology. But there is one aspect of the struggle that I have never looked at, and that is its humanity. Who were the men and women who peopled this extraordinary episode in Iberian history? What were their experiences, their hopes, their fears? And, above all, perhaps, what did they suffer? Aided by the great wealth of memoirs and other material bequeathed us by the conflict, in this book I try to answer these questions. To a certain extent this task has already been undertaken in respect of the British army, but Wellington's soldiers were by no means the only participants in the Peninsular War, and, for all the privations and hardship which they endured, they were certainly by no means its chief victims. Though material is sometimes lacking, I have endeavoured to do my best to give a voice to those who previously have had none: the defenceless civilians who cowered under bombardment in towns such as Zaragoza and Tarragona, starved to death in the great famine of 1812 and were the universal prey of men in uniform, whether they were British, French, Spanish or Portuguese. It has been a humbling experience, and one that I have found deeply moving. To read, for example, the anguished words of a woman pleading for help the day before she, her husband and her young son were killed in a prison massacre is not a comfortable experience, while it is hard not to feel pain on coming across such stories as that of a little child of no more than two years old who was found by a police inspector in Madrid's Calle del Carmen late one evening in 1811: abandoned by his parents or simply lost, he had been crying in the street all day and knew only that his name was Juan. To quote Wilfred Owen, in short, 'My subject is war and the pity of war'; in addressing this theme, I have also constantly had in my mind the words of General Sherman, 'War is hell and I intend to make it so.'

In part, then, this work is a reaction against those who have portrayed the Peninsular War simply as a catalogue of battles and campaigns in which Wellington and Castaños, Soult and Marmont, move this division here and that division there. But from all this it follows that *Peninsular Eyewitnesses* is also a contribution to the Napoleon debate. One may discuss the reasons why Napoleon decided to intervene in the Iberian Peninsula *ad infinitum*, but in the end it is impossible to absolve the emperor of responsibility for the conflict, the result being that those who continue to admire Napoleon must necessarily reflect on the scenes portrayed in this book and ask themselves whether their hero still emerges unsullied. To my mind, there is but one answer, and it is my most earnest hope that this book will in some way serve to challenge those who still see Napoleon as some great benefactor of humanity, not least because it reflects the wishes of at least some of those who were there. To quote the British brigadier Robert Long, 'It would be curious to see a correct return of the casualties that have occurred on either side since the commencement of this sanguinary contest, and, having ascertained it, I should like to inscribe the totals in letters of blood on the walls of every room occupied by the demon who has occasioned it, though he would only grin, perhaps, with ferocious delight.'[2] The correct return of the casualties called for by Long will probably never be obtained, but a variety of records allow us to recover the names of at least a selection of those lost in the conflict, and one such group – the people of the little

Aragonese *pueblo* of Utebo (in 1808 its inhabitants numbered just 493) who died from illness and wounds in the second siege of Zaragoza – has been chosen to represent all those who would otherwise have no memorial.[3]

That this is not a history of the Peninsular War goes without saying. There is simply not the space to describe every encounter between the Allies and the French, and I trust that if readers want more detail they will forgive me if I refer them to my *Peninsular War: a New History*. At the same time, too, I am to some extent bound by the limits of what is available: there is more British material than French, more French material than Spanish, and more Spanish material than Portuguese (indeed, there is no Portuguese material at all: consultation with a variety of Lusitanian scholars has confirmed that Portugal did not produce even a single personal memoir). In a variety of ways, such factors cannot but dictate the shape of the book, while readers are also reminded of many of the problems that any author has to face when working with memoir material. What one gets is often something written many years after the event by men whose memories were distorted by the passage of time, and who had frequently been heavily influenced by reading histories of the conflict such as the one published by William Napier, who had a variety of axes to grind and who knew the value of a good story. No one, then, should be under the illusion that everything in these pages is necessarily 'true', and it is in fact the case that the whole issue of the 'memorialisation' of the Peninsular War – the process by which it was constructed as a historical memory – would be an excellent subject for some up-and-coming doctoral student. But, to return to *Peninsular Eyewitnesses*, the issue matters rather less than might be expected in that what is described is not so much event as experience, and in terms of memory this is something that is much more likely to stand the passage of time. This is not the end of the problems, of course – old soldiers are renowned for their tall stories – but the reader can be assured that there is nothing in these pages that is not at the very least plausible.

Another practical matter that has arisen in writing this book is the issue of language. Even in English, spelling and, especially, punctuation did not always correspond to modern forms, and for ease of reading I have had no hesitation in modernising both. As for the many passages that I have translated from French or Spanish, I have again endeavoured to render these in such a way as to make them accessible to the reader. At times this has meant reflecting the spirit of a passage rather than sticking to a literal translation, but every effort has been made to do so in a way that I felt reflected the mood and intentions of the author, and I trust that none of those involved will come back to haunt me for any errors I have committed in this respect. Very occasionally, too, a particularly rambling approach has forced the introduction of changes in the sentence order. Once again, however, this has been handled with great care, and the result has in no case altered the emphasis or meaning. Finally, there is the issue of the rendering of place names. In the original this is often erratic in the extreme, and I have for obvious reasons sought to ensure that the modern form is always used, while at the same time eliminating some of the more glaring and outdated anglicisations that litter the memoirs of Wellington's army, in defence of which I have no hesitation in recurring to the Duke's own insistence to his 'exploring officers' that place names should always be rendered accurately and in the form in use in the country concerned.

My thanks are many. At Pen & Sword, Rupert Harding has been the soul of patience, while at the same time deserving credit for the idea on which this book was based. At A.M. Heath & Co. my agent, Bill Hamilton, has never ceased to give me support and encouragement. In Spain, Jesus Maroto has as usual been the soul of generosity, as has, among others, Herminio Lafoz Rabaza. In all the libraries in which I have worked – the chief examples are the Biblióteca Nacional in Madrid, the British Library in London and the Sydney Jones Library at the University of Liverpool – the staff have been as kind as they are efficient. My employers at the University of Liverpool are owed many thanks for the travel support I have received from them, as are my colleagues for the patience with which they have endured my frequent absences. Additional travel support, meanwhile, came from the Universidad Autónoma de Barcelona via the good offices of my friend and colleague, Antonio Moliner Prada, in respect of the research project entitled 'Cultura y Sociedad en la Guerra de la Independencia' (HUM 2005–01118) funded by the Dirección General de Investigación of the Spanish Ministerio de Educacion y Cultura. Very special mention must be made, too, of the various institutions and individuals who have contributed to the plate sections: Philip Haythornthwaite, Richard Tennant, Kenneth Crumplin and Andrew Jackson have all been generous in the extreme (in which respect readers may like to know that a splendid set of photographs is available from Richard at dicksue.tennant@tesco.net, while thanks are also due here to Juliet McConnell of the National Army Museum, Concepción Ocampos of the Museo del Prado, Lt. Col. G.S. Nichol and the Trustees of the Devonshire and Dorset Regiment, the Regimental Headquarters of the Scots Guards, and the Taylor Library at Pen & Sword. Less attractive than the illustrations but just as useful is the index, and here I was lucky to have the help of Emily Stephens. As for the text, it would be much less elegant than it is were it not for the careful ministrations of Sarah Cook as copy-editor.

And, finally, my wife – truly the last widow of the Peninsular War – and children have continued to keep the home fires burning during my long absences 'on campaign': for them, especially, I hope that this project will prove worthwhile.

Charles Esdaile
Parque del Retiro, Madrid, May 2007

Dramatis Personae

French

Jean-Baptiste Barrès, lieutenant, Sixteenth Regiment of Light Infantry.
Pierre Baste, captain, Sailors of the Guard.
Auguste Bigarré, *aide-de-camp* to Joseph Bonaparte.
Elzéar Blaze, lieutenant, Young Guard (?).
Sébastien Blaze, pharmacist, Second Corps of Observation of the Gironde.
Thomas Bugeaud, captain, 116th Regiment of Light Infantry.
Gaspard de Clermont-Tonnerre, *aide-de-camp* to Joseph Bonaparte.
Jean-Roche Coignet, sergeant, Grenadiers of the Imperial Guard.
André Delagrave, *aide-de-camp* to General Junot.
Jean-Pierre Dellard, colonel, Sixteenth Regiment of Light Infantry.
Hippolyte d'Espinchal, captain, Second Regiment of Hussars.
Antoine Fée, pharmacist, staff, I Army Corps.
Charles François, captain, First Legion of Reserve.
Louis François Gille, quartermaster-sergeant, First Legion of Reserve.
Aymar de Gonnecourt, captain, Sixth Regiment of Cuirassiers.
Jean Grivel, captain, Sailors of the Guard.
Abel Hugo, general.
Jacques-Louis Hulot, captain, Sixteenth Regiment of Foot Artillery.
Eugène Husson, *adjutant-majeur*, Eighth Provisional Infantry Regiment.
Laure Junot, wife of General Junot.
Pierre de Lagarde, Ministry of General Police.
Louis Lagneau, surgeon, Twelfth Regiment of Dragoons.
François Lavaux, sergeant, 103rd Regiment of Line Infantry.
Louis François Lejeune, *aide-de-camp* to Marshal Berthier.
Jean-Baptiste Lemonnier-Delafosse, captain, Thirty-First Regiment of Line Infantry.
Marcellin de Marbot, *aide-de-camp* to Marshal Murat.
André François Miot de Melito, intendant of the royal household.
Joseph de Naylies, lieutenant, Nineteenth Regiment of Dragoons.
Pierre le Noble, commissary, II Army Corps.
Jean Noël, captain, First Regiment of Horse Artillery.
Charles Parquin, lieutenant, Twentieth Regiment of Light Horse.
Jean-Jacques Pelet, *aide-de-camp* to Marshal Masséna.
Maurice de Tascher, lieutenant, Twelfth Regiment of Light Horse.

British

John Aitchison, ensign, Third Regiment of Foot Guards.
George Bell, ensign, Thirty-Fourth Regiment of Foot.
Robert Blakeney, ensign, Twenty-Eighth Regiment of Foot.
Andrew Blayney, general staff.

Charles Boutflower, surgeon, Fortieth Regiment of Foot.
Robert Brindle, seminarian, Colegio de San Albano, Valladolid.
William Brooke, major, Forty-Eighth Regiment of Foot.
Thomas Browne, lieutenant, Twenty-Third Regiment of Foot.
Thomas Bunbury, ensign, Third Regiment of Foot.
Charles Cadell, ensign (?), Twenty-Eighth Regiment of Foot.
John Cooper, private, Seventh Regiment of Foot.
Edward Costello, private, Ninety-Fifth Regiment of Foot.
William Dent, surgeon, Ninth Regiment of Foot.
John Dobbs, lieutenant, Fifty-Second Regiment of Foot.
Joseph Donaldson, private, Ninety-Fourth Regiment of Foot.
John Douglas, First Regiment of Foot.
Charles Doyle, lieutenant-colonel, Eighty-Seventh Regiment of Foot.
Benjamin D'Urban, lieutenant colonel, Quartermaster General's department.
George Farmer, private, Eleventh Regiment of Light Dragoons.
Augustus Frazer, major, Royal Horse Artillery.
Alexander Gordon, captain, Fifteenth Regiment of Light Dragoons.
Alexander Gordon, *aide-de-camp* to Sir Arthur Wellesley.
William Grattan, ensign, Eighty-Eighth Regiment of Foot.
John Green, private, Sixty-Eighth Regiment of Foot.
Howell Rhys Gronow, ensign, First Regiment of Foot Guards.
James Hale, private, Ninth Regiment of Foot.
Basil Hall, lieutenant, HMS *Endymion*.
Anthony Hamilton, private, Forty-Third Regiment of Foot.
John Harris, private, Ninety-Fifth Regiment of Foot.
Peter Hawker, captain, Fourteenth Regiment of Light Dragoons.
William Hay, lieutenant, Twelfth Regiment of Light Dragoons.
George Hennell, gentleman-volunteer, Forty-Third Regiment of Foot.
James Hope, ensign, Ninety-Second Regiment of Foot.
Thomas Howell, private, Seventy-First Regiment of Foot.
George Jackson, Foreign Office.
William Jacob, Member of Parliament.
William Keep, ensign, Twenty-Eighth Regiment of Foot.
John Kincaid, ensign, Ninety-Fifth Regiment of Foot.
William Lawrence, private, Fortieth Regiment of Foot.
John Leach, captain, Ninety-Fifth Regiment of Foot.
Charles Leslie, ensign, Twenty-Ninth Regiment of Foot.
Robert Long, general staff.
James Macarthy, captain, Fiftieth Regiment of Foot.
Benjamin Miller, sergeant, Royal Artillery.
John Mills, ensign, Second Regiment of Foot Guards.
Stephen Morley, private, Fifth Regiment of Foot.
Adam Neale, surgeon.
James Ormsby, chaplain, staff of Sir Arthur Wellesley.

John Patterson, captain, Fiftieth Regiment of Foot.
Andrew Pearson, sergeant, Sixty-First Regiment of Foot.
Robert Porter, artist.
Joseph Moyle Sherer, lieutenant, Thirty-Fourth Regiment of Foot.
George Simmons, lieutenant, Ninety-Fifth Regiment of Foot.
Harriet Slessor, British civilian, Oporto.
John Stepney, ensign, Third Regiment of Foot Guards.
William Stothert, captain (?), Third Regiment of Foot Guards.
William Swabey, lieutenant, Royal Horse Artillery.
William Tomkinson, cornet, Sixteenth Regiment of Light Dragoons.
Charles Vaughan, Fellow of All Souls' College, University of Oxford.
William Warre, *aide-de-camp* to General Beresford.
William Wheeler, private, Fifty-First Regiment of Foot.
Samuel Ford Whittingham, British liaison officer, Spanish Army of Andalucía.
George Wood, lieutenant, Eighty-Second Regiment of Foot.

Spanish
Agustín Alcaide Ibieca, inhabitant of Zaragoza.
Antonio Alcalá Galiano, student, Madrid.
José María Blanco y Crespo, teacher, Madrid.
Toribio Bustamente, government courier, Medina de Río Seco.
José Clemente Carnicero Torribio, priest, Madrid.
Faustino Casamayor, bailiff, Real Audiencia, Zaragoza.
Juan Domingo Palomar, hospital administrator, Alcalá de Henares.
Joaquín Encinas de los Arcos Zahonero, inhabitant of Salamanca.
Francisco Gallardo, procurator, Real Chancillería, Valladolid.
Juan García de León y Pizarro, senior official, Ministry of State.
Pedro Agustín Girón, lieutenant colonel, Regiment of Provincial Grenadiers of
    Andalucía.
Francisco de Paula Guervos, lieutenant, Santa Fée infantry regiment.
Antoni Perich y Viader, parish priest, Sant Jordi Desvalls.
Juan Antonio Posse, parish priest, San Andrés del Rabanedo.
Juan Manuel Sarasa, private, Zamora infantry regiment.
Luis de Villaba, colonel, First Regiment of Artillery (?).

Miscellaneous
Heinrich von Brandt, lieutenant, Second Infantry Regiment, Legion of the Vistula.
Dezydery Chlapowski, Polish Light-Horse Regiment, Imperial Guard.
Andrzej Daleki, private, Ninth Regiment of Line Infantry, army of the Grand Duchy of
    Warsaw.
Jozef Mrozinski, lieutenant (?), First Infantry Regiment, Legion of the Vistula.
Albert de Rocca, lieutenant, Second Regiment of Hussars, French army.
Auguste Schaumann, British Commissariat.
Andreas von Schepeler, Prussian exile.
Robert Semple, American adventurer.

Chapter 1

Iberia in Revolt

At the beginning of 1808 no one would have considered it possible. Spain was a docile ally of Napoleon and Portugal a country abandoned by its rulers and firmly occupied by a large French army. Yet by the end of the year the entire Iberian peninsula was in the grip of a great insurrection against the emperor and Lisbon was firmly in the hands of British troops. How this change had come about is one of the strangest stories of the entire Napoleonic period, but it is one that has been told many times elsewhere, not least by the present author. In consequence, it will here suffice to give only the barest details. In the summer of 1807 a Napoleon Bonaparte fresh from the greatest triumph of his career – the defeat of the Russians at Friedland and the subsequent negotiation of an alliance with Tsar Alexander I of Russia – received a sudden and unwelcome slap in the face. Under the very noses of a French army, a British fleet and expeditionary force attacked Copenhagen and sequestered the Danish fleet. Unable to accept this blow to his prestige and anxious in any case to find new sources of glory, Napoleon cast about for a riposte and found exactly what he wanted in the neutral but pro-British state of Portugal. With the willing assistance of the Spaniards, whose rulers were eager to reverse Spain's loss of the neighbouring kingdom in the 1640s, by October 1807 a large army was therefore bearing down on Lisbon under General Junot. But just at this very moment a major political crisis broke out in Spain. Thanks to years of war, epidemic and natural disaster, Spain was at one of the lowest ebbs in her entire history with trade and industry at a standstill and the population wracked by famine and disease. All this, meanwhile, was laid at the door of Manuel de Godoy, the extraordinary adventurer who had since the 1790s been the favourite of the king and queen, Charles IV and Maréa Luisa.

That Godoy was venal and corrupt there is no doubt, just as it is also the case that his foreign policy – in brief, temporary alliance with France – had brought with it terrible costs while at the same time failing to deliver the benefits for which he hoped. Yet he was not the villain of legend. A scion of the petty nobility, he had from the beginning faced the hostility of the great magnates, while his espousal of a variety of reforms of the type associated with the reign of King Charles III (1759-1788) had antagonised many of Spain's élites, including, not least, the Catholic Church. From the mid-1790s elements of the clergy and the aristocracy had begun to intrigue against him, while the fact that many of Godoy's reforms – for example, his abolition of bullfighting and expropriation of the lands of the Church – had had a serious impact on wide swathes of the populace made it easy for them to buttress their manoeuvres with a veneer of populism. In the first years of the nineteenth century fuel was added to the flames when the heir to the throne, Prince Ferdinand, became ever more convinced that Godoy was out to seize the throne for himself. As such, the prince, who was, to put it mildly, distinctly lacking in intelligence, was an obvious target for manipulation, and very soon a group of conspirators had in effect colonised him as a useful figurehead under whom they would be able to turn back the tide of royal reformism. However, Ferdinand was not just a tool in their hands, but also a means by which they could mobilise ever greater levels of popular support, and so in a mounting propaganda offensive the prince was made out to be a veritable 'Prince Charming' who would remedy all Spain's ills and usher in a new golden age. Yet the more hatred of Godoy was stoked up, the more it was feared that the favourite would make a bid for the throne in the wake of the death of Charles IV (something that was generally judged to be a likely occurrence given the king's age and increasing infirmity). In order further to reinforce their position, the conspirators therefore encouraged Ferdinand to make overtures to Napoleon and, in particular, seek a Bonaparte bride. The result was crisis: tipped off by person or persons unknown, Charles jumped to the conclusion that a plot was afoot to oust him and quickly had Ferdinand and his chief supporters arrested.

However much it was justified, this move proved catastrophic. In the first place, public opinion was outraged, for the whole affair was held to be a dastardly plot to get rid of Ferdinand. And, in the second, it led directly to Napoleonic intervention. Despite what has often been written, the emperor appears to have had no fixed intentions in respect of the Spanish monarchy. French troops had been pouring into northern Spain certainly, but they were primarily there to safeguard the communications of the troops who had been sent to Portugal. However, the French ruler was already gravely dissatisfied with Spain as an ally, and the discovery that the court was riven with faction was in consequence one that was most unfortunate. Political disruption in the Iberian peninsula was not something Napoleon could afford, but at the same time the idea took root in his mind that a Spain ruled by a Bonaparte monarch would be a Spain that would be able to contribute far more to the imperial war effort, while her increased naval power would enable him to get his hands on the wealth of Spanish America.

Yet even now catastrophe might have been averted. All the reports from Spain suggested that the best option would be to overthrow Charles IV and Godoy, and install Ferdinand on the throne in their stead, and there is some evidence that Napoleon was still toying with this idea as late as January 1808. At this point, however, the emperor swung decisively in favour of turning Spain into a satellite kingdom with one of his brothers on the throne. Though it is clear enough that there was nothing holding the French ruler back – his contempt for the Spanish army was as massive as his conviction that any popular resistance could be crushed with the proverbial 'whiff of grapeshot' – precisely why he reached this decision is uncertain: perhaps he simply could not resist a fresh *tour de force* of the sort that had been buttressing his power and reputation ever since 1796; perhaps, too, his hand was forced by events in the eastern Mediterranean and the Balkans where Russian pressure was forcing him inexorably into an attack on the Ottoman Empire. But, whatever the reason, at the end of February French troops suddenly seized Spain's chief border fortresses and marched on Madrid. It was truly a make-or-break moment, and, beyond that, one which Napoleon was to regret for the rest of his career.

Mutiny at Aranjuez

By the end of 1807 thousands of French troops had entered Spain. Among the men marching in the ranks of the corps commanded by General Dupont was Louis François Gille. Born in Paris on 29 February 1788 to parents who are described as bourgeois rentiers, Gille had been a rather sickly boy who had entertained dreams of becoming an actor, but in April 1807 he was conscripted into the army, becoming a private in the 1eme Légion du Reserve. Soon promoted fourrier (quartermaster-sergeant), in December of the same year he found himself in Spain. An honest observer, he was later to admit that the onward march of the occupation forces was accompanied with much disorder:

> Pancorbo is situated at the foot of two high mountains. A fort crowns the higher of the two and commands the road. The sight piqued my curiosity, and, despite my fatigue, I decided to pay it a visit. The rocks were covered with snow and it was only with the greatest difficulty that I managed to reach the summit. Inside the fort I found . . . several cannon and piles of cannon balls. If it should ever come to war, I could see that it would be very advantageous to hold the position. On the side that overlooks the road, the mountain forms an absolute precipice . . . while on the side that overlooks the town the slope is still so steep that when a group of soldiers, who had doubtless climbed up to that spot for the same reason as me, threw some of the cannon balls down the hill for fun . . . they picked up such a speed that one of them . . . knocked flat one of the houses. Immediately the whole town was in an uproar, while, as for us, the crash put an immediate end to our promenade.[4]

Very soon, then, Gille began to encounter signs of hostility:

> I was billeted on my own in a house outside [Vitoria]. I only saw a woman there when I went there to deposit my things, but, coming back from an errand a while later, I encountered a brown-skinned man with a thick beard and a pair of black eyes that were shadowed by bristling eyebrows. He was occupied in fitting a new flint to a fowling piece, and appeared to be a day labourer. He had a hard air about him, while his manner was not at all pleasant: watching me out of the corner of his eye, he turned to his wife, and appeared to ask her what he should do with me. We spent the evening in silence sitting by the fire: it was impossible to engage them in conversation as at this point I had no knowledge of their language. The time to turn in having arrived, I left my hosts, and went to the room which they had given me. I was not frightened, but even so I thought that I had better take some precautions. The bed was . . . very heavy, and I could not move it, but I stacked all the chairs that were in the room in front of the door (unfortunately, this could not be locked from inside) in such a manner that no one could come in without knocking them over and waking me up on account of the noise. My musket and sword, meanwhile, I placed beside me. Nor did I have any reason to regret all this. I had hardly been asleep two hours when I was awoken with a start by the noise of the chairs I had placed against the door being knocked over. The Spaniard whose features had inspired little confidence in me was coming into my room. In one hand he held a lantern, while the other one was hidden in the cloak in which he was swathed. I lay perfectly quiet,

but in my hand I held my sabre, which I had had the sense to take out of its scabbard. Having taken a turn around the room – I think he was looking for my weapons – the Spaniard approached my bed and made as if to withdraw his hand from beneath the blanket. At once I sprang up and shouted, 'What do you want?' Immediately he stopped dead, and frightened by my expression, mumbled a few words in Spanish which I did not understand. With my sword I pointed to the door, and he did not hang about. Piling the chairs up against the door again, I went back to bed and soon fell asleep . . . but after that, a soldier of the company always lodged with me.[5]

If the Spaniards were feeling sore, it was not surprising, for the presence of a French army was never easy. Among the witnesses to the realities of occupation was Robert Brindle, a young seminarian from Lancashire who was studying at the college which the English Catholic Church had maintained at Valladolid since the late sixteenth century:

The soldiers were quartered in private houses and brought distress and misery into every family. Their right to anything which they chose to covet few had the hardihood to call into question. If complaint were made, it [had to] be proffered to a French officer, and insult or an additional grievance was the usual result. If any man dared to raise his hand in defence of his wife and children, he was immediately hurried to the prison, and before the lapse of many hours consigned to the gallows. Daily instances occurred where the husband generously sacrificed himself in defending the virtue of his wife and children. Such was our state in time of peace.[6]

In so far as the conduct of the French army was concerned, it did not help that, in a gesture typical of the extreme over-confidence with which Napoleon approached the Spanish venture, the troops he had dispatched across the Pyrenees were in large part raw recruits. Another of the men commanded by General Dupont was Sébastien Blaze, a native of Avignon and the second son of a family of some property and status who had become a pharmacist in the army's medical services:

I joined the Second Corps of Observation of the Gironde at Valladolid . . . On 15 March we conducted manoeuvres in a plain outside the town, and the divisional commander General Malher was killed by a ramrod which a soldier had carelessly left in the barrel of his musket. An inspection was immediately made of all the arms of the regiment that had fired the fatal volley to discover the culprit, and it was found that no fewer than eighteen ramrods had been shot away in the same fashion.[7]

As yet, however, friction remained relatively low-level. Most Spaniards were still convinced that the French had come to Spain to overthrow the hated Godoy and replace Charles IV with Ferdinand VII. For an insight into the thinking of the educated classes, we can turn to José Clemente Carnicero Torribio, an ecclesiastic living in Madrid:

The French troops continued to enter in ever larger numbers. After their treacherous plans were revealed, it was often said that they should not have been allowed to pass. But who could have stopped them? The army was split up all over the place, while public opinion had been thoroughly alienated by the predominance of Godoy. All that an attempt to block the way would have done would therefore have been to give Napoleon a pretext to declare war on Spain and send the full weight of his forces against her so as to achieve her conquest. And, far from waging a determined war against him, the people of Spain would have been so anxious to overthrow the yoke of Godoy that they would have seconded his efforts. In any case, we were being told that the French had come to protect Ferdinand, of which it was held to be proof that the emperor had offered him the hand of one of his nieces in marriage . . . In the year 1801 Napoleon had again sent a large army to conquer Portugal. This had got as far as Salamanca and yet, as soon as he changed his mind, he withdrew the troops concerned without molesting the Spaniards in the slightest. Why would the same thing not happen on this occasion? In so far as the troops in Castile were concerned, the newspapers gave out on the one hand that their purpose was to aid the ones that had been sent to Portugal, and on the other . . . that it was to escort him when he came to . . . Madrid to . . . bring down Godoy and marry his niece to Prince Ferdinand. These conjections, meanwhile, were strengthened by the fact that Godoy was known to be planning to move out of his magnificent palace and selling much of the exquisite furniture which had filled its rooms . . . These ideas were so commonplace that little girls in the poorer quarters were singing rhymes which attributed all these removals to the coming of Napoleon.[8]

Along with the rest of Dupont's forces, Blaze soon found himself bearing down on Madrid. When the threat to the capital brought about a military coup that placed Ferdinand on the throne the joy of the populace knew no bounds. Louis François Lejeune was a 32-year-old officer of Alsatian stock who had made a great name for himself as an artist and had been sent to Spain to report on the situation for Napoleon's chief-of-staff, Marshal Berthier:

The troops of the emperor had been received as friends throughout the peninsula . . . Everywhere our soldiers were welcomed as liberators, and all along my route I found towns, villages and even isolated houses prepared to celebrate the expected arrival of the emperor. On every road laurel branches had been cut down to form triumphal arches beneath which the emperor, the redresser of the grievances of the people, was to pass . . . The Spaniards had long been discontented at the position occupied by Manuel de Godoy . . . Spanish sailors had shed their blood in our service at Trafalgar, a Spanish army under the Marqueés de la Romana had fought side-by-side with the French in . . . Germany, and the loyal populace, who now received us as if we were their brothers, impatiently awaited the day when the emperor should arrive at Madrid. They hoped that he would replace the hated minister and restore the royal authority to Charles IV, or place it in the hands of his son, Ferdinand.[9]

That none of this was wishful thinking is suggested by the wild scenes that had greeted the fall of Godoy. One eyewitness here was an inhabitant of Salamanca named Joaquín Encinas de los Arcos Zahonero:

On 22 March there arrived the – for many reasons – great news of the serious disturbances that had . . . put an end to the primacy of D. Manuel de Godoy. In the afternoon . . . the students rioted and came to the Plaza [Mayor] where they encountered the governor of this city, the Marqués de Zayas. After spending some time throwing stones at the medallion of Godoy which Zayas had put up . . . with great pomp in August 1806, they forced him to fetch a pickaxe and smash it with his own hands . . . Once that was out of the way, they demanded that he should authorise a bullfight . . . which he conceded, and caused the bells of the . . . university and the cathedral to be rung. So crazy were they that that same night they went to the house of the Archdeacon of Salamanca, who was a cousin of Godoy, and there committed a thousand stupidities. The only reason nothing worse was done was that the Archdeacon happened to be away, but even so they still broke all his windows.[10]

In Madrid, meanwhile, there had been similar attacks on those associated with Godoy. José María Blanco y Crespo, who later went into exile in England and became famous as Joseph Blanco White, was a 32-year-old priest from Seville who had the previous year secured a teaching post at a model school established in Madrid by Manuel de Godoy:

Night had scarcely come on when a furious mob invaded the house of Don Diego, the favourite's younger brother. The ample space which the magnificent Calle de Alcalá leaves at its opening into the Prado, of which that house forms a corner, afforded room not only for the operations of the rioters, but for a multitude of spectators, of whom I was one myself. The house having been broken into and found deserted, the whole of the rich furniture it contained was thrown out at the windows. Next came down the very doors and fixtures of all kinds which, made into an enormous pile with tables, bedsteads, chests of drawers and pianos, were soon in a blaze that, but for the stillness of the evening, might have spread to the unoffending neighbourhood. Having enjoyed this splendid and costly bonfire, the mob ranged themselves in a kind of procession, bearing lint torches taken from the numerous chandlers shops which are found at Madrid, and directed their steps to the house of the Prince [of] Branciforte, Godoy's brother-in-law. The magistrates, however, had by this time fixed a board on the doors both of that and Godoy's own house, giving notice that the property both of the favourite and his near relations had been confiscated by the new king. This was sufficient to turn away the mob from the remaining objects of their fury, and without any further mischief they were contented with spending the whole night bearing about lighted torches and drinking at the expense of the wine retailers, whose shops . . . are the common resort of the vulgar. The riot did not cease with the morning. Crowds of men and women paraded the streets the whole day with cries of 'Long live King Ferdinand! Death to Godoy!' The whole garrison of Madrid were allured out of their barracks by women bearing pitchers of wine in their hands, and a procession was seen about the place in the afternoon, where the soldiers, mixed with the people, bore in their firelocks the palm branches which, as a protection against lightning, are commonly hung at the windows.[11]

Celebrations came to a head on 23 March when Ferdinand rode into Madrid from Aranjuez as *el rey deseado*. Antonio Alcalá Galiano was a 19-year-old student and the son of a leading naval officer who had been killed at Trafalgar:

> Mounted on horseback, Ferdinand was accompanied by only a very small suite. He was followed by the Guardias de Corps but his way was not lined with troops in the fashion that is usual when the king and queen arrive in the city or put in an appearance at some public ceremony. However, what was lacking in pomp was made up by the rejoicing of the crowd. This reached a pitch that was higher than anything that can possibly be imagined. In truth, in all the different scenes of popular enthusiasm that I have witnessed, nothing . . . has ever equalled those which I now describe. The cheers were loud, repeated and delivered with . . . eyes full of tears of pleasure, kerchiefs were waved . . . from balconies with hands trembling with pleasure . . . and not for a moment did the passion . . . or the thunderous noise of the joyful crowd diminish.[12]

However, the joy of Ferdinand's accession proved short-lived, for just at this moment Napoleon's pincers snapped shut. Recently sent to Spain as the head of the French forces there, Marshal Murat refused to recognise Ferdinand as King of Spain, while Charles IV was encouraged to protest against the abdication that had been forced on him at Aranjuez and declare it null and void. With father and son ranged against one another, the emperor was in a perfect position to intervene, and so the entire royal family was summoned to a conference with him, along with the unfortunate Godoy. Initially, it was given out that Napoleon was coming to Spain and that the meeting would take place in Burgos or Vitoria, but in fact the French ruler had resolved to hold it at Bayonne. In short, the Bourbon dynasty was riding into a trap. An eyewitness to the movements of Ferdinand in particular was Louis Lejeune:

> A rumour began to spread among us that the emperor meant to place the crown of Spain on the head of one of his own brothers or generals, and the event proved that the rumour was not without foundation . . . Murat was now at Madrid at the head of an army, and in compliance with the wish of the emperor he lost no time in urging the Prince of Asturias [i.e. Ferdinand VII] to go to Bayonne. That prince . . . set off accompanied by . . . an escort so strong . . . that I could not help suspecting that he was to be taken prisoner . . . I had the honour of saluting the prince . . . as he rode through Burgos . . . I was sorely tempted to give him a private hint to escape . . . but to save a prince who inspired me with very little personal interest I should have had to betray the emperor. The situation was very grave and with deep regret I confined myself to my narrow round of duties, leaving deeper issues in the hands of Providence. On his arrival at Vitoria the prince began to suspect the trap prepared for him and under various pretexts put off his departure. But the task of taking him to Bayonne had been confided to a man who knew what he was about, and when the unhappy prince realised the impossibility of escaping from his escort, he allowed himself to be led whither they would without resistance.[13]

Dos de Mayo

By the end of April excitement was at fever pitch. Among those who recorded the atmosphere in Madrid was José María Blanco y Crespo:

> The wildest schemes for the destruction of the French . . . were canvassed almost in public and with very little reserve. Nothing, indeed, so completely betrays our present ignorance as to the power and efficiency of regular troops as the projects which were circulated in the capital for an attack on the French corps which still paraded every Sunday morning in the Prado. Short pikes headed with a sharp cutting crescent were expected to be distributed to the spectators who used to range themselves behind the cavalry. At one signal the horse were to be houghed [hamstrung] with these instruments and the infantry attacked with poignards. To remonstrate against such absurd and visionary plans or to caution their advocates against an unreserved display of hostile views, which, of itself, would be enough to defeat the ablest conspiracy, was not only useless but dangerous.[14]

At this point Charles IV's youngest son, Francisco de Paula, was still in Madrid, but on 1 May rumours spread that he, too, was to be sent to France. By dawn the next day, then, a large crowd had gathered around the royal palace. Alarmed by the growing noise – his headquarters was only a few hundred yards away – Murat ordered an officer named Auguste Lagrange to assess the situation. This, however, proved to be the proverbial red rag to a bull. With stories going around that the 6-year-old Francisco de Paula was in tears and did not want to go, Lagrange was promptly set upon. Seeing the commotion, Murat now took action. Mobilising the nearest available troops – a detachment of the Imperial Guard which he had been given as a personal escort – he ordered them to clear the scene. A few moments later a thunderous discharge rang out, and ten Spaniards lay dead or wounded on the cobbles, the rest of the crowd hastily dispersing in search of shelter. Yet the gunfire had made things worse rather than better. Within minutes, streets throughout the city were full of confused and angry citizens convinced that the French were out to massacre them. Catching up whatever weapons they could lay their hands on, they quickly fell on those Frenchmen unfortunate enough to be caught in the city (albeit there were very few, almost all Murat's 10,000 troops being encamped in the surrounding open country). Something of the atmosphere is conveyed by Alcalá Galiano:

> I was getting dressed when my mother came in looking frightened. All she said to me were the words, 'It has begun'. There was no need to say what it was she was talking about . . . In a moment, having got dressed anyhow, I was in the street . . . Scattered shots began to be heard in the distance . . . On all sides bands of people were beginning to come together, although they were armed in such a ridiculous fashion that they had to be crazy to think that they could do away with French soldiers. I joined one group that was led by a young lad who was some sort of artisan . . . and we headed for the Calle de Fuencarral. But some of them were insisting that we should go to the barracks and join the troops, and others that we should fall upon the French straight away . . . In the course of the argument, one of the men turned to me and asked me what I thought. 'I am unarmed, and am therefore going home,'

I replied . . . One of the others then swore an oath and rounded on me, but, having first taken hold of me and noted my pale complexion, my well-brought-up appearance and my boyish look . . . said to me scornfully, 'You are no good for anything.' Though probably true enough given the task that my new acquaintances had embarked upon, this remark did not please me at all, and so, being close to where I lived, I slipped away, went into my house and then came out again wearing an army bicorn . . . No sooner had I stepped into the street than I encountered an officer and asked him what was going on. At this he asked what unit I belonged to . . . To this I had to admit that I was a student, whereupon he said that I should go home. The garrison, he continued, had been ordered not just to remain aloof, but to restore order by opening fire on the rioters . . . while the French were massing in such numbers that nobody would be able to withstand them. In short, to continue on my way would bring me to a sticky end.[15]

Among the Frenchmen unlucky enough to be caught in the streets was a captain in the Marins de la Garde named Jean Grivel:

I had just crossed the little Plaza de Santo Domingo and was having a chat with our adjutant-major, who was on his way to the Post Office. I myself was on my way to the hospital, and as the two buildings are side-by-side, we decided to walk over together. We had barely gone a few yards when we heard several volleys of musketry at which point the people around us began to run in all directions. Catching hold of a passing priest by his cloak, we asked him what was going on. Seeing that we were French, however, he took to his heels with such speed that part of the cloak got torn off and was left in our hands. A little further on we came across an old Walloon Guard who said to us, 'Gentlemen, if you value your lives, hide your cockades: they are murdering your comrades.' We continued on our way, but, although we were very worried, we did not hasten our steps . . . The Spaniards must have found it a very odd sight to see two officers in full dress decked out in so much gold as to be veritable chalices calmly strolling through the streets amidst the sound of so much gunfire. We were sensible enough not to give any sign of agitation, and I am convinced that the calm we displayed saved our lives . . . At length we arrived at the hospital. An angry crowd had already massed around it and was with difficulty being held back by the picket of fifty men who formed its guard. The main door was provided with an iron grill, and we pulled this shut behind us. It was high time, as the mob had started to throw stones. We then decided that we ought to arm all the sick who could stand. The man who had the key to the armoury was therefore called, but he was unwilling to give it to us and in general played the fool. As there was not a moment to lose if we were to save the hospital, I told him to give me the key or else, but he just made faces at me, so I dealt him a . . . blow with my sabre . . . I have often regretted the necessity of having to draw my sword on so mean a fellow, but I really was doing no more than my duty: the mob were hurling themselves at the door . . . and the lives of the sick were in peril. Pretty soon a detachment of troops reached us from the Prado and restored our communications. At the head of them we encountered Colonel Fréderich of the Fusiliers de la Garde. He was attired in a dressing-gown and a round hat and armed with a sabre that he had taken from a dead trumpeter . . . for the outbreak of the riot had caught him in the bath and he had had no option but to rush out half naked . . . The verve with which we thanked this brave man can well be imagined.[16]

If Grivel and his companions survived, it was in large part due to the vigour displayed by Marshal Murat. Hardly had firing broken out than riders were galloping from his headquarters to summon help from the French camps situated at such suburban villages as El Pardo and Chamartín. Meanwhile, having quickly cleared the street in front of the royal palace, the men who had been protecting Murat's headquarters were already fighting their way towards the heart of the city. Among the men who saw them was José María Blanco y Crespo:

> My house stood not far from the palace in a street leading to . . . the best part of the town. A rush of people crying 'To arms!' conveyed to us the first notice of the tumult. I heard that French troops were firing on the people, but the outrage appeared to me both so impolitic and [so] enormous that I could not rest until I went out to ascertain the truth. I had just arrived at an opening named Plazuela de Santo Domingo, the meeting point of four large streets, one of which leads to the palace, when, hearing the sound of a French drum in that direction, I stopped with a considerable number of quiet and decent people whom curiosity kept riveted to the spot. Though a strong picket of infantry was fast advancing upon us, we could not imagine that we stood in any kind of danger. Under this mistaken notion we awaited their approach, but, seeing the soldiers halt and prepare their arms, we began instantly to disperse. A discharge of musketry followed in a few moments, and a man fell at the entrance of the street through which I was, with a great multitude, retreating from the fire. The fear of an indiscriminate massacre arose so naturally from this initial assault that everyone tried to look for safety in the narrow cross streets on both sides of the way. I hastened on towards my own house, and, having shut the front door, could think of no better expedient, in the confused state of my mind, than to make ball cartridges for a fowling piece which I kept . . . A well-dressed man had in the meantime gone down the street calling loudly on the male inhabitants to repair to an old depot of arms. But he made no impression on that part of the town. The attempt to arm the multitude at this moment was, in truth, little short of madness. In a short time after the beginning of the tumult, two or three columns of infantry entered by different gates, making themselves masters of the town. The route of the main corps lay through the Calle Mayor, where the houses, consisting of four or five storeys, afforded the inhabitants the means of wreaking their vengeance on the French without much danger from their arms. Such as had guns fired from the windows, while tiles, bricks and heavy articles of furniture were thrown by others upon the heads of the soldiers.[17]

Similar scenes, meanwhile, were witnessed by Blanco White's fellow priest, José Clemente Carnicero Torribio, when other troops reached the southern fringes of the city:

Most of the people had nothing other than knives and sticks, while the few fowling pieces that they possessed were for the most part poorly maintained and short of ammunition. Yet despite this, blind with rage and fury, some fired on the French from windows and street corners . . . others flung themselves on their very ranks . . . and still others hurled stones, pieces of furniture and kitchen utensils from the balconies, where they were joined by women armed with cauldrons of boiling water. In short, it really seemed as if there was not a single soul who was not disposed to water the streets with French blood . . . even if it should be at the cost of their own.[18]

However, with thousands of French troops encamped around the city, all the heroism in the world could not save the revolt. Among the troops hastening to restore order was Marcellin de Marbot, a 26-year-old aristocrat who had enlisted in the First Regiment of Hussars in 1799, and had in January 1808 been attached to Murat's headquarters as an *aide-de-camp*:

My orders were to bring the divisions to the Puerta del Sol, and they started at a gallop. The squadrons of the Guard . . . marched first with the Mamelukes leading. The riot had had time to increase: we were fired upon from nearly all the windows, especially the palace of the Duque de Hijar, where every [one] was lined with good shots. We lost several men there . . . but for the moment it was impossible to halt, and the cavalry rode on rapidly under a hail of bullets. In the Puerta del Sol we found . . . a huge compact crowd of armed men . . . On seeing the dreaded Mamelukes arrive, the Spaniards made some attempt at resistance, but the sight of the 'Turks' alarmed the bravest of them too much for their resolution to last long. The Mamelukes, dashing scimitar in hand into the dense mass, sent a hundred heads flying in a trice, and opened a way for the chasseurs and dragoons, who set to furiously with their sabres. The Spaniards . . . tried to escape by the many wide streets which met there . . . but they were stopped by other French columns whom Murat had bidden to assemble at that point . . . The insurgents who had fired so briskly from the Duque de Hijar's palace . . . had had the impudent boldness to remain at their post, and recommenced their fire as our squadrons returned. These, however, indignant at the sight of their comrades' bodies, penetrated into the palace . . . pitilessly massacred every insurgent that they met . . . Not one escaped and their corpses, thrown over the balconies, mingled their blood with that of the Mamelukes whom they had slaughtered.[19]

Only at the army's artillery depot was the French counter-attack met with a degree of resistance that gave it real pause. Exceptionally, a small group of soldiers led by three officers named Luis Daoiz, Pedro Velarde and Jacinto Ruíz had joined the rioters at the depot, and together they had dragged out two field guns to defend the main gates. Yet in a very short time they, too, were overwhelmed, and the French were able to restore order. Reprisals were surprisingly limited – if 113 prisoners were shot, the figure might have been much greater – but the atmosphere in the capital was none the less one of the most abject terror. Let us here again quote Blanco y Crespo:

Hearing that the tumult had ceased, I ventured out in the afternoon towards the

Puerta del Sol, where I expected to learn some particulars of the day. The cross streets which led to that place were unusually empty, but, as I came to the entrance of one of the avenues which open into that great rendezvous of Madrid, the bustle increased, and I could see . . . two pieces of cannon and a very strong division of troops. Less than this hostile display would have been sufficient to check my curiosity if, still possessed with the idea that it was not the interest of the French to treat us like enemies, I had not, like many others who were on the same spot, thought that the peaceful inhabitants would be allowed to proceed unmolested about the streets of the town. Under this impression I went on without hesitation till . . . a sudden cry of 'Aux armes!', raised in the square, was repeated by the soldiers before me, the officer giving the command to make ready. The people fled up the street in the utmost consternation, but, my fear having allowed me instantly to calculate both distances and danger, I made a desperate push towards the opening left by the soldiers, where a narrow lane, winding round the church of San Luis, put me in a few seconds out of the range of the French muskets. No firing, however, being heard, I concluded that the object of the alarm was to clear the streets at the approach of night. The increasing horror of the inhabitants, as they collected the melancholy details of the morning, would have accomplished that end without any further effort on the part of the oppressors. The bodies . . . seen in several places, the wounded that were met about the streets, the visible anguish of such as missed their relations and the spreading report that many were awaiting their fate . . . so strongly and painfully raised the apprehensions of the people that the streets were absolutely deserted long before the approach of night. Every street door was locked, and a mournful silence prevailed wherever I directed my steps . . . A night passed under such impressions baffles my feeble powers of description. A scene of cruelty and treachery exceeding all limits of probability had left our apprehensions to range at large with scarcely any check from the calculations of judgement. The dead silence of the streets since the first approach of night, only broken by the trampling of horses which now and then were heard passing in large parties, had something exceedingly dismal in a populous town, where we were accustomed to an incessant and enlivening bustle. The Madrid cries, the loudest and most varied in Spain, were missed early next morning, and it was ten o'clock before a single street door had been opened. Nothing but absolute necessity could induce the people to venture out.[20]

Far away in Bayonne, the future of the Spanish monarchy had still not been officially settled. In consequence, brought to the *chateau* of Marrac by none other than Marbot, the news of the Dos de Mayo was a most useful windfall as it afforded Napoleon all the pretext that he could need:

From Madrid to Bayonne is . . . 225 leagues, a long journey when one has to ride post with one's sword by one's side without a single quarter of an hour's rest and in a scorching heat . . . I got there on 5 May, covered with dust, at the moment when the emperor was taking an after-dinner walk in the park with the queen of Spain on his arm and Charles IV beside him . . . As soon as the emperor was informed by the *aide-de-camp* on duty that an officer had arrived with dispatches from Prince Murat, he came towards me followed by members of the Spanish royal family and asked aloud, 'What news from Madrid?' The presence of the listeners was embarrassing, and . . . I deemed it wise to do nothing but present my dispatches to the emperor and look steadily at him without answering his question. His Majesty understood me, and retired a few paces to read Murat's report. Having finished, he called me and went towards a solitary garden-walk, asking me all the time many questions about the fighting at Madrid. I could easily see that he shared Murat's opinion and considered that the victory of 2 May must put an end to all resistance in Spain. I held the contrary belief . . . but I had to confine myself to answering the emperor's questions with due respect, and I could only indirectly let him know my presentiments . . . I might, perhaps, have revealed all my thoughts, but Napoleon cut short my thoughts, exclaiming, 'Bah! They will calm down and bless me as soon as they see their country freed from the discredit and disorder into which it has been thrown by the weakest and most corrupt administration that ever existed.' After this outburst . . . Napoleon sent me back to the end of the garden to request the king and queen of Spain to come to him, and followed me slowly reading over Murat's dispatches. The ex-sovereigns came forward alone to meet the emperor, and I suppose he informed them of the fighting at Madrid, for Charles came up to . . . Ferdinand and said to him in a loud voice and in a tone of extreme anger, 'Wretch! You may now be satisfied! Madrid has been bathed in the blood of my subjects shed in consequence of your criminal rebellion against your father: may their blood be on your head!' The queen joined in heaping bitter reproaches on her son and went so far as to offer to strike him. The ladies and the officers, feeling that this distasteful spectacle was not one for them, withdrew, and Napoleon put a stop to it. Ferdinand, who had not replied by a single word to the objurgations of his parents, resigned the crown to his father that evening, less through contrition than through fear of being regarded as the author of the conspiracy which had overthrown Charles. Next day the old king . . . made over to the emperor all his rights to the throne of Spain on certain conditions . . . Thus was consummated the most iniquitous spoliation which modern history records.[21]

Insurrection

This is not the place to discuss the exact nature of the events that followed the Dos de Mayo. All that need concern us here is that the news that Ferdinand was to be removed from the throne by the French sparked off a series of conspiracies that led to insurrection. By the last week of May, indeed, almost every part of the country that was not physically occupied by the French had risen in revolt under the leadership of a variety of provincial juntas and petty military dictatorships. On the surface, it was a truly uplifting spectacle. Among the first British soldiers to observe the insurrection was a young Scottish gentleman of land-owning stock named Charles Leslie, who was an ensign in the Twenty-Ninth Foot and, as such, briefly visited the Andalusian town of Ayamonte when the brigade to which his regiment was attached stopped there en route for Portugal from Gibraltar in June 1808:

> Being the first English who had landed in Spain since the breaking out of the Patriot cause, we were received with the most enthusiastic demonstrations of joy by the inhabitants. The governor invited all the officers to an entertainment in the evening, and had provided for us billets in all the best houses. The Spanish officers, both of the army and navy, almost crushed us in their fraternal embraces and insisted on carrying us from house to house, and introducing us to all the pretty ladies in the place. These dark beauties gave us the most cordial reception, and sang patriotic songs and warlike hymns, accompanied on the guitar or piano. Some of the naval officers who had been in England repeatedly sang 'Rule Britannia' and 'God save the King!' Their admiration of England's prowess seemed unaffected. In many houses we observed busts of Mr Pitt . . . The governor's supper went off with great harmony. Mutual toasts were given, and bumpers drunk to the perpetual harmony of the two nations.[22]

In reality, however, the truth was far more murky. The fact that many of the civil and military authorities remained loyal to the instructions that had been issued both by Ferdinand VII and the council of regency which had been left behind in Madrid not to resist the French left them wide open to a purge that saw many of them murdered by mobs whipped up by ambitious rivals or subordinates, out for revenge or simply gripped by panic. Typical of the scenes that accompanied the killings were those witnessed in Ciudad Rodrigo:

> It was three o'clock in the afternoon when an extraordinary commotion was suddenly noted in the streets. Large numbers of people having quickly gathered together, this soon became an outright tumult. Throwing aside the bounds of subordination and decorum, the crowds began to shout, 'Death to the governor and the other traitors!' Prepared for this eventuality, the junta asked the bishop . . . to send emissaries to persuade the rioters to desist from their atrocious project . . . but the confusion, the shouting and the sheer density of the crowd prevented their . . . counsel from being heard . . . All was in vain, and . . . by a little past four the governor, one of his adjutants, a French merchant and the postmaster were no more.[23]

Still more graphic is the account of Robert Brindle, who was trapped in his seminary at Valladolid:

> At Valladolid the people seemed to set no bounds to their ardour . . . Arms were called for on every side, but [none] could be procured. The multitude, however, paraded the streets . . . with fowling pieces, pruning hooks and such other weapons as they could procure. From the numerous instances of treachery in those who had official situations the Spaniards suspected their best friends and truest patriots. The Captain General of the province during this time was General Cuesta. Though a true patriot and a skilful officer, yet it was impossible for him to restrain the populace from the most grievous outrages. Don Francisco Ceballos, governor of

Segovia, having been obliged to evacuate that fortress, sought refuge in Valladolid. It since appears that [Segovia] was in the worst possible state of defence [and] that any resistance would only have occasioned . . . the destruction of the town . . . But no sooner had he entered Valladolid than the cry of traitor was raised against him and in a moment the poor man was literally torn to pieces. The Captain General was a spectator of this horrid spectacle, but so far from being able to restrain the violence of the mob [that] the cry was even raised against himself, and a gallows erected for his execution if arms did not arrive before the following day . . . The Captain General had exerted his authority to prevent the English students from being obliged to quit the house, but the mob declared they would burn the college to the ground if we did not join them.[24]

But the trouble was not just confined to the murder of supposed traitors. On the contrary, inflamed by long years of misery, the populace also engaged in overt acts of social protest, this tendency being further inflamed by the continuation of many of the same old faces in the new organs of local government. Tenant farmers protested against high rents; agricultural labourers tried to occupy the land or demanded higher wages; and there was a widespread refusal to pay the tithe. Examples of such unrest are frequent, but perhaps the most dramatic comes from Castellón de la Plana. Thus:

On 19 June [1808] . . . a gang of malcontents assembled . . . in the town, and ran through the streets, disturbing the public peace and shouting 'Long live the King, the Fatherland and the Faith! Death to the traitors!' Having murdered the governor, Colonel Don Pedro Lobo, and a landowner named Felix de Jiménez, they followed these execrable excesses with an attempt on the life of the commissary, Don José Ramón de Santi . . . In addition, the insurgents broke into the Capuchin nunnery, and freed all the prisoners in the public gaols by force.[25]

For a general view of the chaos in one small part of Spain we can do no better than turn to José María Blanco y Crespo. Still at home in Madrid when the uprising broke out, he resolved to flee to Andalucía. It was, as he recalls, a journey characterised by the utmost discomfort:

There were no means of reaching Andalucía but through the province of Extremadura, and no other conveyance . . . than two Aragonese wagons, which, having stopped at a small inn, or *venta*, three miles from Madrid, were not under the immediate control of the French police . . . Summer is, of all seasons, the most inconvenient for travellers, and nothing but necessity will induce the natives to cross the burning plains in which the country abounds. This, however, is mostly done so as to avoid the fierceness of the sun, the coaches starting between three and four in the morning, stopping from nine till four in the afternoon, and completing the day's journey between nine and ten in the evening. We, alas, could not expect that indulgence. Each of us, confined with our respective wagoner within the small space which the load had left near the awning, had to endure the intolerable closeness of the wagon under the dead stillness of a burning atmosphere so impregnated with floating dust as often to produce a feeling of suffocation. Our stages required not only early rising, but travelling till noon. After a disgusting dinner at the most miserable inns of the unfrequented road we were following, our task began again till night, when we could rarely expect the enjoyment even of such a bed as the Spanish *ventas* afford. Our stock of linen allowed us but one change, and we could not stop to have it washed. The consequences might easily be foreseen. The heat and the company of our wagoners, who often passed the night by our side, soon completed our wretchedness by giving us a sample of one, perhaps the worst, of the Egyptian plagues, which, as we had not yet got through one half of our journey, held out a sad increase till our arrival at Seville.[26]

Discomfort was just the start of it, however. As Blanco and the other priest he was travelling with proceeded on their way, it became clear that they were in mortal peril:

We proceeded for two or three days, our feelings of security increasing all the while with the distance from Madrid. It was, however, just in that proportion that we were approaching danger. We had, about nine in the morning, reached the Calzada de Oropesa, on the borders of Extremadura, when we observed . . . a crowd of country people, who, collecting hastily round us, began to enquire who we were, accompanying their questions with the fierce and rude tone which forbodes mischief among the testy inhabitants of the southern provinces. The *alcalde* soon presented himself, and, repeating the account we gave of ourselves and our journey, wisely declared to the people that, our language being genuine Spanish, we might be allowed to proceed. He added, however, a word of advice, desiring us to be prepared to meet with people more inquisitive and suspicious than those of Oropesa . . . As if to try our veracity by means of intimidation, he acquainted us with the insurrections which had taken place in every town and village, and the victims which had scarcely failed in any instance to fall under the knives of the peasantry. The truth . . . of this warning became more and more evident as we advanced through Extremadura. The notice we attracted at . . . every village, the threats of the labourers whom we met near the road and the accounts we heard at every inn fully convinced us that we could not reach our journey's end without considerable danger. The unfortunate propensity to shed blood which spoils many a noble quality in the southern Spaniards had been indulged in most towns of any note under the cloak of patriotism. Frenchmen, of course, though long established in Spain, were pointed objects of the popular fury, but most of the murders which we heard of were committed on Spaniards who probably owed their fate to private pique and revenge and not to political opinions. We found the *alcalde*s and *corregidores* to whom we applied perfectly intimidated and fearing the consequences of any attempt to check the blind fury of the people under them. But no description of mine can give so clear a view of the state of the country as the simple narrative of the popular rising at Almaraz, the little town which gives its name to a well-known bridge on the Tagus, as it was delivered to us by the *alcalde*, a rich farmer of that place. The people of his district, upon hearing the accounts from Madrid, and [of] the insurrections in the chief towns of their province, flocked on a certain day before the *alcalde*'s house, armed with whatever weapons they had been able to collect, including sickles, pickaxes and similar implements of husbandry. Most happily for the worthy magistrate the insurgents had no complaint against him, and on the approach of the rustic mob he confidently came out to meet them. Having with no small difficulty obtained a hearing, the *alcalde* desired to be informed of their . . . wishes. The answer appears to me to be unparalleled in the history of mobs. 'We wish, Sir, to kill somebody,' said the spokesman of the insurgents. 'Someone has been killed at Trujillo, one or two others at Badajoz [and] another at Mérida, and we will not be behind our neighbours. Sir, we will kill a traitor.' As this commodity could not be procured in the village, it was fortunate for us that we did not make our appearance at a time when the good people of Almaraz might have made us a substitute on whom to display their loyalty.[27]

Faced by these disorders, which seem to have been worsened by the growing food shortages brought about by the interruption of normal trade and commerce, the notables who headed the new provincial governments sought refuge in a policy of militarisation, either encouraging men to volunteer for hastily formed regiments of levies or simply imposing conscription. Of this process Charles Leslie was an interested observer:

Ayamonte being but a small town, and the market being but scantily supplied, the number of patriots then in the town made everything extremely scarce, so that we were able to procure only a few vegetables, fruit, bread, etc. The town was crowded with armed peasantry of all ages from seventeen to sixty, eager to enroll themselves under the patriotic banner . . . They were armed with any weapons they could lay their hands on: a few muskets, more fowling pieces, some pikes or poles with long bayonets stuck at the end and many pitchforks. There was as little uniformity in dress as in arms . . . The Patriots having assumed a red cockade, with the cypher FVII worked upon [it], woe to any man who ventured to appear without one. The ladies took a pride in presenting us with this national emblem, embroidered with their own fair hands, as we had been ordered to put them above our black ones.[28]

Among the sort of men observed by Leslie, there was much braggadocio. Typical enough was the encounter recorded by a lieutenant colonel of the provincial militia named Pedro Agustín Girón:

I will not omit an incident that paints a good picture of the epoch. I was just leaving a meeting with the Junta [of Ronda] when a man accosted me. He was dressed in a civilian jacket and a floppy hat, but was adorned with aiguillettes as well as a sword and pistol, and handed me a dispatch from a Major Echavarrí who had been named, or so he said, commander of the Army of Córdoba. In this we were exhorted to march to join Echavarrí immediately . . . At this I asked this strange emissary how many men his master thought the French were bringing against him, but his sole reply was 'Nobody: four boys and four Germans, and these last are only waiting for you sluggards to turn up before they surrender.' This was typical of the idea of the enemy that had been allowed to get about. Unfortunately, it was entirely erroneous, but it was just the thing for getting the people to hurl themselves into battle. Its progenitors, however, were not the ones who would have to get them out of it again.[29]

Yet these improvised soldiers were in no state to fight the French in the open field. For a good example of the sort of spectacle which they presented we can do no better than turn to Girón's description of the forces raised in Córdoba:

Half a league from the city we saw a great crowd of horsemen coming towards us along the road, and after a short while we saw that it was General Echavarrí followed by a numerous mass of poorly mounted and worse armed men that he called his cavalry. There were more than 1200 of them, most of them on horses, and the rest on mules. They had saddles of every style – and some of them none at all – and arms of various centuries ranging from the dagger to the rapier. Such was the confusion in which they rode that, as they went by, they left a saddled horse abandoned in the road.[30]

The inevitable result of putting such men up against the invaders was soon illustrated all too well. Having been sent across the Sierra Morena to enter Andalucía and seize the vital port of Cádiz, the division of General Dupont encountered Echavarrí's men at the Puente de Alcolea a few miles east of Córdoba. Among the men facing the Spanish general was Pierre Baste, a company commander in the Marins de la Garde who had been born in Bordeaux almost forty years earlier. The Spaniards were in a strong position with three battalions of infantry and a battery of artillery drawn up in entrenchments commanding the bridge and the armed civilians who formed the bulk of their forces were arrayed on the heights behind, but there was nothing they could do to check the French onrush:

It was scarcely 5am when the entire division was deployed in front of the enemy. The weather was magnificent and presaged a day of extreme heat. Having deployed his forces and placed the artillery in battery on a small hill, the commanding general sent orders to the *voltigeurs* and the Marins de la Garde to establish themselves on both sides of the bridge . . . Despite the brisk musketry, wishing to reassure myself it had not been mined . . . I managed to establish a small number of *marins* . . . supported by *voltigeurs*, beneath the bridge . . . Having assured myself of the solidity of the bridge, I sent my report to the commanding general, who sent one of his *aides-de-camp* to determine how the bridge could be taken. We had already been exchanging fire on all sides for nearly an hour when the general ordered the Garde de Paris . . . to take the bridge by storm . . . Alerted by the *voltigeurs* to the fact that the regiment was approaching in column I climbed the bank of the river, followed by several of my soldiers, in order to enter the trenches at the same moment that our troops would arrive, their muskets at the ready. We were . . . some 15-20 paces from the earthworks when the Spaniards opened fire and left us with about 100-120 casualties. Only a few of my men were struck – undoubtedly due to the impetuosity with which they threw themselves at the barricades, each helping the other to climb up; the net result was that within 6-8 minutes we found ourselves on the bridge – 25-30 troops from the *voltigeurs*, the Garde de Paris and the Marins de la Garde, with seven officers and a colour. We tore along immediately – bayonets to the fore – and fell on the Spaniards . . . We should have inevitably been overcome were it not for the fact we were followed, after an interval of two minutes, by a group of sixty soldiers whose numbers grew with every passing second, and had we not been given covering fire by the 3rd Légion de Reserve, drawn up in line of battle to left and right of the bridge. In less than a quarter of an hour the first attacking column had not only the bridge in its power, but also the buildings on the other side, as well as the position where the enemy battery was. All the peasants found in the trenches were massacred; we pursued the Spaniards for half an hour and came to a halt only half a league beyond the bridge on the Córdoba road, to wait there for the rest of the division, which took position on the olive-crowned heights.[31]

For an alternative view, we can turn to the memoirs of Pedro Agustín Girón, as he was commanding one of the few battalions of regular infantry that the Spaniards had available to block Dupont's path at the bridge:

After bombarding us for quite a time with their cannon . . . the enemy attacked the outpost blocking access to the bridge. Running short of munitions as they were, the men of the small detachment holding it were compelled to give up their positions and fall back . . . The two battalions of grenadiers and the half-battalion of the Regimiento de Campo Mayor . . . then opened fire on the enemy, but, while they held up the enemy for some time, they lost far more casualties than they inflicted . . . At the same time, as was only to be expected given their greater numbers and higher quality, the enemy had soon done what they needed to force their way across the bridge, and, with them all but upon us, we had no option but to retreat. As for all those who had made such a big noise in Córdoba, from General Echavarrí downwards, not a single one of them put in an appearance at the bridge: indeed, the battalions of peasants who were with us fled at the very first shots.[32]

Pursuing the fleeing Spaniards, the French soon arrived before the walls of Córdoba. What followed, alas, was not a pretty story:

It was close to 2.30pm when the bulk of the division came close to Córdoba. At our approach, the Spanish abandoned their position . . . and our troops launched themselves into the town at the charge. We found it deserted by the Spanish troops, who were fleeing in the greatest disorder . . . But it became impossible to restrain the greed of the soldiers who, running through the streets with bayonets fixed, forced passage for themselves everywhere and spread throughout the houses in order to pillage. An early column, still marching in closed ranks, arrived in one part of town to be met by musketry from the windows of several streets; this fact led us inevitably to the persuasion that the inhabitants had taken up arms and were defending themselves. So a form of street-to-street combat broke out and served as a pretext for our soldiers to sack Córdoba and deliver it up to all the horrors of a town taken by assault. The soldiers scattered by platoons or singly, fully armed and unmoved by any representation made to them. Murder and pillage were soon joined by the rape of women, virgins and nuns, the theft of sacred vessels from the churches – sacrilege accompanied by the most atrocious circumstances. Some officers – even some generals – demeaned themselves by indulging in such dishonour, even when grief-stricken parents sought to solicit the protection of the first officers they encountered. Happily for the name of French honour there were some sensible and generous souls who, in saving more than one family, protected them from the outrageous behaviour of a soldiery even more difficult to rein in once they had broken all the leashes of discipline. I had the good fortune to be able to save several women and some Spanish men who would otherwise have become victims of the soldiers' blind fury. Called to the aid of a woman in the greatest distress, I was almost forced to kill three frenzied members of a light battalion who, despite my efforts and the entreaties of the unfortunate woman, persisted in forcing their brutal attentions on her daughter, a charming young woman . . . All kinds of disorder characterised this awful day and the scenes of desolation for which Córdoba provided the stage. The heat was so excessive and the soldiers so pressed by thirst that, without pausing to ask for drinks, they descended into the cellars and used their muskets to break open the great casks they found there in ranks, such that within a quarter of an hour they were swimming in wine and were drinking it without a break. By evening these same soldiers who had fought so well at daybreak could have been dispersed and overwhelmed by a thousand determined and well-led men. There was, however, a benefit to the town in the outbreak of drunkenness that seized almost all the soldiers of the division; they soon succumbed to the inevitable need for rest and sleep, and this preserved Córdoba from a total sack – and perhaps its utter destruction.[33]

Bailén

In northern Spain the French on the whole had the better of the fighting that had everywhere blazed up between their forces and the insurgents. If, as we shall see, the invaders were checked at Zaragoza, a large Spanish army was beaten at Medina de Río Seco and on 20 July Joseph Bonaparte, who had at length been named King of Spain by Napoleon, entered his capital. In La Mancha and Andalucía, however, the French were soon in trouble. No longer was foraging, for example, a simple matter. Here and there the inhabitants of towns and villages such as Valdepeñas tried to defend themselves against enemy incursions, while there emerged the first signs of an even more worrying form of resistance. Quick to appreciate the value of irregular warfare, the Junta of Jaén had formed a number of guerrilla bands, while a variety of local notables copied their example and assembled private armies of their own. Very soon, then, Dupont's communications were under attack. Typical enough was the experience of Captain Charles François, a 33-year-old veteran of the Egyptian campaign who was originally from the village of Guinchy in Picardy. A company commander in one of the second-line formations that formed the bulk of the first Army of Spain, at the beginning of July he was sent to the town of Linares with a convoy of wagons and three companies of infantry to requisition the contents of the local powder mill:

> I arrived . . . at the town, presented myself . . . before the *alcalde* and showed my order. He gave us every assistance . . . and we took half a ton of powder and 1,500 pounds of balls, which we put in the carts. My mission being accomplished, I caused bread, meat, rice and a bottle of wine apiece to be given to the soldiers, and they prepared their meal on a plateau overlooking the town . . . I left at 9pm, and had hardly started before there came a shot that wounded one of the sharpshooters, so I formed sections with the carts between and continued my march, but was hardly more than half a league from the town when I was attacked on all sides. I formed square with the wagons inside and continued my march, blazing away in all directions . . . until five o'clock in the morning, when I entered a wood where, very fortunately, I found a company of sharpshooters which the general had sent to meet me.[34]

Another Frenchman who experienced this early outbreak of guerrilla war was Eugène Husson, an infantry officer who had been born at Reims on 17 March 1786 and was now adjutant-major in the hastily improvised Eighth Provisional Regiment. Part of the division of General Gobert, this force soon found itself trudging southwards across La Mancha in an attempt to reinforce the corps of General Dupont:

> On 5 June and the days that followed we passed through Ocaña, Tembleque, Madridejos, Villaharta and Manzanares, all of them little towns of the province of La Mancha, a region rich in wheat and wine, and one whose inhabitants appeared to be less lazy than those of the other provinces through which we had passed. We had to burn Manzanares, which is the largest of these places. Its inhabitants had massacred two hospitals that the army of Dupont had left behind . . . Four hundred sick French soldiers had been put to death in the most unworthy fashion. Some had been thrown into ovens and others into ditches full of hot coals, while others had been hung up in chimneys . . . and burned to death little by little. I myself found a French dragoon still in his uniform hung up in just such a fashion and with his feet horribly burned in an isolated house three hundred paces outside the town on the main road south in which I established an advanced post.[35]

Another witness to the massacre of the inmates of the French hospital at Manzanares was Louis François Gille who had been sent south with a further division of reinforcements under General Vedel:

> Walking out into the gardens and other enclosures that surrounded the town, I found my senses assailed by the most frightful scene. About fifty bodies that had not yet been buried allowed us to make our own judgements in respect of the barbarism of these cowardly assassins. Some had been beaten to death; others had had their heads smashed in by axes; and still others had in a refinement of cruelty been plunged alive into cauldrons of boiling oil: the limbs of these unfortunates had been so contracted by the action of the fire that a man of the height of five feet and six

inches now arrived at one of hardly three. Leaving this scene of horror, I set out for my billet. About half way back I heard a confused babble of voices, and very soon I came across a woman being dragged along in the midst of a group of French soldiers. The mutilated body of a French dragoon had been found in her house . . . and she was being taken to prison on the orders of General Vedel. What became of her I never found out.[36]

The stories of Spanish atrocities undoubtedly grew in the telling and many of the accounts that have come down to us stretch credulity to their limits: it is, for example, especially hard to accept the claim that the poverty-stricken inhabitants of La Mancha had sufficient spare olive oil to boil captured Frenchmen alive. The invaders, however, were not in a mood to ask questions, and responded with great brutality. Indeed, freed from the constraints they might have observed in areas of, as they saw it, greater civilisation, the troops were increasingly out of control. For example, at the village of El Viso del Marqués, a place where graffiti scrawled by the invaders may still be observed on the walls of the great Renaissance palace that once belonged to the victor of Lepanto, Alvaro de Bazán, there was great disorder:

> On 24 June we left Manzanares . . . with the aim of reaching Valdepeñas. The inhabitants having all fled their homes, this place proved a complete desert. El Viso did not offer us any more in the way of resources, but, even in this state of want, it proved a most unfortunate conquest. Despite the orders that had been issued forbidding pillage, the soldiers were soon spread out through the town in search of food or plunder. Hardly any of them found anything other than a few cellars filled with brandy, but this was enough. In an instant the . . . camp was full of containers of the stuff; and a great part of the rank and file were completely drunk. If we had been attacked, it would have been the end of us: we could not have made the least defence.[37]

Arriving at El Viso the next day, a 22-year-old cousin of the Empress Josephine named Maurice de Tascher who was serving as a lieutenant in one of the invaders' ragtag provisional cavalry regiments found it little more than a ghost town:

> Few sights have caused me so much horror as the one I encountered when we rode into this town. It was entirely deserted. The most terrible noise would have caused me less disquiet than the oppressive silence and solitude with which we were greeted . . . The only people I could find were three old women of between seventy and eighty, and their brother, who was a dotard of eighty-four, all of whom had taken refuge in the palace . . . It had been necessary to smash in the door of every house and it was clear that pretty soon the need to find food, the excitement of the sack and the soldiers' greed for gold had overcome all the soldiers' inhibitions . . . In consequence, every step that I took filled me with sadness and despair. How they must hate us![38]

South of the Sierra Morena, meanwhile, the forces of General Dupont had drawn back from Córdoba to Andújar. With his communications threatened by the insurrection and a large Spanish regular army massing against him under General Castaños, the French commander eventually decided to retreat, but the operation was not well managed, and the French army became strung out along the high road to Madrid, enabling the Spaniards to throw two divisions of regulars across its line of march. The result was that both Dupont himself and a large part of his forces were cut off, and suddenly found themselves having to fight a battle to get through. Already, however, the men with him were extremely tired, having set out from Andújar in the early evening and marched all through the night. At the rear of the column with the baggage train was to be found Jean Grivel:

> At seven o'clock in the evening we evacuated the town and set out for Bailén . . . As can be imagined from the time of year, it was extremely hot, and the dusty road along which we had to march . . . was very tiring on account of the fact that we had to travel at the same speed as the numerous wagons that accompanied us. We were constantly having to sort them out, and . . . the frequent halts delayed us a great deal. I do not know if the enemy had guessed our intentions . . . but we found them drawn up across our path and ready to give battle . . . We had no food and almost no water, and were wearied by the fatigues of the night . . . in a word, in a real fix.[39]

Among the French reserve was Pierre Baste:

> Battle was now joined at every point of contact. We sought to face up to every movement of the enemy, whose numbers so exceeded ours. We hoped to find a gap in the line, or at least to bring the enemy to a halt, just until the arrival of General Vedel who, we were told, was just four leagues from the battlefield. We tried several attacks on different parts of the enemy line, and took advantage of the ability to form our columns hidden from the enemy's fire, as a result of the heights we had seized. But we were truly exhausted, and were marching from one place to another. The various units of our cavalry made superb charges, which would have resulted in taking the enemy's principal artillery battery if the infantry had been able to follow. Each unit had taken an enemy flag during the heat of the action. A Spanish regiment had been overcome by 100 cuirassiers of the 5th Regiment commanded by Captain Verneret; they had traversed the Spanish lines three times. Both armies had equal motivation for making extraordinary efforts. Our motivation was simply to pass through and to force the position; the Spanish objective was to hold firm. Each army was threatened with being caught between two forces; we, by the principal Spanish force that we had left behind on the heights of Andújar during our retreat and which could, by consequence, arrive in our rear at any minute; and General Reding by the arrival of General Vedel, who had set off from La Carolina and therefore could not be too far from the battlefield . . . But huge mistakes characterised our manoeuvres. Pannetier's brigade could not occupy its position before 10am. This last reinforcement was composed of troops whose approach march had been so rapid that they arrived totally breathless. The baggage train had held them up. They could do nothing but present themselves and be immediately thrown into disorder. The enemy's artillery was of heavier calibre than ours. The latter would have produced an entirely different result had we been able to employ it in concentrated manner.

But we never had more than four pieces in battery and frequently fewer . . . Our troops, brought to a halt by the whole enemy line, tried once more to renew their attacks. The task of the cavalry was even more difficult, since they had to manoeuvre on ground cut up by ravines and planted with olive trees. General Reding, reinforced by the forces of the Marquis de Coupigny, began to extend his front further and further in order to outflank us on the right . . . Two new charges, prosecuted blow for blow by General Privé, achieved only minor advantages . . . In vain the commanding general paraded before us the Spanish colours that had just been taken by Verneret's squadron of cuirassiers . . . The two flags were greeted, it is true, by cries of 'Vive l'empereur!' But that was the limit of the ardour and the enthusiasm of our troops. They were exhausted from fatigue and devastated by the heat. Their starvation was so great that, no longer able to support their arms, they threw them to the ground and waited where they were without moving. The battle had been going on since 3am and already half the day was spent. There simply was no spirit left for another bayonet charge – this had already been tried three times without success. Only the intrepid Marins de la Garde demonstrated a resolution none could overcome. The commanding general, seeing no sign of the arrival of Vedel's division, losing faith in the ability to break the enemy's strong line . . . and having also been informed of the impending arrival of Lieutenant-General La Peña's advanced guard on the field, despaired of the day. The defection of part of the Swiss troops rattled his morale . . . More than a third of our line troops were now *hors de combat*. In such a dire situation, the commanding general – already vanquished, one might say, by the general despondency as much as by the strong resistance of the enemy – resolved to . . . arrange a cease-fire.[40]

With Dupont's men all but out of the fight, there now arrived – much too late – General Vedel's division, which had been sent on ahead to secure the passes that carried the high road to Madrid through the mountains of the Sierra Morena and into La Mancha. Arriving full in the rear of Reding and Coupigny, this fresh force fell on the few units that they had left to watch the road. Among the first French soldiers on the scene was Captain François:

The First Legion [of Reserve], of which I was part, took two guns, three caissons and 800 prisoners of the [Irlanda Regiment]. At that moment I was ordered to attack a chapel where the Jaén [militia] regiment was posted . . . I sounded the charge, and my young soldiers received the Spanish fire, crying out 'Vive l'empereur!' At the moment when a Spanish officer waved a white handkerchief as a sign of surrender I was hit by a bullet in the right hip which knocked me over in the brushwood. I lost in this affair nineteen men [killed] and thirty-three wounded, myself included . . . As it was dusk, the men sent to pick up the wounded did not find me, as I had crawled into the brushwood and was unconscious from loss of blood. In the night I came to and found myself alone, surrounded by my dead *voltigeurs* and expecting the same fate . . . The next morning the Spanish soldiers and peasants came to the field of battle to pick up the weapons and search the dead. Two peasants found me, and, seeing I was alive, insulted me, pulled me out of the brushwood, searched me, took my watch and my belt, which contained eighty-three *napoléons* . . . tore out my earrings, and left me despite my prayers that they would either kill me or take me to the ambulance [i.e. dressing station] at Bailén. They replied that I was a brigand and had lived long enough, and went away insulting me. A few minutes later some other peasants came, and I persuaded them to take me to . . . Bailén. I cannot describe what suffering I went through to get there: I was weak from loss of blood, and had passed a whole night on the battlefield.[41]

For the soldiers of Dupont's army, the capitulation was the start of a terrible ordeal. From the very beginning, indeed, they were subjected to threats and harassment, as witness Captain François's account of events at the town of El Arahal:

Being convalescent and walking with difficulty, I had made the journey from Morón [de la Frontera] on a donkey . . . The inhabitants, seeing that I was wounded and my trousers covered with blood, insulted me in the most outrageous manner: many of them threw stones and mud at me. I cannot describe how much I cursed my fate. On 1 September there arrived 200 men of the Alcántara regiment, who were supposed to guard us. As a preliminary, they sabred three of our soldiers who had asked permission to fetch water . . . About eight in the morning, a crowd of peasants assembled before our lodgings, threw stones at the window and insulted us. They displayed their knives and cried, 'By noon you will have ceased to live: your heads will be cut off!' Our guards did not interfere with the mob, but laughed and seemed pleased to see us insulted.[42]

Nor was it just the men who had actually fought at Bailén who had to surrender. Left behind at the pass of Despeñaperros to guard the road to Madrid, Husson saw none of the campaign that followed, but in accordance with the terms of Dupont's capitulation he and his men still had to lay down their arms. Marched into Andalucía to await repatriation – an agreement that was never honoured – they, too, found that their lot was likely to be grim in the extreme:

On 25 July we crossed the Guadalquivir accompanied by a furious crowd that slit the throats of all those who could not follow the column and arrived at a place called Menjibar on the right bank . . . From there we were taken to the town of Archidona in the province of Granada . . . Having got to that town, however, we discovered that we were to be conveyed to Málaga and thrown in prison. To reach that city, we had to . . . pass through the town of [Antequera]. This is a big enough place, but its inhabitants proved exceedingly barbarous. No sooner had we arrived than these tigers fell upon us. Not content with having taken my horse and all my belongings, they tied me to a tree and stripped me of all that I had . . . A bemedalled Spanish officer took my boots and breeches, and gave me in exchange several blows from his stick . . . a pair of rough sandals and . . . some cotton trousers. The pillage was general . . . The next day . . . we took the road for Málaga. This proved most hazardous. To enter the place we had to pass through an immense crowd of people shouting for our heads. They were kept off by the strong guard which had accompanied us, but they nevertheless followed us all the way to our prison, hurling abuse at us and subjecting us to a hail of stones. Having reached the prison, we were then set on in the courtyard [by the guards] . . . and deprived of the little money that a few of us had been able to keep hidden. Only once we had got inside the building was there any shelter and even then we could hear the savages outside demanding, 'Are they going to be killed tonight or tomorrow? Are they rich? Will we do well for ourselves?'[43]

The calvary of the prisoners of Bailén had only just begun. Meanwhile, in counterpoint to their sufferings, and in part, perhaps, their cause, was the mood of exaltation that now gripped Patriot Spain. Present with the army of General Castaños as it advanced on the Spanish capital in the wake of Bailén was Samuel Ford Whittingham, the 36-year-old son of a Bristol wool merchant, who had travelled extensively in Spain prior to his purchase of a commission in the First Life Guards in 1804, and had been attached to the Spaniards as a liaison officer:

On our passage through La Mancha to Madrid, I was taken to the house of a woman who had obtained great celebrity from the murder of a number of French soldiers. In the courtyard of her dwelling there was a well of very good water, but the rope for drawing it up was very short, and you were obliged to stoop forward in order to be able to drink out of the bucket. Whenever an incautious soldier came to the well and bent over to drink, she came behind him and, seizing him by the legs, tumbled him into the well. She had, I understood, put eight men to death in this fashion. The triumphant march of General Castaños to Madrid far exceeds my powers of description. On entering the gate of Atocha, our steps were directed to the chapel to hear mass. The crowd was immense and at the church door one of the *manolas*, a stout, handsome woman, threw her arms round my neck with such affectionate violence that down we came at full length together on the floor, she exclaiming all the while, 'God bless the Englishman, the delight of my soul.' The burst of laughter was not quite in harmony with church gravity, but Castaños long enjoyed the joke, and the Englishman's fall became a standing dish at his table.[44]

In the capital there were now no French troops, Joseph Bonaparte having ordered a retreat to the Ebro. It was, however, some days before any Spanish forces arrived to take over, and even then it was not Castaños's men who got there first. For a Spanish eyewitness to the liberation of Madrid, we can turn to Alcalá Galiano:

On 14 August the first of the troops who had triumphed in the provinces entered Madrid. They were Valencians who had been placed under the command of General Don Pedro González Llamas, an old man. Among them came some veteran units who were dressed and arrayed in the style of the Spanish army of those days. But the majority of our new guests wore the baggy breeches of Valencia with cloaks draped over their shoulders while their long, badly combed and greasy locks were covered with round hats decorated with patriotic cockades, ribbons embroidered with slogans and little images of the Virgin or the saints. In general, the aspect they presented was most singular, with something of the ridiculous and a great deal of the ferocious, while their actions were no better than their appearance. Once inside the capital, they mixed with the worst part of the common people, and gave themselves over to replacing the peace that, however imperfect, had more-or-less reigned hitherto with riot and disorder . . . The cry of 'Death to all traitors' constantly interrupted their cheers, and pretty soon it became known that they had murdered someone in the Plaza de la Cebada and then gone on to drag the corpse through the streets . . . General Llamas went to calm them down, but he was treated with little respect and even insulted, and was in fact at grave risk of being murdered by these . . . madmen. All the decent people of the capital were in consequence seized with a terror that was just as bad, if not even greater, than they had felt under the domination of the French . . . On 23 or 24 August there arrived the troops of Castaños. We gave them a warmer welcome than we had accorded those of Valencia . . . on account of the greater grandeur of the events in which they had taken part and the unequalled importance of the results. The enthusiasm of the population was immense . . . Among those who excited the most curiosity and attracted the most applause were the Lanceros de Jeréz with their Andalusian dress . . . and their lances improvised from bull-pricks . . . it being said of them that they had run through whole strings of cuirassiers without the latter's armour being any use at all.[45]

Also in Madrid was Sébastien Blaze, who had been left behind to help care for the many sick who had been too weak to leave the city with Joseph's forces and now fell into the hands of the victorious insurgents:

Hardly had the French army left . . . the city than the population rose *en masse* . . . The Spanish army had still not arrived, and, the doors of the hospital having been thrown open to them, the *canaille* threatened us with their daggers . . . On 5 August the army finally arrived, and marched through the streets from six o'clock in the morning till midday. The populace gathered to greet them at the Puerta de Atocha. One can easily imagine the joy that was shown by one and all: shouts of 'Long live Ferdinand! Long live Castaños!' rang out on all sides. Thereafter, to celebrate the glory of Spain's arms every day was marked by bullfights, balls and spectacles and entertainments of every sort.[46]

The general excitement, while understandable, was not conducive to putting the Spanish war effort on the sort of footing that was necessary if Spain were really to fight Napoleon. Of this period the reminiscences of Robert Brindle are far from untypical:

Our unwelcome visitors now left us, as we hoped, to return no more. Their precipitate retreat made us believe that even the hardy veterans of France could not stand against the enthusiastic valour of the Spaniards. Every place resounded with acclamations of victory, and there was scarcely one Spaniard who did not already imagine their troops at the gates of Paris and Bonaparte tottering on his throne. Such, indeed, was the enthusiasm that if any feared another eruption from the French, it would have been looked upon as treason to express such fears. This state of affairs continued for two or three months during which time not one unpleasant tiding was permitted to reach our ears . . . We reposed great confidence in the Spanish army and . . . as we heard for some time no song but the song of victory, we were unwilling to change our tune.[47]

Zaragoza

With the Spanish insurrection against the French, fighting had broken out in many parts of the country, but some of the fiercest battles were to take place around the city of Zaragoza. Almost ungarrisoned and protected only by weak medieval walls, the city had no option but to rely for its defence on armed civilians. Galvanised by José Palafox y Melzi, the local nobleman in the royal guard who had orchestrated the uprising in Aragón, the populace had sprung to arms, but the crowds of improvised levies that were sent out to attack the French forces bearing down on the city were routed in actions at Mallén and Alagón, and by 15 June some 5,000 enemy troops had reached the city under the command of General Charles Lefebvre-Desnouettes. Among the men about to attack the city was Jozef Mrozinski, a 34-year-old Galician nobleman who had enlisted in the newly formed Legion of the Vistula in 1807, and had just entered Spain as an officer in the latter's first infantry regiment. In a tribute to French over-confidence, Lefebvre-Desnouettes decided to storm the walls straight away. At Mallén and Alagón, the Poles had seen Spanish levies turn and run without firing more than a few shots, but hardly had the attack started than it became clear that Zaragoza itself would be a different matter:

> General Lefebvre formed a column with those companies of Polish infantry which he had to hand, and these immediately followed the fleeing enemy in formation of attack towards the Puerta del Carmen. Because of the density of the olive groves and gardens that surrounded the city, it was only possible to discern the gate . . . at a distance of 60 *sazen* [i.e. approximately 120 yards]. The Spaniards had stationed some guns before it, and the moment that the column appeared . . . they opened fire. The first shots killed Captain Karol Emmerych, Lieutenant Mierzwinski and fifteen grenadiers . . . The sudden loss of these brave men . . . might easily have confounded the little column, but, obeying the voice of Colonel Chlopicki [the commander of the First Regiment], the soldiers kept going until they had reached the very gate in spite of an intense fire that struck down ten more men including Ensign Ambrozy Borakowski. The Spaniards might not have had any troops capable of resisting an army as experienced as our own on the field of battle, but they did not lack a few dozen brave-hearts who preferred to defend the gate to the death rather than let themselves be driven from it. There therefore began a bloody fight, and the defenders of Zaragoza for the first time saw the enemies checked in their attack. This cheered them, and whole mobs of them now began to rush towards the gate. Crowding into the houses that overlooked it, they opened fire from the windows and roofs on our men who could not see them to fire back . . . In vain were two French guns brought up to the gate: they fired dozens of shots into the city, but the thick walls of the houses occupied by the inhabitants were hardly scratched, while the cannon had pretty soon been left without any means of moving them . . .

Now the *zaragozanos* were winning . . . With a hail of fire criss-crossing our columns from all directions, General Lefebvre recognised the need to fall back from the walls of the city and gave the order to retreat.[48]

What renders this resistance the more remarkable is that the city's defenders were almost leaderless, their commander General Palafox having taken to his heels at the approach of the enemy on the pretext that he had gone to look for reinforcements. Among the defenders was Agustín Alcaide Ibieca, a wealthy man who was later to write the chief Spanish history of the siege:

> The situation could not have been more critical . . . There were but fifty trained gunners in the city; they had very little in the way of munitions, and there were almost no other troops . . . Enemy columns were advancing on the walls from all sides, while in the streets there was nothing to be seen but crowds of excited people. They had few arms, but were yet full of passion: every man, indeed, saw himself as a soldier, or, better, as a general, and was therefore eager to opine on what should be done and tell everyone else what to do. Ready to see traitors on all sides, they were seizing anyone they deemed suspect: for example, the garrison's chief engineer, Don Antonio Sangenis, was arrested for no better reason than that he was seen taking notes on the city's defences . . . Having been summoned to decide what should be done, the town council was about to commence its discussions when a group of men burst in brandishing blunderbusses and threw them out of the chamber, saying that they were going to fire on the enemy from the balconies . . . The walls of the Casa de Misericordia were lined with people while others jammed the balconies, the windows and even the roofs of the buildings . . . that lined the walls as far as the Puerta del Carmen, together with those of the monastery of Santa Engracia and the convent of the Incarnation, but, while some were armed, many had come for no other object than to watch the fight. Had the convents of the Discalced Augustinians, the Trinitarians and the Capuchins, all of which were . . . outside the walls, been occupied, they might have caused the enemy terrible casualties, but there were hardly any men in any of them.[49]

For a Spanish view of Lefebvre's assault, we may turn to Faustino Casamayor, who was born to a family of some substance in Zaragoza on 15 February 1760. The son of a bailiff in the city's Real Audiencia, he studied law at its university and eventually took over his father's job while at the same time working as an administrator for one of Zaragoza's grandees:

> About one o'clock the French troops approached the city . . . from their stations on Monte Torrero and around [the hermitage of] Santa Barbara, whereupon we immediately opened fire upon them . . . with the cannon placed at the Portillo, Carmen and Santa Engracia gates. The battle went on for a long time, and was marked by many vicissitudes. The Carmen gate, for example, was smashed open by artillery fire, and the enemy broke in, only for all the men concerned to be either killed, taken prisoner or thrown out again. The same thing happened at the Santa Engracia gate. The French got into the square behind it, but the artillery that had

been placed on the walls of Santa Inés drove them to take shelter in the cavalry barracks, and they were then killed by the forces we had stationed in the Casa de Misericordia. All this was accompanied by a display of valour on the part of the inhabitants that has few equals: seeing that the French were inside the walls, they rushed to confront them with no other protection than their own noble breasts and forced them to retreat by dint of a hail of fire . . . The people were in great confusion, but this in no way interfered with the unparalleled heroism which they displayed . . . This was especially true of the women who from the very beginning of the attack kept the defenders supplied with water, wine and brandy and, mingling with their very ranks . . . reanimated their spirits and in this fashion helped them to defeat an enemy who was as daring as he was ferocious. The destruction that we suffered was very great. Many beautiful trees were felled by cannon balls while the convents of the Augustinian Friars and the Discalced Trinitarians were badly damaged, along with the Casa de Misericordia and the cavalry barracks; indeed, having first been sacked, these last two edifices were set on fire . . . The enemy dead amounted to 700, while our own losses were quite serious, for the enemy fired on us the whole time with howitzers, while the lack of skill which characterised our men gave rise to many misfortunes . . . The action lasted till past seven in the evening, at which point . . . the French fell back, taking with them a number of prisoners.[50]

This was a severe setback for the French, and it was many days before they returned to the attack. With the French once more gathering for an assault, the defenders were suddenly struck by calamity. Once again the observer is Faustino Casamayor:

All of a sudden on the stroke of two o'clock in the afternoon the powder magazine that had been established in the Escuelas Públicas blew up with results that were so dreadful that it makes one feel faint just to think of them. The building itself was completely wrecked while the diocesan seminary and the greater part of the houses on the southern side of the Coso [i.e the broad street in the centre of the city that served as its main square] were heavily damaged. Indeed, almost all the inhabitants of the latter perished in the ruins, along with a number of the seminary's teachers . . . Anxious to succour the dying, many priests and religious immediately rushed to the scene, while the people living nearby attempted to recover the corpses of those who had been caught up in the disaster. The explosion was the result of some burning cigar ash falling on a consignment of gunpowder that was being loaded into some carts to be taken to the convent of San Agustín. Every single one of the carters perished along with their teams and the men who were loading the powder, and such was the force of the explosion that their remains were flung far beyond the city walls. So badly hit were the houses in the area immediately adjacent to the site that they are in a state of complete collapse, while the noise of the explosion was so loud that it was heard more than ten leagues away. There is hardly a pane of glass left in the whole city, and everyone has been plunged into the greatest consternation at the loss of so many lives.[51]

Nor was this tragedy the end of the city's travails. Once again the story is taken up by Casamayor:

> At midnight precisely [on 1 July] the French opened the most horrible bombardment . . . Never having been experienced before in Zaragoza, this new accident of war caused the greatest alarm to all the inhabitants. Seeing the streaks of fire that filled the sky, the people rushed into the streets, commending themselves to the care of Our Lady of the Pillar, whose protection they regarded as their only hope of surviving the peril in which they found themselves . . . The place where most people headed was the square in front of the basilica, and, seeing how many of the shells flew over the building and fell into the Ebro, they took heart at this sign that Our Lady so much favoured our cause. All the more was this the case given the fact that a shell which plunged through the roof of the basilica and blew up . . . near the chapel of San Joaquín . . . did not hurt any of the people taking shelter there. The bombardment did not cease with the coming of morning . . . and in fact the latter saw the opening of a furious battle as many of the defenders had rushed to the walls. Because the enemy had emplaced their guns very close to the city, the struggle was very cruel and bloody. Indeed, this was one of the most dreadful days that we had yet experienced . . . The fire reached so violent and continuous a pitch that success began to be despaired of.[52]

Yet Zaragoza remained undaunted. When the French finally launched a fresh assault five days later, they were met by fierce resistance. As before, Mrozinski and his men were well to the fore:

> The attack on the Puerta del Carmen was directed by General Lefebvre. Some of the companies were equipped with ladders and others with hand grenades . . . After a signal had been fired by four cannon, the assault began . . . There was not a single spot at which the Spaniards did not offer resistance. Every building . . . had been provided with loopholes; the streets leading to the gates had been entrenched and protected by cannon that had been placed so they could fire across them; ditches protected the weakest sections of the wall; and the Spaniards had prepared hidden mines which they now exploded. Nevertheless for two hours every attempt was made to get through these obstacles, the soldiers surging round the walls and trying desperately to find a way to get at the enemy . . . Among the dead were Ensign Bartkowski of the Second Regiment and the Glowazewski brothers, who were serving in the same company as its lieutenant and ensign . . . Eager to avenge their death, the latter's men fearlessly pressed right up to the walls of the city only for the enemy to kill almost all of them. Finally, seeing that entry into the city was impossible, General Verdier had to order the troops to suspend the assault and return to their encampments.[53]

Amid the chaos there occurred one of the most famous incidents of the entire war. The story is recounted by Charles Vaughan, a Fellow of All Souls' College, who had spent most of the last few years travelling on the Continent and had now come to Spain to experience the war at first hand. Employed as a volunteer courier by the British embassy, he visited Zaragoza shortly after the siege:

> The attack of the enemy seemed to be directed principally against the gate called Portillo . . . The sandbag battery before the gate . . . was gallantly defended by the Aragonese. It was several times destroyed and as often reconstructed under the fire of the enemy. The carnage . . . throughout the day was truly terrible. It was here that an act of heroism was performed by a female to which history scarcely affords a parallel. Agustina Zaragoza, about twenty-two years of age, a handsome woman of the lower class of the people, while performing her duty of carrying refreshment to the gates arrived at the battery . . . at the very moment when the French fire had absolutely destroyed every person that was stationed in it. The citizens and soldiers for the moment hesitated to re-man the guns, [but] Agustina rushed forward over the wounded and the slain, snatched a match from the hand of a dead artilleryman, and fired off a twenty-four pounder. Then, jumping upon the gun, [she] made a solemn vow never to quit it alive during the siege, and, having stimulated her fellow citizens by this daring intrepidity to fresh exertions, they instantly rushed into the battery, and again opened a tremendous fire upon the enemy.[54]

With the French beaten off once more, there followed a formal siege. For several weeks, then, the invaders busied themselves digging approach trenches and constructing batteries for their cannon. Eventually, all was ready, and, after a sharp bombardment, 4 August saw the French attack the city for a third time. This time there was no mistake. As Alcaide Ibieca recounts, the defenders were quickly driven from their shattered walls:

> At length the day dawned . . . At the first rays of the sun, the enemy's seventy guns all opened fire in cadence, and such was the shock that it felt as if everything must be shaken off its hinges. Only the most vivid imagination could describe so awful a scene. Meanwhile, we could see the French infantry advancing to the left and right of the castle . . . Our own guns kept up a determined response, but at Santa Engracia large parts of the wall . . . were brought down upon them, and many men were buried by the débris . . . The Torre del Pino forms the salient point of the angle between the Puerta de Santa Engracia and the Puerta del Carmen, and it put up a most vigorous defence, but the defenders also lost many dead. Sent there at the head of a squad composed of a sergeant, two corporals and twenty-four privates, Sub-lieutenant Narciso Lozano . . . lost one of the corporals and no fewer than twenty-two of the privates . . . Despite the heavy losses they were suffering, the enemy redoubled their efforts . . . and, having got across the River Huerba, managed to enter the gardens of Santa Engracia and the Campo Real by means of the two breaches that had been blown in their walls. Although they came under heavy fire from the buildings overlooking the gardens, more and more of them got in . . . and they then began gradually to work their way round to take the . . . various gates in the rear. Lieutenant Colonel Escanero was wounded, along with the artillery officer Don Salvador de Orta . . . and at this the commander of the men who had been defending the gardens . . . ordered his men to fall back. The enemy's fire,

meanwhile, was getting worse and worse, and the number of explosions multiplying by the minute, while the defenders were falling in droves, some of them crushed by falling masonry and others cut down by bullets or shell fragments . . . With every second the situation was getting more critical . . . A sub-lieutenant of the Voluntarios de Aragón named Don Antonio Arruc sought to rally a group of men who . . . were on the point of giving way, but he was wounded by a musket ball and had to be carried away . . . Seeing that the French had occupied Santa Engracia, the men manning the walls beside the Torre del Pino dragged the two cannon that had been stationed there . . . back to the entrance of the Calle de Santa Engracia . . . After seven hours' of fighting the Torre del Pino then itself fell into the hands of the enemy, and this meant that it was also necessary to pull our guns back from the Puerta del Carmen . . . When I think of Zaragoza's situation at that moment, I am quite overcome and the pen falls from my hands . . . Large numbers of soldiers and civilians alike were falling back on the Plaza de la Seo in great confusion, throwing away their arms, while crowds of people also jammed the bridge across the Ebro. Full of zeal and enthusiasm, the commandant of the Puerta de Angel, Colonel Don Cayetano Samitier, tried sword-in-hand to hold back the fugitives, but his cries were . . . drowned out by the shrieks of the women.[55]

With the Spaniards falling back in ever greater confusion, Verdier's troops were soon threatening to erupt into the Coso. This time Mrozinski found himself fighting in the Santa Engracia sector:

The capture of the monastery of Santa Engracia . . . opened the way into the heart of the city. Led by Generals Verdier and Lacoste, the column . . . poured down the Calle de Santa Engracia. This had been blocked by the enemy with ditches and ramparts armed with cannon, while the Spaniards kept up a heavy fire from the houses, the roofs and the church towers. In consequence, the strength of the attacking force was soon being reduced. It was necessary to fight for every house, and not just every house, but every floor and every corner . . . while new combats were required to clear the side streets. At length the First Regiment and a battalion of the Seventieth Line, or rather detachments of both units, reached the Coso . . . All the exits from this street were blocked off by ditches and barricades . . . and a large battery in the centre of the street covered the way in from the Calle de Santa Engracia . . . This was immediately stormed by a group of Poles, but, while they drove off the defenders, the Spaniards in the buildings overlooking the battery were quickly able to wipe out this band of heroes . . . At this point Colonel Henriot arrived with the 14th Line, which had been advancing up the . . . Calle de Santa Engracia behind the First [Regiment of the Legion of the Vistula] and burst into the Coso . . . The appearance of this unit must have shaken the defenders a little, for all of a sudden a priest rushed into the street with his arms stretched out in the shape of a cross. He was praying in a loud voice and was accompanied by a girl who appeared to be no more than about twelve years old and was dressed up as the Virgen del Pilar. In the midst of so much gunfire and death, the image of the priest and the girl took hold of everyone and for a moment there was silence. The soldiers were stunned by the strange vision at first, but then they became impatient and opened fire on the priest. However, the latter was not touched by their shots, and walked calmly away. No sooner had he reached cover than from every roof and every window there blazed forth a horrible fire, and the rain of bullets was such that the new attack proved unsuccessful.[56]

On the same day Mrozinski was also involved in fighting at the General Hospital, a large complex of buildings that had to be captured to secure the flanks of the lodgement the assault troops had occupied within the city:

> The conquest of the general hospital occasioned the most appalling scenes that could possibly be imagined. In a desperate attempt to get away from the fires that were consuming the building, the wounded dragged their shattered limbs along with the last of their strength, wrapped up in bloodstained sheets, while some of them flung themselves from the windows, only to fall straight on to the bayonets of the soldiers below. Amid all this heartbreak, the cells of the lunatics had been opened, and they were rushing about singing, laughing and chanting depending on the manner in which their madness affected them. Those who escaped the flames and the bayonets of the soldiers (who were themselves more than a little maddened by this bloody combat) were taken back to Monte Torrero.[57]

With the French occupying a corridor of territory leading right to the heart of the city, Zaragoza should now by rights have fallen. But there was to be no surrender. Completely exhausted, the attackers lost all impetus, while the Spaniards began to recover their courage and press in against the flanks of the salient. Yet it was a grim time for the defenders. Among the miserable civilians who could do nothing but cower from the French shelling was Faustino Casamayor:

> For the past two days . . . for want of meat the sick have had nothing but soup made from herbs. Indeed, there has been no meat on any table in the city, and this has greatly upset the people. There are so many dreadful sights . . . things were already bad enough. It is very sad to see so many churches closed, so many priests and religious wandering the streets, so many widows and mothers lamenting . . . the fury of the enemy, so many houses abandoned or in ruins, so many people trying to find new homes in streets that have not yet been destroyed by the fighting, and finally so many people with no other remedy or comfort than to make their way to Nuestra Señora del Pilar . . . And all the time the enemy remain in the city pillaging and destroying, killing and wounding.[58]

Had things gone on in the fashion described by Casamayor, in the end Zaragoza would probably have fallen, but in the end the city was saved. Shaken by the news of Bailén, as Alcaide Ibieca recounts, Verdier decided to retreat:

> It soon became clear that the enemy were going to raise the siege . . . In the afternoon of 13 August they called for a parley, and we assumed that this would just

be the same old blather, but it turned out that they wanted to return a number of prisoners, among them General Palafox's old tutor, Padre Basilio . . . Then at nightfall they set fire to their base on Monte Torrero. The stores of timber . . . burned particularly furiously, and the great pyramids of fire made for a most startling sight . . . Finally, round about twelve o'clock there came a terrible explosion which shook all the buildings in the city. The unexpected shock filled us with fear for a moment, but then we realised that the enemy had blown up the monastery of Santa Engracia and were withdrawing from their positions . . . At three o'clock in the morning some peasants went out to Monte Torrero, and, climbing over the defence works by the light of some burning mattresses and bedding, found it strewn with rubbish and discarded objects of all sorts . . . With the retreat of the French now a certainty, the news was greeted with much joy, but to many people it seemed like a dream. Nor was this surprising: such had been the weight of our suffering that it was hard to take in such wonderful news.[59]

Vimeiro

So accustomed are British readers to thinking that the Peninsular War did not begin until the first action of Sir Arthur Wellesley took place at Roliça on 17 August 1808 that the preceding accounts of the fighting at Bailén and Zaragoza ought to serve as a useful corrective. From 1 August 1808, however, a British army under Sir Arthur Wellesley did indeed start to disembark roughly half-way between Lisbon and Oporto. As Charles Leslie recounts, it was not the easiest of beginnings to the campaign:

All was now bustle on board. Animation shone in every countenance. Our anxious hopes of being employed in active service were about to be realised. Everyone was occupied in selecting the few articles requisite for a campaign, and getting their heavy baggage properly secured. This was effected with no small trouble. A tremendous swell caused the ship to roll in the most violent manner and everything was slipping and flying about. We got into flat boats soon after midday, but the process of disembarkation soon became a tedious and dangerous operation. Owing to the swell and dreadful surf, only a few boats could approach the beach, where Portuguese fishermen were employed in wading to meet them and conduct them to the shore. During this we had to remain for hours tossing and rolling about till our turn came. Several boats were upset, and one containing a part of our grenadiers lost arms and everything, and the men narrowly escaped with their lives. It was late when we reached the army . . . It was so dark that we had some difficulty in finding our tents, and, in regard to food, nothing whatever could be got, so we had to content ourselves with a morsel of ship's biscuit and a glass of rum from our haversacks. We then wrapped ourselves in our cloaks and lay down on the . . . grass, eagerly seeking repose after our fatigues.[60]

Advancing south proved harder than had been expected. An isolated French division put up a sharp fight at Roliça, while it was a long, hot march through rough country. Among the men was Thomas Howell, an 18-year-old from Edinburgh who had grown up in a

background of genteel poverty and joined the Seventy-First Foot after a fit of stagefright
had put paid in the most humiliating of fashions to an attempt to become an actor:

> On our leaving the ships, each man got four pounds of biscuit and four pounds of
> salt beef cooked on board. We marched for twelve miles up to the knees in sand,
> which caused us to suffer much . . . for the marching made it rise and cover us. We
> lost four men of our regiment who had died of thirst. We buried them where they
> fell.[61]

For the British army the first major action of the Peninsular War came at Vimeiro, a small
village near the sea where 21 August saw the bulk of Junot's forces hurl themselves upon
the British in an attempt to throw them into the sea. Not a major battle by later standards,
it was quickly resolved in favour of Sir Arthur Wellesley. The main fighting took place in
the centre of the British line around a low hill to the immediate south of the village of
Vimeiro itself. Among the defenders were the famous Ninety-Fifth Rifles in whose ranks
was to be found Benjamin Harris, a young shepherd from Blandford, who had been
conscripted into the army under the terms of the legislation creating the so-called Army of
Reserve in 1802 and then volunteered for foreign service. Deployed in open order in
advance of the main line, he was among the first men to open fire on the four battalions
with which an over-confident Junot first attempted to drive the British from the hill:

> I myself was soon so hotly engaged, loading and firing away, enveloped in the smoke
> I created, and the cloud which hung about me from the continued fire of my
> comrades, that I could see nothing for a few minutes but the red flash of my own
> piece among the white vapour clinging to my very clothes. This has often seemed
> to me the greatest drawback upon our present system of fighting, for while in such
> a state . . . until some friendly breeze . . . clears the space around, a soldier knows
> no more of his position . . . than the very dead lying around . . . The French, in great
> numbers, came steadily upon us, and we pelted away upon them like a shower of
> leaden hail. Under any cover we could find we lay, firing one moment, jumping up
> and running for it the next, and when we could see before us we observed the
> cannon balls making a lane through the enemy's columns as they advanced,
> huzzaing and shouting like madmen.[62]

In command of Harris's company was Captain John Leach, who had obtained a
commission in the Seventieth Foot and served in the West Indies before transferring into
the Ninety-Fifth Rifles:

> The night before the battle I belonged to a picket of about 200 riflemen . . . We were
> posted in a large pine wood . . . About eight o'clock in the morning . . . a cloud of
> light troops, supported by a heavy column of infantry, entered the wood, and,
> assailing the pickets with great impetuosity, obliged us to fall back for support on
> the Ninety-Seventh Regiment. As soon as we had got clear of the front of the
> Ninety-Seventh . . . that regiment poured in such a well-directed fire that it
> staggered the resolution of the hostile column, which declined to close . . . with
> them. About the same time the second battalion of the Fifty-Second, advancing

through the wood, took the French in flank, and drove them before them in confusion. On the pickets being driven in, I joined my own brigade, which was on the left of the Ninety-Seventh. Here the business was beginning to assume a serious aspect. Some heavy masses of infantry, preceded by a swarm of light troops, were advancing with great resolution . . . against the brigade on which our battalion was posted. In spite of the deadly fire which several hundred riflemen kept up on them, they continued to press forward . . . until the old Fiftieth Regiment received them with a destructive volley, following it instantly with a most brilliant . . . charge with the bayonet.[63]

There followed two other French attacks, both of them unsuccessful. Watching the action from a position in the rear of the British line was Londoner Stephen Morley, a private in the Fifth Regiment of Foot, who had enlisted in 1804 and since served in Hanover and South America:

Our situation was on the slope of an eminence. We saw our people promptly advance against the enemy's masses, which were formed in column, and with which they boldly attempted to break the British lines. The attempt was vain, although they were ably assisted by their [cannon] and howitzers, from the latter of which we saw the balls rise high in the air; after describing many of the segments of a circle, they generally fell between our people who were advancing and ourselves. Dense smoke soon after enveloped the belligerents. It was then we found our situation irksome: many of our officers too high spirited to be thus shut out of the glowing scene actually left us and ran into the battle.[64]

In this part of the fighting there occurred one of those curious incidents that are found on any field of battle. Anthony Hamilton was a runaway apprentice from Donegal who had joined the Forty-Third Foot as a volunteer in 1806 or 1807. At Vimeiro his battalion suffered a higher rate of loss than any other unit in the British army, and the story that he recounts must therefore be regarded as being doubly remarkable:

Our regiment, the Forty-Third, was posted close by the road that entered the village. The enemy advanced upon us with determination and valour, but after a desperate struggle on our part were driven back with great slaughter. It was not only a hot day, but also a hot fight, and one of our men by the name of MacArthur who stood by me, having opened his mouth to catch a little fresh air, [was struck] by a bullet from the enemy [which] entered his mouth obliquely, which he never perceived until I told him his neck was covered in blood. He, however, kept the field until the battle was over.[65]

For a French view of the action we can turn to Jacques-Louis Hulot, a 35-year-old captain in the Sixteenth Regiment of Artillery, who was commanding a battery of field guns attached to the four grenadier battalions that made up Junot's reserve. Preoccupied with his battery, Hulot observed little of the battle until he suddenly found the victorious redcoats bearing down on his position:

Hardly had the reserve arrived on the field when it set off in column of platoons . . . with its two batteries off to one side. Captain Brun, who was an *aide-de-camp* of the commander of the reserve artillery, Colonel Foy, then brought us an order to support the attack with my battery . . . on the right of the infantry and the other on their left . . . Complying with this order, I took up the position that had been indicated to me, but it was too low down: the enemy's cannon balls might just have flown over us, but I could only use howitzers, while their musketry was still a nuisance. I was just looking around for somewhere better to place my pieces when I saw Colonel Vincent of the engineers and an *aide-de-camp* of the general in chief bringing up some orders in a style that betokened little good. Just at this moment a column of English troops hove into view and made as if to rush my battery. I had my gunners load canister, but just at that moment a crowd of fugitives streamed past and masked the enemy from my sight . . . We tried in vain to stem the panic by falling back a short distance and occupying a small village that stood behind us. Barricading the main streets, I set my guns up to cover the few ways in, but such was the press that they were in several instances overturned, while I myself was almost knocked down despite being on horseback. Not a single one of my gunners abandoned the battery, and, had I but had a single battalion of infantry, I think I might have . . . gained sufficient time for the rest of the army to rally. But at that moment I might just as well have been crying out to a crowd of deaf people. All that I could do, then, was to drag my guns to the rear, and this managed to execute despite the heavy fire of the English.[66]

Some miles to the north-east of Vimeiro, a French flanking force had been trying to get round Wellesley's rather exposed left flank. Posted near the village of Ventosa was the Twenty-Ninth. As Charles Leslie remembered, the French seem initially to have advanced quite cautiously, covered by a thick screen of skirmishers. At all events, the first assault, which was delivered by the three-battalion-strong brigade of General Solignac, was preceded by a considerable period of skirmishing:

Scarcely was this victorious achievement and repulse of the enemy accomplished by the right wing when we on the left wing were attacked with great vigour. The enemy attempted to turn the extreme left of our lines, so that the Twenty-Ninth, being on the right, had at first little to do. But the light companies of the Twenty-Ninth, Eighty-Second and Fortieth regiments were warmly engaged in skirmishing close in our front. Our men were ordered to lie flat down on the ground, yet we lost a considerable number. We found it rather difficult to keep the men still, as they were impatient to get forward, particularly as they were under a galling fire, and were not allowed to return a shot.[67]

At length the French abandoned their skirmishing and rushed forwards. Facing them in the first instance were the Seventy-First Highlanders and with them Thomas Howell. It was a nerve-wracking moment. As Howell recounts:

They came upon us crying and shouting to the very point of our bayonets . . . I felt my mind waver: a breathless sensation came over me . . . I looked along the line. It was enough to assure me. The steady determined scowl of my companions assured my heart and gave me determination. How unlike the noisy advance of the French![68]

In the event, however, it was not much of a combat: advancing uphill, and confronted by superior numbers, the French were quickly routed. Present in the same brigade as Howell was a private of labouring stock in the Light Company of the Fortieth Foot; William Lawrence, from the village of Bryant's Piddle in Dorset, had enlisted in 1806 at the age of 15 after running away from the master builder to whom he was apprenticed:

> A large body of French made their appearance in our front. Our artillery greeted them pretty sharply, ploughing furrows through them with ball and throwing them into a confused state, after which our columns advanced under General Spencer, our cannon still playing over our heads, until we got within a short distance of the enemy when we fired and charged them, driving them from the position they had occupied after some very severe fighting . . . and capturing about seven pieces of artillery with ammunition wagons.[69]

The fight, however, was not quite over. Yet another French brigade – that of General Brenier – had been sent even further north than that of Solignac, and now launched a surprise attack on the victorious British. Among the men facing them was Lieutenant George Wood of the Eighty-Second Foot:

> A strong French regiment . . . advanced to within half a pistol shot of us when a tremendous point-blank fire ensued. This not proving effectual, 'Charge!' was the word vociferated from flank to centre, but on their seeing us come to this awful position of destruction in the art of war, they had not courage to withstand our impetuous movement, for, just as we were in the act of crossing bayonets, to the right-about they went in the quickest time. We followed as rapidly, driving them from their artillery . . . passing it on the right flank at the same time as the Seventy-First did on the left, and I trust we had an equal share in the honour of capturing them . . . It was near this spot that I saw, as we advanced, a Scotch piper of the Seventy-First Regiment lying wounded. This, however, did not prevent his cheering his comrades on to glory with their national music.[70]

With Junot's army completely beaten, the way was now open for the complete destruction of the French presence in Portugal. From this fate, however, the invaders were saved by the untimely change in the command of the British army that placed it in the hands of, first, Sir Harry Burrard and, second, Sir Hew Dalrymple. In reserve in the ranks of the Ninth Foot was James Hale, a militiaman from Gloucestershire who had joined the regular army in April 1807:

> Just in the midst of our glory we were ordered to halt, and were not permitted to advance any more that day, which caused great murmuring among the army, in particular in such regiments as had not been engaged, for every soldier seemed anxious to push on as we could plainly see that a great part of the French army

would have been our prisoners . . . had we been permitted to continue the advance . . . As Sir Arthur Wellesley was riding up and down in front of our brigade, the men loudly called out to him from one end of the line to the other, saying, 'Let us advance! Let us advance! The enemy is in great confusion!', but his answer was 'I have nothing to do with it: I have no command.' We were astonished to hear him say, 'I have no command', and in a short time, instead of advancing, we were ordered to take up our former position.[71]

Following the battle the British troops for the first time received an intimation of the sort of war in which they had become involved:

We remained at our advance until sunset, then retired to our camp ground . . . On my return from the pursuit . . . the birds of prey were devouring the slain. Here I beheld a sight . . . even more horrible: the peasantry prowling about, more ferocious than the beasts and birds of prey, finishing the work of death and carrying away whatever they thought worthy of their grasp. Avarice and revenge were the causes of these horrors. No fallen Frenchman that showed the least signs of life was spared. They even seemed pleased with mangling the dead bodies. When light failed them, they kindled a great fire and remained around it all night, shouting like as many savages. My sickened fancy felt the same as if it were witnessing a feast of cannibals.[72]

In view of the hostility of the Portuguese peasantry, the relief exhibited by many of the French prisoners was entirely understandable. Amidst the carnage of the battlefield, it was evidently this that most struck Leslie:

After resting some time on our arms, we marched back to the bivouac with bands playing and colours flying. It was amusing to see many of the French soldiers who had been taken prisoners, or who had come over to us, marching along with our men with shouldered arms and fixed bayonets, apparently in the greatest good humour, and all expressing anxious wishes to be sent to England. Two genteel-looking young men who were among the prisoners told me that they were conscripts torn from their homes, and that when their regiment gave way they threw themselves down, pretending to be wounded, in order that they might fall into our hands. Fatigue parties having been left to bury the dead, many of our men had possessed themselves of the French white linen frocks, and it was grotesque enough to see Highland soldiers strolling about the bivouac in these dresses. The field of battle after the action presented a curious feature from so many lying killed and wounded. There were quantities of letters and papers strewed about in all directions. I picked up a bill for several hundred francs payable in Paris, from which it appeared that the poor fellow who had owned it had gone as a substitute, and had received this bill in part payment. Many of the letters were from parents and friends, but not a word of politics was to be found in any of them.[73]

Other observers of the battlefield were less insouciant. Adam Neale, for example, was a surgeon with Anstruther's brigade who had observed the attack of Solignac's troops at close quarters:

Close to the spot where Major General Ferguson's brigade received the attack of the French stood a small farmhouse into which it had been determined to carry the wounded. Thither I repaired and witnessed a scene the most distressing. Around the building, whose interior was crowded with the wounded, lay a number of poor fellows in the greatest agony, not only from the anguish of their wounds, many of which were deplorable, but from the intense heat of the sun, which increased the parching fever induced by pain and loss of blood. Two fig trees afforded the scanty blessing of a sort of shade to the few who were huddled together beneath their almost leafless branches. Over the surrounding field lay scattered fragments of arms and military equipment of every description – caps, muskets, swords, bayonets, belts and cartouche boxes covered the ground, on which were also stretched in many an awful group, the friend and foe, the dying and the dead . . . On entering the cottage to survey the sadly interesting group within, I recognised . . . I could be useful . . . to a great many who, but for my interference . . . might have remained for many hours in excessive pain. To several, [however,] a simple inspection of their wounds, with a few words of consolation, or perhaps a little opium, was all that could be done or recommended. Of these brave men, the balls had pierced organs essentially connected with life, and in such cases prudence equally forbids the rash interposition of unavailing art and the useless indulgence of delusive hope . . . A hospital mate was . . . left in charge of them till the morning, and . . . [at] eleven o'clock at [night] I left them to proceed towards [Vimeiro] accompanied by Staff Surgeon F____. The night was so dark that it was necessary to have recourse to a Portuguese guide . . . On crossing the fields to get to the . . . road, I shuddered as we involuntarily stumbled over many an unburied corpse of man and horse. We found the road almost impassable from the number of tumbrils and artillery wagons of the enemy which were broken down in every direction. Our ears were saluted on passing the churchyard by the heavy moaning and exclamations of the wounded French, with whom the church and the cemetery were crowded. 'Ah, mon Dieu, mon Dieu! Le sang coule: je meurs, je meurs!' At length, with a great deal of difficulty, we reached Vimeiro. The streets . . . were choked up by the long line of ox wains bearing in from the fields the wounded, whose haggard countenances appeared more wretched from the glare of the torches which blazed around them and increased the horrors of the impressive scene.[74]

Someone else who tried to assist the many wounded was James Ormsby, a chaplain attached to Wellesley's headquarters:

The day was employed in burying the dead and conveying the wounded to the beach to be embarked in the transports . . . Having ascertained these most important concerns in a military view, the still, small voice of humanity led me to the hospital in Vimeiro where the wounded French, to the number of about 400, lay. A novice in such scenes, the sight affected me deeply. They were principally young men . . . Many operations had been performed, and the surgeons said few of them could survive. To one I addressed myself, and lamented the horrors of war, commiserating his pain . . . He replied with a mixture of pride and indignation that he gloried in his wounds and that war was the greatest happiness of his life. To such a disputant I had nothing to rejoin, but to wish his recovery, and that he might be doomed to bear the miseries of peace, and the inconveniences of two legs, two arms and the natural features of his face for the remainder of his days.[75]

Vimeiro had cost the British army less than 800 other casualties. Even so, for an army that had never had more than 10,000 men engaged in the fighting, the 'butcher's bill' was by no means inconsiderable. When news arrived that Dalrymple had compounded his suspension of the action of 21 August by negotiating a convention which allowed the French to return to France in British ships, there was much discontent, and all the more so as there followed a slow and uncomfortable march through the hills of central Portugal in the baking heat of summer. Particularly miserable were the officers and men of the Twenty-Eighth Foot, a unit which, after spending months at sea as a result of a fruitless expedition to Sweden, had disembarked just too late to take part in the battle. A scion of the Anglo-Irish ascendancy from Galway, Robert Blakeney had obtained a commission as an ensign at the age of 15 in 1804:

> This, our first march . . . was severely felt, since . . . we had been for upwards of four months cooped up in miserable little transports. The men had scarcely the use of their limbs and, being so long unaccustomed to carry their packs, to which were now added three days' provisions and sixty rounds of ball cartridge, in this their first march, with the thermometer between ninety and one hundred, many were left behind . . . Nor did the officers suffer less than the men. Being mostly very young, and, with the exception of those who were at Copenhagen, where little or no marching took place, never having seen a shot fired, they were totally ignorant of the nature of a campaign. Means of transport being very difficult to procure in Portugal and Spain, we all overloaded ourselves, carrying a boat cloak . . . a partial change of dress . . . three days' provisions . . . an extra pair of boots . . . a stout charge of rum . . . a case of pistols and a liberal quantity of ball-cartridge, and generally a heavy spy-glass. Thus heavily equipped, many of us commenced our first day's march in the Peninsula.[76]

Even reaching Lisbon proved a disappointment. For a good portrait of the Portuguese capital in 1808, we can turn to Robert Porter. The son of an army surgeon, Porter had been born in Durham in 1777 and from an early age displayed such talent as an artist that he had obtained a scholarship to the Royal Academy. After making his name through a series of dramatic canvasses illustrating various actions in the War of the Second Coalition, he had been commissioned to paint a number of murals by Alexander I of Russia and duly travelled to St Petersburg, where he fell in love with a Russian princess, only to have to flee to England following the peace of Tilsit in 1807. Always something of an adventurer, Porter had naturally seen the Peninsular War as a great opportunity to further his career, and had therefore attached himself to Wellesley's army as one of its more unusual camp followers:

On a nearer approach to Lisbon . . . the cleanliness which the external whiteness of the houses shining in the sun leads one to expect vanishes, and the miserably plastered dwellings present themselves in their true colours, bespattered with dirt of every description and rendered almost intolerable by the accumulated filth and the raging heat which draws their honours reeking up to heaven. On disembarking I landed some distance from the suburbs. The foul imagination of Dean Swift himself could not prefigure the scene that presented itself: a chaos of nastiness, poverty and wretchedness lay on every side. Rags or nakedness seemed the condition of every person who approached me, except now and then I saw a man enveloped in a mass of cloak in no better state, hung in . . . folds about him, leaving to the fancy the animated filth it concealed . . . While I am on this delectable subject (for, as it first strikes the senses on entering Lisbon, it must, perforce, be the first noticed), I cannot but remark that a nocturnal custom . . . is most religiously observed in this ever-steaming capital. As soon as night casts her sable mantle over the city, the inhabitants collect their libations, and pour them out in rich potations upon the earth beneath. In fact, few seconds pass without the foot passenger being saluted, or, most probably marked, by a *jet d'eau*, or something worse, from the teeming windows of the houses. Should the unlucky perambulator chance to be within reach of the torrent, I fear he would emerge with other ornaments hanging to his dress than the spangling globules of clear water. A brother officer of mine is so afraid of these green and yellow cascades that he never walks to his quarters at night without bearing above him the friendly shade of an umbrella.[77]

With Lisbon still full of French troops – the arrangements to send them home took a few days to organise and for a little while the rival armies not only mingled in the streets together but even mounted guard together side by side – the city was extremely crowded, and finding a billet therefore often proved a difficult task. One of those looking frantically for accommodation was Chaplain Ormsby:

On arriving at Lisbon, I had very great difficulty in procuring an apartment at one of their noisy and nasty hotels . . . There was such an assemblage of voices and language as Babel could scarcely have surpassed. Between the master and his waiters, there was a Greek, an Italian, a Swiss, a German, a Spaniard and a Portuguese, and, as they all spoke in a very high key and happened to choose exactly the same moment for utterance . . . I threw myself on their compassion and entreated that they would take it in rotation and speak but two at a time, as I might then be able to ascertain whether they could supply me with any . . . supper. They were amused, even to laughter, at the unreasonable absurdity of this request, and evidently entertained a very mean opinion of my understanding.[78]

* * *

Thus ended what may be regarded as the first phase of the Peninsular War. Repeatedly humiliated in Spain – for they had not just been defeated at Bailén and forced to abandon the siege of Zaragoza, but also driven from the walls of both Gerona and Valencia – the French had withdrawn into defensive positions behind the River Ebro and, in Catalonia, the city of Barcelona, which was soon being loosely blockaded by a large Spanish army. And, however disappointing the end of the campaign as far as the British Army was concerned, Portugal was free. But the war was not over. Never in his entire career had Napoleon suffered so bad a blow to his prestige, and for that very reason he could not quietly draw in his horns, restore the Bourbons to the throne and pray that the whole débâcle would soon be forgotten. On the contrary, Bailén and Vimeiro must needs be avenged, the British chased into the sea and Spain and Portugal taught a lesson they would never forget. Very soon then, preparations were in train for a new campaign, and one that would in truth be very different.

Chapter 2

The Revenge of the French

In Spain, Portugal and Britain alike, Bailén and Vimeiro induced a mood of great self-confidence, and, indeed, euphoria. Napoleon had been worsted and humiliated, and the reputation of the *grande armée* left in tatters. There were, of course, disappointments and frustrations – the convention of Sintra had, for example, taken much of the shine off victory in Portugal – while more sentient observers were warning that the French were very far from beaten. Yet, for all that, it was a moment of real hope and excitement: for the first time it seemed that Napoleon's grip on the continent of Europe might be loosened. So it was that, in Germany in particular, revenge-minded Prussian soldiers and enthusiastic nationalist writers began to dream of organising an insurrection of their own. Early in 1809, for example, we find the future Prussian chief-of-staff Neithardt von Gneisenau organising a network of committees to prepare an Iberian-style revolt, and the poet Heinrich von Kleist writing a grandiloquent ode in honour of the defender of Zaragoza, José Palafox, as well as translating an anti-Napoleonic catechism published in Spain in 1808 into German. Echoes of the events in Spain and Portugal are also to be found in the preparation of the Tyrolean insurrection of 1809, while both inside and outside the Portland administration in London a variety of members of the British establishment seized on the idea of popular revolt as the new way forward in the struggle against Napoleon. Indeed, even in France there were those who were shaken to the core by the failures across the Pyrenees and began to question the sustainability of the Napoleonic epic. But the French ruler was not beaten, and within the space of a few months he would reveal to the world not only the partial nature of the setbacks he had suffered in 1808, but also the extent of his commitment to victory in the Iberian peninsula: the prestige of French arms had been sullied, and in the eyes of the emperor only total victory could set things to rights.

The Calm before the Storm

In both Spain and Portugal the chief priority facing the new political authorities that had emerged from the turmoil of the insurrection of the early summer was the restoration of order and the mobilisation of the nation for total war: such was Napoleon's desire for revenge and his ability to take drastic action that only the most whole-hearted commitment to the struggle could have saved the Iberian insurgents. In Portugal it proved relatively easy to establish a new central government: across the ocean in Brazil, the Portuguese monarchy was still intact and this gave both direction and focus to the efforts to restore order. However, in Spain the situation was very different. In the first place, Bailén made for a considerable degree of over-confidence, not to say complacency. In the circumstances what was required was clear and responsible leadership. This was not entirely lacking: many men in public life were well aware of the need to build an effective government and a new army.

But they were hardly operating in propitious circumstances. There was, for example, much rivalry among the different provincial juntas, some of which certainly had designs on imposing themselves on their fellows, and even of assuming the national leadership. With some difficulty a new government known as the Junta Suprema Central was formed, but this found that not only was there much resistance to its authority but also many of its subordinates were fiercely opposed to one another. While the Spaniards were struggling to put their house in order, meanwhile, the French house was simply being ordered. From far away, then, masses of troops began to converge on the Spanish frontier. Among the men of Marshal Mortier's Fifth Corps was a diminutive 34-year-old infantry sergeant in the 103rd Line named François Lavaux, who had fought at Hohenlinden, Austerlitz and Jena after being conscripted in 1798 in his native Champagne village of Rivière-les-Fossés:

> In Germany all was profound peace. In the midst of this, however, our eyes were drawn to the . . . bloody picture afforded by the Spanish revolution. With tears in our eyes we contemplated the murder of our brothers-in-arms in their very beds, and cried out with one voice, 'Vengeance! Let's go! These brave lads . . . must be avenged immediately!' On 9 September 1808 we broke camp . . . From Breslau – the capital of Silesia – to Madrid, it was but a stroll: I made it at least 700 leagues. Leaving Silesia behind us, we crossed Prussia, and then passed through Bayreuth, Bamberg . . . Schweinfurt . . . Wurzburg and Heidelberg. Crossing the Rhine at Spire, we traversed Landau, Wissembourg, Haguenau, Saverne, Phalsbourg, Saarbrouck, Blamont, Lunéville and Nancy. In this last place our passage was as brilliant an affair as anything I can remember. The inhabitants received us with gestures of the warmest friendship. They had prepared a great feast to celebrate the return of the *grande armée*. Nothing was lacking . . . Every soldier had his place at table, military music accompanied the meal, and in the evening there was a free theatrical performance.[79]

In general, the mood in the French army was one of great confidence, but the few men who had served in Spain before in 1793-95 or 1801 warned their comrades of a region of Europe that was, at the very least, devoid of creature comforts. Among these 'old sweats' was Jean-Roche Coignet, a sometime shepherd boy from Druyes-les-Belles-Fontaines in the Department of the Yonne, who, now aged 32, was at this point a sergeant of grenadiers in the Old Guard:

> Early in October, the emperor issued orders for us . . . to start for Bayonne. I said to my comrades, 'We are going to Spain: beware of the fleas and the lice! They root up the straw in the barracks and run about over the pavement like mice. Let drinkers beware too: the wine of the country is fierce stuff: a drop of it lays you low.'[80]

To return to events in Spain, the general confusion was to a certain extent covered by a veneer of enthusiasm, in which respect let us turn to the memoirs of George Jackson. An experienced diplomat who had previously served in a variety of postings in central and northern Europe, Jackson arrived in La Coruña on 20 October 1808 with the new British ambassador, John Hookham Frere:

By ten o'clock . . . the governor . . . with a few *hidalgos* and deputies came on board, and, after an immense deal of complimentation and a trifling amount of business had been got though, we began the ceremony of landing, for which three gaily decorated boats were in waiting . . . When we had all taken our places and were about to strike off from the ship, the interesting fact was announced to the anxious spectators that lined the shore, by a salute from the *Semiramis*, which was immediately returned from the batteries by twenty-one guns. Onward we went and at last set foot on Spanish soil amidst the never-ceasing shouts and acclamations of thousands of excited people of every age, sex and condition. The air may indeed be said to have been rent by the loud *vivas* that resounded around us, *vivas* for the *ingleses*, for Ferdinand VII, for the Junta, and for many other persons and things too numerous to particularise . . . The day was very fine, and the *tout ensemble*, not forgetting the variety of picturesque costume and the veils of the women – which, by the way, serve for anything but concealing their charms – formed a spectacle of which I have given you a very faint description, but which will ever be to me a most interesting recollection, let the results of our efforts be what it may. The enthusiasm of the inhabitants . . . is something I could hardly have imagined, much less can I describe it. The women appear particularly forward in the cause, a zeal which has extended even to the convents . . . However, to return to the landing place, when we had with no small difficulty reached the top of it, the governor, mounting a richly caparisoned horse, led the way, while we followed in suitably decorated carriages, dragged by the populace, to the government house, attended by escorts of the new levies, of horse and foot, and the whole town of Coruña at our heels, their shouts only interrupted by the fizzing of crackers, explosions of rockets, and the banging of another salute from the ships and batteries. Arrived at last at our destination, we were introduced to the Junta of this province, assembled in form in their state chamber, in the centre of which is a crimson velvet throne with a large portrait of Ferdinand VII suspended upon it. This ceremony ended, we proceeded in nearly the same way as we had arrived to the house of the Duke of Viraques, apparently the best in the place, and which the duke had most obligingly prepared for our reception. By this time it was two o'clock, and we were to dine with the Junta at five . . . The intervening three hours were fully occupied in receiving innumerable visits from the inhabitants of the town, some individually, others in bodies, but they seemed all equally devoted to the cause, and grateful to us for our assistance. This is the more pleasing because La Coruña and the other towns on the coast have been the greatest sufferers from the war with England from the almost total cessation of their commerce. At the appointed hour we were again, with all due honours, conducted to the state chamber, and were received by the same people, who, as the Junta is composed of persons of various grades, differed much in their dress and appearance, but were alike earnest and enthusiastic in the greeting they gave us. From the state room we were ushered into a large hall where covers laid for at least a hundred wished to show the superabundance of their sentiments of gratitude towards us. By the profusion of the viands and wines they had provided for the repast, for the table might be said, in a far less figurative sense than the expression is usually employed, to have groaned under the number of dishes that were served on it. For my part, had there been but a third of that number, and those less highly flavoured with garlic, I should not have thought the banquet less sumptuous. From the dinner table we had to proceed to the theatre . . . As you may suppose, it was filled almost to suffocation. As soon as we entered, the whole of the audience rose . . . 'God save the King' was struck up and 'Rule Britannia' followed, with the same huzzas and *vivas* that had greeted us in the morning repeated at the end of each. When we had full half an hour of this, the play began. It had been selected for the occasion, and every word that the audience fancied bore an allusion to England was received with bursts of applause . . . The piece . . . commenced by a representation of Ferdinand in prison and George III coming to his assistance. Afterwards Boney is introduced, utterly confounded by the successive accounts which Joseph and Murat – frightened out of their wits and running breathless on the stage – bring him of the Spanish successes. This precious piece concludes with a scene of the infernal regions, where Pluto and Proserpine are represented tormenting the three brothers Bonaparte, while, in the background, George and Ferdinand appear seated in the clouds, serenely contemplating the god and his wife at their work. In the grand finale, Pluto strikes Bonaparte under foot, 'God save the King' strikes up and the curtain drops. Never before was, I think, such a pack of stuff and nonsense imagined . . . but they say that the effect is good and serves to keep up the spirit of the people. It was just one o'clock in the morning when we got home, and never in all my life was I more gratified to betake myself to my pillow.[81]

Yet enthusiasm did not equate to efficacy. A plan of campaign was adopted, but this amounted to little more than letting the various Spanish generals pursue pet schemes of their own whose only effect was to make the Spanish armies ever more vulnerable to a French counter-attack. Among sentient observers there was therefore much alarm. Attached to the headquarters of the Army of the Centre, for example, was the British liaison officer Samuel Ford Whittingham:

Everything is now settled and tomorrow I go off to the army. We occupy the right bank of the Ebro, and the French the left . . . Our whole force may amount to 100,000 men. But at least 30,000 of them are not yet near the scene of action, having been detained by a complete want of clothing. Yet there is no time to be lost if we mean to attack the French before the arrival of their reinforcements . . . For the first time in my life . . . my heart misgives me, and forbodes no good. I fear the result of this action. The French are concentrated, and we are considerably scattered. Their troops are all equal; ours, some bad and some good. They have the advantage of unity of command; we are directed by three generals, all independent of each other . . . The enthusiasm of the Spaniards is worthy of their cause, and their bravery such as you would wish your best friend to possess. But we are not yet organised, and . . . I cannot help entertaining some doubts of the issue of the first battle.[82]

With the government unable to function effectively, meanwhile, the troops were soon suffering from serious shortages of all kinds. Among the forces caught up in the cold and rain that characterised autumn in the Cantabrian mountains of northern Spain was the division that had been sent to Denmark in 1807 under the Marqués de la Romana. Rescued by the Royal Navy, this had recently been landed at Santander and numbered among its members Juan Manuel Sarasa, a 23-year-old soldier of the Zamora infantry regiment from the Navarrese town of Ollo:

> We were encamped in the Berrón district for fifteen days. For the first three we received no rations of any sort until the evening of the third when some cattle arrived. So great was our hunger that we did not bother to butcher them properly, but simply hacked off such chunks as we could. The meat we set to roast, but, absolutely overcome, we snatched it from the fires before it was barely warm. As for bread we received none at all. I bought a loaf for 100 *reales* . . . and to eat it I had to hide it from my comrades.[83]

Had the provincial authorities been able to stand in for the floundering Junta Central, some of the soldiers' suffering might have been eased. In practice, however, in many instances they were still worse. In Zaragoza, for example, José Palafox seemingly had little to offer the Spanish war effort other than demagogy. Let us here quote the verdict of an artillery officer named Luis de Villaba who was currently serving in his forces:

> The astonishing disorders that took place in Zaragoza . . . would fill a book . . . Appointments and commissions, few of them merited, were lavished on all sides for no good reason, many of them going to deluded youths without experience and some of them even to persons of noted criminal conduct. Mere stonemasons were promoted to be captains in the Royal Corps of Engineers, and their advice was preferred to that of real engineer officers. A guard of honour was created for Palafox . . . and given rich costumes in the style of times gone by while thousands of soldiers who had fallen sick were left without . . . shelter or support. The newspapers were full of bare-faced sedition: libels were published against persons of the highest character and merit, while the dispositions and announcements of higher authority were openly criticised (indeed, the Central Junta was never recognised in Aragón) . . . Finally, all the maxims and military doctrines that might have led us to victory were ignored or trampled underfoot, while all those that would bring us to ruin with bloodshed as copious as it was useless were adopted . . . To sum up, we can say that General Palafox was a staunch vassal of King Fernando VII, but, being both very young and lacking in training and experience, he became infatuated with the idea that nobody else could . . . defend the Fatherland and chose those at his side very badly.[84]

If the Spanish authorities at every level exhibited a curious mixture of frivolity and incapacity, there was one issue that even the most well-disposed and assiduous of regimes would have found difficult to cope with. Thus, far from being united behind the war effort, the masses of the populace were in effect bitterly opposed to it. Though sometimes prepared to defend their homes against attack, they had not risen in revolt in May 1808 to fight for the Old Order as such, but rather to revenge themselves on the propertied classes for years of misery. In practice, however, the rising had brought few changes at the local level – the provincial juntas, for example, were universally manned by representatives of the Church, the town councils, the army and the nobility – and the British forces who began to enter Spain from October onwards therefore quickly began to discover that the reality of the Spanish war was very different from what they had been led to expect. To quote Auguste Schaumann, a 30-year-old Hanoverian exile who had worked as a post office official in his native country before fleeing to England and enlisting as a commissary, in which capacity he was currently attached to the Thirty-Second Regiment of Foot:

> The people here have the effrontery to look upon the English troops as exotic animals who have come here to engage in a private fight with the French, and now that they are here all the fine Spanish gentlemen have to do is to look on with their hands in their pockets . . . The more one sees of the Spaniards, the more discouraged one gets. Everything that has been so blatantly trumpeted in the papers about their enthusiasm, their great armies and the stampede to join them is simply lies. It often looks as if Spain were not even willing to defend herself. In all the hamlets, villages and towns, the inhabitants . . . lounge about in their hundreds, completely apathetic, indifferent and gloomy, and sunk in their idleness. Is this the daring, patriotic and impetuous race about which the press have raved so bombastically?[85]

In similar vein is a letter from the surgeon Adam Neale, that was written to a friend at home from Salamanca:

> I have hitherto been . . . among the most sanguine in the Spanish cause, but since my arrival here I have witnessed so much apparent apathy and indifference that . . . I cannot help at times asking myself if I am in the midst of Spain. The beings I see muffled up in long cloaks, sauntering . . . in listless indifference under the piazzas, are so very different from that bold impassioned race which my heated imagination has been contemplating that I wish rather to believe myself in the midst of a Spanish city in Paraguay or Peru.[86]

Finally, such troops as there were frequently behaved with the greatest indiscipline. Francisco de Paula Guervos, for example, was a volunteer from Andalucía who found himself sent to Catalonia:

> Every day I hate these people more: they have no God but money, and for it they would sell their fatherland, their families, their saints and anything else that comes to hand . . . Much vaunted though it is, the Army of Catalonia is nothing but a collection of bands of thieves who, under the name of *somatenes*, enter the towns and villages in almost the same manner as the French . . . the only difference being that they are rather more skilful when it comes to robbing them.[87]

From Burgos to Madrid

A variety of adverse circumstances, then, dogged the Spanish war effort. Now commanded by Sir John Moore, meanwhile, the British forces in Portugal had also been having many difficulties, and as a result were still many weeks from being ready for battle. At the end of October, however, time ran out. Since the beginning of September, nemesis had been gathering in the shape of the immense reinforcements that were pouring across the Pyrenees at the behest of Napoleon. With a powerful striking force now gathered along the upper reaches of the River Ebro in Navarre and the Basque provinces and the emperor himself almost on the scene, early in November the French struck. Minor fighting had been going on in the vicinity of Bilbao since late October, but the first real blow came just outside Burgos at the village of Gamonal where on 10 November Napoleon himself came up against the Army of Extremadura under the inexperienced Conde de Belveder. Dezydery Chlapowski was an *aide-de-camp* of Napoleon who had served in the Prussian army from 1801 to 1806 and then enlisted in the forces that were being raised to fight for the French in Poland:

> Our first march took us to Irun. We only caught up with the emperor at Burgos where he had halted because the main Spanish army was drawn up on the plain before the city. As soon as the leading body of our army had arrived, that is, one corps . . . of three infantry divisions, a division of dragoons and half of the Guard, he deployed them, not in line, but in battalion columns with skirmishers in front. The skirmishers went into line, and the artillery must have fired about 500 rounds at the enemy. We could see confusion breaking out in their ranks. They only tried one charge.[88]

As was frequently the case in this campaign, the aftermath of Gamonal was a grim affair. A senior official of the French foreign ministry, André Miot de Melito was a close personal friend of Joseph Bonaparte, who had served as his Minister of the Interior in Naples and had now been appointed to the post of intendant of the royal household:

> As we approached Burgos, we crossed the site of the affair of 10 November. It was still strewn with corpses, although the sad spectacle which it presented did not make as painful an impression on me as the state of that great city at the moment of our entrance. Absolutely deserted, almost all the houses had been pillaged and their furniture smashed to pieces and thrown in the mud; part of the city was . . . on fire; a frenzied soldiery was forcing every door and window, breaking down everything that stood in the way, and destroying more than they consumed; all the churches had been stripped; and the streets were encumbered with the dead and dying. In short, although it had not been defended, the city exhibited all the horrors of an assault.[89]

That horrors aplenty took place there is no doubt. Even the cathedral, where a group of monks had gone into hiding in the tower, was the scene of violent death, one witness to such a scene being Jean-Roche Coignet:

> Our horse-grenadiers put up their chargers inside the fine old arches, which were filled . . . with bales of cotton. They were about to feed their horses, when, at the foot of the small stairway [leading to the tower] there appeared a little boy of eleven or twelve . . . As soon as one of them saw him, he ran back up the stairway, but the grenadier followed him and caught up with him at the top of the steps. As soon as he reached the landing, the little boy entered with him. The door closed, and the . . . little boy came down again, showed himself as before and another grenadier followed him . . . The little boy returned a third time, but a grenadier who had seen his comrades go up the stairway said to those who had just returned from feeding their horses, 'Two of our men have already gone up to the belfry, and have not returned. They may have got shut up . . .

We must see about it at once.' So they started off in pursuit of the child. They . . . mounted the narrow stairway . . . burst open the door, and found their comrades lying there with their heads cut off and bathed in their own blood. Our old soldiers became perfectly enraged. They slaughtered those scoundrels of monks: there were eight of them, and they had all sorts of ammunition, provisions and wine. It was quite a fortress. We threw . . . the little boy out of the windows and down into the garden.[90]

Nor was Gamonal the only disaster to strike the Allied cause on 10 November. On the same day that Belveder was attacked before Burgos, Blake's Army of the Left was hit in the Cantabrian mountains at Espinosa de los Monteros. Ensconced in a strong position and in part composed of the veteran troops who had been rescued from Denmark by the Royal Navy, however, the Spaniards put up a good fight. Among the defenders was Juan Manuel Sarasa:

We had hardly taken up our positions when the enemy attacked us with great impetus, but their arrogance came to grief in the face of the valour and serenity of our division. Letting our opponents approach to within ten paces, with every volley we brought down an entire column. The enemy repeated their attacks with fresh troops, but each time . . . they were beaten back, leaving mountains of corpses in front of our lines.[91]

There is considerable exaggeration here – French casualties in the whole battle have been estimated at only 1,000 men – but even so the French had been roughly handled, and had Blake slipped away that night the battle would have gone down as a Spanish victory. But, rendered over-confident by his success, he elected to stay put. At first, indeed, his men were still full of fight. The 34-year-old son of a peasant from Cahors, Jean-Pierre Dellard was the colonel of the Sixteenth Light Infantry:

As soon as [the Spaniards] saw us, they . . . sent out . . . a very large number of skirmishers to harass our right from behind the shelter of a stone wall which flanked it. Seven small artillery pieces of a sort carried by mule-back, together with a battery stationed in front of their line, then opened up on us with canister and wounded a number of men.[92]

This resistance, however, was not sufficient to deter the French from pressing home the assault. Unusually, however, the attack came not in serried columns, but rather as a very thick skirmish line that was constantly reinforced, and peppered the defenders with musketry. With many senior officers down, the section of the Spanish line targeted by the French, which was held by a division of raw levies from Asturias, collapsed. Attacked in both front and flank, the rest of the army fell back in its turn. Among the last to retreat were the men of La Romana:

With the river barring our route just behind us and the enemy in possession of the only bridge . . . there was no option but to wade across . . . Once on the other side we had to climb a very steep slope . . . exposed to the terrible fire which the enemy directed at us from the other bank. In this short time I was hit by seven bullets, but fortunately not one of them cost me a scratch. When I saw the state in which they had left my clothes, I raised my gaze to heaven and gave thanks to the Almighty.[93]

Conducted in incessant rain and snow through some of the highest mountains in Spain, however, the retreat that followed broke the Army of the Left as a fighting force: barely half its 40,000 men reached León, and those that did were penniless, starving, disease-ridden and lacking arms and ammunition. As La Romana wrote on 9 December after being ordered to take over the command from the unfortunate Blake:

> I have now assembled 20,000 men . . . but I can make no movement against the enemy because I have neither any cavalry nor a greater supply of musket cartridges than forty rounds per man. I lack many arms which the troops lost in their disorderly retreat and many units have no camp kettles in which to prepare their meals. There is not a *real* in the army's coffers, and the troops have not been paid for the last month . . . The draught and pack mules have not been paid for, and their owners work with the greatest ill will.[94]

With a huge gap now torn in the Spanish line, the French forces fanned out to exploit their success. Temporarily attached to the VI Corps of Marshal Ney was the brigade of light cavalry that included the brown-jacketed Second Regiment of Hussars. Present in its ranks was a young officer named Albert de Rocca. A scion of one of the leading families of Geneva, de Rocca had joined the French army in search of adventure in 1805. As Rocca records, he and his fellows took part in the great flanking manoeuvre by which Ney was sent to envelop the rear of Castaños's Army of the Centre:

> On the fifteenth of November, our brigade of hussars went to Lerma to join the corps of Marshal Ney . . . On the sixteenth, Marshal Ney's corps went from Lerma to Aranda: the inhabitants always abandoned their dwellings at our approach, carrying with them into their mountain retreats all their most precious possessions. The solitude and the desolation which victorious armies commonly leave behind them seemed to precede us wherever we came. In approaching the deserted towns and villages of Castile, we no longer saw those clouds of smoke, which, constantly rising through the air, form a second atmosphere over inhabited and populous cities. Instead of living sounds . . . we heard nothing within the circle of their walls but . . . the croaking of the ravens hovering around the high belfries. The houses, now empty, served only to re-echo tardily and discordantly the deep sounds of the drum or the shrill notes of the trumpet . . . As soon as the main guard was posted, at a concerted signal the soldiers left the ranks, and precipitated themselves all together tumultuously, like a torrent, through the city, and long after the arrival of the army shrieks were still heard, and the noise of doors [being] broken open with hatchets or great stones.[95]

While Marshal Ney was trying to take Castaños in the rear, considerable forces were moving against him down the valley of the River Ebro under Marshal Lannes. The account left by Marbot, who had in the course of the autumn been reassigned to his personal staff, is brief and to the point:

> Napoleon ordered Lannes to go to Logroño, take command of the Army of the Ebro [i.e. Marshal Moncey's III Corps] . . . See what the presence of a single capable and energetic man can do. This army of recruits, which Moncey had not dared to lead

against the enemy, was set in motion by Lannes on the day of his arrival, and marched against the enemy with ardour. We came up with him the following day, the twenty-third, in front of Tudela, and after three hours' fighting the conquerors of Bailén were driven in, beaten, [and] completely routed, and fled headlong towards Zaragoza, leaving thousands of dead on the field. We captured a great many men, several colours and all the artillery: a complete victory. During this affair I had a bullet through my sabretache.[96]

Another *aide-de-camp* who observed the fighting was the Pole, Dezydery Chlapowski:

The Spanish corps . . . stood in a strong position in the hills, which were perhaps too steep as artillery on such heights cannot fire downwards effectively . . . Before dawn, two infantry divisions set off up the hillside in four columns with skirmishers out in front. The Spanish outposts half-way up fired at them and retired to the summits, from which the artillery opened a heavy fire. For two hours the French columns did not stop, and their skirmishers duly reached the ridge line. An officer came down to the marshal with the news that the whole Spanish corps was retiring and was everywhere in chaos.[97]

Among the forces marching directly on the Spanish army at Tudela from the French assembly area around Vitoria and Miranda de Ebro was the Second Regiment of the Legion of the Vistula. Born in 1789 in part of Poland that had recently been annexed by Prussia, Heinrich von Brandt had originally enlisted in the Prussian army, but had transferred to the Legion of the Vistula following the demobilisation of his regiment in 1807. At the battle that followed at Tudela on 23 November, however, he and his comrades saw little action:

Tudela was a tremendous boost for French morale as the Spanish army was composed of Castaños's Andalusians, the victors of Bailén, and the Aragonese of Palafox, full of pride after their . . . defence of Zaragoza. They fled in complete disorder . . . The battle had raged sometimes this way, sometimes that, from morning to night, but none of our troops had been engaged for more than two hours at any one time. Habert's brigade had taken part in an attack on the heights, but my battalion had been placed in reserve at a considerable distance from the enemy and where only the noise of the cannon and the shrill whistling of cannon balls overhead could make us believe we were on a field of battle. That part of the enemy which fled towards Zaragoza was pursued as far as Alagón . . . This whole stretch of road was littered with corpses, mostly volunteers without uniforms, as the cavalry had shown them no quarter. These corpses would lie unburied for some weeks.[98]

After the battle the Army of Aragón and a considerable part of the Army of the Centre took refuge in Zaragoza. Realising that the city was a strategic cul-de-sac, however, Castaños led most of his surviving troops southwards in a desperate bid to reach Madrid. With them was Samuel Whittingham:

Before the battle of Tudela, I had been attacked by rheumatic fever and confined to my bed for many days. Towards the close of the action, General Graham called on me to say that all was lost, and that I must be moved forthwith, or I should be taken prisoner. As all my horses were too gay and unsteady for a sick man, the general had brought one of his own, a strong steady horse, quite equal to my weight. A pillow was placed on the saddle, and I was carried downstairs and lifted into it. But my sufferings were beyond human endurance, and, after proceeding about three miles to the village of Ablitas, I was taken off the saddle and thrown on a mattress. About ten o'clock at night, General Castaños and the principal officers of his staff arrived. We had been completely defeated [and] were in full retreat upon Cuenca, [and] the French were pursuing. The general directed that I should be carried downstairs, and placed on a mattress in a little covered cart, which had been secured, and that without a moment's loss of time I should proceed on the road to Cuenca. The whole of my body was at that time so inflamed with rheumatism that I could only be turned in bed by lifting up the sheets on which I was extended. Yet in this dolorous state I was forced to make a journey of 300 miles in a cart without springs in the depths of winter and over abominable mountain roads. Castaños had kindly directed his principal medical officer to accompany me to Cuenca, and one very cold morning before daylight, Doctor Turlán (that was his name) requested that I would permit him to enter the cart and share my mattress with him. I readily consented, but we had not proceeded half a mile when the cart was overturned and pitched down a precipice. In the fall the unfortunate *médico* got under the mattress, and, as Santiago [the name by which Whittingham was known in Spain] with his feather weight remained upon it, the poor doctor was nearly suffocated. His cries and screeches were quite terrific . . . The arrival of a few straggling soldiers put off the doctor's evil hour. They dragged me out by the feet and again set the cart upright, but nothing could induce Turlán to re-occupy a share of my mattress.[99]

While Castaños's army was being hounded at Tudela, Napoleon was heading for Madrid at the head of a force of 45,000 men composed of the Imperial Guard, the corps of Marshal Victor and the heavy cavalry divisions of Latour-Maubourg and Lahoussaye. As the emperor's *aide-de-camp*, Lejeune, remembered, this march was accompanied with precisely the same scenes witnessed by the corps of Marshal Ney:

> Whatever may have been the consideration shown by our advanced guard for the inoffensive inhabitants of the towns we passed through, they all fled before us, fearing reprisals for the assassinations of which some of them had been guilty, and abandoning to us their houses, convents and churches . . . These buildings, deserted as they were, offered irresistible temptation to the cupidity of our soldiers, and, in spite of the severe punishments inflicted by their officers, every inch of them was ransacked from the chapels to the crypts . . . and all that could be removed carried off.[100]

Naturally enough, such behaviour spread much panic among the population. For a view of the situation in Valladolid, let us turn to the English seminarian, Robert Brindle:

> All was now bustle and confusion. The French were said to be at the gates of the city . . . Men, women and children [were] wandering up and down uttering the most painful cries and with terror and dismay painted on their countenances . . . The doors of the nunneries were thrown open by the bishop's order, and many venerable

ladies who for the space of fifty years had never trodden unhallowed ground were now obliged to leave the grave which they had prepared for themselves.[101]

Very soon the emperor's forces were confronted by the last remaining Spanish army in central Spain, a scratch force of second-line troops commanded by General Bénito San Juan. This was drawn up so as to block the Pass of Somosierra, a defile in the Sierra de Guadarrama traversed by the main road from Madrid to Burgos and the French frontier. Among the first men to come up with them was Lejeune:

> On the twenty-ninth the emperor and his suite had established their headquarters at the base of the Somosierra, where they were joined by Marshal Victor, who at once led his troops into the pass through a fog so dense that they could not see two paces before them. In spite of this the marshal made his men climb into the forests on either side of the main road, the enemy having occupied the summits, where they considered themselves impregnable behind the deep excavations they had made. General Bertrand, one of the *aides-de-camp* of the emperor, had instructions to repair the road and render it practicable for our cavalry and artillery. Napoleon, however, impatient at the delay caused by the necessary work, told me to push a reconnaissance party into the mountain till I came upon the enemy, when I was to return and report as to their numbers and position. I soon came up with General Bertrand, who had not yet completed his task, and then pressed on by a rapid ascent. I had traversed about a couple of miles without seeing anyone, when a Pole who was one of my party made me a sign that he could hear the Spaniards talking. I dismounted at once . . . and crept noiselessly forward till I was arrested by the sound of . . . a number of people talking Spanish. I then turned aside and walked along the edge of the road to try and find out the extent of the entrenchment, which seemed to me to contain some twelve or fifteen guns. After having reconnoitred the position so far as was possible in the dense fog, I was returning down the mountain to my horse, when . . . I suddenly found myself face to face with a battalion silently advancing upon me. Although quite close to the men, the fog was so thick that I first took them for a French corps, and I said to the officer marching at their head, 'You had better not advance in this direction. There is a ravine you cannot cross.' At these words the whole column took aim at me, and I shouted as I came nearer, 'Do not fire! Do not fire! I am French!' At that very instant I discovered my error, for it was a Spanish corps climbing up from the base of the mountain. My position was indeed critical, and I hastened to call out in Spanish, 'Do not fire! Do not fire! I have three regiments here which will cut you to pieces: the best thing you can do is to surrender to me, who can do you no harm.' The Spaniards seemed uncertain what to do and hesitated . . . but they quickly dispersed on the left and disappeared in the fog . . . Their panic saved my life, and as soon as they were out of sight I ran back to my men. I hastened to return to the emperor and told him all I had done . . . He then ordered General Montbrun to advance with his cavalry, in spite of all obstacles, protected by the infantry, which now had time to crown the heights. Montbrun, at the head of a body of Polish cavalry, galloped up the mountain, fell upon the

Spanish entrenchments and sabred some of the artillerymen at their posts, but the roughness of the ground, combined with the volley of grapeshot which met him, compelled him to retreat and rally his men beyond the range of the guns. In the thick of the hail of shot, the Poles recognised the emperor himself and . . . returned to the charge, overcame all the obstacles which had deterred them at first, carrying everything before them and penetrating into the very heart of the formidable position of the Spaniards, who were unable in the fog to see how very small the attacking column was. The cavalry of the guard followed the movement [and] every one of the Spanish gunners . . . was cut down.[102]

The cost to the Poles – sixty men out of the eighty-eight in the single squadron that had made the charge – was heavy, however, and, typically enough, as Chlapowski remembered, it was a considerable time before the wounded received any proper attention:

> Two days after the battle of Somosierra, about which we had been told on the way, we reached the battlefield itself. There were still several bodies of Polish light horsemen in the snow which continued to cover the summit . . . We stopped for half an hour in the village of Somosierra, where we found some severely wounded men had not yet been transported. They told us about the charge by Dziewanowski's squadron, claiming all the officers and over half the men had been killed . . . While we were there, ambulances came to take the rest of the wounded to Madrid. From one of the surgeons I learned that, as a reward for the charge of Somosierra, the emperor had promoted . . . the regiment straight from the Young to the Old Guard, and . . . also ordered the whole Guard to present arms to the squadron as it passed by.[103]

At Madrid, meanwhile, the Junta Central had been trying to shore up its tottering defences. As Jackson wrote in his diary on 25 November:

> The [Central] Junta, having learnt that Romana was stopping for a day or two with the northern army to get it together again and reorganise it after the battle of the tenth [and eleventh], sat down and wrote a *belle lettre* to Castaños . . . telling him that the fate of Spain was in his hands, etc. . . . A proclamation has been issued to the inhabitants of Madrid, and there are 8,000 stand of arms in the city, but it is yet undetermined whether an attempt shall be made to defend the capital or not. Two other proclamations respecting the new levy have also appeared containing the exemptions, which according to the new plan are very few, every man unmarried, including the nobility, being subject to it from the age of sixteen to forty. Besides this an honorary militia, similar to our volunteers, is to be established. All this, as far as it serves to keep up the spirit of the people, is well enough, but beyond this these measures are evidently futile at a moment when events . . . render the execution of them impracticable.[104]

With the French now just a few miles away, however, the Junta Central had no option but to evacuate Aranjuez and head for Seville. Behind them, meanwhile, Madrid was a hive of activity. Among those left behind in the capital was a prominent official of the Ministry of State named Juan García de León y Pizarro:

The capital presented a grandiose spectacle: on all sides both sexes ran . . . to pull up cobbles, dig up earth, carry stone . . . The docility and zeal shown by the populace . . . were amazing . . . The least word was enough to have them throwing metal cooking utensils and items of wool and cotton from the balconies to help make bullets and wadding. In order to hold up the French inside the city windows were stuffed with mattresses, while the streets were blocked with . . . furniture of every sort.[105]

Yet with the capital devoid of any proper defences and in a state of the utmost confusion, the reality was that Madrid was completely indefensible. When the French appeared before the city on 2 December, there was a brief show of resistance at the barricades – the impact of the French cannon balls may still be seen on the Puerta de Alcalá – but after a single day popular enthusiasm for the struggle evaporated, whereupon the junta that had been left to govern the city laid down its arms. With the enemy at the gates, large numbers of the inhabitants chose to flee. Among them was Juan García de León y Pizarro:

At daybreak I saw thousands of people who had also chosen to leave Madrid fleeing in the greatest disorder. Entire families were on the move, and on all sides the most touching and lamentable sights were to be seen. An old man in his eighties was being supported by a son on the one side and a daughter on the other, and this last with a baby in her arms, and three or four small children clustered round her legs. A woman with two babies in her arms had run out of milk and was begging anyone who passed by to take at least one of her children and give them a drop . . . It has been estimated that at least 14,000 people fled Madrid that day, although the majority were forced to turn back after having been attacked, mistreated and robbed by the French patrols that were circulating round about . . . Aided by the dense fog that had arisen that morning, I managed to get to Móstoles . . . At this point the sun came out and I looked around for something to eat, but, together with Alcorcón, the town had been destroyed by fugitives from the Army of Extremadura, and I could only obtain a little wine . . . Moving on, I came upon the Duque del Parque, Puñónrostro and various other people of my acquaintance, and one of them let me ride his horse for a little while . . . and gave me a chicken wing and a little bread . . . Finding the country through which the high road passed devastated by the stragglers who had preceded us, and the road itself made very dangerous by soldiers who were firing in all directions at hens, pigs, cows, goats and anything else that moved, we abandoned it and took to a by-way in the hills, but all around us the countryside rang to the sound of so much shooting that one might have thought that a battle was going on.[106]

Having taken Madrid, Napoleon proceeded to issue a series of decrees that established the social and juridical foundations of his new Spanish monarchy. Meanwhile, the fall of the capital produced a general collapse in the Allied position in central Spain. What little remained of the Army of the Centre – during the retreat from Tudela it had lost fully half its men – had on 2 December been at Guadalajara. Too late to try to save the capital and deprived of its commander, who had been recalled by the Junta Central, it then fled eastwards and eventually reached Cuenca where command was assumed by the Duque de Infantado. Its sufferings, meanwhile, had been terrible. To quote its new commander:

I saw a ruined army and troops who presented a most distressing experience. Some were entirely barefoot, others almost naked, and all disfigured . . . by the most ravenous hunger (there were many who had had no bread for eight days . . . and many had died along the roads and in the mountains). They appeared more like corpses than men ready to defend their fatherland.[107]

But Spain was not yet beaten. Among the foreign observers present in the Patriot zone was an erstwhile officer in the Prussian army named Andreas von Schepeler who had come to Spain to take part in the war against Napoleon:

The burning imagination of the nation attributed all the fruits of the negligence of the government and the disunion and lack of skill of the generals to treason. The proclamations and false reports spread by the juntas added to the excitement, but they did have a good side as well as a bad one, as the most dreadful blows failed to awaken the Spaniards from the dream that they were superior to the enemy. Heed, then, was paid not to the soldiers who had fled Madrid, but rather to those men . . . who swore that the inhabitants of the capital were resolved to defend themselves. Even as late as the end of December newspapers in the south were claiming that Madrid was putting up a brave resistance. And for a long time even after that the army of La Romana, which had in fact fled into the wilds of southern Galicia in a state of near total collapse, was being put about as having 40,000 men by the same papers, and even appeared with the same number of British troops in the Sierra de Guadarrama annihilating an enemy army . . . The departure of Napoleon from Madrid and his pursuit of Moore was something else that contributed to this illusion . . . while his sudden departure for Paris woke up every last spark of hope.[108]

Hope, then, was not yet dead, but under the impact of defeat there followed what amounted to the temporary collapse of the social order. A near-victim of this state of affairs was General Castaños who, in deference to the orders that he had received from the Junta Central, was now travelling to the new temporary capital of Seville:

I left the army on the sixth [of December] . . . taking with me an escort of thirty cavalry and fifteen infantry. In other circumstances, this would have been quite sufficient or even too many, but the number is but small . . . when the people respect neither justice nor government, and, with the greatest scandal, carry out whatever excesses . . . are stirred up by wicked agitators full of the execrable reports spread by the prodigious number of deserters and stragglers from the armies. According to these men, all the generals are traitors who have been bribed into selling out the soldiers and leading them into a slaughterhouse. These charges are supported by ideas that are grosser and more ridiculous than the ravings of the insane, and stem from the desire that their crimes have instilled in them to avoid being arrested and treated as criminals, but unfortunately the unreflective populace has listened to them and given them credit.[109]

Such was the anger of the populace in respect of Castaños that at the village of Miguel Turra a mob tried to storm the house in which he had lodged for the night, the general only escaping by slipping out through a rear door. At Talavera de la Reina, however, as Jackson records, a similar riot had tragic results:

> The roads swarm with the officers and men of the dispersed army of Madrid, some on foot, some on horseback, and many with hardly any clothes to their backs: in a word, much such a scene as I witnessed two years ago at Brunswick after the battle of Jena. San Juan, who was really a very clever officer and one of the best men, and who was on his way to the Junta to endeavour to effect some new arrangements, has been murdered at Talavera. He was almost the only man who behaved as he ought, but some of the fellows who were running away, to cover their own shame, raised the cry of traitor against him, when the populace of Talavera, incensed at what had recently happened, without further inquiry or consideration fell upon him and killed him, mangling him with their *cuchillos* in a most savage manner . . . Such is the unfortunate state of affairs at present. The people give way to the most unbridled indignation, and the most licentious expression of it. Every man in command is now a traitor, and anarchy and confusion seem to be making rapid strides.[110]

Also struggling across La Mancha was the 19-year-old Antonio Alcalá Galiano. Much alarmed by the news that the French had breached the Sierra de Guadarrama, and married just two weeks before, he had immediately set out for Andalucía with his mother and his new wife:

> It really was something to travel in Spain at this time. Every town was excited at the misfortunes that the state had suffered, while they were dominated by the ferocious passions that had given birth to the current war. In consequence, anyone who came from the provinces that had been . . . occupied by the enemy was looked on with suspicion . . . and, flight being regarded as the fruit of treason, they were often subjected to the most barbarous treatment. Many people . . . fell victim to blind fury shown in many small towns at this time. In this respect I can put forward a true anecdote that perfectly illustrates the disposition of the Spanish people in 1808. We had arrived at Manzanares . . . and had just settled down in the room that we had been given in the inn, when it was entered by one of the servants, a tall and well-built young fellow of somewhat sinister appearance. Much alarmed . . . we kept quiet, and it was therefore he who broke the silence. 'You see before you,' he said, 'the man who has killed more Frenchmen than anyone else in La Mancha.' Having said this, meanwhile, he proceeded to regale us with tales of the most barbarous and repugnant atrocities, in which respect he placed great weight on those in which he had taken part himself on the assumption, one presumes, that their very savagery made these excesses . . . proofs of his heroism and devotion to the Fatherland. A French hospital had been left at Manzanares . . . without adequate protection and every last one of the patients put to the sword, and the young man boasted of having taken a leading role in this event . . . However great, our patriotism did not extend so far as to allow us to approve actions of such barbarity, or even to listen to them with equanimity . . . but we refrained from saying anything in the hope of avoiding an unpleasant experience. Nevertheless the intruder went one step further than

simply recounting his deeds. Thus, after a moment of silence and indecision typical of the common people when they find themselves having to address someone of superior rank, he said, 'And here, too, you have someone who is sworn to kill every traitor.' Seeing that we had good reason to be frightened, we answered, in chorus, 'Well done! Traitors are even worse than Frenchmen!' At this he perceived either that we had not understood him properly, or that we did not wish to understand him . . . and so, after a fresh pause that was rather shorter than its predecessor, he said, 'They say that all those who come from Madrid are traitors.' All dissimulation was now gone, and it was clear that we were in imminent danger. Not knowing what else to do, I said to him, 'But why are they traitors?' 'Because,' he replied, 'they have fled so as not to have to fight the French.' To my great good fortune, I then had the sort of idea that tends to get one out of situations of great danger. 'The French? What are you talking about? Haven't you heard the news? The French have suffered a great defeat, and hardly one of them remains in Spain.' Such nonsense was always very welcome to men of his sort . . . With his rage swept aside by the joy of victory, he left us in peace . . . and the next morning we continued on our way.[111]

The March of Sir John Moore
For British readers, the most well-known episode of the winter campaign of 1808 is the intervention of the British army commanded by Sir John Moore. On this force there rested great hopes in the Spanish camp. One observer of the troops who began to gather at the designated rendezvous of Salamanca was one Joaquín Encinas de los Arcos Zahonero:

> There are no troops of higher quality in the whole world . . . The punishments were cruel: for very small things, they were sentenced to 1,100 lashes, and many of those who suffered such penalties died as a result; the men who carried them out were the drummers. On Sundays they had communion services out in the fields without any more in the way of ceremony than the following. The chaplain wore a cassock, and, leaning on a couple of drums, he read from two books, answered only by a soldier who was stationed three paces behind him. This went on for three-quarters of an hour, and at the end of this time the soldiers, who had attended the service drawn up in a hollow square fully armed and accoutred, each ate a little piece of bread . . . The whole time the only people who took their hats off were the chaplain and his assistant. Nor are their burials any different: all they do is to read something over the corpse for a little while and then lay it in the ditch of the cemetery, where it is buried.[112]

Yet hopes of succour – and it should be remembered that until as late as the beginning of December, if not even later, there was little recognition in most of Spain that there was any need for foreign troops – could not sweep aside centuries of xenophobia and cultural prejudice. Nor, meanwhile, were matters helped by the drunkenness that tended to characterise officers and men alike, heavy drinking being something that was not only uncommon but also abhorred in Spain. There was therefore, at best, a lukewarm response to the British presence, as witness, for example, the recollections of Sir Robert Porter in respect of the minor border fortress of Alcántara:

The governor proved a beast – a vulgar, uncivil animal with little power to serve us and less inclination. He was asleep when we called on him. Indeed, all seemed asleep to the feelings we brought along with us. They received us . . . with an inhospitality they durst not have ventured had they not believed us to be friends. We were wretchedly quartered and the governor's excuse was that he had no authority to force the people to receive us into more respectable houses. The interior of the city is nasty, filled with crumbling walls and churches in a desolate state. Dirt reigns here with equal sway as in Portugal. And my expectations of receiving a comforter under these ills from the civility of the people and their blazing enthusiasm evaporating in the general coldness of the place, I could only ruminate within myself on the romantic fables we had heard . . . If these indolent, arrogant Alcantarans be specimens of the army we are to join, I cannot augur a very brilliant campaign.[113]

At Ciudad Rodrigo, it seems, things were even worse. Among the troops who passed through the town were the Fiftieth Foot and with them Captain John Patterson:

A more atrocious set of men we never had the honour of being acquainted with, and so much did they appear in favour of our enemies that we were convinced they would gladly have delivered us into their hands if it had been in their power to do so. An officer of the Seventy-Ninth unfortunately got involved in a dispute, and, while passing through one of their dark and narrow streets, was barbarously assassinated by an unknown hand.[114]

When Moore arrived at Salamanca early in November, fresh problems emerged. The French were on the move – indeed, had very quickly broken through – but a variety of difficulties, not the least of which was Moore's own mismanagement and failure to obey orders, meant that the full British army could not be got together until the end of the month at the very earliest. With matters in this state, it came increasingly to appear that the British army would not intervene in the campaign at all. However, at length Moore got all his troops together, while news arrived, first (and falsely, as it turned out), that Spanish resistance was stiffening, and, secondly, that the French had no idea that the British were present at Salamanca in strength. So far as Moore was concerned, it was not much of a hope, but in the circumstances to retreat without a fight would be disastrous, the consequence being that mid-December found the British forces on the advance. Battle was not long in coming: on 21 December Moore's cavalry commander, Lord Paget, led a brigade of hussars against some French dragoons and *chasseurs* who were quartered in the Leonese village of Sahagún de Campos. The Fifteenth Hussars were among the troops involved in the action, and with them Captain Alexander Gordon:

On our arrival at Sahagún we . . . discovered the enemy formed in a close column of squadrons near the road to Carrión de los Condes . . . Lord Paget immediately ordered us to form open column of divisions and trot, as the French, upon our coming in sight, made a flank movement, apparently with the intention of getting away, but the rapidity of our advance soon convinced them of the futility of such an attempt. They therefore halted, deployed from column of squadrons, and formed a close column of regiments, which . . . made their formation six deep . . . As soon as the enemy's order of battle was formed, they cheered in a very gallant manner and immediately began firing. The Fifteenth then halted, wheeled into line, huzza'ed, and advanced. The interval between us was perhaps 400 yards, but it was so quickly passed that they had only time to fire a few shots upon us before we came upon them . . . The shock was terrible: horses and men were overthrown, and a shriek of terror, intermixed with oaths, groans and prayers for mercy, issued from the whole extent of their front. Our men pressed forward until they had cut their way quite through the column. In many places the bodies of the fallen formed a complete mound of men and horses, but very few of our people were hurt . . . The French were well posted, having a ditch in their front which they expected to check the impetus of our charge; in this, however, they were deceived . . . My post being on the left of the line, I found nothing opposed to my troops, and therefore ordered 'Left shoulders forward!' with the intention of taking the French column in flank, but, when we reached the ground they had occupied, we found them broken and flying in all directions . . . Notwithstanding this, there was a smart firing of pistols and our lads were making good use of their sabres . . . At this time I witnessed an occurrence which afforded a good deal of amusement to those who were near the place. Hearing the report of a pistol close behind me, I looked round and saw one of the Fifteenth fall. I concluded the man was killed, but was quickly undeceived by a burst of laughter from his comrades, who exclaimed that the awkward fellow had shot his own horse, and many good jokes passed at his expense. The mêlée lasted about ten minutes . . . There was not a single man of the Fifteenth killed in the field, [but] we had about thirty wounded, five or six severely, two of whom died the next day.[115]

Encouraging though this success was, the sequel was a great disappointment. Pressing on towards the French forces he had elected to attack, on the afternoon of 23 December Moore received news that massive French forces had crossed the Sierra de Guadarrama and were heading north to attack the Allies. Knowing that the game was up, Moore immediately turned his army around and headed for the safety of Galicia. That he did so was just as well, for the French were pressing on at speed led by Napoleon himself. Marcellin de Marbot was with the emperor's headquarters:

Next day a furious snowstorm, with a fierce wind, made the passage of the mountains almost impassable. Men and horses were hurled over precipices. The leading battalions actually began to retreat, but Napoleon was resolved to overtake the English at all costs. He . . . ordered that the members of each section should hold one another by the arm. The cavalry, dismounting, did the same. The staff was formed in similar fashion, the emperor between Lannes and Duroc . . . and so, in spite of wind, snow and ice, we proceeded, though it took us four hours to reach the top.[116]

Present with the pursuing French troops was the Polish cavalryman Dezydery Chlapowski. As his recollections show, Napoleon's forces were forced to contend with conditions that were just as bad as anything faced by the British, as well as with a dangerous enemy:

> The British army had marched from Salamanca towards La Coruña where a fleet of transports awaited it. The emperor wanted to intercept [Moore's] path through Valderas and Astorga. But several days of rain saved him, for the British were on a metalled road, and our road from Medina to Astorga was just a dirt track. There was snow, rain and very cold temperatures, and the earth became such a mire that it took three days to march to Valderas instead of one. Horses and men sank deep into the mud. The older Grenadiers of the Guard said it reminded them of Pultusk. I was told that some soldiers who could not keep up with the column took their own lives for fear of falling into the hands of the Spanish guerrillas whose bands were roaming the country. General Lefebvre-Desnouettes had gone on ahead . . . with the Chasseurs-à-Cheval of the Guard, and . . . forded the River Esla by the town of Benevente. On the plain before the town he was attacked by a whole division of British cavalry . . . The general was forced to retreat . . . and was himself captured with about sixty *chasseurs* on the river bank as he had wanted to cross over last . . . Even among those who got back across the river, many were wounded from pistol and carbine shots. Many displayed great bruises on their shoulders, backs and even faces, and told us the English always struck with the flat of their swords instead of the point, for their swords were too broad and they did not know how to thrust them as the French did. The emperor sent a few of us off to right and left . . . in search of boats . . . About 1,000 paces away in a deserted village behind some undergrowth I found some boats . . . On these we ferried some light infantry across to the enemy bank . . . A division of cavalry and some artillery arrived next on the river bank. The emperor made the cavalry column close up to form a solid block . . . and ordered it to march into the river above the ford to form a living dam. The water level downstream of them fell, and the emperor ordered the artillery to cross, which it did without even getting its ammunition wet. He followed right behind with the staff . . . That same night the emperor sent me from Benevente to Marshal Bessières, who had marched off a few hours before with a whole division to Astorga. The night was dark, the road was invisible, and there were no trees to mark its route. I led my horse by the reins and followed the tracks of the marshal's cavalry, which had gone before me. I caught up with the marshal two miles down the road at La Baneza at about two in the morning. We marched through Astorga and that day joined forces with the advanced guard of Marshal Soult who was coming up from León. It was commanded by General Colbert. Bessières's division remained at Astorga and Colbert went on as far as Manzanal. A little beyond Cacabellos he encountered some Scottish infantry in a good defensive position. He rode through the village with one platoon, for, while he was waiting for his infantry to come up, he wanted to study the ground. The enemy fired a few shots, and a musket ball hit Colbert square on the forehead, and he fell dead on the spot.[117]

In reality, Colbert was shot not by a Highlander but by a soldier of the Ninety-Fifth Rifles named Tom Plunket. But the general point holds good in that the British were anything but a broken force. That said, the retreat to the coast was scarcely the brightest moment in the history of the British army. As the British fell back, so drunkenness, exhaustion – at one point Moore forced his men to march for thirty-six hours without a break – hunger and discontent led to widespread straggling. Though some battalions held together well enough, the path of the army was therefore marked by a trail of arson, theft, rape and murder. Stories of the disorders witnessed during the retreat are legion. Typical of the horrors inflicted on the civilian populace is the sight seen by Alexander Gordon on 1 January 1809:

> In the afternoon we passed through a large village which had been completely gutted by fire. The wretched inhabitants were sitting amidst the trifling articles of property they had been able to seize from the flames, contemplating the ruins of their homes in silent despair. The bodies of several Spaniards who had died of hunger and disease, or perished from the inclemency of the weather, were lying scattered around and added to the horrors of the scene. The village had been burned by some of our infantry.[118]

One place that suffered very badly was Bembibre. To quote Robert Blakeney:

> Bembibre exhibited all the appearance of a place lately stormed and pillaged. Every door and window was broken, every lock and fastening forced. Rivers of wine ran through the houses and into the streets, where lay fantastic groups of soldiers . . . women, children, runaway Spaniards and muleteers, all apparently inanimate . . . while the wine oozing from their lips and nostrils seemed the effect of gunshot wounds . . . The music was perfectly in character: savage roars announcing present hilarity were mingled with groans issuing from fevered lips disgorging the wine of yesterday; obscenity was public sport.[119]

Such were the conditions faced during the retreat that the desire to seek oblivion was entirely understandable. Marching with the Seventy-First Foot was Thomas Howell:

> There was nothing to sustain our famished bodies or shelter them from the rain or snow . . . Fuel we could find none . . . The road was one line of bloody foot-marks from the sore feet of the men, and on its sides lay the dead and dying. Human nature could do no more . . . We felt there was no hope . . . There was nothing but groans, mingled with execrations, to be heard between the pauses of the wind. I attempted to pray and recommend myself to God, but my mind was so confused I could not arrange my ideas. I almost think I was deranged . . . How I was sustained I am unable to comprehend. My life was misery. Hunger, cold and fatigue had deprived death of all its horrors . . . Words fail me to express what we suffered.[120]

Marching in near continuous rain and snow, even those troops who remained with the colours presented a sorry sight. The Spanish muleteers deserted, wagon after wagon was abandoned, and even the headquarters' supply of ready cash had to be thrown into a ravine. Meanwhile, the road became littered with dead men and horses and abandoned equipment of all sorts, the many blazing supply dumps only adding to the appearance of rout. About the only comfort to be had from the situation, had the soldiers had the strength to think about it, was that the French were suffering just as badly. Far to the rear was Joseph de Naylies, a cavalry officer with the corps of Marshal Soult, who had joined the Nineteenth Dragoons in 1805. We pick up his story at the moment that his unit set out from Astorga on 1 January:

> After having marched all day, we found ourselves on the summit of a high mountain . . . There we were assailed by a terrible storm: men and horses were blown over by the wind, while the eddying snow prevented us from seeing further than four paces. The road that we followed the next morning – the Coruña highway – was one of the best in Spain, but, as the snow had frozen as soon as it had fallen, it had been turned into a sheet of ice. In the middle of these mountains, at the spot where the road from León joins the Coruña highway, we found fifty or so carts full of wounded Spaniards whose drivers had deserted them . . . They were members of the corps of La Romana which Marshal Soult had beaten in the vicinity of León. Most of these unfortunates had died in the course of the terrible night we had just passed, and the survivors begged us to kill them. We could do nothing to help them as we were in a deplorable condition ourselves: oppressed by cold, covered with snow and leading their horses . . . on foot, many of our riders were fainting from exhaustion and want.[121]

As for the British soldiers, typical enough was the experience of Stephen Morley:

> We had neither an adequate supply of food or clothing, and our feet were dreadfully hurt from want of shoes; many were actually barefooted . . . The poor women were deeply to be pitied. One of them . . . with no covering but her tattered clothes . . . gave birth to a son . . . The road all the way was strewed with men unable to proceed . . . Discipline was forgotten, none commanded, none obeyed . . . Seeing smoke issue from a large building off the road, I crawled rather than walked to it. It was something like a barn, and full of our men who had made a fire. I found a spare corner, and, putting my pouch under my head, fell into a sound sleep . . . When I awoke, I was told the army . . . had gone on.[122]

The French then coming up, Morley was taken prisoner, like many such men. The group that he was with put up a fierce fight, however, one of the few bright spots of the retreat being the manner in which bands of stragglers repeatedly clubbed together in desperate 'last stands'. But isolated acts of heroism were hardly enough to redress the balance, still less to assuage the feelings of the Spaniards. Let us turn, for example, to the account of the Marqués de la Romana:

> The English have seized . . . the mules and oxen that drew our army's artillery, munitions and baggage train; they have insulted and mistreated . . . our officers . . . They have stolen all the mules of the . . . inhabitants of Benevente and the *pueblos* of the Tierra de Campos, and have left a multitude of carts abandoned by the wayside, some of them broken down and others smashed up on purpose. They have without necessity killed and eaten the oxen that pulled these carts and have not paid

their value. They have killed three magistrates and various other inhabitants. After allowing anyone who wanted to drink their fill without paying a penny, they have poured away all the wine in the cellars. They have not paid for the carts and animals that they have used to move their women and their immense baggage trains. In some *pueblos* the commissaries have refused to give receipts for the supplies made available to them by the justices, while in others they have arbitrarily reduced the sums that were asked of them. In a word the French themselves could not have found agents better calculated to whip up hatred of the British than the army commanded by General Sir John Moore.[123]

That the British army behaved extremely badly there is no doubt. About the only things that can be said in its defence is that it was badly misused by its commander – Sir John Moore pushed the men onwards at a rate that was quite disproportionate to the danger in which they stood once they had entered Galicia – and that it had good reason to complain of the Spaniards. At long last a Spanish force had appeared in the shape of La Romana's Army of the Left, but it was in no state to fight, having just been badly beaten at Mansilla de los Mulos by Marshal Soult. Let us here quote the cavalryman Alexander Gordon:

> The brigade marched . . . from La Bañeza at one o'clock leaving several houses on fire . . . Within half a league of Astorga we found a picquet of the . . . German Legion . . . The officers told us that the Spanish army, estimated at 120,000 men was in the town and adjacent villages, and that it was determined that our combined forces should await the arrival of the French army . . . It is difficult to conjecture how such an absurd report could have gained credit; the town was in fact occupied by the Marqués de la Romana's corps, in consequence of which we found it difficult to obtain quarters. This Spanish force amounted to about 6,000 men in the most deplorable condition. They were all ill-clothed; many were without shoes and even without arms; a pestilential fever raged among them; they had been without bread for several days and were quite destitute of money . . . I spoke to some of the men who were evidently suffering from famine and disease: they declared they had eaten nothing for three days, and, when we gave them the remains of our dinner and money to buy wine, their expressions of gratitude were unbounded.[124]

To this further evidence, as it was supposed, of Spanish incompetence, was added much anger at the general failure of the populace to offer anything in the way of resistance. In Schaumann's words:

> The apathy with which the inhabitants of this mountain country . . . have witnessed our misery is revolting. They were to be seen in large armed hordes far away from us in the mountains . . . when . . . they might have been very useful to us and covered our retreat. But not only did these puffed-up patriots . . . give us no assistance, but they also took good care to remove all cattle and all foodstuffs out of our way . . . and in addition murdered and plundered our own men who fell out left and right along the road.[125]

To have expected much more of the populace was scarcely realistic. Terrorised by the

British and French alike, they were also assailed by the desperate troops of La Romana, as witness the experience of Juan Antonio Posse, the parish priest of the village of San Andrés del Rabanedo:

> The streets and houses . . . were strewn with the dead and dying. What with the stench and filth of the former and the cries and groans of the latter, a more horrible spectacle had never been seen . . . All this was accompanied by robbery, insult and outrage as men besieged by hunger or accustomed to a life of crime assailed road and home alike. Seeing me come out of a privy, a group of stragglers went in and searched the excrement, believing that I must have gone in to hide some money . . . It was not possible to move an inch without exposing oneself to every sort of vexation.[126]

In general, indeed, the unfortunate populace suffered terribly. Galicia was a poverty-stricken district at the best of times, and the passage of the armies in consequence produced scenes of the utmost misery. Passing through Manzanal, for example, Schaumann forgot his own cold and hunger long enough to look around him a little:

> I looked into one of the huts. The fireplace was in the middle, and the smoke went whither it listed, up to the roof or out at the door. The fuel consisted of moist heath . . . the smoke of which makes the eyes smart horribly. The family in this particular hut consisted of a tall, old . . . witch and three ugly children, of whom two were suffering from a hectic fever. Everything was extremely dirty: their hair was matted together and they never seemed to have washed since the day of their birth. Round the woman's neck hung a rosary . . . She did nothing except sit over the fire, and shake with cold and misery, and the whole place presented a picture of the most appalling misery. For several more miles now, the road was knee-deep in mud and snow . . . Starving inhabitants of the country fled . . . past us with faces distorted by fear, despair and vindictiveness, and the weaker among them, the aged, the children and the women, laden down with their belongings and perishing from fear, and from the rains, the storms, the snow and the hunger to which they had been exposed night and day, sank in the mire at our feet imploring in vain for help which we could not give even our own men.[127]

But on both sides starvation and despair ensured that compassion was in short supply. Benjamin Miller was a 32-year-old corporal in the Royal Artillery from the Dorset village of Melbury Osmond, who had enlisted in 1796:

> When we came to Villafranca [del Bierzo], the Spaniards shut their houses on us, and we were ordered to break them open . . . and make our lodgings good for the night. Me and four more broke open a house where they had plenty of wood and would not give us any. I went downstairs to take some, but they had some Spanish soldiers to guard it. They said one to the other, 'Kill him', and began to push me about . . . One of them very luckily pushed me against the stairs. I immediately ran up, and told the four men to be on their guard or we should all be killed. One placed himself behind the door and I and the other three stood with our swords drawn. In

a few minutes up came three Spanish soldiers with large staves and knives. The man behind the door ran one of them through, and I cut down another and the third had three swords on him. We left them all for dead . . . We made the door secure inside and kept all in, both the man of the house and his family. We then pulled down a partition that went across the room and broke up the chairs and stools to warm ourselves. We saw some hams hung up and a basket of eggs. We asked them to sell us some and offered double the value, but they refused. [So] we took one ham and as many eggs as we could and fried [them] . . . On our road to La Coruña we burned down a village because the people would not sell us anything.[128]

At length the bulk of the British forces reached the hills above La Coruña (where it should be noted that the populace proved far more welcoming), only to find that there were no transports in the harbour. In fact they turned up within two days, but the delay was none the less sufficient to allow the French to come up, leaving Moore with no option but to turn at bay. Before the battle that could not but follow, however, yet another horror had come to pass. Once again, it is Captain Gordon who takes up the story. As he wrote in his diary on 13 January:

The whole town was thrown into considerable alarm at about nine o'clock this morning by a tremendous explosion, which shook the buildings like an earthquake. A number of windows were broken by the concussion, and the inhabitants . . . rushed into the streets – many of them half-dressed and with terror in their countenances – and, falling upon their knees, began to repeat their 'Aves' with an energy proportioned to their fright . . . The account I heard of the cause of this explosion . . . was that Sir John Moore had ordered a magazine to be destroyed . . . as there was not time to remove the powder it contained, amounting to 1,500 barrels. It was said, however, that there was another depot of nearly 5,000 barrels in an adjoining building, but that this circumstance was concealed . . . by the Spanish officer in charge of the magazine. The consequence was . . . an explosion infinitely more violent in its effects than had been calculated. Some of the men who were employed on this occasion were blown up. The inhabitants of the village in which the magazines were situated had been sufficiently warned of their danger . . . but they paid little attention to the cautions they received, and it is probable that many of them perished owing to their obstinacy as the place was reduced to a heap of ruins.[129]

On 15 January the French arrived before the city. Helping to man Moore's front line the next day was Benjamin Miller:

On 16 January 1809 I was ordered out with the guns attached to the 'forlorn-hope' pickets to keep the enemy's advance picket at bay . . . Some sharp skirmishing took place between the pickets, and several men were killed or wounded; we drove them back to their lines and continued firing until Generals Moore and Baird, who were standing by the gun which I commanded, came and looked over the wheel . . . with a spy glass, and said to me, 'Don't fire any more . . . for I don't think it will come to a general engagement' . . . In the course of the day, having had nothing to eat, we sent six men . . . to a small village, Elvina (which the Spanish peasants had been obliged to leave), to seek for plunder. They had got some potatoes, a pan of butter and some fowls, but just as they were leaving the place some French riflemen came down and fired on them. They were obliged to drop their plunder and with difficulty got back to the guns. One man brought about half a bushel of potatoes. These were boiling when . . . a shot came and knocked the kettle off the fire. We filled our pockets with them and ate them while fighting our guns.[130]

In the battle that followed Miller and his colleagues were badly outclassed by the French. Only nine light guns remained on shore to support the weary redcoats, and even these few were scattered along the length of the line in twos and threes. In the French camp, by contrast, Marshal Soult, who had headed the last stages of the pursuit, had no fewer than forty guns, and, as a commissary named Pierre Le Noble recalled, a number of these were dragged into a prominent hilltop position:

Having occupied [Monte Mero], Marshal Soult immediately realised that it was an excellent position from which to open fire. As cannon placed there could enfilade the English line, he saw that this could do it great damage. Orders were therefore quickly given to the commander of the artillery . . . to establish a grand battery there. We did not control any road that led to the position, and, given . . . the nature of the terrain, the obstacles that had to be overcome to get artillery up there can easily be imagined. However, our gunners again proved that there was nothing they could not do, and by the morning of the sixteenth we had eight cannon and two howitzers in battery.[131]

The French attack was at its most dangerous on Moore's right. Here the defenders included the Black Watch and with them an anonymous 23-year-old private soldier whose memoirs were collected and published in 1821:

The enemy were then seen advancing in two very large compact columns down on our brigade: this seemed to be our planned attack. Sir John was soon on the ground where the attack was expected to be made. Our artillery fired a few shots, and then retreated for want of ammunition. Our flankers were sent out to assist the pickets. The French soon formed their line and advanced, driving the pickets and flankers before them, while their artillery kept up a close cannonade on our line with grape and round shot. A few of the Forty-Second were killed, and some were wounded . . . We had not then moved an inch in advance or retreat. Sir John came in front of the Forty-Second. He said, 'There is no use in making a long speech, but, Forty-Second, I hope you will do as you have done before.' With that he rode off the ground in front of us . . . This ground . . . was very bad for making an engagement, being very rocky and full of ditches, and a large valley between the two positions. The French army did not advance very rapidly on account of the badness of the ground. Our colonel gave orders for us to lie on the ground at the back of the height our position was on, and, whenever the French were within a few yards of us, we were to start up and fire our muskets, and then give them the bayonet. They came up the hill cheering as if there were none to oppose them, we being out of their sight. When they came to the top of the hill, all the word of command that was given was 'Forty-Second: charge!' In one moment every man was up . . . and every shot did execution. They were so close upon us we gave them the bayonet the instant we fired . . . and many of us skewered pairs, front and rear rank. To the right-about they went, and we after them . . . When we had driven them in upon their other columns, we ourselves retreated . . . and took the advantage of a ditch that was in the valley from which we kept up a constant fire on the enemy till dark . . . All the time I was in that ditch I was standing up to the knee in mud. I had a narrow escape here: it was within a hair's breadth. In assisting a man that was wounded to the top of the ditch, we were no sooner upon it than a shower of grape shot was poured upon us which killed the wounded man and my comrade, who was helping him up: I got the feathers blown out of my bonnet by one of the grapes.[132]

Also heavily involved in the fighting on the right flank was Robert Blakeney and the Twenty-Eighth Foot:

The enemy's dark columns were seen advancing from three different points, and with rapid pace literally coming down upon us, cheered by their guns which sent their shot over their heads but plunged into our line, which at the same time was raked from right to left by their grand battery. During these primary operations we became the reserve, but continued so only until the commander of the forces should ascertain to a certainty where the enemy intended making their fiercest attack, and, as to the point where this was to take place, Sir John Moore was not mistaken . . . On our right two heavy columns descended against Baird's division. One passed through Elvina, a village about midway between our two lines . . . This column made direct for Baird's right, obliging the Fourth Regiment to retire their right wing, and then advanced into the valley. The other column attacked the whole front of Baird's division . . . The enemy's column [that had] passed by Baird's right, flushed with the idea of having turned the right of the British army . . . moved sternly forward . . . But as they advanced, they met the reserve coming on with an aspect as stern and determined as their own . . . We painfully recollected the wanton carnage committed on . . . defenceless stragglers . . . and the many cold nights we [had] passed in the mountains of Galicia . . . The haughty and taunting insults, too, of our gasconading pursuers were fresh in our memory . . . Thus urged forward . . . we soon came to the charge, and shortly the opposing column was dissipated.[133]

Throughout the battle Sir John Moore had been in the thick of the fighting, encouraging his men, keeping watch on the enemy and directing the movement of his forces. Several times cannon balls had passed close to him: indeed, one had struck the ground beside his horse. Just as the Forty-Second were going forward, however, a lucky shot smashed into his left shoulder and all but tore it completely away. So close to him that their horses were all but touching was staff officer Henry Hardinge:

The violence of the stroke threw him off his horse onto his back. Not a muscle of his face altered, nor did a sigh betray the least sensation of pain. I dismounted and, taking his hand, he pressed mine forcibly, casting his eyes very anxiously towards the Forty-Second Regiment, which was hotly engaged, and his countenance expressed satisfaction when I informed him that the regiment was advancing. Assisted by a soldier of the Forty-Second, he was removed a few yards behind the shelter of a wall . . . The blood flowed fast [and] the attempt to stop it with my sash was useless from the size of the wound. He assented to being removed in a blanket. In raising him for this purpose, his sword . . . touched his wound and became entangled between his legs. I perceived the inconvenience and was in the act of unbuckling it when he said in his usual tone and manner, 'It is well as it is: I had rather that it should go out of the field with me . . .' He was borne by six soldiers of the Forty-Second, my sash supporting him in an easy posture.[134]

Taken to a house in La Coruña, the British commander died a few hours later. But the French had been foiled: with Soult's men too battered and exhausted to intervene, the bulk of the British forces got away by sea the next day. That said, the survivors were a lamentable sight when they arrived home. Among the troops who got back was John Harris:

Nothing . . . could exceed the dreadful appearance we cut on the occasion of the disembarkation from La Coruña, and the inhabitants of Portsmouth, who had assembled in some numbers to see us land, were horror-stricken with the sight of their countrymen . . . with feet swathed in bloody rags, clothing that hardly covered their nakedness, accoutrements in shreds, beards covering their faces, eyes dimmed with toil (for some were even blind), arms nearly useless to those who had them left, the rifles being encrusted with rust and the swords glued to the scabbard.[135]

Fresh Disasters

While the British army had been retreating through León and Galicia, fierce fighting had continued elsewhere. In La Mancha, for example, an ill-managed Spanish stab at the capital had produced a major disaster at the town of Uclés. Far to the north, meanwhile, fighting was also continuing in Aragón. Isolated by the retreat of the Army of the Centre, Zaragoza was once again under siege. At first, however, the news from the city seemed cheerful enough. Thus no sooner had the battle of Tudela been fought than the inhabitants threw themselves into the task of strengthening the defences. For a typical view, let us turn to Palafox's friend and admirer Charles Doyle, the latter being one of the many British liaison officers who had been sent to Spain:

Such was the spirit of the inhabitants that upon the 27th and the 28th [of November] there was not a moment's cessation of work during day or night and every individual of every class was at work at the batteries . . . The ladies . . . and hundreds of women of the lower class . . . [had] formed companies in order to supply the different batteries with provisions, etc., during the siege which the people seem to desire. At the head of these heroines is the Countess of Bureta, cousin to General Palafox, who set the same example during the late siege, and whose conduct seemed to inspire the inhabitants with the greatest zeal and devotion to their country.[136]

Unfortunately, while Palafox's leadership might have been inspirational, the Aragonese commander was no general, and no sooner had the French closed in than it became apparent that he had committed a cardinal error. The artillery officer Luis de Villaba, indeed, was openly scornful:

> Palafox obstinately refused to leave an army in a position where it could relieve the city . . . All the troops were concentrated in Zaragoza and . . . in this fashion 35,000 men were shut up within the walls despite the fact that there was neither sufficient food, nor sufficient billets . . . Within four days of the city coming under siege, however, we see his brother, Don Francisco, leaving via the River Ebro in search of . . . reinforcements. What an astonishing spectacle! General Palafox had said that, if he left an army outside the city, the government would use it for other objects and leave both Zaragoza and the Kingdom of Aragón to their fate, and yet, four days into the siege, we find him calling for the rest of Aragón to send him reinforcements, thereby leaving itself all the more uncovered.[137]

By late December the city had been formally invested. Inside the defences the mood wavered between hope and despair. Among the many civilians sheltering in the city as the French siege operations gathered pace was Agustín Alcaide Ibieca:

> As the relief force whose coming was constantly being announced never seemed to arrive, while the number of sick was multiplying rapidly, the populace began . . . to guess that the outlook was one of complete ruin. Whether it was because Palafox had heard that Perena had managed to get some troops together or news had reached him from some other part, on 17 January there appeared a very interesting issue of the gazette . . . In brief, what it said was as follows. In Catalonia the French had been defeated: Reding had an army of 60,000 men and was marching to our rescue with a strong division, while the Marqués de Lazán had chased the invaders out of the Ampurdán and crossed the frontier, spreading fear on all sides and enriching his men with large amounts of booty. Elsewhere, another division was coming to relieve us under the Duque de Infantado, while Blake and Romana had, together with the British, defeated Napoleon and killed 20,000 men including Ney and Savary . . . The news spread with the speed of lightning . . . and at five o'clock all the cannon on the walls joined in three great salvoes. The bands of every regiment then played for an hour on the battlements in the very sight of the enemy, who were also loudly taunted and made the butt of many sarcasms. Meanwhile, the streets were illuminated, torches placed on the Torre Nueva, and the church bells rung, at which signs of rejoicing the people could not contain themselves . . . and started firing their weapons in the air to such an extent that anyone would have thought a full-scale battle was going on . . . While all this was happening, the French did no more than salute us with a few bombs, but at ten o'clock at night they let fly with a furious

bombardment . . . It is not easy to imagine how tense the situation was in those moments. Many families had absolutely nothing; those of the sick who were not still struggling to undertake work of the most arduous sort on the defences were filling every cellar; and every moment one and all feared that one of the thousands of shell splinters that rent the air . . . would take off their heads . . . In the first days of the siege, many people had immediately fled with their bedding to the Pilar basilica, and, particularly around the sanctuary, this had very soon become crammed with sick, some of them lying on the floor and others on beds. So loud were their lamentations, and so distressing the sight of the people nursing them attending to their bodily necessities, that a zealous group of ecclesiastics drove them out of the building for fear that it would be utterly profaned. Compelled to seek shelter elsewhere, many ignored the orders . . . forbidding such a practice, and took cover beneath the arcades in the market place, only to find that here they began to be assailed by cold and wet . . . while at the same time experiencing the horrors of a famine that got worse by the day.[138]

With the masses of troops at his disposal, Palafox might well have made life very difficult for the besiegers, but such sorties as he sent out were the work of small groups of men only, and were therefore easily repelled. Within the city, meanwhile, the results of his determination to concentrate all the forces of Aragón quickly became all too apparent. As Lejeune writes:

Fresh meat and vegetables were altogether exhausted, and there was nothing to eat but fish and salt meat . . . All the mills on the Ebro were in our hands, and the besieged had no means of grinding the corn of which they still had considerable quantities. True, they had made a few handmills, but they were altogether inadequate, and the people had to be content with grain merely crushed or bruised. This unwholesome diet did almost as much harm as actual famine would have done, and to these evils was added the terror inspired by the bombardment, which had already lasted three weeks. Most of the inhabitants had taken refuge in cellars, thinking to be safe there, but . . . the air of these damp retreats, far too small for the numbers crowded into them, was foetid and vitiated in the extreme, so that there was really more danger in breathing than in sharing in the defence in the open. Already these evils combined had caused an epidemic which claimed some 300 victims per day . . . Many were no longer strong enough to remove their dead from their houses, and those corpses which were carried into the streets or to the doors of the churches remained there without burial. Often bombs would burst and shatter the dead to pieces, tearing them from their tattered bloodstained shrouds so that at every turn the most horrible sights met the eye.[139]

Aided by Palafox's incapacity, the French had soon breached the walls and on 27 January they advanced to the assault. Ill-led though they may have been, the defenders none the less put up a desperate struggle. As Heinrich von Brandt remembered, the day was no battle of Tudela:

The main assault, made on 27 January, was one of the bloodiest days of the siege. Since dawn our batteries had concentrated their fire on widening the breaches. At nine o'clock those units designated for the assault moved forward. The column meant to break into the garden of the Santa Monica convent was 400-men strong and composed of the Fourteenth Line and part of the Second Regiment of the Vistula Legion. A second and smaller column had to storm a breach to the left of this and close to one of the principal batteries of the besieged – that which bore the name of their illustrious leader Palafox. A third column formed by a battalion – my own – of the Second Regiment of the Vistula Legion was directed to the right of the Santa Monica convent and the San Agustín monastery towards the Casa González, a stone building jutting out . . . towards the Ebro and linked to the defences by a covered way . . . Of all the attacks on the right only one achieved even partial success – that on the breach by the Palafox battery. The . . . assault on the Casa González, in which I took part, failed completely. We . . . just managed to get into the building, but were met by such a heavy fire . . . that we fell back rather quickly. Major Beyer . . . was seriously wounded, and the captain of my company, a certain Matkowski from Cracow, had a leg shattered by roundshot and fell into enemy hands.[140]

Eventually, as Faustino Casamayor recounts, the French got inside the city:

This day [i.e. 27 January] our enemies assailed us with a fire that was as furious as it was constant: bombs, shells and cannon balls did not cease to fall upon us for a single moment and the result was that many buildings suffered heavy damage. Just before eight o'clock they launched an attack on every point between the Puerta Quemada and the Puerta del Portillo. So terrible did this attack appear that it was necessary to sound a general alarm. At the sound of the bells, the defenders ran to their posts, but, although they waged a most vigorous defence, the French got across the Huerba and established themselves in the gardens of both Santa Engracia and San José. Another forty who got into the city's oil press were all killed, but such was the panic that gripped the area that inhabitants and religious alike fled their homes and convents and did not check their flight until they had reached the Pilar basilica. At one o'clock there came a second assault . . . and bitter fighting raged at every gate until nightfall, in the course of which the Real Audiencia was unfortunately set on fire with the loss of both its archives . . . Firing went on all night, but the enemy nevertheless managed to capture the battery that covered the Puerta del Carmen; to occupy all the gun positions between that point and the convent of the Trinitarians; to get into the Carmelite convent . . . the Plaza de Santa Engracia, and the Capuchin convent and the houses that surround it; and finally to reoccupy the city's oil press . . . and all this despite incurring terrible losses: everything they gained, indeed, they paid for in blood . . . As for the inhabitants, all they could do in this dreadful situation was to take shelter in the Pilar basilica.[141]

Another Spanish eyewitness was Agustín Alcaide Ibieca:

At midday the enemy army advanced . . . Full of ardour, the column that had set off from the mill of Goicoechea crossed the short space that separated it from the right-hand breach and were not checked by the detonation of two mines at its feet. A number of the enemy were blown apart, but their losses were not serious, and many of them succeeded in getting to the summit. This, however, had been foreseen and a fusillade of fire from . . . the windows overlooking the breach, not to mention the two cannon . . . that had been placed in the gardens of the convent of Santa Monica, left the ground covered with corpses and checked the impetus of their advance. Frustrated at having been brought to a halt by this fresh obstacle at the very moment they had thought themselves on the brink of triumph, with great daring they struggled to overcome it no matter what the cost. Yet this they soon found to be an arduous endeavour. Supported by some grenadiers, their pioneers sought to open the way, but such was the weight of musketry and canister . . . that met them that all they achieved was to increase the number of the fallen. Instead of getting into the city, they therefore had to content themselves with a lodgement in the very breach, and even this they were only able to sustain with great difficulty and at the cost of continual losses . . . With the air thick with smoke, at nightfall the town-crier announced that French losses had amounted to 6,000 men. This was an exaggeration, but it encouraged the common people and the air rang with cheers. And it is true enough that . . . many of the enemy had bitten the dust and thus paid a heavy price for their daring. Meanwhile, the firing continued, albeit at a somewhat slower rate than before.[142]

Had the French been able to press on, it is just possible that the city might have been completely over-run, but by the end of the day they were too weary to advance any further and this gave time for the defenders to regroup, and, indeed, encouraged them to fresh efforts. There followed one of the most savage episodes of the entire war. Like von Brandt, Jozef Mrozinski was with the Legion of the Vistula:

The *zaragozanos* did not just fight for each house, but for each floor and even each room. Monks appeared in the streets with sabres buckled on over their habits, encouraging the men to fight harder or get on with the task of repairing the defences (not that they were inactive themselves: many of them helped make up cartridges and joined in the task of distributing them among the defenders, while others attended to the spiritual needs of the defenders under fire or spurred on the soldiers not just with words but with their own example). Even the women took part in the defence, Palafox having in at least one proclamation encouraged them to follow the example . . . of the amazons of old. Thus they distributed ammunition among the defenders, and, given that the latter included many of their sons and husbands, more than one of them took up arms to avenge their fall, some of them even getting military decorations. Nor was it just women of the lower classes who joined the fighting: in the ranks there were also to be seen beautiful and well-dressed young ladies . . . The valour of these female warriors provided an example for the officers while their presence, which beyond doubt awoke in them the hope of a sweet reward, inspired them to fresh efforts.[143]

Faced by the most obstinate resistance, the French could only make progress by the use of an approach that was slow, painstaking and very costly. As Marbot, who was attached to the besieging forces' headquarters, remembered:

To attack such men by assault in a town where every house was a fortress would have been to repeat the mistake committed during the first siege, and to incur heavy losses without a chance of success. Accordingly Marshal Lannes . . . adopted a prudent method, which, though tedious, was the best way to bring about the surrender . . . of the town. They began in the usual way by opening trenches until the first houses were reached, then the houses were mined and blown up, defenders and all; then the next were mined and so on. These works, however, involved considerable danger for the French, for, as soon as one showed himself, he was a mark to musket-shots from the Spaniards in the neighbouring buildings . . . Such was the determination of the Spaniards that, while a house was being mined and the dull thud of the rammer warned them that death was at hand, not one left the house which he had sworn to defend. We could hear them singing litanies, then, at the moment when the walls flew into the air and fell back with a crash, crushing the greater part of them, those who had escaped would collect about the ruins and, sheltering themselves behind the slightest cover . . . recommence their sharpshooting. Our soldiers, however, warned of the moment when the mine was going off, held themselves in readiness, and no sooner had the explosion taken place, than they dashed on the ruins and, after killing all whom they found, established themselves behind bits of wall, threw up entrenchments with furniture and beams, and in the middle of the ruins constructed passages for the sappers who were going to mine the next house . . . The huge fortified convents could not be destroyed, like the houses, by mining; we therefore merely blew up a piece of their thick walls, and when the breach was made sent forward a column to the assault. The besieged would flock to the defence, and in the terrible fighting which resulted from these attacks we suffered our principal losses.[144]

As Lejeune remembered, one such assault came on 10 February at the convent of San Francisco:

At three o'clock in the afternoon . . . the charge [was] fired and the terrible explosion flung to a great height in the air a huge portion of the convent and the cloister. Hardly had the mass of falling debris reached the deep . . . crater which the explosion had opened, before the . . . men flung themselves into the convent and charged the retreating enemy with the bayonet . . . We had hoped that the Spanish would have been intimidated by the magnitude of this disaster . . . but our sudden attack only increased their fury. They contested every inch of ground . . . We had to pursue them to the very roofs . . . and those of us who were below saw many fling themselves from the top . . . rather than yield to their conquerors . . . Never in any war was there . . . a more terrible scene than that presented by the ruins . . . The . . . surrounding suburbs . . . were rendered horrible by the quantities of mutilated human remains with which they were strewn. Not a step could be taken without stumbling over torn limbs . . . hands or fragments of arms.[145]

Amid the chaos Faustino Casamayor continued to record his impressions of the battle:

28 January. Today the fire of the enemy was more horrific than can possibly be imagined, and exceeded anything that had been experienced in the preceding days . . . The enemy continued to maintain themselves in the oil press and the Carmelite convent, and, although many of them perished in consequence of the heavy fire directed at them by our troops . . . they never ceased to fire back at us, with the result that our positions were strewn with bodies. The picture that Zaragoza presents is melancholic in the extreme: the very atmosphere seems full of fire, while on all sides one sees nothing but ruins . . . and carts full of dead bodies . . . It is impossible to describe everything that is taking place, but the picture offered by the chapel of Nuestra Señora del Pilar is on its own enough to make an impression on the boldest of spirits, for all the inhabitants have taken refuge there and gone so far as to spread their bedding on the very steps of the sanctuary, evidently believing that only by crouching in the very shadow of their only source of aid and comfort can they hope to survive.[146]

For the attackers, too, Zaragoza had become a veritable calvary. As Mrozinski recounts, very soon the attackers were completely exhausted:

The number of our troops was simply insufficient to shut in an army of 50,000 men that was defending itself in such a fashion . . . To attack the city there were available just two divisions, those of Grandjean and Musnier . . . In all [their] seven regiments had just 9,000 men. Half of them had to be on duty in the city every day, and, while there, they had to mount guard on the houses that had been occupied, keep up with the task of building the necessary siege works and mount attacks on the enemy positions . . . The two divisions suffered terribly while the men were exhausted by their labours and discouraged by the difficulties which they had to overcome every day. Yet, for all that they were driven a little bit further back towards the centre of the city every day, the Spaniards continued to demonstrate a spirit that was quite unquenchable . . . The fact was that the daily combats and extraordinary efforts which they were forced to make became a real torment for the soldiers who could see no end to the bloody struggle . . . It is true that they could see plenty of signs of the state into which their opponents had fallen. Mountains of unburied corpses lay in the streets and the courtyards that we occupied . . . but all this suggested to them was that we were fighting for a graveyard.[147]

Not surprisingly, morale in the imperial camp was badly shaken. Among those caught up in the battle was Thomas Bugeaud, a 34-year-old captain in the 116th Regiment of Line Infantry. Of noble stock, he had enlisted as a private in 1804 and fought at Austerlitz and been wounded at Pultusk. As he wrote to his sister on 12 February:

We are still before this cursed, this infernal Zaragoza. Although we took their ramparts by storm more than a fortnight ago and are masters of part of the town, the inhabitants, stirred up by the hatred they bear us, by the priests and [by] fanaticism, seem to wish to bury themselves under the ruins of their city after the pattern of old Numantia. They defend themselves with incredible determination and make us buy the smallest victory very dear. Every house, every convent holds out like a citadel, and every one has to be besieged by itself . . . You may imagine how many men such a war must cost . . . Our brigade has already lost two generals . . . There is not a day when there are not some officers among the dead . . . If we get all the advantage from this war that is expected, it will be bought very dear. But the most fearful thing is to think that our labours and our blood may not be of use to our country.[148]

Among the wounded was Marcellin Marbot. Ordered to lead an assault on the convent, he was shot by a Spanish sniper as he was inspecting the powder charges that had been placed to blow a hole in the walls:

I felt no pain at first and thought that the adjutant standing by me had inadvertently given me a push. Presently, however, the blood flowed copiously: I had got a bullet in the left side very near the heart. The adjutant helped me to rise, and we went into the cellar . . . I was losing so much blood I was on the point of fainting. There were no stretchers, so the soldiers passed a musket under my knees, and thus carried me through the débris of this quarter . . . to Marshal Lannes's headquarters on the outskirts of the town. When they saw me arrive, all covered with blood . . . the marshal and my comrades thought I was dead. Dr Assalagny assured them to the contrary, and hastened to dress my wound . . . To find the object Assalagny . . . turned me on my face and examined my back. Hardly had he touched the spot where the ribs are connected with the spine than I involuntarily gave a cry. The projectile was there. Assalagny then took a knife, made a large incision, perceived a metallic body showing between two ribs and tried to extract it with the forceps. He did not [at first] succeed, though his violent efforts lifted me up until he made one of my comrades sit on my shoulders and another on my legs. At length he succeeded in extracting a . . . bullet of the largest calibre.[149]

Yet the Spaniards, too, were under pressure. With the French inching ever closer, even the Pilar basilica was now under fire. Among those who had taken refuge there was Faustino Casamayor:

8 February. Today was one continuous hail of fire. Zaragoza suffered things that those who did not see them will never believe. Such was the damage to its buildings that it really seemed that nothing would be left standing . . . The Pilar basilica was left filled with rubble and debris from several bombs which smashed through the vaulting and frescos above the sacristy and the chapel of Santa Ana, the noise which they made when they blew up being such that it really seemed that the whole place was coming down. This did not occur, but even as it was things were bad enough. Many confessional boxes were smashed up; a hole was blasted in the floor; and the

walls and pillars . . . were so peppered with fragments that they will serve as a perpetual reminder of this catastrophe. Meanwhile, all the lights were blown out, while the church was filled with smoke so thick that it was impossible to see anything. Yet not even this was sufficient to drive the people from the feet of our patron, and the litany continued to be chanted before her holy image.[150]

As the days went by, so Casamayor's writing became ever more dramatic:

14 February . . . There was firing all day in the Coso. The enemy managed to seize the convent of San Francisco and kept up a continual barrage from its tower. Meanwhile, in the Jesuit convent they deployed a battery of six guns with the aim of bombarding the palace of His Excellency . . . Today things reached an extremity of anguish . . . Bread is so short that . . . guards had to be placed on all the bakehouses . . . while the soldiers have been reduced to eating biscuit. As for the sick, there are now so many that 300 people are dying a day; so many are the bombs, meanwhile, that no one can give them holy unction. And, if there are many sick, there are very few doctors, not that it matters as most of the dead are falling victim not to the epidemic but misery, hopelessness and want of spirit.[151]

By the middle of February, indeed, few men were in a fit state to fight. Living cheek by jowl with the defenders, Frenchmen such as Lejeune had a grandstand view of the city's agony:

The struggle became more bloody as the defence grew more concentrated. The population decreased in a most alarming manner, and every day ten times as many perished from typhus as the day before . . . There were no longer any regular hospital attendants; the medicines for the sick were exhausted, and rice water was all that was left to assuage their sufferings. The unfortunate invalids had nothing but a little straw on which to rest on the pavements of the long, cold, vaulted passages which form the entrances to all the houses in Saragossa. There they died of hunger or were consumed by the fever without a hand to give them a cooling draught. The Countess of Bureta and the women who had devoted themselves to succouring the wounded were now either dead themselves or scarcely able to drag themselves to their nearest relations. Gangrene set in rapidly in the slightest wound; the few sentinels . . . were to be seen sitting shivering on the stone benches wrapped in their cloaks, their weapons dropping from hands no longer strong enough to hold them, and many actually died before they could be relieved.[152]

For a Spanish view, let us again turn to Alcaide Ibieca:

The need to do something was growing by the minute, for Zaragoza was hovering between life and death . . . Smoke from burning buildings filled the atmosphere . . . Along the front line . . . all the doors and windows were protected with sandbags, boards and mattresses, and the streets blocked by barricades and ditches. Here were to be seen the craters opened by explosions, and there the shell of the same buildings that they had brought down, while the mountains of wreckage were strewn with . . . dismembered limbs in the most horrifying fashion. There were hardly any munitions, for powder and bullet were being consumed far faster than they could be made, while food was equally short, for the large quantity of grain that still existed in the magazines could not be ground into grain sufficiently quickly by . . . the mills that had been improvised beside the Ebro. All the private stocks of flour in the city had been given up . . . and, as for any other type of food, there was absolutely nothing to be had at any price. Every cellar . . . was crammed full of people taking shelter, many of whom were prostrated by illness and close to death . . . In fact, wherever one looked, there was nothing to be seen but the sick and the dying. More than forty convents and private houses had been turned into hospitals for the troops who had fallen ill, but these had almost no assistance of any sort, and were dying in a state of the utmost abandon and misery . . . The market place, in particular, offered a scene that brought tears to one's eyes. Many unfortunates whose houses had been destroyed or who had sought shelter from the bombardment had set up home under its arcades, and they were lying on filthy mattresses or even the very paving stones, bewailing their fate . . . In the streets dead bodies blocked the way at every step, while in churches such as that of San Felipe they lay in piles for want of anyone to bury them . . . and had become the prey of hungry dogs. Such memories chill one's blood, and my pen cannot record them any more: death had been enthroned in Zaragoza, and . . . it really seemed as if all the furies had come to exterminate her.[153]

The end finally came when French forces overran the Arabal suburb on 18 February. With Palafox himself almost dead from typhus, the Spaniards finally collapsed. Following the negotiation of surrender terms, the remnants of the garrison marched away to captivity on 21 February. Behind them lay not only a city in ruins, but one whose population had been decimated: in all, out of the 100,000 or so Spaniards in the city when the siege began, some 54,000 had died, of whom only about 20,000 were soldiers. One of the first men to look around was Heinrich von Brandt:

We went first to the famous church of the Pilar, which was quite close by. We had to make our way along the riverbank in order to avoid the barricades and the still smoking ruins. The square in front of the church was one of those scenes impossible to forget. It was clogged with praying women and children, coffins, and the dead for whom there were no coffins. In some places there were as many as twenty corpses piled on top of each other . . . Inside the church the priests, present in numbers and at all the altars, found they could not fulfil all of their many tasks. The doleful congregation crowded under the portals and filled the aisles, the floor of the nave had vanished under kneeling figures in black whose sobs intermingled with the psalms . . . [and] the smoke of the countless candles drifted up to the vaulted roof which had been riddled by our shells. Still more sinister was the Calle de Toledo. Here the population had sought refuge from our bombardment. Under the arches, and in indescribable confusion, there lay children, old people, the dying and the dead, all kinds of furniture and emaciated domestic animals. There was a mound of corpses, many stark naked, piled in the middle of the street; here and there fires were burning around which these poor people were attempting to cook their food.

Above all it was the children, thin and with the bright eyes of fever, that were painful to behold . . . I have since then been present at many scenes of slaughter. I have seen the Great Redoubt at Borodino, one of the most infamous horrors of war. Yet nowhere have I felt the same emotion as I did at that moment and perhaps the sight of suffering is far more poignant than that of death.[154]

* * *

The fall of Zaragoza is a convenient moment at which to conclude our survey of these climactic months of French revenge. Madrid had been recaptured; Barcelona had been relieved; the Spaniards had been beaten in five major battles and at least six actions of lesser import, and left without a single one of their field armies in a fit state to take the field; and the British had been, if not routed, then subjected to a severe drubbing. Allied casualties had been severe – some 5,000 British troops and perhaps ten times as many Spaniards (though many men of both nationalities who were taken prisoner managed to escape and in many cases rejoined the struggle) – and awkward questions had been left hanging over the willingness to continue the struggle of both the Portland administration and the Central Junta, the latter having also been considerably discredited and left in charge of a motley collection of territory rent by faction fighting and popular unrest. Also in question was the very alliance between Britain and Spain, Moore's campaign having both provoked a torrent of mutual recriminations and shattered the illusions which each of the two powers had about the other. Laid to rest, too, had been Napoleon's two chief demons of the summer of 1808: the Spanish troops who had triumphed at Bailén had been humbled at Tudela and Somosierra, while Zaragoza had been pounded into surrender. With even the British stand at La Coruña put down as a French victory, well might Napoleon, who left for Paris on 17 January, have felt that he could return to France and leave *l'affaire d'Espagne* to his subordinates, who were given a detailed set of plans to which they were expected to adhere. But the war was not over. Moore had disobeyed the orders of the Portland administration in respect of the march of the British forces into Spain, and been extremely badly served by some of his subordinates. Moreover, his conduct at Salamanca had been extremely churlish and his handling of the retreat through León and Galicia marked by an excess of haste that cost his unfortunate men very dear. Yet by striking, however briefly, at the French in northern Spain, Moore had arguably saved the Allied cause, for so many of the imperial forces had been drawn into Old Castile, León and Galicia that there were none left to drive on to Lisbon and Seville. In this, of course, the desperate stand of the defenders of Zaragoza also played its part, but the fact was that the battered Central Junta was given sufficient time in which to rebuild at least a façade of political authority and to reconstitute its armies. By the time the story of Moore's retreat reached London, then, there was no way that the Portland administration could abandon Spain to its own devices. Whatever Napoleon might think, the Peninsular War was far from over.

Typical soldiers of Wellington's army: a line infantryman, a heavy dragoon and a Scottish Highlander. In the field such men would have presented a much more battered appearance. (*Philip Haythornthwaite*)

Portuguese volunteers: these figures appear to represent some of the units raised in the first days of the uprising in Portugal in June 1808. (*Philip Haythornthwaite*)

A rifleman of the Ninety-Fifth Regiment of Foot. Universally known as the Ninety-Fifth Rifles, this unit has been much mythologised, but was none the less equipped with the highly accurate Baker rifle. (*Philip Haythornthwaite*)

A captain of the Fifty-Second Regiment of Foot, the unit in which John Dobbs served. (*Philip Haythornthwaite*)

A Spanish hussar. This figure depicts a trooper of the pre-war army, but is also representative of many of the Spanish cavalry and guerrilla units raised after 1808. (*Philip Haythornthwaite*)

An infantryman of the Legion of the Vistula. Under the leadership of such officers as Von Brandt and Mrozinski, this unit of Polish auxiliaries served at the siege of Zaragoza and afterwards helped garrison Aragón. (*Philip Haythornthwaite*)

An officer of the Ninety-Fifth Regiment of Foot. This was the uniform worn by several of the diarists featured in this work, including Leach, Kincaid and Simmons. (*Philip Haythornthwaite*)

A light infantryman and gunner of the pre-war Spanish army. In mute testimony to the supply difficulties experienced by the Spanish forces, the former is wearing a pattern of uniform that had officially been replaced in 1807. (*Philip Haythornthwaite*)

The main gate of the citadel of Pamplona. On 16 February 1808 French soldiers secured the citadel by pouring across the bridge in mock flight from a snowball fight that had been staged on the glacis. (*Charles J. Esdaile*)

The northern front of the royal palace in Madrid. The first shots of the Peninsular War were fired here on the morning of 2 May 1808 by a squad of French troops lined up at the approximate spot from which the picture was taken. (*Charles J. Esdaile*)

In a scene immortalised by the famous Spanish painter Francisco de Goya, the squadron of mamelukes of the Imperial Guard that had accompanied Marshal Murat to Spain battles with the populace of Madrid in the square known as the Puerta del Sol. (*Museo del Prado*)

Citizens of Madrid die at the hands of French firing squads at the Monte de Príncipe Pío on the western outskirts of the city on the night of 2/3 May 1808. (*Museo del Prado*)

During the sieges of 1809 parts of Zaragoza were reduced to a state reminiscent of Stalingrad. Here we see the devastation left in the wake of the great explosion that destroyed the city's main powder magazine on 27 June 1808. (*Taylor Library*)

The ruins of Zaragoza's general hospital. During the night of 3 August 1808 the French bombardment of the city caused panic among the 2,000 sick and wounded who had been given shelter in the building, and many were killed by bursting shells and falling masonry as they fled into the streets. (*Taylor Library*)

Desperate French troops surrender to their Spanish opponents in the wake of the battle of Bailén. (*Philip Haythornthwaite*)

Olive trees on the battlefield of Bailén in rear of the main French position. Exhausted and demoralised, the survivors of Dupont's forces fell back into these groves to seek shelter from the sun. (*Charles J. Esdaile*)

The bridge over the River Rumblar some miles west of the battlefield of Bailén where Captain Grivel sat out the battle. The bridge one sees today, though built more or less in the same style as the original, dates from 1929. (*Charles J. Esdaile*)

The River Rumblar just to the west of the bridge. This shallow stream, which is here seen photographed in April rather than July, was the only source of water for the whole of the French army. (*Charles J. Esdaile*)

The Seventy-First Regiment of Foot, among whose ranks was numbered Thomas Howell, repulse the brigade of General Solignac at the battle of Vimeiro. (*Taylor Library*)

Vimeiro viewed from near the spot where Captain Hulot's battery was stationed. (*Andrew Jackson*)

The campaign of La Coruña was marked by a number of successful British cavalry charges. Here detachments of the Tenth and Sixteenth Light Dragoons pounce on an unwary French advanced guard near Benevente on 29 December 1808. (*Taylor Library*)

British line infantry and rifles deployed to protect the retreat of Sir John Moore's army. Carried out in bitter winter weather, the retreat to La Coruña was marked by much disorder on the part of the British army. (*Taylor Library*)

The convent of Santa Monica in Zaragoza. In the attack on the city on 27 January 1809 the defenders repulsed every French attempt to take the building. (*Charles J. Esdaile*)

A romanticised French view of the assault on the monastery of Santa Engracia during the second siege of Zaragoza. (*Taylor Library*)

An artistic representation of the defence of the convent of Santa Monica. (*Philip Haythornthwaite*)

A house in the Calle Doctor Palomar that still shows damage from the battle for Zaragoza. (*Charles J. Esdaile*)

The battlefield of Medellín viewed from Marshal Victor's headquarters. The Spanish army advanced directly towards the camera in a long concave arc. (*Charles J. Esdaile*)

The French cavalry general Antoine Lasalle, whose light cavalry division played a crucial role at the battle of Medellín. (*Taylor Library*)

The seminary occupied by the British forces at Oporto. (*Andrew Jackson*)

French infantry advance from the eastern outskirts of Oporto in a desperate attempt to push the British back across the river. (*Taylor Library*)

The valley to the north of the British position at Talavera. (*Richard Tennant*)

The battlefield at Talavera looking north-westwards towards the Cerro de Medellín from the French centre. (*Richard Tennant*)

The Third Foot Guards at Talavera. In reality bodies of infantry rarely came to such close quarters. (*Regimental Headquarters of the Scots Guards*)

The battle of Talavera. (*National Army Museum*)

Civilian refugees flee the advance of the French armies. (*Museo del Prado*)

Women being raped by soldiers. British, Portuguese, French and Spaniards all engaged in such atrocities. (*Museo del Prado*)

Chapter 3

Recovery and Counter-Attack

In the second half of December 1808 there can have been few observers who would have wagered on the survival of the Patriot cause in Spain and Portugal: every Spanish army had been beaten; the British expeditionary force commanded by Sir John Moore was threatened with encirclement in León; Madrid was in the hands of the French; the Central Junta was in flight; and Portugal was defended by little more than a rabble of armed levies stiffened by a handful of British troops Moore had left behind in Lisbon. Yet just a month later the sense of crisis had passed: thanks to the campaign of La Coruña and the desperate defence of Zaragoza, the French had been unable to march on Lisbon and Cádiz and finish off the Allied forces, while Moore had managed to save his army by retreating through the wilds of Galicia and making contact with the British fleet. Given something of a breathing space, the Central Junta was able to rebuild its battered forces while in Portugal the council of regency that had been established in the wake of the battle of Vimeiro was able to proceed with conscription and receive fresh help from Britain. According to Napoleon, it was yet but a short step to finishing the job – such was the political dissension in the Spanish camp, in fact, that the impression seemed far from outlandish even now – but for the most part the French had lost the strategic initiative. Instead of sweeping all before them, indeed, in Portugal, Catalonia and southern Spain they faced a series of counter-attacks, their problems being exacerbated by the outbreak of popular insurrection in Galicia and the emergence of the complex phenomenon known as *la guerrilla*. Thanks to all this, by midsummer the Allies were on the offensive and even threatening to retake Madrid. In the event they were to be forestalled, but Napoleon's dreams of rapid victory had gone for good, while in the person of the newly ennobled Lord Wellington – at this stage he was but a viscount – there had emerged a champion whom the best of his marshals were never able to overcome.

People's War
Despair though the British might have done of the Spanish armies and their leaders, many of them kept faith with the notion that the Spanish people were wholeheartedly committed to the struggle against the French. Even as they fell back through the wilds of Galicia, from Moore downwards there were therefore plenty of observers who hoped that great days lay ahead for the Patriot cause – that, to be more specific, the experience of French occupation would cause the people to shake off what was seen as the torpor of centuries. And no sooner had the last British ship departed from La Coruña than in Galicia at least that dream seemed to become reality. For a good account of events in just one area, let us turn to the *Semanario Político, Histórico y Literario de la Coruña*, a liberal newspaper that appeared in Galicia after the French evacuation of the province later in the year:

On 25 January . . . General Fournier entered Mondoñedo with 700 cavalry. On the following day he sent 150 of them to the town of Ribadeo. No sooner had they arrived than they demanded bread, meat, wine, eggs, hay, barley and firewood from all the villages roundabout . . . These demands were backed up by all kinds of threats that were made only too credible by the robberies and other iniquities already committed in the places through which they had passed . . . All this led a number of honourable and distinguished patriots to persuade the peasantry that they should refuse to supply the rations which had been demanded of them . . . and within twenty-four hours the parishes of Cogela, Balboa, Sante, Villaosende, Cedofeita and Vidal had come together and elected as their chief Don Melchor Díaz de la Rocha. On the twenty-ninth of the same month, 320 peasants armed with fowling pieces, pitchforks and pikes presented themselves in the early morning . . . 200 of them being sent to occupy the heights overlooking the bridge on the road from Mondoñedo to Ribadeo [at Nuestra Señora del Puente] and the others to watch Quintalonga . . . On the same day the 200 peasants blocking the road at Nuestra Señora del Puente attacked a group of Frenchmen travelling from Ribadeo to Mondoñedo. In this action five Frenchmen were killed . . . whereas our peasants suffered no losses at all, being sheltered from the enemy horsemen by walls and ditches. On the thirtieth the enemy . . . attacked Quintalonga, only to be thrown back by the 120 peasants who held that point . . . As a result of these happy successes, our countrymen took heart and their number increased considerably.[155]

The Galician example was something of a special case, for the men responsible had not just sprung to arms in a spontaneous effort to defend their homes, but were rather members of a local militia known as the *alarma* that had been organised by the local authorities. Far more common in terms of popular resistance was the phenomenon of the guerrilla band – the small group of armed civilians waging war on the invaders from the shelter of hideouts in the rugged mountains that criss-crossed the zone of French occupation. In this respect there has been much exaggeration. Many of the leaders were, at best, adventurers, while the rank and file were often deserters on the run from the regular army, or peasants or day labourers who had only taken up arms because otherwise they faced starvation. In the worst instances, then, the bands were mere gangs of bandits who were little different from the similar groups that also thronged the Patriot zone. As the artillery officer Luis de Villaba later wrote:

The guerrillas who go by the name of Patriots should be exterminated: they are gangs of thieves with *carte blanche* to rob on the roads and in the villages. If some of them have brought benefits, the damage that others have wrought is one thousand times greater . . . Those who believe these bands . . . to be very useful are many, but if they meditate on the desertion from the enemy that has not occurred for fear of being murdered . . . the burnings and other disasters suffered by the villages . . . the many highwaymen and bandits who carry out their crimes under this pretext, and finally the manner in which their disorder and independence has caused all kinds of evil, they will understand how far the disadvantages outweigh the benefits.[156]

One must, then, be cautious, but, for all that, there is no doubt that the best of the bands made genuine efforts to harass the French. Toribio Bustamente, for example, was a guerrilla who played a leading role in the struggle in Extremadura:

> I have the honour to inform Your Worship of the humble services which the guerrilla band under my command has performed . . . in defence of King, Fatherland and Religion. Receiving news on 1 May that enemy soldiers were pillaging the towns of Villanueva de la Serena, Don Bénito and La Haba, I led my men to Villanueva where I discovered a party of seventy mounted Frenchmen who had come to seize wine and supplies. Although I had only thirty followers, I opened a heavy fire upon them whereupon they took flight in the most shameful and precipitate fashion. At this I pursued them as far as the gates of Medellín. They left six dead behind them and I took two cavalry horses and seven others that they had impounded from civilians to carry their booty. On our side we had but one man wounded and one horse killed.[157]

Among the irregulars there were also leaders of real genius and commitment. One of the early heroes of the struggle was a peasant from Old Castile named Juan Martín Díez. Nicknamed El Empecinado – 'Stick-in-the-Mud' might be a possible translation – he spent the early part of 1809 harassing the French in a broad district stretching from Aranda de Duero to Valladolid. Among those who met him at this time was the English seminarian Robert Brindle:

> Though elevated at this time to the rank of colonel, [El Empecinado] had not cast aside the dress of the peasant. His hat was the same as that worn in many places by the peasants with a small crown and broad brim and was fastened under his chin by an old ribbon . . . A carbine was fastened to his side by a silk handkerchief and he had a sword on the opposite side [and] a brace of pistols . . . and a large knife in a sash tied round his middle.[158]

Even if few of the guerrillas possessed the energy and charisma of El Empecinado and even, too, if the level that they were operating on was little higher than that of the common bandit, even the French recognised that at least some of them were something other than brigands. The son of an *émigré* aristocrat, Hippolyte d'Espinchal had enlisted in the French cavalry following the return of his family from exile in 1801:

> These forces were composed of both cavalry and infantry. In so far as the former were concerned, they were mounted on steeds of a rather scrawny build, equipped either with high Spanish saddles or others taken from French dragoons and hussars. Meanwhile, the dress and armament of the men corresponded with the variety of their horse furniture. On the one hand, one saw French coats, colpacks, infantry shakos and broad-brimmed hats . . . and on the other lances, muskets and sabres of every pattern. All this was typical enough of irregular troops, of course, and yet in one respect their costume had a certain degree of uniformity: almost all of them wore brown jackets decorated with red turnbacks and bars of lace and numerous rows of buttons in the style of our postillions. As for the infantry, they were armed

with a mixture of English, Spanish and French muskets, a part of them with no bayonets, as well as sabres and cutlasses of a variety of origins; few had packs, while their cartridge boxes were generally fashioned in the form of a belt. As for their dress, they had brown jackets and trousers in every imaginable colour, while their footwear was in very poor condition. In general, they had the aspect of a mass of peasants marching and fighting without order, whose courage was stimulated by nothing more than their numbers, the hope of pillage and the enjoyment of massacre.[159]

Taken as a whole, the irregulars also had a considerable impact on the French. Typical enough in this respect were the views of Louis Lagneau, a surgeon attached to the Twelfth Dragoons:

> The guerrillas represented a great danger to our communications. Irregular troops formed by volunteers from among the villagers and townsfolk and directed by the first man of authority who happened upon the scene – a priest, a shepherd, a smuggler – frequently attacked the small detachments sent out to escort our convoys (no one, indeed, could travel on their own) . . . Hiding among the rocks and laying ambushes for us in the gorges, they took care to profit from every advantage offered them by the mountainous terrain.[160]

Isolated Frenchmen might be murdered for no other reason than such money as they might be carrying, but the cruelty that often accompanied such crimes – gratuitous violence and torture were a common feature of Iberian banditry – created a terrifying legend that all too often became reality. Marcellin de Marbot, for example, had a grim experience in the vicinity of Agreda while carrying dispatches from the Ebro valley to Madrid:

> After Tarazona there is no more high road. The way lies entirely over mountain paths covered with stones and splinters of rock. The officer commanding our advanced guard . . . gave me a troop horse and two orderlies, and I went on my way in brilliant moonlight. When we had gone two or three leagues we heard several musket shots, and bullets whistled close past us. We could not see the marksmen, who were hidden among the rocks. A little further on we found the corpses of two French . . . soldiers, recently killed. They were entirely stripped, but their shakos were near them . . . Some little distance further we saw a horrible sight. A young officer of the Tenth [*Chasseurs à Cheval*], still wearing his uniform, was nailed by his hands and feet, head downwards, to a barn door. A small fire had been lighted beneath him. Happily, his tortures had been ended by death, but, as the blood was still flowing from his wounds, it was clear the murderers were not far off. I drew my sword; my two hussars handled their carbines. It was just as well we were on our guard, for a few minutes later seven or eight Spaniards, two of them mounted, fired on us from behind a bush. We were none of us wounded, and my two hussars replied to the fire, and each killed his man. Then, drawing their swords, they dashed at the rest. I should have been very glad to follow them, but my horse had lost a shoe among the stones so that I could not get him into a gallop. I was the more vexed

because I feared that the hussars might let themselves be carried away in the pursuit and get killed in some ambush. I called them for five minutes; then I heard the voice of one of them saying in a strong Alsatian accent. 'Ah! You thieves! You don't know the Chamborant Hussars yet. You shall see that they mean business.' My troopers had knocked over two more Spaniards: a Capuchin mounted on the horse of the poor lieutenant . . . and a peasant on a mule with the clothes of the slaughtered soldiers on his back. The emperor had given strict orders that every Spanish civilian taken in arms should be shot, and, moreover, what else could we do with these two brigands, who were already seriously wounded, and who had just killed three Frenchmen so barbarously? I moved on, therefore, so as not to witness the execution, and the hussars polished off the monk and the peasant.[161]

Another Frenchman with tales of fear and horror was Aymar de Gonnecourt, the 25-year-old son of an *émigré* who had returned to France in 1804, enlisted in the cavalry as a gentleman-volunteer, and was now a captain in the Sixth Cuirassiers with a position on the staff of General D'Avenay. As such he now found himself stationed in the town of Zamora:

Two . . . events happened at Zamora that may give a notion of the kind of life we led. The general gave a ball, and everything presentable at Zamora came there with the greatest delight . . . But, lo and behold! Just at midnight, when everyone was trying to enjoy himself and make some pleasant acquaintance, information reached us that the Spaniards were attacking the Toro gate. The general gave me orders to hasten to the infantry quarters, take three companies and go to the gate with all speed . . . As soon as I was outside, I heard some musketry, but it did not seem in great force . . . The infantry were already under arms in their quarters. I took three companies . . . and ran with them towards the . . . gate. But before I got there I perceived that the firing did not come from thence, but from the higher part of the town commanding the Duero . . . Having visited the . . . gate and ascertained that there was no attack, I left one of my companies there, and with the other two proceeded in the direction of the fire . . . and, on coming up, found a sergeant in a most extraordinary state of excitement. He told me that, on going towards a market about twenty paces from there, with a roof supported by a great many posts, he had seen an assemblage of armed Spaniards with fires lighted . . . He had cried out, 'Who goes there?', and, instead of answering, they had put out the fires and returned musket shots at him, [and] that he had been replying for half an hour, but had . . . not received any other shots than those that had brought on the affair. The matter was examined into and it was ascertained that some twenty oxen had been . . . lodged with their drivers in the place in question; that the unfortunate sergeant had been struck with hallucination; that no shots had been fired upon his force of fifteen men patrolling the streets, that . . . scared by the . . . challenge, [the drivers] . . . had tried to extinguish their fires without reply; and that then firing had begun and killed most of the oxen, happily without hitting the men, who had thrown themselves on the ground at the first shots . . . I have related this unimportant incident to give a slight notion of the anxious and disturbed life we led during these

Spanish campaigns . . . A few days after the adventure that I have just related, a guard of four men and a corporal that we kept a few hundred paces in front of the Toro gate were surprised during the night, and their throats cut without the least noise to give the alarm. This guard could only have been surprised by some neglect of duty, for it was placed in a little isolated building, very substantial, which should have been kept shut at night . . . Now the door had been found open without any mark of breakage, and the men . . . killed by poignards without making any defence. We supposed that they had made acquaintances among the Spaniards, as was often the case, and fallen victims to treachery. A corporal of the garrison was also found hung up by the feet in the shop of a butcher . . . with whom he had made acquaintance. The butcher, assisted no doubt by some accomplice, had opened the corporal as one opens a pig, and removed the whole of his inside, [and] then . . . made his escape.[162]

Faced by these attacks, the French responded with repression. General Abel Hugo was governor of Avila:

At El Escorial there was a division of dragoons under the command of General Lahoussaye . . . [but] this received orders to follow the army, whereupon I was instructed . . . to take over the task of watching over its lines of communication in the area between Las Rosas and Villacastín. In consequence, I posted pickets wherever I could, but they were insufficient in number . . . and therefore could not prevent peasants discontented at the vexations from which they were suffering or simply attracted by the hope of booty from hurling themselves on our convoys and taking the lives of the wagoners in a manner that was as unworthy as it was cruel. I was obliged to make an example to put an end to these murders, and for this purpose singled out a number of undesirables from the village of Las Vegas de Matute who had been arrested at my orders and handed over to a court martial in consequence of the part they had played in the killings. In dealing with them, use was made of the customs of the country: after they had been executed, their heads were placed above the door of the parish church, while their bodies were displayed on a gibbet that marked the highest point of the Madrid-Valladolid high road. Meanwhile, copies of the sentence that had been pronounced against them were nailed up in all the main villages of the district under my command and especially those close to the high road . . . Despite the quiet maintained by its own inhabitants, the area around Villacastín was also frequently the scene of the murder of isolated soldiers . . . In response, I got together all the *alcaldes* and other local notables . . . and made clear to them the necessity of introducing strong measures that would put an end to these crimes. Their elaborate replies failing to satisfy me in the slightest, I was obliged to tell them that, unless they organised the necessary patrols and personally watched over the security of such Frenchmen as might pass through the area, I would hold not only them but also their town responsible for anything that took place in the district.[163]

Yet neither exemplary executions nor the threat of further reprisals made the slightest difference. With the Spanish economy in a state of collapse, for many country dwellers, in particular, violence was quite literally the only means of survival. In large parts of the occupied territories, then, the French were forced to engage in full-scale military operations. Fighting in the wilds of eastern Aragón, for example, was the infantryman François Lavaux:

All the élite companies were got together: the aim was to drive off the brigands who from time to time raided our lines, and cut us off from every supply of food. On 15 January [1809] we left the vicinity of Zaragoza to march in the direction of Valencia. We found the brigands barricaded in a little town called Alcañiz. After a sharp fight we got into the place, and it was given over to us for pillage . . . Having murdered everyone and looted everything in sight, we stayed on for another six weeks . . . The brigands attacked us several times, but they could achieve nothing . . . However, whenever they caught someone from our side, they subjected him to martyrdom. Their tongues and nails were torn out, and then they were roasted alive. This was done by thrusting the victim into a fire as far as the middle of his body, and then leaving him to die amidst the embers.[164]

Atrocity, however, was met by counter-atrocity. Basil Hall, a young British naval officer serving in a warship off the coast, witnessed the fate of the Galician town of Corcubión when it was visited by a French punitive column:

We rowed smartly up the bay, but had scarcely doubled the point . . . at the entrance of the harbour, when we observed . . . the French soldiers pouring into the wretched town from both sides of the valley. Many of the inhabitants rushed to the fishing boats on the beach, and, leaping into them indiscriminately, pushed into the stream. As we rowed up the harbour, we met hundreds of these poor people, half-dressed, screaming, and struggling hard to get beyond the reach of shot. Others fled along the sides of the hills towards the bay, hoping to be picked off the shore by boats or . . . to conceal themselves . . . among the rocks. Of these fugitives, great numbers were brought down . . . by the fire of the enemy . . . So completely hemmed in . . . were these wretched people that escape was almost impossible. The horror and confusion of this frightful spectacle were increased by the conflagration of the town, in the streets of which deeds of still greater atrocity were going on.[165]

For the men caught up in such fighting, it was a trying time: no one, it seemed, could be trusted. Among the troops operating in Extremadura was Andrzej Daleki, a peasant from the district of Krotoszyn who was conscripted into the Polish army formed by Napoleon at the end of 1806 and sent to Spain in 1808:

Marching towards the Portuguese frontier, we camped in a village. On the following day, we continued our advance, but a general officer remained behind with a single company of infantry, though why I do not know. The general then continued on his own, leaving the infantrymen to follow on behind. However, when the latter did so, the peasants sent them the wrong way and they ended up in the midst of [a band of irregulars]. We marched to help them, but it was too late: the Spaniards had already massacred them, and all we could do was to bury their bodies. Going back to the

village, at first we found nobody there. Captain Jasielski remained with most of the
. . . battalion on a hillside outside the village, but a group of about ten of us were
sent into the village to see if we could find any food and at the same time come up
with any clues as to who had been responsible for the attack. At first we did not see
a soul, but, going through the houses, we . . . at length found a woman who had just
given birth lying in a bed. We let her alone, but when we got back we went to the
captain who said, 'Go back to the house tonight: somebody is bound to visit the
woman.' So we did as we were told and, sure enough, we found a young man sitting
on the bed. In accordance with our orders, we arrested husband, wife and child alike
and brought them back to the camp. The captain ordered us to respect the woman,
who was very weak. We therefore made a fire for her and ordered her to sit down
beside it with her child. The husband, however, remained a prisoner. In the
morning the woman was taken back to the house, and we then marched away, taking
the man with us as a guide . . . But he led us straight towards [some Spaniards]. The
captain was a decent person, but he now got very angry. In a low voice he ordered
us to run towards some nearby trees before the Spaniards saw us. Happily, we
escaped, and when we had got far enough away he ordered us to bind the man's
hands behind his back, tie him to a tree and flog him.[166]

Unused to fighting irregular opponents, the French were hampered not just by their
vulnerability to being tricked by the local populace, but also by want of familiarity with the
methods and tactics they needed to employ. Heinrich von Brandt, for example, found
himself trying to garrison the town of Barbastro as part of the brigade of General Pierre
Habert:

Barbastro, which Habert's brigade occupied for close on three weeks, is no doubt
quite a pleasant place in times of peace, but in times of war it is one of great danger
on account of the labyrinth of canals, olive plantations, vineyards and other walled
enclosures which surround it. Habert, so confident in open country, was not half
the man he should have been in such a terrain. He personally organised the
positioning of the outposts after an all too brief reconnaissance, and his dispositions
left much to be desired. Any method in our security measures was obscured by a
host of pointless duties which wore out the soldiers without adding to their safety.
There was, above all, a lack of basic organisation. Each battalion was ordered to
provide men to guard first this place and then that and consequently never grew
familiar with its surroundings. This constant rotation . . . was deeply troubling in a
terrain so suited to surprise attack. We had sentries carried off . . . by invisible
enemies every night. It would have been better to assign each battalion a permanent
post and for them to report back to the commander details of any movements or
activity in their sector . . . These constant setbacks undermined the morale of the
troops . . . With each new misadventure the general would rage and take his
frustration out on the populace and even his own soldiers. The soldiers soon began
to take this as just another example of the bad feeling so prevalent in our armies in
Spain.[167]

Even among the leaders of the invasion, then, the belief began to grow that the situation was spiralling out of control. Born on 12 April 1768 at Painpol, Pierre de Lagarde was the son of an official of the crown estates, who had become first a college teacher and then, following the Revolution, a bureaucrat. After service in the Ministries of Marine and Foreign Relations, he transferred to the Ministry of General Police, and in January 1808 was appointed head of the new 'General Intendance of Police' that was being established in Portugal. Expelled from that country with the rest of Junot's forces after Vimeiro, he was now waiting for a chance to take up his position once again, while at the same time keeping Napoleon informed of events:

> For several days I have been at Valladolid . . . This is where the danger begins . . . It is towards Olmedo and [the Sierra de] Guadarrama that the brigands, of whom there are supposed to be 400-500, attack and kill. Several of the posts set up along the road . . . have been carried off to the number of thirty or forty men at a time. The *medecin en chef*, Desgenettes, was held up and only escaped death thanks to the unexpected arrival of a French patrol. The *chef d'escadron*, Thomas, one of the best officers in Your Majesty's gendarmerie, was killed, or at least made prisoner . . . Any French soldiers who travel the road on their own are killed . . . In the last few weeks alone, eight or ten couriers have been captured, thereby exposing the secrets of Your Majesty and Your Majesty's august brother to . . . the leaders of the insurrection and British headquarters. As for the road via Somosierra, it is absolutely impracticable without an escort of three or four men . . . The fact is that, following the failure of its efforts in the field, the country is preparing itself for a veritable Vendée.[168]

What Lagarde failed to point out to the emperor, however, was that in the district of which he wrote in particular, but also elsewhere as well, the behaviour of the French troops and their commanders could not but tend to undermine the restoration of order that was so much desired. Born in Paris on 27 November 1779, Gaspard de Clermont-Tonnerre had gone to Naples with Joseph Bonaparte and was now serving as one of his *aides-de-camp*:

> The officer in charge of the whole of Old Castile was General Kellermann. Renowned as much for his cupidity as he was for his bravery in battle, from the moment that he succeeded Marshal Bessières, he had . . . burdened the whole extent of his jurisdiction with enormous requisitions with the intention of selling the foodstuffs concerned back to the people whom they had just been stripped from, ruined though they now were. All means of raising money were deemed good, and it was claimed that general officers went in person from village to village, arresting the mayors in order to force them to pay up. As a result, the whole of the north-west of Spain was ready to take up arms.[169]

With the challenge of the irregulars strengthened by the fact that the 'little war' also involved flying columns of regular troops and a variety of local militias, the consequence of all this was clear enough. On the one hand demoralisation set in among the soldiers actually in Spain, while on the other alarming stories began to circulate on the home front. Among the reinforcements sent across the frontier in 1809, for example, was Antoine Fée, a native of Issoudun and a keen amateur botanist who had obtained a commission as a pharmacist. His experiences, one suspects, must have been replicated many times over:

> At that time Spain was being called the Frenchman's tomb, and the sadness with which I was bade farewell suggested all too well that my return was at the very least regarded as being something that was very doubtful . . . Having boarded the stage coach, I soon lost sight of . . . my home town . . . Much affected by the scenes that had accompanied my departure, I gave myself over to the full bitterness of my regrets . . . New travellers soon got on board . . . One of them was an official in the corps of hydrographic engineers who was going back to Spain . . . after having temporarily escaped it, and he was clearly much annoyed at having to serve there again . . . He drew me a picture of the Peninsula that was scarcely encouraging, and his remarks would have seemed exaggerated had they not been confirmed . . . by various soldiers whom we met at the stopping points we passed along the way. Nobody was richer in terrifying details than a commissary we met at Angoulême. He depicted Spain in colours that were so sombre, and spoke of the excesses to which both sides had given themselves over in so pessimistic a manner, that we were plunged into the most profound sadness. Not being able to believe in such barbarism, however, I supposed the narrator to be something of a poet, and yet, as I soon learned, he was in reality . . . speaking no more than the simple truth.[170]

Spring Offensive

Thanks on the one hand to the march of Sir John Moore and on the other to the growth of irregular resistance, the tide of French conquest was sufficiently slowed down for the Junta Central to rally its armies. Protecting Andalucía were two main forces: the Army of Extremadura under General Cuesta, and the erstwhile Army of the Centre under, first, the Marqués del Palacio, and then the Conde de Cartojal. With the attention of the French pulled towards the north of Spain, the Junta even enjoyed the initiative. In reality the auguries for anything other than a defensive campaign were not very good: in mid-February the Spanish forces in Catalonia had essayed an attack from their new base at Tarragona, only for them to be heavily defeated at Valls. At the same time, as many Spanish officers recognised, the uprising of 1808 had left Spain with an army whose quality left much to be desired. Yet the government was under heavy pressure on the home front. On all sides its authority was being challenged, and this in turn meant that it had little option but to embark on a search for military victory as the only means of asserting its position. For good or ill, then, there was no option: the Junta Central had to win a battle. In this respect, the main clash came in Extremadura where General Cuesta advanced to attack the corps of Marshal Soult which had recently struck southwards from the Tagus valley to threaten Badajoz. Initially, the reports were encouraging enough. Present with the Spanish forces was Benjamin D'Urban, an officer in the Quarter-Master General's department, who had been attached to Cuesta's headquarters as an observer:

> Early this morning the army got orders to march . . . The French advanced guard

showed itself on the heights [and] Cuesta made a disposition, and, indeed, a very good one, but it . . . proved only a strong reconnaissance, which, very foolishly descending from the heights, was enveloped and cut off by the regiments of Almansa and Infanta . . . A colonel of cavalry and seventy men [perished], the Spaniards making no prisoners.[171]

But when the two forces clashed at the town of Medellín on 29 March, Patriot hopes were dashed yet again. The story is taken up by Jackson:

> The battle began at 1pm in a plain between [Don] Benito and Medellín, no one – not even his confidential *aide-de-camp* – being acquainted with Cuesta's intentions. He deployed his whole force, leaving no reserve, obliqueing to the right and left into one long line extending a full league, but, by so doing, a great space was left in the centre of which the French did not fail to take advantage. His line being formed, he did not immediately begin the attack, for which a very favourable opportunity offered while the French were deploying, but suffered them to form theirs, when the action began along the whole line at once. The Spanish infantry behaved nobly. Though great numbers were without shoes and almost without clothing, they advanced with a coolness and resolution that would have done credit to veteran troops and drove back their adversaries.[172]

What happened next is described by the hussar Albert de Rocca, who was present on the field with General Lasalle's cavalry division:

> We retired for two hours slowly and silently, stopping every fifty paces to face about and present our front to the enemy in order to dispute our ground with him before we abandoned it . . . As we retired, the cries of the Spaniards redoubled; their skirmishers were so numerous and so bold that they frequently forced ours back into the ranks. They shouted to us . . . that they would give no quarter . . . The Spaniards had sent six chosen squadrons against our single one; they marched in close column; at their head were the Lancers of Jérez. This whole body began . . . to quicken their pace in order to charge us when we were retiring. The captain commanding our squadron made his four platoons . . . wheel half round to the right. This movement being made, he adjusted the front line . . . as quietly as if we had not been in presence of the enemy. The Spanish horse, seized with astonishment at his coolness, involuntarily slackened their pace. Our commandant profited by their momentary hesitation, and ordered the charge to be sounded. Our hussars . . . then drowned the sound of the trumpet . . . by a . . . terrible shout of joy and fury. The Spanish lancers stopped; seized with terror, they turned their horses . . . and overthrew their own cavalry, which was behind them . . . Our hussars mingled with them indiscriminately [and] cut them down without resistance, and we followed them to the rear of their own army . . . Our dragoons . . . took advantage of the uncertainty of the Spanish infantry, which seemed shaken by the flight of the cavalry, and made against the Spanish centre a brilliant and fortunate charge . . . In an instant the army that was before us disappeared like clouds driven by the wind. The Spaniards threw down

their arms and fled, the cannonade ceased and the whole of our cavalry went off in pursuit of the enemy.[173]

In the midst of the chaos Cuesta tried vainly to restore order. As he later recounted:

> The left had arrived within half a pistol shot of the first enemy battery and was advancing with the bayonet to take it, when a strong force of enemy cavalry . . . charged to rescue it. Our infantry did not stop, but the Almansa and Infante line cavalry regiments, and . . . the Imperial Chasseurs of Toledo wavered . . . and, abandoning our array, fled at the gallop . . . I was behind . . . our left at the time, and seeing the flight of the three regiments, quickly rode over to contain the disorder . . . The corps of grenadiers, which was still advancing on the battery . . . was shouting, 'What is this? Come back! They are ours!' But it was all in vain. The cavalry could not be rallied, and so the enemy got into the rear of our infantry and achieved their disunion.[174]

In this imposing battle – some 22,000 French troops faced 24,000 Spaniards – the Patriot cause suffered terribly. It was in all probability, in fact, the bloodiest single day in the history of the Spanish army. Few of the families of those involved ever found out what happened to their loved ones, but, here and there, stragglers from the carnage did manage to make their way home. An American adventurer who had come to see the war at first hand, Robert Semple decided to try to travel from Lisbon to Gibraltar via Seville and Granada:

> Our protracted stay at Posadas enabled me to witness one of those scenes which mark, as it were, the very outskirts of war, and affect us more than those of greater horror. A poor woman of the place had been informed that her only son was killed in battle, and she, of course, had given herself up to grief, but this very morning a peasant arrived with certain intelligence, not only that her son was living, but that he was actually approaching the village, and not above a league distant from it. The first shock of these tidings overpowered the mother's feelings: she ran out into the street, uttering screams of joy, and telling everyone she met that he was not dead . . . and, so saying, attired as she was, she hurried into the road and soon disappeared. But what can describe her return? Her son lived, but, alas, how changed since she last saw him! His arm had been carried away by a cannon ball, the bandages on his wound were dyed with blood, he was pale and emaciated, and so weak that he was with difficulty supported on his ass in a kind of cradle by the help of a peasant who walked by his side. On the other side walked his mother, now looking down at the ground, now up to heaven, but chiefly on her son with anxious eyes and a countenance in which joy and grief, exultation and despondency reigned by turns or were strangely mingled together.[175]

Nor was it just a question of those who had died or come home a shell of their former selves; the gaps in the ranks inevitably had to be filled by fresh drafts of recruits:

> On leaving the place . . . we had not proceeded far when we saw a great number of parties approaching towards us and in a manner covering the plain. I first imagined

them to be inhabitants of Castro who had been spending their Sunday on the country, but on their nearer approach they appeared to be composed entirely of men and youths, who, I was informed, had been drafted, from the most part from about Baena, for the army. This was occasioned by a recent decree of the Junta calling upon this part of the country for men, and granting very few exceptions to such as were able to carry arms. Nothing could give a more striking picture of the patience and implicit obedience of the Spaniards to their government than was presented by these successive groups which had . . . suddenly relinquished their homes in strict obedience to a single decree of a self-appointed junta. Some were old men with grey hairs, riding on asses; others striplings under fourteen years of age, playing with each other as they went along the road. Most were silent, but some laughed and sang, while others with downcast eyes and melancholy looks appeared with difficulty to refrain from tears. In this manner at least 1,200 men and boys passed in review before me ere sunset, nor was it possible to behold so many individuals torn from their homes and peaceful occupations, and to reflect how many mothers, wives and sisters were at that moment plunged in sorrow for the departure of those so dear to them . . . without cursing from the bottom of my soul the ambition and perfidy of that man who was the sole cause of this misery and distress . . . [Having arrived at Baena] I took a moonlight walk with one of the inhabitants through the streets . . . I everywhere observed a profound silence . . . unusual in a Spanish town on so fine a moonlit Sunday evening, but . . . my companion sufficiently accounted for it. 'Could you behold the interior of these houses', said he, 'you would find scarcely one family of which the women are not in tears.'[176]

Commitment Renewed

In the aftermath of the retreat of Sir John Moore, it would not have been surprising if the British government had withdrawn its forces from the Peninsula. However, thanks in large part to the efforts of the Foreign Secretary, George Canning, it was instead decided to reinforce the small British force that had been left in Portugal, and restore its command to Sir Arthur Wellesley, who was naturally anxious to refurbish the laurels that had been tarnished by Sintra, while at the same time being possessed of clear views as to how Britain might this time make a success of her intervention. In the event this decision was one day to lead to the liberation of the entire Peninsula, but in the first instance Wellesley's object was limited to the defence of Portugal. Here the situation had since January 1809 become very grave. Indeed, it was not just the battle of Medellín that made 29 March 1809 a black day for the Allied cause in the Peninsula: that same day some 200 miles to the north-west French forces stormed the Portuguese city of Oporto. Despite the insurrection that had broken out in Galicia, in February the corps of Marshal Soult had set out to invade Portugal from the north. The campaign that followed proved a difficult affair. In the first place, there was the little matter of the weather. As the French commissary Pierre Le Noble remembered:

From 2 February onwards it never ceased to rain: veritable torrents fell from the clouds, and the least stream became a great river. Much swollen, the Miño burst its banks and presented a barrier that was all the more difficult to cross in view of the army's lack of bridging equipment . . . Between them, wet and inanition caused many men to fall sick: on 15 February the hospital of Pontevedra had around 500 invalids, and by the evening of the sixteenth 400 had been admitted at Tuy.[177]

With the main coastal road into Portugal blocked by floods, not to mention several substantial fortresses, Soult's men had to embark on a long and circuitous march to the inland city of Orense, while the local militia known as the *alarma* made a determined attempt to contest their passage. As Joseph de Naylies remembered, in the towns of Maurentan and Ribadavia, in particular, there were scenes of terrible savagery:

Reaching . . . Arbo, we learned from a peasant, who was caught among some rocks, that the inhabitants of all the neighbouring cantons had taken arms against us . . . The majority of these people had got together at the village of Maurentan. One could only approach this place via a long defile lined with hedges and overhung with rocks that ended at the river Sachas, a small stream that at this point fell into the Miño. To reach the town, one then had to cross a very long and very narrow bridge, and this was defended by 1,000 . . . men, barricaded, and blocked by *chevaux de frise*. Yet if we wanted to continue on our way, there was nothing for it but to take both bridge and town. In consequence, the division deployed into battle order in the shelter of the defile, and 200 dismounted dragoons advanced towards the village . . . At first the Galicians showed signs of wanting to fight – we were horsemen, and, not realising that our men could fight on foot with the bayonet as well as on horseback, they believed that they could easily turn back a force of cavalry marching without infantry support in a region of gorges and mountains – but when they saw that the dragoons were armed with carbines and coming on on foot, they let loose a single volley and fled . . . into the village. Hidden in the buildings, they opened fire on us again, but by then the bridge had been forced. In a few moments the first houses had been stormed, and very soon the whole village was on fire. The flames took everyone who was still alive . . . More than 400 Spaniards died in them, whereas we lost just two dragoons . . . The inhabitants of Maurentan had abandoned the village, and hidden in the hills; they were pursued and a great number killed . . . On 18 February our division met up with the rest of the corps near Melón. We bivouacked at the village of Coto, while the infantry [divisions] were distributed roundabout. Two battalions occupied Ribadavia, and they were there attacked by a cloud of peasants who had come down from the mountains. The courage of the French overcame that of the multitude who opposed them, and, after a bloody combat in which many of the Galicians lost their lives, the remainder fled back into the hills. When we marched through the town the next day, we did not see a single inhabitant. Under the walls of the town, I saw a horrible tableau that summed up the effects of this odious war. Lying nude and disfigured in the midst of a pile of corpses, I saw the bodies of two women. One of them was middle-aged: beside her lay a musket, while she was wearing a cartridge box and a sabre . . . and had been killed by a bullet in the chest while fighting in the ranks of the Galicians. The other, who was entirely naked and could not have been more than seventeen years old, had evidently joined a group of peasants in trying to pull a mounted officer from his horse: she had been cut down by a blow from a sabre that had split her skull in two.[178]

The Portuguese, alas, were in no state to face invasion. The regular army was still being rebuilt and practically the only troops in a fit state to fight the French were the men of the tiny Loyal Lusitanian Legion, a volunteer force recruited in and around Oporto by the English adventurer Sir Robert Wilson (curiously enough, many of his men were not Portuguese, but rather Galicians who had fled to Portugal to avoid conscription only to find no other means of supporting themselves). Among the substantial British expatriate community there was therefore much disquiet. An English girl named Harriet Slessor wrote in her diary:

It appears extraordinary to see how the inhabitants of this town, as well as the country people, persist in their confidence that there is not the least danger of the French coming again so soon. They even say, should they venture, they are confident that Porto is in a fine state of defence, as well the resolution of the country people to attack the French on their way from Spain. One very material reflection that has not occurred to these good people is that of what description are those who have come forward to their defence. Troops there are none. The good bishop with his motley attendance, most likely, on a day of confusion and attack, will be making the best of his way to Lisbon, or wherever he may be most secure, not to be kidnapped by the French. The country people declare they will fight. It is true they flock together in great numbers. Thousands, I have not a doubt, will assemble, and very few among the number that have been taught the use of arms. They are willing to think, and I believe do think that as long as the enemy does not appear, that they are capable of performing wonders. But let a formidable French army present itself, well disciplined, full of ardour for conquest and rapine, [and] how soon will confusion, dismay and distraction be mingled in the probable destruction of thousands?[179]

Nor were things any better in Lisbon. On his arrival in the Portuguese capital, Robert Semple encountered a depressing spectacle:

When it could no longer be concealed that the English and Spanish armies in Galicia were retreating, [and] . . . that the English force in Lisbon was making every preparation to embark at the shortest notice . . . the government made an animated appeal to the people, reminded them of the former glory of the Portuguese name and called on them to assert it. The enthusiasm created by these appeals was very great, but, had the French advanced, it would in my opinion have proved less fatal to them than to the stragglers of the English rearguard. Happily this was not put to the test. The streets, the squares, the quays, were lined with ranks of volunteers whose arms, equipment and movements were most various and whimsical. The greater proportion carried pikes; some were armed with fowling pieces, some with bayonets screwed on poles; some with small-swords, with daggers [or] with pistols . . . Here and there . . . were seen halberds and pikes of curious and ancient workmanship, which had probably been wielded in the wars of the fifteenth century and, after lying long in dust and darkness, were now dragged forth to light. The assortment of the men was as various as their arms. The tall and the short, the lean and the corpulent, the old man and the stripling stood side-by-side. At the word of command some turned to the right and others to the left; [meanwhile,] some parts of the line advance while others remained stationary. In short everything was ridiculous except their cause, and that was most sacred.[180]

After fighting two battles against forces of Portuguese levies that were easily put to flight, the last days of March saw Soult and his men reach the city of Oporto. This had been fortified by a line of redoubts and other entrenchments, but when the French attacked the town on 29 March they quickly broke through. The scenes that followed were possibly among the worst of the entire war. One French eyewitness was Auguste Bigarré, the 33-year-old son of a magistrate from the Breton island of Belle-Isle, who had in 1806 become an *aide-de-camp* of Joseph Bonaparte and was currently the latter's emissary at the headquarters of Marshal Soult:

On the twenty-ninth at seven o'clock in the morning Laborde's division marched on the enemy entrenchments with shouldered arms. Having got through the advanced works, it fell on the Portuguese line with the bayonet and, overcoming it at every point, put it to flight. Having followed in the rear of this movement, the French cavalry . . . charged the fugitives. Dealing mighty blows with their sabres, they inflicted real carnage upon them and rode pell-mell into Oporto mixed up with their ranks. I entered the town with the first battalions of the Seventeenth Line Infantry, and went straightaway to the bridge across the Douro at which spot the most dreadful slaughter took place. Imagine 12–15,000 souls crowded together on the bank of a river crossed by a bridge of boats, whose centre has been pushed under the water. Imagine that mass . . . pressing forward to cross the bridge. Imagine those unfortunates being hurled into a gulf whose existence they only discovered at the last moment. Imagine them being exterminated by . . . Portuguese guns on the left bank of the Duero and the bayonets of the French at their heels. . . Mercifully, this scene of carnage only lasted for one hour, but . . . for eight days afterwards one saw husbands, fathers and brothers dredging the river . . . for their wives, their children, their parents and their friends.[181]

Another French soldier to witness the last moments of the fighting in Oporto was Joseph de Naylies:

Here and there fighting was still going on in the streets, but a heavy hand was being used against anyone who was caught with arms in their hands. For some hours the city was then prey to all the horrors of an assault. I was fortunate enough to save a young girl who was about to become the victim of a number of drunken infantrymen. Looking up from the street where we were formed up in column, I saw a girl try to fling herself from a balcony, only to be roughly pulled back through the doorway by a number of men. Running up the stairs, sabre in hand, I threw myself upon these brigands, but I was knocked down by one of them. The blow drew blood, and I was only saved by the fact that in his drunken state he failed to take proper aim. Attracted by the noise, three dragoons then ran in and helped me to chase them away.[182]

The French occupation proved a grim affair. An English officer of the Eighty-Second Foot named George Wood who had been billeted in Oporto at the time of the French arrival later returned to the house in which he had stayed to find it in a shocking condition:

> To witness the destruction occasioned in this beautiful residence was truly pitiable . . . the fine balustrades [were] broken; the chandeliers and mirrors were shattered to pieces; all the portable furniture had been taken away and the remainder either wantonly burned or otherwise destroyed; the choice pictures were defaced, and the walls more resembled a French barrack than the abode of a Portuguese *fidalgo* from the obscene paintings that were daubed upon them. The beautiful garden was entirely ransacked; the charming walks and fragrant bowers torn up and demolished; the fountains broken to pieces.[183]

To explain how Wood managed to get back to Oporto, we must turn to the doings of the British army. As we have seen, after some discussion it had been agreed that the British army should continue to operate in Portugal. Command of the forces involved, which were quickly rebuilt with troops sent out from Britain, was restored to Sir Arthur Wellesley, and a substantial British force was soon marching against the troops of Marshal Soult. By 11 May the redcoats were facing the city on the south bank of the river Douro, and the following day the discovery of a few boats that had not been removed by the French enabled Wellesley to attempt a daring amphibious assault. Seizing a prominent convent that overlooked their crossing point, the first troops across the river fought off a series of desperate counter-attacks. So far was the garrison from being daunted, indeed, that some of its bolder spirits even tried to take the fight to the enemy. Thomas Bunbury, for example, was a 17-year-old ensign in the Third Foot:

> I was posted at the iron gateway of the courtyard with orders to let in any of our men, but to exclude their pursuers. These, however, entered the garden, and endeavoured, as I afterwards learned, to get between us and the river so as to prevent the passage of more troops coming to our assistance. The affair was rather more serious in the orange grove and garden, but five or six youngsters . . . all as giddy and thoughtless as myself, sallied out . . . and, never looking behind us, proceeded to attack the different small parties of the French who were coming up to reinforce their companions in their attempt upon the seminary. The advancing French made a great noise when marching, every small party having a drummer thumping away with all his might, and against these poor devils of drummers our fire was principally directed. We shot several, and our opponents did not seem to get on well

without them, and, as they were driven before us, our officers armed themselves with the French muskets. All this was well enough as long as we were going ahead and we had very few of our party hurt, but at length we were brought to a stand by a party of the enemy taking post behind the walls of an enclosure to oppose our further progress. In our advance we had been reinforced, and had now about twelve or thirteen men, among them a most singular character, a German rifleman who could not or would not speak a word of English . . . With some loss we reached a cottage, the garden of which was walled round. The door was barred in such a manner as to prevent our admission, and we were therefore obliged to dispense with this citadel and confine ourselves to defending the garden wall. For a time we continued to beat back every advancing force that came against it. At length it became evident that our party, from its advanced and isolated position, was attracting considerable attention from the enemy, who, accompanied by a large Newfoundland dog, seemed determined to drive us from the garden. We inflicted a heavy loss on our assailants during their advance, but a fine young fellow who led them succeeded in reaching the wall. Our friend the rifleman was all this time investigating the contents of a pack he had brought in, but, observing the officer on the wall . . . he took a very deliberate aim, and tumbled the fellow over. This so discouraged the rest that they got back again, and, to our great delight, ran away as fast as their legs would carry them . . . This being the first time I was under fire, I may be asked what were my feelings on the occasion. Being a giddy, hare-brained fellow, I do not suppose that I reflected at all upon the matter. It seemed to me capital fun.[184]

With the attention of the French distracted by events at the convent, a number of bold spirits among the inhabitants rushed to the quayside and seized a number of boats which they proceeded to take across the river to Wellesley. In consequence, by the end of the day, the British were pouring into the city. Among them was an officer of the Third Foot Guards named William Stothert:

The Guards now received orders to advance, and were embarked as they reached the Douro under the superintendance of Colonel Donkin with the most perfect regularity. Although harassed by a fatiguing march of eighty miles in four days . . . no sooner were they on the opposite shore than the whole began to run up the steep streets of Oporto, and continued their exertions until the head of the column was ordered to halt. In passing along, the brigade was cheered with repeated shouts . . . by the inhabitants, who hailed the British as their deliverers. The smiles of the young ladies at the balconies, their white handkerchiefs waving as the troops approached, and the prayers of the aged, accompanied with tears, for their success, formed a most interesting scene. The way was somewhat obstructed by the artillery and wagons of ammunition which the enemy had abandoned in his retreat. Amid these lay the bodies of the dead and wounded Frenchmen, already stripped by the Portuguese and exhibiting a most painful sight.[185]

The brunt of the fighting in this part of the battle, however, was borne by the Twenty-Ninth

Foot. The first troops to get across the river at the new crossing point, they had advanced through the streets amidst the same scenes of jubilation described by Stothert, and pushed on in pursuit of an enemy that now seemed bent on nothing but flight. Among the men involved was Lieutenant Charles Leslie:

> On gaining the upper part of the town, we observed some of the enemy through an opening . . . Here our leading company, the grenadiers, began to fire upon them. They made little resistance, and made off in haste and confusion, abandoning . . . some ammunition wagons. Many were killed and wounded by our fire, and we left sentries to protect the wounded as the Portuguese mob was threatening to kill them. On getting clear of the town we turned to our left into an open space with a wall, in passing which the enemy, who occupied a rocky height on our right, opened a smart fire upon us. We did not stop to return it, but pushed on and immediately attacked the enemy, whom, after a smart skirmish, we drove from the heights. This was their last stand. We now had a splendid view of their whole army in retreat. We reformed and rushed down after them. They made no fight – every man seemed to be running for his life – and threw away their knapsacks and arms, so that we had only the trouble of making many prisoners every instant, all begging for quarter and surrendering with great good humour.[186]

Another British soldier who was in at the death was Captain Peter Hawker of the Fourteenth Light Dragoons, whose regiment had crossed the river a little further east with some soldiers from the King's German Legion and was now well placed to harass the retreating enemy:

> Our passage of the river was effected about a league above Oporto . . . On landing, we took our position on a height where we had an uninterrupted view of the town . . . We could see for several miles in every direction, and distinctly observe the whole of the enemy's cavalry retreating. Orders were then given to make an attempt to cut off some of the rear troops, but these orders were recalled before the squadron had proceeded a quarter of a mile as the general soon perceived that the enemy's covering party was too strong for us. After rejoining the German Legion battalions on the height, we descended to the valley, making a flanking movement for some distance parallel to the Douro with a view to advancing as a reserve in the rear of those engaged. While General Murray was making a momentary reconnoitre, a staff officer came up with the information that one of our regiments was very hard pressed, and that the cavalry must advance immediately for its support. On this we hastened forward as fast as was possible from the nature of the ground, and, after surmounting many impediments among the stone walls, got into the main road on reaching the outskirts of the town. Our infantry here extended along the road. We then formed up in threes, [and] passed all our lines at a full gallop, while they greeted us with one continued huzza. After this, going almost at full speed, we cleared our infantry and that of the French appeared. A strong body was drawn up in close column with bayonets ready to receive us in front. On each flank of the road was a stone wall, bordered outwardly by trees, with other walls projecting in various

directions so as to give every advantage to the operations of the infantry . . . On our left, in particular, numbers were posted in a line with their pieces rested on the wall which flanked the road ready to give us a running fire as we passed. This could not be but effectual, as our left men . . . were nearly [touching] the muzzles of their muskets, and barely out of the reach of a *coup de sabre*. In a few seconds the ground was covered with men and horses. Notwithstanding these obstacles, we penetrated the battalion opposed to us, the men of which, relying on their bayonets, did not give way till we were nearly close upon it, when they fled in great confusion . . . After many efforts we succeeded in cutting off 300, most of whom were secured as prisoners, but our own loss was very considerable . . . For my own part, my horse being shot under me the moment after a ball had grazed my upper lip, I had to scramble my way on foot amidst the killed and wounded . . . The town of Oporto, to which we retired, exhibited a scene of the greatest confusion: the streets were strewed with dead horses and men, and the gutters dyed with blood. This night the town was illuminated in honour of our success. The effect, however, could not be very brilliant as the late exactions of the French had left the inhabitants in a state to testify their joy more by good will than by deed.[187]

The stiff resistance encountered by Hawker was very much a last ditch effort, however. Taken totally by surprise, Soult's men were by now in a state of complete disorder. As Le Noble remembered:

General Foy had been wounded, and General Delaborde thrown from his horse and badly bruised. Three hundred of our men had been killed or taken prisoner. The battery of light artillery, which covered the retreat, had had all the horses of its first piece shot down in a narrow street in the suburbs, and had had to be abandoned for want of any way to get the men past the obstruction. In the few moments in which an effort was made to clear the way eight men were shot dead.[188]

The French, then, took to their heels. Hasty though their departure was, however, the soldiers still had sufficient time to take out their wrath upon the unfortunate inhabitants. For this, however, they paid a heavy price. As the German commissary Auguste Schaumann remembered:

At midday . . . I passed a field where the French had bivouacked. All the furniture and even the crockery had been taken from the houses of a neighbouring village and brought into the field. The beds and the mattresses lay in rows in the mud. The drawers from the various articles of furniture had been used as mangers. Wardrobes had been transformed into bedsteads and roofs for the huts. The chairs, staircases and window frames had been used . . . as fuel for the kitchen fires . . . All the crosses and statues of the saints on the road had been thrown from their pedestals, and the almsboxes in front of them broken open and plundered, while all the altars and chapels had been ruined and polluted. In the churches even the graves had not been spared, and the sanctuaries had been rifled. Altar candlesticks, arms and legs of apostles and saints, torn vestments, chalices, prayer books and the like, mixed up with straw and filth, lay all about them. In one chapel there were a number of French prisoners with an English guard over them. I saw one well-dressed Portuguese at the head of a band of peasants offering the English sergeant ten gold florins to give the prisoners up. The cruelties perpetrated at this period by the Portuguese hill-folk against the French soldiers who fell into their hands are indescribable. In addition to nailing them up alive on barn doors, they had also stripped many of them, emasculated them, and then placed their amputated members in their mouths – a ghastly sight![189]

With the French on the run, there followed a determined attempt at pursuit. As Hawker remembered, however, this was a task that proved far more demanding than the actual battle:

Our regiment assembled at two in the afternoon, and about three marched for Vila Nova. Fifty campaigns may not produce greater miseries than we had to encounter before we reached this place. We started on a very bad road in a wet evening, and, by the time we were soaked to the skin, it became so dark that we could not see our way, of which the guide himself had an imperfect knowledge even by daylight. After crawling on till the horses were totally knocked up, and the men scarcely able to keep their eyes open, we were cheered with some lights, which indicated our approach to a village. We all thanked our stars that we had at last found the quarters. We had, however, soon the consolation to find that we had wandered to the wrong place, and were quite out of our path to Vila Nova. We had then to wait while another guide was pressed, and the hamlet . . . was so crowded with infantry that not one of us could get under an empty shed. After sitting, benumbed with cold, for nearly an hour, we proceeded with our new conductor, who was a lame fellow [and] consequently a very slow goer . . . It was so dark we were forced to be every moment hallooing to each other to avoid being lost, and the men so repeatedly mistook the road that we had often to stop and sound the bugle for half an hour at a time before we could get them together. We were the whole night without the least shelter in an incessant pour of rain, scrambling with our horses among the rocks, expecting every moment to be thrown down, and, in places where the safety of our lives required dismounting, we had to wade through deep streams of water occasioned by the torrents of rain . . . We were latterly every now and then dropping asleep on our horses quite exhausted, and shivering the whole time with cold. After suffering every hardship that could attend upon a mere march, we reached Vila Nova where we had to remain an hour in the streets, the rain still continuing. At last some sheds were provided and we filed off. It was then past six o'clock, which extended the duration of our drenching to sixteen hours. Our servants were lost so that we had neither meat, drink nor clothing. I got into a stable where, on some dirty straw, I slept in my wet clothes till two o'clock in the afternoon.[190]

Another British soldier who experienced the miseries of this campaign was John Cooper, a 23-year-old sergeant in the Seventh Foot. Originally from the hamlet of High Startforth near Barnard Castle, he had escaped the misery of life as a farm labourer by volunteering for the militia, subsequently transferring to the Seventh Foot:

The rain fell heavily and the roads became very bad. Sometimes we had to wade knee-deep in mud and water. We might have avoided many bad parts of the road, but the general would not allow any break in the column, so through thick and thin both officers and men had to splash. One day, after being well wetted, we were turned like bullocks into a damp church. What followed was really ludicrous. The building was large and lofty, and I think the whole regiment was bundled into it. . . All were cold, hungry, tired and ill-humoured. Fires were wanted and fires were made. Smash went the forms; down came the priests' stalls. The crashing of wood, the bawling and swearing of hundreds in the building [and] the choking smoke that completely filled the edifice were awful, and when darkness set in the place was a perfect pandemonium. During the uproar, a large box of large wax candles . . . was found. Many of these were . . . lighted in different parts of the church, and the scene was complete and fit for Hogarth's pencil . . . At this period the English troops made sad work in Portugal by plundering the inhabitants. No sooner was the day's march ended than the men turned out to steal pigs, poultry, wine, etc. One evening . . . a wine store was broken open, and much was carried off. The owner, finding this out, ran and brought an officer of the Fifty-Third, who caught one of our company named Brown in the act of handing out the wine in camp kettles. Seizing Brown by the collar, the officer shouted, 'Come out you rascal and give me your name!' Brown came out, [and] gave his name as Brennan; then, knocking the officer down, he made his escape and was not found out.[191]

Yet rain and other hazards notwithstanding, the pursuit went well enough. As Allied forces were closing in upon it from several different directions, the Second Corps was only able to escape by abandoning its baggage and artillery and taking to precipitous goat tracks. By these means Soult and his men succeeded in escaping all pursuit. The cost, however, was very high. Let us here turn to the cavalryman Joseph de Naylies:

At the village of Santiago de Rubias we entered Galicia. Hope stirred once again in our hearts on setting foot on Spanish soil: we hoped that we would soon be back in touch with the other army corps, and that we would all receive news from France, news of which we had been deprived for more than seven months. The continual rain and the dreadful roads strewn with rocks had destroyed the footwear of the infantry, while for eight days the majority of the soldiers had eaten nothing but parched maize. In consequence, unable to bear all these privations, a great number of them had died. Others had fallen out along the way: although they faced the certainty of being murdered, they could not go on any more and were deaf to all entreaty. The infantry suffered far more than we did, and so their morale was badly affected. In view of this the Marshal ordered each regiment of cavalry to transport fifty wounded infantrymen, these men being put on our horses which we then led on foot . . . Laden with their knapsacks and with their muskets balanced across the saddle bow in front of them . . . in any other circumstances, they would have looked very funny to us, but their pale and defeated faces, and their naked and bloody feet meant that we felt no other sentiment than pity . . . On 19 May our advanced guard, which was formed by the Third Swiss Regiment, entered Alaraz. The red uniform of these soldiers occasioned a very singular mistake: the inhabitants had heard that the French army had been exterminated and that the English were about to enter Spain, and so they took the Swiss to be soldiers of that nation. Hailing them as their liberators and calling down a thousand curses on the French, they rushed to offer them food and wine. One of them, who had a musket, boasted that he had murdered several Frenchmen, and demanded to be allowed to lead the regiment against them immediately. However, the arrival of our own infantry put paid to the error, and all concerned scurried to hide their bravado for a more appropriate occasion.[192]

The defeat of Soult's army changed the face of the war. Encouraged by continued Spanish resistance and what appeared to be a strengthening of the position of the Junta Central, Wellesley made imaginative use of the very limited latitude he had been given in his instructions to take part in a joint offensive with the Spaniards whose aim was the liberation of Madrid. Advancing into Spain, the British came up with Cuesta's Army of Extremadura near the Puerto de Miravete. Cuesta had his forces drawn up ready to receive them in a grand review, but the impression that his men made on the British was none too favourable. Among those present was Andrew Pearson, a 26-year-old Northumbrian who was originally from the village of East Thornton. A sergeant in the Sixty-First Foot, he later claimed to have been shanghaied into the army under the influence of drink, but this story of illegal enlistment may well have been an invention designed to cover the fact that in 1813 he deserted after falling foul of an unjust officer. A literate man of some intelligence, he was at all events a sharp observer:

> Falstaff's ragged regiment would have done honour to any force compared with the men before us. They were undisciplined, badly armed, and . . . almost naked. I can assure the reader that it was with the greatest difficulty we could avoid laughing right out of our faces, when officers out at elbows and knees stalked past carrying rusty old swords not worth lifting off the road. Hundreds of men with the most haughty countenances sported coats of many colours, while their inexpressibles bore unmistakable testimony to the difficulty experienced by the wearers in keeping the rags pinned about their legs.[193]

If the Spanish troops appeared a dubious quantity, their commander, who was 60 years old and still suffering from the effects of the bruising he had sustained at Medellín, did not exactly inspire confidence either. Let us here quote the Guards officer William Stothert:

> The Spanish leader appeared an infirm old man, so much so that he is obliged to be lifted into his saddle, and, as he cannot remain long on horseback, an ancient family coach drawn by six mules is in constant attendance . . . He was considered a man of strict honour and to possess an invincible hatred of the French, but his dilatory and half-digested measures did not seem calculated to be of much service to his country.[194]

While the appearance of the Spaniards may have given cause for concern among some of Wellington's soldiers, for the moment there were more pressing concerns. To quote George Wood again:

> We soon arrived at Plasencia where we halted a few days. This was certainly a most oppressive situation: in Portugal we had experienced the most distressing cold and wet weather; it was now as suddenly become as intensely hot, and we had very little except the olive trees, which we were prohibited from cutting, to screen us from the scorching rays of a sun almost vertical . . . We were infected and annoyed beyond measure by the scorpions and centipedes crawling over us, and the mosquitoes stinging us in such a manner that I have frequently seen officers and men with their eyes so swollen that they could not see out of them for some hours.[195]

For William Lawrence, by contrast, the chief problem as the Allied armies advanced up the Tagus valley was rather the food:

> From Oropesa we advanced through a country abounding with difficulties, the army suffering much during this march from the heat of the weather, the long exposure, insufficient food . . . bad roads, and illness being very prevalent. Our provisions rarely exceeded two pounds of meat a day, and sometimes a pint of wheat took the place of one of the pounds of meat with occasionally, but very rarely, a little flour. Our way of cooking the wheat was to boil it like rice, or sometimes, if convenient, we would crack the kernel between two flat stones and then boil it, making a kind of thick paste out of it. This having so little bread or other vegetable substance to eat with our meat was one of the great causes of illness.[196]

Eventually, the situation became so bad that, thoroughly exasperated with his Spanish allies' inability to supply his needs, Wellesley resolved to advance no further. Yet battle came anyway, for the French launched a sudden counter-attack. After a day of confusion in which Wellesley himself was almost captured when a British outpost he was visiting east of the river was taken by surprise, by the evening of 27 July the British and Spaniards stood shoulder-to-shoulder in a reasonable defensive position that stretched from the river Tagus at Talavera due north to a prominent hill called the Cerro de Medellín. The battle that followed was by no means an easy victory for the Allied forces. The full force of the French assault fell on Wellesley's troops, and for once their commander had been unable to find them a position in which they were sheltered by a reverse slope. Already the scene of a surprise attack in the depths of the previous night, during which the French had temporarily seized the summit, the Cerro de Medellín was defended by General Hill's division. Among the troops involved was the Twenty-Ninth Foot, and with it Charles Leslie:

> As the sky began to redden with the first blush of the morning sun . . . our light company and others of the brigade were thrown out as skirmishers to cover our front. The still of the morning was broken by no warlike sound: a solemn silence prevailed on both sides. Our view was extensive, and the scene before us was most imposing and sublime. While we were contemplating this, Sir Arthur Wellesley

rode up in rear of our regiment . . . and, then going to the front, seemed to survey the enemy with great earnestness. Much about the same time we could plainly discern Joseph Bonaparte and a large suite of staffing . . . coming up at full gallop in rear of the French masses in our front. All was yet breathless silence, when we perceived the smoke of a gun curling up through the air, and heard the report of a single cannon. This appeared to be the signal for putting the enemy's columns in motion. We were not detained long in suspense: in a moment a tremendous cannonade opened upon us.[197]

On the Cerro de Medellín there was some cover, but in the centre of the line it was a different story. Let us again quote Andrew Pearson:

> Just as my company got into line, the captain told me to close the files to the right, and . . . at that moment a round shot passed through the bodies of the front and rear rank men, killing them both. I was struck with one of their muskets on the breast and stunned for a few minutes . . . A sergeant who assisted me up instantly reeled and fell, and was carried about six yards to the rear. I ran to him and inquired if he thought himself mortally hit, when he replied that the shot was in his pack. I at once examined it . . . and putting my hand into it brought out a twelve-pound shot.[198]

The first attack came at the Cerro de Medellín, where Leslie now found himself in the thick of the fighting:

> We could . . . see the French skirmishers dash up and push rapidly on, while the columns immediately in front of us got in motion, advancing towards us . . . General Hill, seeing the overwhelming force that was coming against us, gave orders that the light troops should be recalled, and the bugles sounded accordingly. The skirmishers were closing in and filing to the rear with all the regularity of field-day and parade exercise, which the general observing, [he] called out, 'Damn their filing: let them come in anyhow.' In order to cover the advance of their columns, the enemy continued the terrific cannonade, which became so destructive that we were ordered to lie down flat on the ground . . . At length the French column of attack . . . began to approach us, when our brigadier general . . . said, 'Now, Twenty-Ninth! Now is your time!' We instantly sprang to our feet, gave three tremendous cheers, and immediately opened our fire, giving them several well-directed volleys, which they gallantly returned . . . We then got orders to charge, which was no sooner said than done. In we went, a wall of stout hearts and bristling steel. The French did not fancy such close quarters. The moment we made the rush they began to waver, then went to the right about. The principal portion broke and fled but some brave fellows occasionally faced about and gave us an irregular fire. We, however, kept . . . following them up, firing, running and cheering. In the midst of the exultation . . . I received a ball in the side of my thigh about three inches above the right knee. The sudden and violent concussion made me dance round and I fell on my back . . . As I found myself unable to rise, I called for assistance, but in the noise and hurry of battle no one seemed to take notice of me. At length my friend, Andrew Leith-Hay,

perceived me. He raised me up, and then, taking the musket out of the hand of Corporal Sharp of my company, he directed him to conduct me out of the action.[199]

With the repulse of the French from the Cerro de Medellín, there followed a brief lull in which soldiers from both sides freely mingled as they sought to draw water from a little brook that ran between the two armies. Very soon, however, the cannonade was resumed. Behind the centre of the Allied line, the German commissary Schaumann was an awed spectator of the bombardment:

> The thunder of the artillery, combined with the whizzing and whistling of the shot, in such an attack resembles a most dreadful storm, in which flashes of lightning and claps of thunder follow one another in quick succession, and cause the very earth, not to mention the heart in one's breast, to shake and quiver . . . At midday, owing to the insufferable heat, the fire on both sides was somewhat abated, but at two o'clock the French again opened a fierce attack supported by small and heavy guns. A Spanish powder magazine blew up in front of our cavalry, and with it a gunner was flung aloft and sailed through the air with arms and legs outspread like a frog . . . I was trying to ride back into the town when I overtook one or two bandsmen . . . who, with sad and solemn faces, were escorting a dead officer thither. His head was swathed in a handkerchief, and his body, which was clothed only in a shirt, a pair of pants and some socks, hung athwart a horse's back . . . A German sharpshooter . . . looking quite black in the face from the sun, the dust, the gunpowder and perspiration, ran from the raging battle and flung himself on the ground in an exhausted condition, assuring me that he had fired off sixty charges. His tongue was cleaving to his palate with thirst; he was unable to fire any longer, and hardly ten of his company were still alive. I rode through Talavera to see how matters stood with the Spaniards. It was impossible to see what was happening in the olive woods, but . . . now and again . . . a party bearing wounded would appear . . . Hardly had I reached my house in order to refresh myself and my horse a little . . . before a terrific outburst of gunfire announced the opening of a fresh attack . . . The Spaniards, unaccustomed to the endurance of the English and losing heart at the sight . . . dashed headlong in masses through the town, and, mixed up with vast quantities of baggage, blocked the streets . . . I watched this appalling tumult . . . with amazement . . . Even the inhabitants were packing and taking flight. Just opposite my quarters there lived a wonderfully beautiful married woman who, with the help of her family, was trying to load and mount a mule. Every time she attempted to mount, however, the madly hurrying throng would swing her mule and its load so sharply round that the load always fell down beneath the animal's belly. It was interesting to watch this woman's passionate rage: screaming, tearing her hair out, weeping . . . wailing, and imploring all the saints to hear her appeals – her expression changed every moment.[200]

The afternoon attack that sparked off the panic in the Spanish lines was a ferocious affair. Yet the British infantry stood firm at every point and drove off their assailants. Among the defenders was Andrew Pearson:

Major Smith of the Royal Artillery having descried the arrival of King Joseph and Marshal Jourdan . . . he ordered two batteries of guns to the spot, jocularly remarking, 'Yonder come some big-wigs, and we will bid them good morning.' The salute of the major did skilful service, but it failed to daunt the royal commander, who ordered the army to advance in columns of grand divisions . . . They accordingly advanced, the front ranks firing from the hip, and, when within fifty yards of the ravine, they halted and opened a murderous fire on our columns. Sir Arthur Wellesley immediately saw that were the divisions allowed to stand they would be cut down, and he accordingly ordered them to lie down . . . The French, gaining courage from our apparent cowardice, advanced across the ravine and moved up the opposite bank. It was too much for us to lie any longer, and, leaping up, we gave the well-known British cheer and charged. This was a movement for which they were not prepared, and we soon broke their front ranks, when they immediately fell back on the dense columns in the rear.[201]

Also present in this action was Anthony Hamilton, who was currently serving not with his own Forty-Third Foot, but rather in a 'Battalion of Detachments' cobbled together from invalids and stragglers from the army of Sir John Moore:

On the first indication of the enemy's intention, General Sherbrooke gave orders that his division should prepare for the charge. The assailants came on over the rough and broken ground in the valley with great resolution, and in the most imposing regularity, and were encountered by our troops with their usual firmness. The whole division, as if moved by one powerful and undivided impulse, advanced to meet them, and, pouring in a most galling and destructive fire, their ranks were speedily broken and they gave way . . . In this battle I was severely wounded by the explosion of a bombshell, and was left for dead on the field till the engagement was over. My skull was fractured, in consequence of which I have since suffered fatally [sic] from the wound.[202]

These accounts are, however, too sanguine. The first French onrush was certainly repelled, but a number of British troops proved too eager in their pursuit, and were driven back in great disorder by the substantial French reserves. For a moment it appeared that Wellington's line had been broken, but the troops who began to push into the gap were counter-attacked by some of the men holding the Cerro de Medellín, among them Thomas Bunbury of the Third Foot:

In the afternoon the battle was renewed. The French again attacked the height where we were stationed, and the head of their column came in contact with our grenadiers and No. 1 . . . Company . . . The officer carrying the king's colour, Ensign Maners, called on me to follow him. Accordingly, we placed ourselves at the head of the grenadiers, while Nos 1 and 2 Companies wheeled to their right and, enveloping the enemy, prevented them from drawing into line. It seemed for a while as though neither party would or could give way, and the smoke obstructed the view except when the flashing of the powder showed the grim faces and moustaches of our opponents. At length a French trumpet sounded what we took to be a retreat, and it was responded to by a cheer from our men. Off went the enemy down the hill in the greatest disorder, and some of our fellows in following paid dearly for their rashness, as I am sorry to say that a number of them were found shot in the back by their own comrades.[203]

On the British right the great French attack was beaten off more easily, however. A private soldier who left an account of this phase of the action was John Cooper, who, as a member of his battalion's light company, began the battle manning a picket line in the vineyards and olive groves that filled the space in front of the British position:

> By and by the cannonading nearly ceased, but it was only a prelude for more serious work: the enemy were massing for attack. The death cloud was gathering blackness and soon burst with fury. Several columns were set in motion and directed towards different parts in our line. One of these, after threading its way among the trees and grape vines, came up directly in our front, and, while deploying, called 'Españoles', wishing us to believe that they were Spaniards. Our captain thought they were Spaniards, and ordered us not to fire. But they soon convinced us who they were by a rattling volley. We instantly retired upon our regiment, which sprang up and met the enemy . . . but, our men being all raw soldiers, [this] staggered for a moment . . . Our colonel, Sir William Myers, seeing this, sprang from his horse, and, snatching one of the colours, cried, 'Come on, Fusiliers!' 'Twas enough. On rushed the Fusiliers and the Fifty-Third Regiment and delivered such a fire that in a few minutes the enemy melted away, leaving six pieces of cannon behind, which they had not had time to discharge. While [we] were charging the enemy, a Frenchman fell in his hurry and was collared by a brutal sergeant of ours, who exclaimed, 'I'll kill a Frenchman for once', and then deliberately shot the poor fellow dead . . . For a considerable time the combatants were enveloped in a mighty cloud of smoke. This, with the thunder of the artillery, the roll of musketry and the huzzas of our men as they pushed back the masses of the foe, was one continuous uproar . . . Another lull in the storm and fresh formations. 'Here they come again,' said many voices, [and] so they did, but we were ready and gave them such a warm reception that they speedily went to the right about. As in their first attack, they . . . left several . . . cannon, which we secured as before. After these two attacks and smart repulses, we were not troubled with their company any more.[204]

After the battle the combatants faced the usual scenes of horror: over 13,000 men had been killed or wounded. George Wood was with the so-called Second Battalion of Detachments (Anthony Hamilton, by contrast, was in the First Battalion of Detachments). With a mere thirteen dead and eight wounded, this unit had escaped very lightly. For all that, however, Wood still faced an exhausting few hours:

> Night now began again to draw her sable veil between these murderous hosts of mortals . . . By this time I became much exhausted for want of food, for the meat that we had taken half-cooked with us, had, from the heat, become so full of

animalculae that I could eat but little of it; I therefore gave it to the man next me, who, not being quite so nice, gobbled it up in a moment. Bread, however, was out of the question, and water only to be procured by going into greater danger. In this state . . . I fell fast asleep for an hour or two as soundly as if I reclined on the softest couch. The dawn reappeared, and one of the men roused me from my slumber, which indeed he had some trouble in doing . . . We again stood to our arms, but it appeared the enemy had got enough of it, for they . . . under cover of the night, had taken the opportunity of retreating from the scene of action . . . We then heard a few shots, and learned that they proceeded from the Spaniards, who were shooting the wounded French. There was in consequence an officer and twenty men from each brigade immediately sent out to protect and gather together the wounded enemy . . . This was a most unpleasant duty: the scenes of horror I here witnessed, I cannot . . . describe, but one circumstance I cannot help noticing. On passing the ravine where the contest had been most severe, I perceived that a quantity of high sere grass which grew there had taken fire from the wadding of the guns, and the poor fellows who had fallen there, wounded and deprived of the power of escape, were literally burned to death, which gave them all the appearance of pigs that had been roasted.[205]

The aftermath of the struggle is also graphically described by Andrew Pearson:

Sir Arthur ordered the army to burn the dead and not bury them. This was certainly a more convenient though to not a few a more revolting way of disposing of our comrades . . . I had just begun to write out a list of the killed, wounded and missing men of my company, my knapsack being my writing desk, when the sergeant major, who was severely wounded, came crawling to me and stated that I had been appointed orderly sergeant to the commander-in-chief, and that I was at once to proceed to headquarters to assume my new duties . . . I was not long in setting out for Talavera, and, on entering the town, a most appalling sight presented itself. The streets were lined with the dead and dying, indiscriminately heaped up in piles, a narrow passage to enable us to pass along being the only space unoccupied by the carcasses of the soldiers. The first man that caught my eye was a corporal of my company, who was dragging himself along, carrying his bowels in his clasped hands. He had been cut across the abdomen by a grape shot, but he did not go far till, from pain and exhaustion, he fell down and died. I then came on another comrade who had been severely wounded in the leg . . . but, on speaking with him, I found him almost insensible. The groanings of the wounded were the only sounds that greeted the ear, and painful they were, while each man, as he passed along between the piles of the dead and dying, seemed borne down with grief and horror.[206]

Some eighty miles away in Madrid, meanwhile, the French had been thrown into a panic by the rapid approach of so many Allied troops. One eyewitness to what transpired was Joseph Bonaparte's *aide-de-camp* Gaspard de Clermont-Tonnerre:

Up until 22 July all was quiet – profoundly peaceful even – but then, all of a sudden Marshal Victor announced that a large army made up of British, Spanish and

Portuguese troops was on the point of crushing him. At three o'clock in the morning on the twenty-third, the king duly marched off with his reserve, while on the twenty-fourth orders arrived for his treasury, those of his ministers who were still in Madrid and the rest of the garrison to join him. All that was left in Madrid was the First Spanish Regiment, a battalion of gendarmes and a minimal garrison in the fortress of the Retiro . . . Needless to say, the result was that a general alarm had soon spread to the French civilians living in the city . . . On all sides, people could therefore be seen making for the Retiro, and within twenty-four hours not a soul remained behind.[207]

If the French and their supporters responded to the Allied advance with terror, among their opponents the mood was one of wild excitement. As the priest José Clemente Carnicero Torribio remembered:

> A friend entered my room. Seeing me in my accustomed state of calm, he exclaimed, 'What! Do you really have such phlegm? Don't you know that people are running through the streets full of joy . . . because King Joseph has surrendered with his entire army? We are Spaniards again, and our troops are coming to take possession of . . . the palace this very afternoon.' 'I am delighted to hear it,' I replied, 'but we had better watch out to make sure it is not a trick to get us to reveal our true feelings so that we can be pounced on later.' 'Watch out all you like,' he answered, 'but I am telling you that it is the truth. Come and see for yourself.' We went round various streets . . . and in all of them we saw proof of what my friend had said. In some there were great crowds of people fraternising with unarmed Frenchmen . . . In others groups of men, women and children were running up and down congratulating one another at the happy news. And in still others groups of young girls from the poorer quarters were sallying out . . . to greet and make much of our men. It was being said that they had already entered the city, that General Castaños was already in the palace with a guard of halberdiers, that the British had come . . . In short, there was not a soul who did not appear to believe the good news.[208]

Very soon, of course, the hope of rescue receded, but, if this was so, at least the sight of the French wounded provided some consolation:

> Although some of the more compassionate were filled with pity, for many citizens the sight of . . . entire wagon trains filled with wounded entering the city every minute . . . was a source of the utmost satisfaction. Some had lost limbs; some were nursing broken bones; some were being driven to utter the most lamentable screams; some were in their last agonies; and some were pleading for death . . . So excessive was the number of victims that even the general hospital's many . . . rooms were not enough to take them, and it proved necessary to requisition . . . the women's hospital . . . and . . . the magnificent monastery of San Francisco . . . and even then the carts were kept waiting at the doors for many hours.[209]

Aftermath

Victory had not come cheaply at Talavera, but the terrible losses suffered by Wellington's forces could not disguise the fact that the French had been thoroughly beaten. Within a matter of days all sense of triumph had been dissipated, however. At Talavera Wellesley and Cuesta had together faced the full weight of the French armies in central Spain. This was not entirely unexpected, but the Allied plan had called for another force – General Venegas's powerful Army of La Mancha – to move up to the river Tagus in the vicinity of Aranjuez and hold itself ready to pounce on Madrid should the French move all their troops to fight the Allied forces marching on the capital from the west. For various reasons, however, Venegas moved with the utmost caution, and the forces facing him, then, were therefore allowed to slip away to join those of Marshal Victor. Still worse, the Allied position at Talavera soon found itself under threat from the rear as the French had determined to evacuate Galicia and were consequently able to hurl a great mass of troops against the Tagus valley. All but surrounded, Wellesley and Cuesta had no option but to flee into the barren mountains south of the river. The events that followed put a great strain on the alliance. There were more quarrels over food; a large number of British wounded who had been left to the care of the Spaniards had to be abandoned to the enemy; and Cuesta's forces were taken by surprise and routed at the Puente del Arzobispo. For a French view of this action, which was largely gained by their cavalry, we can turn to Joseph de Naylies:

> At about two o'clock in the afternoon on 8 August the corps of the Dukes of Treviso and Dalmatia, which had been deployed behind a hill which protected them from the fire of the enemy, marched forward in columns of attack . . . it being the job of the cavalry to ford the river so as to take the enemy in the flank, as well as to carry with them a number of sappers who were charged with the job of dismantling the barricades that blocked the bridge so as to open the way for the infantry. In all, twelve regiments had been massed for this task, four of them light. The Eighteenth and Nineteenth Regiments of Dragoons asked for the favour of being allowed to cross first, and this they got. After a short harangue designed less to stimulate our courage than to make us sensible of the honour that was being done to us, our general plunged into the river. The Eighteenth followed his example, but the horses found the going difficult on account of the soft sand of the river bed and the swift current, while enemy canister fire wreaked havoc . . . Nevertheless, no sooner had fifty dragoons got together on the left bank, than they threw themselves on the enemy batteries and overwhelmed them. Many of the Spanish gunners were cut down beside their pieces, but others were forced to turn the guns round and aim them at their comrades, many of whom were already in flight. Some 8,000 or 9,000 strong, the Spanish infantry sought vainly to get itself into battle order, but the Eighteenth and Nineteenth Dragoons, both of which had now got across the river, charged them vigorously, and drove them back at every point. Meanwhile, having dismounted, the sappers we had carried across the river had reached the bridge and were pulling down its defences in order to open a passage for the infantry. A regiment of Spanish hussars sought to restore the situation and advanced on our disordered squadrons, but, though the

moment was certainly an opportune one, they were not up to taking advantage of it, and turned aside at the last minute. As we were pursuing these hussars sword in hand, we suddenly descried a mass of cavalry debouching from the village of Azután . . . This proved to be the Duque de Alburquerque, and with him 4,000 élite cavalry . . . The advance of this force was so rapid that in an instant it was upon us. It was formed in three lines, each of which was more than 100 paces broader than the front presented by our two little regiments. Cheering loudly, the Spaniards shouted the charge, and their lines could be seen opening out in order to envelop us. As for us, we rode forward to meet them, and succeeded in closing the distance half-way before coming into contact with them. Pretty soon, then battle was joined, and a general mêlée developed in which everyone was so jammed together that men were literally fighting one another hilt-to-hilt . . . So bad did our chances appear that Marshal Soult at first wanted to fire upon the cloud of dust that was all that he could see as the only means of stopping the enemy. Had he used this dreadful measure, the odds against us were so great that it is probable the enemy would have lost six men for every one of ours, but in the end it was not employed as we gained the victory: suddenly realising that the rest of our cavalry had crossed the river, the Spaniards broke and fled in all directions. A battery of light guns that had been deployed in an advantageous position on the bank of the river did them much damage as they did so, while we pursued them for two leagues along the Tagus: the sabres of all our men were covered in blood . . . We bivouacked for the night at the village of Villar del Pedroso . . . The sun had gone down long since and the hour had arrived when the earth should have been covered in shadows, but the sky was lit up as bright as day. A fierce fire had broken out thanks to the . . . dry grass that covered the vast plain that extended southwards from the Tagus at Arzobispo having been set alight by the shells of the artillery. Across a space of two leagues a wall of fires pushed on by a strong wind could be seen consuming all that offered it nourishment. Its speed was truly terrifying – I saw a whole wood of evergreen oaks consumed in an instant – while the moans of the wounded who were struggling to escape the fire, not to mention the cries of despair uttered by those unfortunates who could not flee, filled one's heart with the most painful sentiments.[210]

To cap it all, Venegas loitered too long in the vicinity of the Tagus, and was badly beaten at Almonacid de Toledo. Of this action we have a good account from the pen of Pedro Agustín Girón, who commanded a division on the Spanish left:

Our dispositions were bad; indeed, one could say that they were non-existent. The men were scattered here and there as if by the whim of God, and there was nothing to suggest the existence of plan, inspiration or idea . . . The enemy had from the very first moment shown every sign that their main effort was going to fall upon our left, and they lost no time in attacking it with the greatest determination . . . Seeing one of our battalions putting up a good fight in the plain below the heights on which we were stationed, I decided that I ought to support it and marched to do so at the head of the first Battalion of the Guardias Españolas, but I had not gone far when it broke and fell back in the greatest disorder, this leaving me with no option but to deploy in line in an attempt to hold the enemy. However, the force bearing down on me was so great that I realised that I would not be able to hold my own in the plain . . . and so I fell back . . . in an attempt to reach the heights again. Unfortunately, I had not got further than half-way up the slope, when the troops who had been fighting on my right further along the heights . . . routed. I immediately plunged among the fugitives in an attempt to rally them and get them back on to the ridge, but all my efforts proved futile. All of a sudden the enemy appeared on the crest of the ridge and opened fire upon us. I tried to get the Guardias Españolas and the Ecija militia to respond, but the men from the broken division crashed into them and disordered their ranks . . . A skilful general might still have been able to achieve something at this point, but Venegas did nothing at all until, finding him, I told him that we ought at least to try to fight the enemy . . . Agreeing with me, he told me to counter-attack the enemy with three battalions from my division . . . Putting myself at the head of these troops, I deployed them in column at the edge of an olive grove . . . and sent out a company of skirmishers to see if anything lay hidden among the trees. Coming back, these reported that the grove was full of enemy troops . . . whereupon I ordered the troops to make ready to open fire . . . Instead of doing so, however, two of the three battalions concerned were seized by panic and went off at top speed. All that I was left with was a single battalion – as it happens, the Ecija militia. Putting myself at its head . . . I got it to open fire on the nearest enemy column, and was able to do it considerable damage, and, indeed, to keep fighting until an order for a general retreat reached me and I led it off the field.[211]

Among the British forces, needless to say, the product of all this was great anger. For a succinct account of how the situation was perceived, let us turn to a letter written by Alexander Gordon, who was one of Wellesley's *aides-de-camp*, to his brother Lord Aberdeen, from Jaraicejo:

Although the affair at Talavera was the most brilliant possible, yet Sir Arthur was obliged to forgo following up his success from his having received certain intelligence of Soult, Ney and Mortier being close in his rear, and whose united forces made upwards of 30,000 men. He accordingly resolved to cross the Tagus and take up a position on its left bank. On the fourth we retired from Talavera to Oropesa. Having left all our sick and wounded who could not be moved at Talavera . . . Sir Arthur had agreed with Cuesta [for the latter] to remain at Talavera until the enemy should appear. However, to his astonishment he received a letter from him that evening saying he intended retiring his army that night without giving any reason for it, no enemy having appeared. We crossed the river at the bridge of Arzobispo, and after a most fatiguing march through the passes over the mountains we arrived . . . at Deleitosa. Here we remained some days, and should have remained longer but moved here to give way to the Spaniards. Their army in the first instance was to have defended the bridge of Arzobispo . . . They remained one day [and] were attacked by the French. Four hundred cavalry swam across the river after a short time [and] put theirs to flight. The infantry ran away; the French took twenty guns and turned them against them. Thus was this most important bridge lost. But the Spaniards will not fight, will not maintain a position, will do nothing, are the damn'dest set of cowards . . . We receive not the least assistance from the country and have been starved: government will soon be obliged to believe what the whole army said last year of the Spanish cause, and what is the opinion of the commander and everyone in this [force] . . . If the Spanish cause was bad last year, it is desperate this. They have no spirit, no exertion. You never even hear a 'viva' now: all is terror at the sight of a Frenchman; whole villages are deserted . . . One more word with regard to the Spanish army and I have done. Its head, Cuesta, is an old infirm fool. His army is radically bad and never will be better.[212]

Despite Gordon's hints, it is probably unfair to claim that the Spaniards deliberately deprived the British of food: the fact was that in poverty-stricken Extremadura there was simply none to be had. Yet, whatever the cause, the fact is that real hunger assailed the British troops. A humorous observer of the misery which they endured was Captain John Leach of the Ninety-Fifth Rifles:

A march of twelve hours brought the British army to Oropesa, but, owing to the intense heat of the weather, the want of water, and the scarcity of provisions for many days before, the road was covered with stragglers . . . As [we had] neither bread, meat nor rations of any kind, General Crawford ordered that any animals in the shape of cattle, sheep or pigs which could be found in the extensive woods in which we halted for the evening should forthwith be put in requisition for the troops, and never do I remember having seen orders so promptly obeyed. A most furious attack was instantly made on a large herd of pigs which, most fortunately for us, little dreamt of the fate that awaited them . . . It would be useless to attempt a description of the scene of noise and confusion which ensued. The screeches and cries of those ill-fated swine as they met their death . . . and the rapidity with which they were cut up into junks [*sic*] with the hair on, and fried on the lids of camp kettles or toasted at the fire on a pointed stick . . . was quite incredible, and, I must add, truly ludicrous . . . At midnight we resumed our march, the main body of the army proceeding by the road towards Trujillo, and our division taking its route through a tract of mountainous country with orders to reach the bridge of Almaraz with the least possible delay . . . The time which we passed at this spot, although sufficiently monotonous, was such as one is not likely to forget. To the best of my belief, not one issue of bread was made to the troops during the fortnight; [instead] an exceedingly coarse kind of flour, mixed with bran and chopped straw, and in very small quantities, was issued by the commissariat. This, moistened with water and made into a sort of pancake, was baked on a camp-kettle lid and speedily devoured. The only regret was that the quantity was so very small . . . Now and then half-a-dozen antiquated goats, which the commissary contrived to take by surprise in the mountains, found their way into the camp-kettles . . . One day we were so fortunate as to stumble on some beehives in the gum cistus with which the mountains abound, and in a shorter time than I have taken to relate the capture, the honey and the comb were consumed . . . In short, if any corpulent person despairs of reducing his weight by the means usually adopted, I strongly recommend a few weeks' change of air and scene at Almaraz, taking especial good care to observe the same rules and regulations for diet, and to roast himself throughout the day at the foot of a shadeless olive tree . . . If that fails to have the desired effect, I give him up and can prescribe nothing further.[213]

Having crossed the Tagus, Wellington's army continued to retreat on the haven of Badajoz. As Cooper remembers, matters had now gone beyond a joke:

We continued our march for three days [by] bad rocky roads and then halted near the river Ibor. This was a desolate region, truly nothing but rugged mountains on all sides . . . Notwithstanding our weak state through want of food, we had to drag the artillery by ropes up some steep mountains, as horses could not keep on their feet. Great numbers of these animals died. Stores and cannon were buried. Men looked like skeletons. Our clothing was in rags; shirts, shoes and stockings were worn out and there was no bread. All we got was a pound of lean beef each day; happy was the soldier that had a little salt . . . Tents during this campaign we had none, nor yet blankets. We slept in the open air, and this was the mode: the greatcoat was inverted and our legs were thrust into the sleeves . . . There were also plenty of snakes, scorpions [and] centipedes to be had for nothing. Sleeping one night as usual under some dry branches . . . a scorpion having crawled up one of the men's . . . sleeves stung him severely. The poor fellow bawled loudly, jumped up, threw off his coats, and caught the venomous rascal. His arm instantly turned blue, and he was in hospital several days.[214]

As usual, however, the worst of the suffering befell the wounded. Many of those who had fallen at Talavera had had to be abandoned to the care of the French, but Wellesley's retreat had led a number of men to make a desperate bid for escape. Among those struggling along in the wake of the British army were Charles Leslie and a fellow officer named Stanus, who had managed to procure a horse and a mule with the aid of no less a person than General Cuesta:

We found ourselves in a wretched plight owing to the motion of the animals and the hanging of our legs in riding. Our wounds became much irritated and painful, while the poor hobbling animals were almost done up. After a few miles we fortunately overtook some covered Spanish provision wagons. We offered the driver of one of them a dollar to give us a lift, which was accepted. We got on for some miles in this way, but at length the road became so blocked up with artillery, baggage, stores, etc., that the wagon could not proceed. We therefore remounted our Rosinantes and passed through the Spanish army and . . . reached our bivouac about two o'clock in the morning. Our people were just then getting under arms to march off; we, however, secured one of the cars supported for the wounded, and then stretched ourselves on the ground near a large camp fire. We rested our exhausted frames while our servants prepared fresh poultices for our wounds, which being dressed, we continued our route in rear of the army, not in a triumphal car, but . . . in a vehicle of the most primitive construction, being no other than a few planks nailed to a frame with a pole in front of which oxen were yoked. The frame was placed in two low wheels, each consisting of solid pieces of wood into which the axle tree was blocked so that, instead of the wheel going round the axle tree, they all went round together, there being two pieces of wood under the frame . . . scooped out to fit the axle tree. The friction was very great and occasioned a noise . . . like the drone of bagpipes. On this miserable machine we placed some straw covered with our blankets, and we were then laid upon it with our small modicum of baggage for pillows. Four sticks were stuck into holes in each corner of the frame and a blanket fastened on them to form a canopy to protect us from the scorching sun, and two lean kine with slow and measured steps dragged us along. Such was our equipage.[215]

With the army in dire straits, even catching up with their comrades brought the wounded little succour. Hit by a bullet in the leg at Talavera, Peter Hawker had made an epic escape from the French and eventually managed to rejoin the main column at Trujillo:

During our pass through this desert country, we were literally starving, and had the utmost difficulty in procuring bread, even at an imposing price. As to wine and spirits they were not to be heard of, and there was scarcely a bit of meat to be bought. Our horses and mules, which were chiefly fed with stale chaff, were nearly as famished as ourselves. For my own part I believe my life was owing to the goats: their owners, the Patriots, refusing to send me a little milk, I contrived to get this nourishment by stealth, making the guide fill my bottle every day . . . we came to a herd of these animals. To complete this wretched retreat, we were everywhere annoyed with fleas, bugs and body lice.[216]

Eventually the British army reached Badajoz where it found plenty of food and was in general able to recoup its strength. The privations had left many men sick, however, while spirits were by no means high. Let us here quote a letter written home with all the insouciance of youth by a young ensign named John Aitchison of the Third Foot Guards, who had enlisted in the army in 1805 and served in the expedition to Copenhagen:

The truth must at last appear: I expected it would . . . How I pity fallen greatness! For rapidity of movement and able dispositions in a battle, my Lord Wellington certainly merits much applause, but the late campaign in Spain has diminished in a considerable degree the credit for generalship which he acquired by the brilliant success that attended his former operations. There is but one opinion of the late campaign . . . In arranging and directing his operations with the Spaniards, my Lord Wellington appears entirely to have forgot the indolent habit and inactive disposition of the people with whom he had to co-operate, nor does he appear to have bestowed much consideration on the nature of the country through which he had to march. [Also] the small supply, nay extreme deficiency, of medical stores showed he entertained no apprehension of a reverse. In short, ere he had quitted Abrantes with his army, he had already triumphed in imagination in Madrid . . . The grand error of our commander-in-chief seems to me to have been to place too much reliance on . . . the Spaniards: from this has resulted the discomfiture of the combined army. But I am also of an opinion [that] the great miseries which our troops have suffered are in no small degree to be attributed to a presumption of infallibility which Lord Wellington appears to have entertained for his own plans . . . I think every man ought to have confidence in his abilities, and, as there is always a chance of success when the stake is great, I have no objection to [risking] it. But ere the safety of an army be committed, the commander-in-chief ought first to weigh all the circumstances.[217]

The retreat of the British army made perfect sense in almost every respect, but it was long to remain a sore point in Anglo-Spanish relations. All the more was the case as it inevitably brought with it the devastation of yet more Spanish towns and cities. One such was Coria, which was occupied by the cavalry brigade of which Joseph de Naylies was a member:

It was already quite late when we got to Coria. We bivouacked in an olive grove outside the town, but we had no other food than some biscuit we had been given at Galisteo. As soon as sentries had been posted and the horses tethered to trees, the soldiers went into the town, which was deserted. Equipped with great candles which they had stolen from the churches, they battered down the doors with axes, and ransacked every chest and cupboard on the pretext of searching for food . . . The unfortunate place was pillaged all night. Greed knew no limits among our soldiers: inflamed by the tales spread by men whose searches had already proved successful, they did not even respect the sanctity of the grave . . . Behold the atrocities to which we are led by the woeful system of making war without magazines. A soldier who has been given no rations believes that anything goes, and in consequence it was impossible to stop evils that were being done under our very eyes . . . Every day I cursed the author of this hateful war, and called down on his head the same ills for which he had been responsible . . . As for the unfortunate inhabitants of Coria, left to wander in the surrounding mountains, they soon learned of the devastation, whereupon their hatred for us increased still further.[218]

Nor was the devastation limited to Coria. As de Naylies discovered when his regiment was sent back towards Madrid, large parts of the Tagus valley had also been laid waste by the French:

My regiment was bivouacked for some days in the vicinity of Cazalegas. Situated near the high road to Madrid, this unfortunate village had been entirely reduced to ruins in consequence of the battle of Talavera. Once upon a time it had been rich and prosperous, but now there remained just four families, and they were living as beggars. On the day of the battle it had been made use of by our army as its chief field hospital: the houses were still full of corpses, and these exuded an odour that was quite insupportable, while, four months on, one could still see amputated limbs lying in the streets amidst the debris . . . Attracted by the remains, large numbers of . . . vultures came to the place from the surrounding countryside to gorge themselves on human carrion . . . The numerous troops who had passed through the district had reduced it to the most awful state of misery. We could not buy bread, while we could not even find barley or hay for our horses . . . Wood being very rare in the valley of the Tagus, the men who had gone before us had burned all the furniture, all the doors and all the window frames, and we were therefore left with no other resources than that of pulling down the houses altogether.[219]

* * *

With the Talavera campaign at an end, we can again take stock of the war as a whole. The first point to note in this respect is that once again the Anglo-Spanish alliance was under considerable strain, for the campaign in the Tagus valley had reinforced British doubts about their Spanish allies. In the eyes of most British observers, the organs of political authority that had emerged in Patriot Spain were at best utterly incapable of organising an effective war effort, and, at worst, downright malignant; the Spanish army was poorly commanded and completely unreliable; and the Spanish people were hostile both to their allies and to the struggle against Napoleon. Yet the Spaniards were just as angry. In the first place, British diplomacy was frequently very tactless, as witness, for example, the repeated attempts that were made to station a British garrison in Cádiz even when there were no French troops for hundreds of miles. In the second, Britain's soldiers were all too often not just badly behaved, but inclined to be contemptuous of Spanish culture and society. In the third, there was a strong feeling that Britain was less than fully committed to the war in Spain, and that Wellington was in addition far too cautious. And, in the fourth, the Spaniards could with some justification feel that the performance of their forces was persistently underrated by the British: there were defeats, certainly – there were even shameful outbreaks of panic – but the majority of the soldiers involved in battles such as Medellín and Talavera had fought well enough, while whole episodes of the war went seemingly unnoticed by their allies; far away in Catalonia, for example, at the time that Talavera was fought the city of Gerona was less than halfway into a heroic siege that in the end lasted for six months and cost the French untold casualties. Feel sore and unappreciated though the Spaniards did, it is difficult to criticise Wellesley, or Wellington as we may now call him, for deciding, as he now did, to suspend direct military cooperation with his Allies: the British army had both been exposed to starvation and only narrowly escaped destruction. But nor can it be denied that in thus restricting his forces to a defensive role the British commander was creating fresh difficulties for the Junta Central. Besieged by political enemies and lacking in credibility and acceptance alike, the Junta Central had been relying on military victory to square the very difficult circle in which it was operating. The failure of the Talavera campaign, then, to bring victory opened it to fresh attacks on the home front, and this in turn was to push it in the direction of launching fresh offensives. This time, however, they would necessarily be delivered without British support which meant that the chances of success were even smaller than before. And, merely by launching such attacks, the Junta Central would further alienate the British, who could not but regard them as foolhardy in the extreme. All in all, it was not a happy prospect, and especially not for the peoples of Spain and Portugal.

Chapter 4

Cádiz Saved; Portugal Defended

As we have seen, the year 1809 had opened with the French very much on the back foot in the Iberian peninsula thanks to Napoleon's decision to throw the bulk of his forces into the headlong pursuit of Sir John Moore. Nine months later, however, the position looked very different. The French had once again been cleared from Portugal, certainly, but in Spain repeated offensives against them had one after another spent themselves and left inter-Allied relations in disarray. In short, the pendulum had once again swung back in the direction of the imperial forces, and all the more so as victory over Austria in the battle of Wagram (5-6 July 1809) meant that Napoleon could once again pour thousands of fresh troops into the peninsula. A new period, then, was about to open in the history of the war, and, what is more, one that seemed unlikely to augur well for the Allied cause: with Wellington's army out of the fight, the brunt of the battle would have to be borne by Spain alone. Yet, as we shall see, all was not lost. On the one hand, Spain was too big a country to be conquered overnight, and on the other Wellington had foreseen the direction in which events were likely to turn, and made certain preparations that were to give the struggle a fresh twist.

Disaster at Ocaña
In the wake of Talavera, the British may well have felt that they had cause for complaint at the conduct of their Spanish allies. However, while pushing for change at the top was understandable, it proved counter-productive in that it was inclined to give fresh encouragement to the Junta Central's many enemies and undermine its authority still further. Still worse, the result was strategic disaster: ever more desperate for military victory, the Junta responded by ordering a fresh offensive. Yet in the wake of the battles of Talavera and Almonacid, the Spanish forces were not in a fit state to take the offensive. Present at the headquarters of the Army of Extremadura was a liaison officer named Phillip Roche:

> I have reason to believe . . . that the actual effective state of the infantry . . . does not exceed 20,000 men, so great has been the desertion since the action of Talavera . . . Four thousand horses have been sent from this army to Seville unfit for service . . . arising from want of forage, bad saddles, neglect and lastly from an infamous practice of purposely giving the horse a sore back [so] that the dragoon may be sent with the horse to Seville . . . Evils of a nature still worse than these exist in the army . . . and when I add that the officers, from the highest to the lowest, speaking generally, are absolutely ignorant of every principle of their profession, and when,

instead of the smallest emulation to forward the discipline of their corps, each man is only desirous of avoiding his duty, how is it possible that anything like success can be expected from such a combination? Between the officers and the men not the slightest confidence exists. The latter are oppressed, cut off from all hopes of promotion beyond that of a sergeant and all appeal against infamy or injustice . . . They are, as you know, ill-fed, worse paid and many almost naked, while honour and rank are heaped upon officers whose conduct in a variety of ways is notoriously infamous.[220]

With matters in this state, when the Spaniards duly moved forwards in La Mancha, the result was never in doubt, and all the more so as they failed to catch the French off-guard, but rather allowed themselves to be attacked at the town of Ocaña. A French eyewitness to the action that followed – the biggest battle in the entire Peninsular War – was François Lavaux, whose 103rd Line found itself drawn up against the Spanish centre:

> The attack was opened by the Fourth Corps, which was composed almost entirely of Germans. At . . . eleven o'clock in the morning, the battle was not going our way: the Germans, indeed, had begun to fall back. The king came to Marshal Mortier, and told him that he was by no means certain that the day would be in our favour. 'Sire,' said the marshal, 'if you will give me the command of the army, I shall answer for it with my head.' The king agreed, and the marshal immediately sent forward the two regiments that constituted the right flank of the corps and the two that made up its left, together with all the *voltigeurs* and other skirmishers. Immediately the firing became very fierce on both sides. We ourselves were showered with case-shot, but the Spaniards almost immediately took flight: it looked as if they thought that the devil himself was at their heels. They abandoned not only the town, but also their baggage and their arms: the ground was absolutely covered . . . My company lost just five men.[221]

From Madrid to the frontiers of Andalucía, the only source of effective resistance to the French was now the guerrillas. In the course of a foraging expedition to the town of Consuegra, Andrzej Daleki made the mistake of getting drunk and falling asleep:

> When I woke up it was dawn, and there was not a single one of our men to be seen. Hearing a noise near my head, I suddenly realised that two Spanish peasants were standing over me. Keeping absolutely still, I played dead, but that did not stop me from hearing what they were saying. 'Look, here's one of those French thieves fast asleep,' said the first. 'Have you got that big knife of yours?' replied the other. 'No, it's not on me.' Bending down, the first one then picked something up off the ground. 'Never mind: here is a big stone. Smash his head in with it quick!' I can still hear these words as if they had been said to me this very day, and I think I will remember them till the day of judgement. I believed my last hour had come. Opening my eyes, I looked up at them. 'Good day, sir, and what might you be up to?' 'What could I be up to? I am flat on my back ill, and unable to move!' 'Scoundrel!' cried the older of the two. 'You might pretend to be ill today, but how

many houses did you sack in the town?' 'Please, gentlemen: I was even weaker yesterday than I am today. How on earth could I have sacked any houses?' 'Well, we'll soon find out,' he replied. 'If we find anything on you, we will kill you!' They then emptied my pack and began to look through my things. At this I really began to sweat because I happened to have a couple of shirts on me that I had found in a house. As to why I had them, you could hardly expect me to march around without a shirt, and I had in any case been obliged to take them by a couple of veterans. More to the point, I had seen the cruelty with which the Spaniards killed their captives . . . One man I saw had had his ears, nose and fingers cut off . . . and then been buried up to the waist in the ground . . . However, in the event they did not notice anything . . . Just then, some more people appeared, and, among them, there was a priest. There was soon quite a crowd milling about and making fun of me, but the priest wished me good day, bade them be quiet and told me to follow him to the parish church. When we got there, he got out some paper and began to interrogate me . . . Meanwhile, many people had gathered round the entrance, most of them women, and they were saying the most dreadful things about me. However, paying them no heed, the priest said, 'Look! This man says he is Polish and Catholic! Let us see if what he says is true.' At this he got two peasants to strip me to my shirt. Luckily for me, he as a result caught sight of a scapular I was wearing at my breast, and, pointing to it, shouted out, 'It is true! He is a Roman Catholic!' At these words everything changed. The shouts and insults died away, and the good priest . . . ordered that I be given a large slice of sausage and a good liquor that the Spaniards call *rosoli* . . . Abruptly turning to the crowd once more, the priest said, 'Listen to me! What would have happened if we had killed him? The French would probably have come back and sacked the town again. In any case, this man is a brother Catholic: had we not treated him with kindness, God would have punished us.' And, turning his back on them . . . he called a boy and told him to get two mules ready for a journey. Filling my canteen with brandy, he also returned my musket and gave me plenty of food . . . The populace saw us off: they fired their guns in the air and the balls whistled round our ears. As for the boy, he set about beating his donkey with a stick . . . and soon had the poor animals dashing along . . . at a rapid pace. Infantryman that I am . . . my teeth were soon snapping up and down like castanets . . . while I bounced about on the donkey's back like a sack of flour. It seems funny enough now, but at the time I did not have the slightest desire to laugh. Still, we found my regiment without any difficulty. I gave the boy something to eat and told him to go home . . . Our general wanted to reward the priest for saving my life, but, when we went back to Consuegra, there was nobody in the place . . . The church had been ransacked and stood with its doors open . . . My heart stopped at the sight of such devastation in a holy place. But there was a war on, so what could one do?[222]

With the situation in Andalucía at the lowest possible ebb, bad news had also come in from Catalonia where the fortress of Gerona had been taken by the French after a six-month siege. Only in parts of northern Spain was the cause of resistance still showing signs of real vigour. In the Basque provinces, Navarre and parts of Aragón commanders such as Javier Mina, Francisco Longa and Juan Díaz Porlier were now causing serious problems to the French. The hussar officer Albert de Rocca, for example, had been sent back to France to gather recruits for his regiment:

Towards the end of the year 1809 I returned to Spain with a reinforcement of eighty hussars for my regiment . . . All the detachments which, like us, were going to reinforce the divers corps of the army of Spain received orders to assemble in the towns of Miranda and Vitoria to be in readiness for an expedition against the Spanish partisans of Navarre and La Rioja . . . [who] held Pamplona in a state of almost perpetual blockade, and were continually attacking the detachments and convoys on their way to the French army in Aragón . . . My detachment of hussars formed part of a corps of four or five thousand men commanded by General Loison. The foot soldiers had left their baggage and even their knapsacks behind them that they might be light for running in the mountains. General Loison and [another corps under General] Solignac marched from Vitoria and Miranda on the sixteenth and threw themselves at once by both banks of the Ebro upon Logroño in the hopes of surprising [Juan Díaz] Porlier in that city. At four o'clock in the afternoon of the seventeenth [of December] we came in sight of Logroño. General Solignac's troops arrived before the town at the same time . . . [and] we flattered ourselves for a moment that we had surrounded the partisans . . . but, to our great astonishment, we soon afterwards entered the town without having to fire a single gun. [Porlier] . . . had been warned of our combined march early in the morning, and had made his escape . . . to the high mountains of Castile . . . The next day General Solignac set out in pursuit of the enemy; at Nájera he met a small Spanish party which he pursued as far as La Calzada de Santo Domingo, fancying that he was to come up with the main body of the guerrillas, but it was a stratagem of [Porlier] . . . to draw us on in the opposite direction to that which he had taken with his little army. General Loison followed General Solignac to Nájera on the nineteenth where we were forced to remain two whole days in order to obtain information concerning the enemy, all traces of whom we had entirely lost. At length on the twenty-first we learned that [Porlier] . . . had taken the road towards Soto . . . We set out again in pursuit . . . We went through narrow, difficult roads, through deep snows . . . When we came within about a quarter of a league of Soto, we were received by a discharge of thirty or forty muskets, and we saw some armed peasants suddenly appear from behind the rocks where they had lain in ambush, and run down the hill towards Soto as fast as they were able . . . Soto is situated at the bottom of a narrow valley crossed by a torrent; beyond the town is a very steep mountain on the side of which a winding road has been made. It was by that road that we saw the partisans retreat before our faces . . . To cover his retreat [Porlier] had left a company of cavalry before the gate by which we had to enter Soto, and at a little distance on the other side of the river he had placed four or five hundred infantry on the rocks and terraces which commanded the town. Whatever happened, these men had it in their power to retire without running the smallest risk after having done us a great deal of mischief.[223]

Another eyewitness to the bitter struggle being waged in the northern provinces was the pharmacist Antoine Fée. Hardly had he crossed the frontier in November 1809, in fact, than he found himself under attack:

At length Briviesca appeared on the horizon. Anxious to get the best billets by right of first arrival, [my friend] Chabrier and I quickened our pace. Thinking much the same as us, a number of other people followed our example, and little by little we drew ahead of the rest of the convoy. There were a number of ladies with us in a couple of carriages, and even a number of particularly quick-footed infantrymen, the whole party numbering around forty people . . . All of a sudden, however, we saw a group of armed men burst from the shelter of some nearby hills, and, albeit in a rather disorderly fashion, draw up in line as if they were going to attack us. Guessing who these fellows were, Chabrier halted our little column . . . Absolutely terrified, the women jumped out of their carriages, and fled to the shelter of a little gully that hid them from sight. Meanwhile, some of the men hid behind the vehicles, a dozen foot-soldiers took possession of a prominent knoll covered in trees, and those of us who were on horseback gathered together in a little squadron in readiness to charge the enemy. In the midst of all this . . . Chabrier came up to me, and with the greatest sang-froid said, 'You have two pistols: make certain that you don't fall into the hands of these wretches alive.' Pretty soon we had opened fire, but hardly had we done so than two squadrons of horsemen suddenly appeared from the direction of a small valley. So great a number of assailants . . . gave us no chance of putting up a fight, but . . . in the event the new arrivals did not turn out to be who we thought they were at all. On the contrary, they belonged to our army, and were, as we soon discovered, the Nassau *chasseurs*.[224]

Yet, march and fight though the guerrillas of the northern provinces might, they could do nothing to affect the situation on the frontiers of Andalucía. All the same, huge areas of the country were still being devastated. Laure Junot, a noted beauty aged just 25, who was reputed to have recently had an affair with the Austrian ambassador Clemens von Metternich, had come out to join her husband, General Junot, and was currently struggling to cross the wilds of Old Castile:

At the time that [I] arrived [Burgos] had for two months been without any authority other than that of those commanders who happened to pass through it . . . The most revolting injustices were being committed by our men, often in reprisal for atrocities that had been inflicted on us, and these outrages were being avenged in their turn so that a chain of disasters had been unleashed of which there was no hope of seeing the end. A desert in which there was nothing to be found but famine, ruin, despair and death . . . extended for four or five leagues in every direction from the town and surrounded it like a belt of misfortune. The barracks and, still more so, the prisons were characterised by the most horrible conditions, while the hospitals were quite unspeakable. And all the way from Bayonne to Madrid there was nothing that even remotely resembled justice: there were neither tribunals nor judges, for everyone had fled or been destroyed by the sword of an exterminating angel. As for the few inhabitants who remained, they no longer cared whether they lived or died . . . and wandered through the badly paved streets of the city like ghosts, the only thing that could be said in favour of their situation being that at least there were no stones for them to hurt their feet upon, for a thick bed of filth covered the ground. In the mud, however, were buried . . . at least a hundred corpses. So mephitic was the stench that the plague could have been caught by breathing it alone . . . Yet Burgos was one of the most important bases in Spain.[225]

In Seville, meanwhile, the Junta Central was in a state of paralysis. Other than the guerrillas, it seemed that the only thing that might stop the French was the sheer size of the country, and their own indiscipline. Fée, for example, was soon trudging across La Mancha with the massive forces gathering for the march on Seville on which King Joseph was now resolved:

Hardly has one lost sight of Madrid than one could believe that it was twenty leagues away. There is no transition between the magnificence of the capital and the misery of the countryside which surrounds it. As we marched in the direction of Toledo, we crossed a plain of killing monotony with neither trees nor houses. Bordered with weeds, the fields . . . offered to the eye nothing but wastes that had been baked completely dry . . . This was not the heart of Europe, but rather some arid steppe on the banks of the Don or the Volga . . . Just before reaching Almagro, I was a witness to the intemperance of our soldiers . . . The chief halt of the day was made near a small village which only our officers were permitted to enter. However, having first obtained permission to do so, the mayor brought out an excellent wine to the soldiers which the latter then proceeded to drink to excess. By the time it was time to go, the drummers could not hold their sticks, nor the soldiers their muskets. Bawling out drinking songs at the tops of their voices, they displayed an infinite tenderness in respect of their officers. Calling them the bravest of the brave, they took their hands and expressed the most touching sentiments, and in several cases officers had to push them away to avoid being greeted in a manner that was still more familiar. There was nothing for it but to wait until the wine fumes had dissipated before getting back on the road again.[226]

Similar scenes were witnessed by an artilleryman named Manière who was serving in Marshal Victor's corps with the Third Regiment of Horse Artillery:

We arrived in El Toboso, the village in which Don Quijote had long ago met Dulcinea, and settled down for the night. In the middle of the night we were woken up by about twenty dragoons who were all singing and making an infernal racket . . . They were all carrying torches . . . and in the middle of them was a baby ass. It was no more than six months old, and they had forced its hind legs into a pair of red trousers, and its front legs into the sleeves of a coat that they had buttoned round

its neck, and then sewn the two garments together across its back . . . As for
headgear, they had cut two slits in some countryman's hat for its ears and fixed it on
its head with some ribbons. At every house they passed they forced the poor creature
to drink some wine, and every time it did so it let fly the most tremendous hee-haws.
Accompanying this band, meanwhile, was a crowd of peasants, all of whom were
exclaiming to one another that the ass had been got up like a true Christian.[227]

On 19 January the long-expected French offensive began:

> Before dawn we were on the road. Although a thin covering of snow lay on the
> ground, we tramped along cheerfully, eager to see that country which we had come
> to conquer, and picked up the main highway a little way north of Santa Cruz [de
> Mudela] . . . Smoke from the Spanish campfires was still rising from the summit of
> the . . . mountains. Dismounted cannon barrels, muskets, sabres, clothing and
> munitions of all sorts lay scattered on the ground, while a number of corpses lay
> scattered among the débris. Everything suggested more that the enemy had taken
> flight than that he was putting up a real fight . . . At length La Carolina came into
> sight with its white houses surrounded by pretty gardens . . . The inhabitants had
> fled. The army had fallen on its opponents like a swarm of locusts and devastated
> everything in sight.[228]

The Siege of Cádiz

The French passage of the Sierra Morena was but the beginning of a blitzkrieg-style
offensive that had soon carried the French to the Straits of Gibraltar and brought down the
discredited Junta Central. With the French conquest of Andalucía, the port-city of Cádiz
came to occupy a pivotal position as both Spain's chief remaining stronghold in the south
and the seat of the new regime that had emerged in place of the fallen provisional
government. As such, it is worth savouring a description of the place that was written by
William Jacob, a Member of Parliament and Fellow of the Royal Society, who arrived in the
city in September 1809:

> The view on entering the bay of Cádiz presents the finest collection of objects that
> can be conceived: on one extremity of the left point is situated the town of Rota, a
> little further the castle of Santa Catalina and the neat city of Santa María; at a
> greater distance on the lap of a lofty hill stands Medina; nearer the sea the town of
> Puerto Real and the arsenal of the Carracas; and on the extremity of the right-hand
> point of land the city of Cádiz. To add to the splendour of the scene, this extensive
> bay was filled with the vessels of different nations displaying their various colours
> against a forest of masts. The whiteness of the houses, their size and apparent
> cleanliness, the magnificence of the public edifices and the neat and regular
> fortifications form together a striking assemblage of objects . . . The best houses
> have brick floors and stone or marble stairs. As the windows generally look into the
> patio or court, they are private and retired and under the house is a cistern which,
> in the rainy season, is filled with water . . . The streets . . . are remarkably well paved,

which may in some measure arise from there being few or no wheel-carriages to destroy the pavement. Coaches are not in use, and most of the streets are too narrow to admit them. Carts for the conveyance of goods are almost unknown. The *gallegos*, or natives of Galicia, a strong and industrious race of men, perform those laborious occupations for which in other cities horse and carts are employed. These men . . . remove the heaviest articles with the utmost facility, and, being frugal as well as industrious, execute their tasks at a very cheap rate. They emigrate from the northern provinces in search of employment in the more southern parts of the peninsula, and every large town is filled with them . . . Though considerable attention is paid to the cleanliness of the streets, none is shown to the entrances of the houses, which are the receptacles of every kind of filth, and, except in the entrances to the houses of the richer class who keep a *gallego* constantly sitting at the door, you are almost suffocated by stenches before you reach the apartments. As this city is placed on a peninsula at the termination of a long sandy isthmus, there is no ground unoccupied, and little can be spared for squares. The Plaza de San Antonio is the only one and is very small, but, being surrounded with magnificent houses and contrasted with the streets (all of which with the exception of a broad street are very narrow), it has a good effect and is the principal resort of the inhabitants . . . The *alameda*, or public walk, is very beautiful: always dry underfoot and furnished with good marble seats on both sides. Being close to the sea, the trees do not thrive and indeed afford very little shade; the cool sea breeze is, however, enjoyed towards evening, and the walk is then crowded with the best company the city contains.[229]

From the land, too, the impression afforded by the city was very favourable:

I left Jérez with my division to march to Chiclana . . . After two hours' marching, we arrived on a hill, and there I saw open up in front of me one of the most beautiful views in the whole world. In the far distance the sea could be seen covered with vessels; in the middle distance there stood Cádiz and its bay; and at my feet there lay the charming seaport and town of Santa María. On the right stood Rota, which is famous for its wines, while on the left lay Medina Sidonia, which was first built by the Moors. A little beyond this last place the sea came in again, and we could see Chiclana, which was surrounded by beautiful groves of trees, and, in the far distance the mountains of Ronda. Nearer at hand, there lay San Fernando . . . next the great shipyard of La Carraca, and finally the . . . pretty town of Puerto Real . . . with, facing it, the Trocadero. The plain that separated the spectator from the sea was taken up with splendid pasturages, through which ran the Guadalete, and the whole of the coast was covered with pine forests, while a multitude of vessels filled the bay.[230]

For one group of observers the arrival of the French army on the shores of Andalucía was a special moment indeed. Marooned aboard their hulks in Cádiz's roadstead, the thousands of soldiers who had been taken by the Spaniards at Bailén were filled with delight. Nor is this at all surprising. As Charles François remembered, conditions on the hulks had been going from bad to worse. Sent to the *Castilla la Vieja* in January 1809, he had already found her in the grip of the utmost misery:

> What was my surprise to find half the soldiers ill, and learn of the death of several officers . . . This terrible disease broke out when the French were first taken to the hulks: it was looked upon as an epidemic. I was struck by the want of order and the dirtiness of the ship. Ten French sailors, also prisoners, were . . . paid by the Spanish navy to clean the ship, but the poor wretches were as ill as the others. All the prisoners were devoid of everything: no food, no water. Several of the wives of the officers were not exempt from the scourge. The air we breathed was pestilential . . . The major of the Third Legion [of Reserve] wrote daily to the Spanish officer charged with the care of the prisoners, but the only reply he received was that there were no military hospitals, and [that] the sick could not be admitted to the civil hospitals . . . For several days we had been short of provisions. We saw a vessel which appeared to be that of our caterer. Our joy was in proportion to our wants, but what was our surprise, and what horror we felt, on finding that the boat was loaded with some fifty naked . . . corpses. Its job was to take the dead from the hulks . . . Every day this boat made its round and never took away fewer than twenty to thirty bodies, most of them with a cord round the neck and towed behind the boat. That was the spectacle that was offered us every morning.[231]

Also on the *Castilla la Vieja* was the apothecary Sébastien Blaze:

> I cannot attempt to describe the transports of joy . . . displayed by my 8,000 companions in misery at the sight of the triumphant French army. Although the sea was in the way, they were only two leagues away. The hope of recovering our . . . liberty made us ready to confront the greatest dangers – they vanished before our eyes, indeed – and the evils of life on the hulks became unsupportable. With freedom waiting on the shore, many men who could swim took to the waves during the night to try their fortune, but all of them drowned or were put to death. Yet neither the unfortunates whom the Spaniards executed before our eyes, nor the corpses . . . that covered the sea were arguments strong enough to dissuade others from risking the same perils for the same object. As the number of escapes continued to multiply, the governor of Cádiz, General Mondragón had a notice put up on each hulk to the effect that all those who attempted to escape would be shot in the event of their recapture. Seeing that this measure was futile, he then published a second order which made us all responsible for one another and condemned two men to death for every man who escaped . . . But these decrees . . . had no effect: we replied . . . that anyone who was executed would go to the scaffold giving thanks for having been rescued from their misfortunes.[232]

Within a short while came still more dramatic proof of the determination of the captives not to give up. One morning a boat bringing food and water out to the hulks was seized by a gang of prisoners led by the Marins de la Garde officer Jean Grivel:

On 22 February we noted when we got up that the wind was in the east . . . and that it was showing signs of blowing vigorously. Deciding to profit by this if some vessel should come alongside during the day, we made sure that we were ready for anything. Breakfast time passed by without anything happening, but about a quarter past ten we saw that one of the large luggers that had been taken from Puerto de Santa María was heading for us. When it arrived, it transpired that it was making a regular delivery of water . . . I strolled over to the rail . . . Having got there, I stretched out my arms: it was the signal we had agreed. Immediately set upon, the Spanish sailors were taken by surprise. Putting up no resistance, they threw themselves into the sea, while I scrambled down onto the boat, shoved my way through the throng and made for the tiller . . . Somebody grabbed the cable that held us to the pontoon . . . but there was no way of cutting it: it was very strong and we did not have an axe. Seeing the difficulty, a cadet who was with us called Dumoustier climbed back onto the pontoon and took advantage of the confusion to let slip the loop that held us firm . . . In a moment we had drifted away and were trying to raise the sail. We had counted on a moment of stupefaction, and this we got. Alerted by the cries of the commissary who had brought the water, the guard on the *Castilla la Vieja* turned out in haste and fired on us at point-blank range, killing *marin* Francisque of the Imperial Guard . . . but for the rest it seemed as if all the Allied gunners who must have been watching us could not believe their eyes . . . The problem was rather the sail. This had begun to flap about in the wind so strongly that it proved hard to get it under control. Luckily a brave cadet named Bellegnic . . . managed to grab hold of it and refused to let go even when this meant being dragged clean out of the boat. His tenacity saved us: in the end we managed to get it fastened down . . . The sail having been run up, we tacked, pushed off from the *Castilla la Vieja* and set an adventurous course through the merchant vessels that stood in our way on all sides. Almost all British or American, the crews of these ships . . . threw their caps in the air and saluted us with their cheers . . . Much less comfort was received from the line of British and Spanish warships we also had to pass. A host of small boats set out after us, while we were also vigorously cannonaded. But nothing could catch us as we were going at full speed, and, so long as the breeze did not fail, or some chance shot bring down the mast, it really looked as if we might escape. I had not, however, considered the possibility that . . . boats might tack their way out into the bay and thereby head us off. I was just . . . telling the army officers on board to lie down to avoid being killed uselessly, when there came a cry from the prow: 'Ship ahoy!' As we had the wind right at our back, the sail stopped me from seeing the vessel in question, but I realised what was going on in an instant. It was a schooner heading straight for us. The circumstances were critical . . . As we had no arms of any sort, had we been boarded, we would have been taken and put to the sword. In a flash of inspiration, I therefore steered straight for the schooner as if I wanted to ram her. Instinctively she avoided a collision . . . We would still have been lost had one of her crew thrown a grappling hook, but very soon we had got clear away, while she did not dare to pursue us on account of her heavier draught. Having escaped that grave danger, we had a reasonable hope of escape . . . And so it transpired: although a few balls peppered our sail, an hour later our boat grounded on the sand . . . and we disembarked among our own people.[233]

In all, thirty-three men got away with Grivel. Even more dramatically, meanwhile, on several of the hulks the prisoners took advantage of the spring storms currently battering the bay to overpower their guards and slip their anchors in the hope of being driven ashore. One such vessel was that which held Sébastien Blaze, but this time the Allied gunners were on the alert. In consequence, its unfortunate passengers found themselves braving a hail of fire, while to make matters worse their ship ran aground some way from the shore:

> The bridge was covered with corpses, piles of dead clogged the gun-decks; and it was impossible to move a step without stepping in the blood or treading on the broken limbs of prisoners who had been torn apart by cannon fire. Mortally wounded victims fell on all sides, and their bodies were immediately torn to shreds by fresh balls that ploughed up the piles of corpses . . . What, then, was to be done? Battered by waves and gunfire alike, we certainly could not expect any help from the land while the wind conserved its violence. In consequence, everyone set to work to build themselves a little raft . . . As soon as their rafts had been completed, most of the prisoners took to the sea . . . But their constructions were not nearly strong enough to withstand the force of the waves and they came to pieces in an instant, leaving their gallant pilots to drown . . . If the tempest had continued, we would all have perished . . . but at last Providence took pity on our misfortunes . . . About four o'clock in the afternoon, the wind fell, and three launches . . . set out . . . and one by one offered us their help . . . Rather than putting alongside . . . they came just close enough to allow people to save themselves by swimming . . . As soon as I saw them set off . . . I descended to the lower gun-deck so that I wouldn't have to jump too far . . . But the gun-ports were shut, and nothing was to be seen but piles of the dead and dying, while I found myself walking through the blood and body-parts that bore sad witness to the fury of our enemies. Seized by horror at this dreadful spectacle, I decided to retrace my steps . . . Just as I was climbing the ladder, a ball passed close to me . . . I was flung full-length on the deck. Feeling a violent blow on my left thigh, I at first thought that the ball had carried off my leg . . . Quickly examining myself, I found that . . . a large splinter of wood . . . had been driven into my thigh, and I had to pull it out with my fingers. The wound was deep and my blood flowed freely . . . But the situation in which I found myself helped me to bear the pain . . . Having bandaged my wound, I . . . jumped into the sea. A launch had been nearby when I entered the water, but . . . by the time I surfaced it was far away. Having no confidence in my ability to follow it . . . I grabbed hold of a rope that was hanging from the side of the ship, and, tossed up and down by the waves, resigned myself to wait for the return of the launches. While I was bobbing around in this fashion, a man slid down the rope . . . He was

terrified by the violence of the waves, and I quickly realised that he had lost his reason. In the excess of his fear, he seized hold of my arms with his hands and gripped my body with his legs. Persuaded that we would both drown if this continued, I roughly shook him off, and made my way to a raft that was tied to the side of the ship. The rope I left to him, but his mind was gone and he could not hold on: an instant later he disappeared, taken by the waves. I remained on the raft for three quarters of an hour . . . All the time the waves were breaking over me. Whenever a big one arrived, I lay flat and let it break over my head . . . At last the launches came back, and, as they were still standing off a little, I abandoned the raft and threw myself into the water. As I swam towards the launches, the breakers repeatedly sucked me down into the abyss, only to lift me up . . . and throw me in the air . . . At last I got alongside and stretched out my arms. Oh God, what transports! My hand touched the gunwale and I clung on for all I was worth. In vain did the waves try to prise me loose: it would have been easier for them to cut off my arms than to make me let go. Holding on with both hands, I tried to pull myself into the launch, but all in vain: cold and fatigue had sapped my strength. But the crew came to my aid. Letting go of their oars, one man grabbed me by the arm and another by the leg, and I fell . . . into the bottom of the launch. Having thrown four other men on top of me, they then set off back towards the shore.[234]

What, though, of events back at Cádiz? In so far as the military events of the siege were concerned, these were of only limited importance. The city being completely impregnable, once a forlorn effort to persuade the garrison to surrender had been rejected, all that could be done was to try bombardment. Large numbers of troops and guns were therefore pushed forward to attack the isolated fort of Matagorda – the only point from which land-based guns could reach the city. For a graphic description of the fighting, we can turn to the memoirs of Joseph Donaldson, a boy from Glasgow whose comfortable commercial background seems to have left him feeling so stifled that he first ran away to sea, and then joined the Ninety-Fourth Foot in 1809, still aged just 16:

At last when everything was prepared, they commenced their operations . . . Five or six batteries, mounting in all about twenty guns and eight or ten mortars, opened their tremendous mouths, vomiting forth death and destruction . . . Death now began to stalk about in the most dreadful form. The large shot were certain messengers where they struck. The first man killed was a sailor . . . The whole of his face was carried away . . . The French soon acquired a fatal precision with their shot . . . killing and wounding men with every volley. I was on the left of the gun at the front wheel. We were running her up after loading. I had stooped to take a fresh purchase [when] a cannon ball . . . carried the forage cap off my head and struck the man behind me on the breast, and he fell to rise no more . . . The carnage now became dreadful: the ramparts were strewed with the dead and wounded, and blood, brains and mangled limbs lay scattered in every direction . . . The action was kept up the whole of that day during which we lost the best and bravest of our men . . . By this time three of our guns were rendered unfit for service, and they had made a great impression on our parapet, with a breach in the end of the bomb-proof . . . It being found that we could not keep the place, boats were sent to convey us to Cádiz.[235]

With Matagorda in their hands, the French could harass harbour, isthmus and city alike. The gunners' efforts, however, proved completely ineffectual and the only result was to swell the confidence of the inhabitants. As Alcalá Galiano wrote:

From December 1810 bombs . . . fired by the enemy batteries had started to fall inside Cádiz. However, these shots . . . came very infrequently, and then only a few at a time. At the same time, in order to carry so far, the projectiles had had to be increased in weight, and were consequently mostly made up of lead without much space for powder. As a result, they caused little damage . . . and in the end little notice was taken of them other than to make them the subject of humour. In theatres and streets, then, a popular couplet was sung . . . 'From the bombs fired by the popinjays, the girls of Cádiz make hair curlers.'[236]

With food abundant in the city, there was in fact no hope of success for the French. Knowing this, Cádiz's assailants became ever more depressed. Let us here quote Fée once again:

Our men were picked off by enemy fire, by illness, sometimes even by suicide. Homesickness, that incurable melancholy . . . carried off a good few more . . . Nobody had a care for the pleasures of the soldiers . . . In those times our men did not receive a free ration . . . of tobacco, while they also lacked the money to buy it. In consequence, the entire First Corps smoked less in a year than the students of a military academy now do in six months. Food was never abundant, while the strong, thick wine distributed to the troops swelled the head without nourishing the body. The army could beat the Spaniards and fight with success against the British, but a still more redoubtable enemy was gradually undermining its strength. Little by little, boredom – something that kills and stupefies just as surely as a narcotic – took control of the best soldiers . . . Meanwhile, the bitterness of our situation was increased still further by the sad fact that we almost never received any mail from our families . . . Nor did we know anything that was happening in France or the rest of Europe. Newspapers or fresh copies of periodicals were rarities . . . Though free on the surface, in reality we were . . . poor exiles in a foreign land.[237]

On top of boredom, there was also heat:

In the month of May the heat became excessive and the thermometer marked 40 degrees centigrade in the shade . . . If you lie perfectly still in a closed room provided with porous water pots . . . that give off a little humidity, and refresh [yourself] with oranges and cold water . . . you can just about stand it, but even these measures are not enough when the wind is in the east. This wind – the solano – comes from Africa where it passes across the sands of the great desert . . . If it blows for several days, the heat becomes stifling, while the nights do nothing to cool things down. At such times streams run dry, plants wither and animals die of asphyxia . . . Man, too, cannot escape its influence . . . He can hardly breathe, and is devoured by an ardent thirst . . . It is, then, all too easy to imagine the sufferings of our soldiers, living, as they were, in the open air and with no better cover than their rough shelters.[238]

By contrast life in Cádiz was very pleasant. To quote Jacob again:

Gaming forms the principal amusement, and is carried on to a very censurable extent in some of the private houses, where parties meet regularly every night and play for large sums at games of hazard. The game now in vogue is called Monte, a species of Lansquenet, but more complicated, requiring little skill and played for any sum the parties may choose to stake provided it does not exceed the amount in the bank: it is quickly decided and consequently the more dangerous. Another game called Pecado – in plain English 'Sin' – is also much practised: it well deserves its name, for the decision is so very rapid that money to a large amount may be speedily gained or lost without the slightest exercise of the mind. At such parties the quantity of gold and silver spread on the table is astonishing, and the rapidity with which it passes from one possessor to another strikingly exemplifies the uncertainty of a gamester's wealth . . . One of the chief amusements of the higher class of inhabitants is the theatre . . . The house is not well calculated for hearing: it is long and narrow, the stage still narrower than the rest of the theatre . . . The first time I visited the theatre the principal performance was a Spanish opera, a species of entertainment rather tiresome even in England where . . . the music is good, the dresses tasteful and the language familiar to the ear, but in this place, where all these requisites are wanting, I should have found it a very unsatisfactory mode of passing my time if the company, the novelty of the scene and the varied dresses of the spectators had not in some measure compensated its want of interest . . . Almost every man in the theatre wore a uniform, but, had 100,000 men been collected from the different European armies, the officers could not have exhibited a greater variety of dress than was displayed in this narrow compass: everyone seems to wear his dress according to his own fancy, and deems it sufficient if it be military without regarding its similarity to others of the same corps. Adjoining the theatre there is a suite of coffee rooms, where all kinds of refreshments are prepared for the company. In these apartments the ladies are seen drinking . . . iced water, and the gentlemen are employed in smoking their cigars, a practice which is carried to a disgusting excess . . . Yesterday, though Sunday, the market was excessively crowded, especially the fish and vegetable markets. The latter was supplied with a surprising profusion of everything in season. Garlic in this place is a most important article, and is sold in strings three or four yards long which are piled in stacks. The market also abounded with onions, grapes, melons, pumpkins, turnips, carrots and celery of a prodigious thickness.[239]

After the excitements of the first months of the blockade, there was little action in the vicinity of Cádiz itself. But in the interior of Andalucía it was a different matter. At first the French occupation seemed to go well enough: King Joseph, for example, was well received in a grand tour he made of the region. It was not long, however, before the early optimism was under threat. The gangs of bandits and deserters who had over-run the countryside under the Junta Central continued to ply their trade, and in the process killed many isolated French soldiers, while amidst the rugged mountains of the Serranía de Ronda the misbehaviour of the invaders and the poverty of the inhabitants combined to produce a general insurrection. Among the soldiers whom we find fighting the insurgents was the cavalryman Rocca. Having crossed the Sierra Morena with his reinforcements, he was now at the town of Olvera en route for his regiment's headquarters at Ronda:

> The priest and the *corregidor* came to us just as we were setting off the next day to ask for an attestation to prove to any French troops who might come to Olvera that they had behaved well to us . . . A few moments after their departure we heard cries of alarm. The townspeople had just murdered six hussars and two farriers who had imprudently gone to a smithy to shoe their horses . . . We mounted hastily, and the [main] body of the detachment followed the adjutant who commanded us to a place of rendezvous about a musket shot from the village. I remained at the bivouac, and kept with me ten hussars to cover the retreat and protect the baggage, which we had not yet got upon the backs of the mules because the Spanish muleteers had fled in the night. One of my comrades soon came back to tell me that our rearguard was on the point of being surrounded, and that the Spaniards were keeping up a brisk fire . . . upon [the rest of] the detachment from the rocks and from the windows of the houses . . . Having no hope of succour, we resolved to cut our way through the enemy. My horse received a ball through the neck and fell. I succeeded in raising him immediately and reached the [rendezvous]. Shortly afterwards my comrade had his arm broken; we saw almost all the hussars fall successively round us. Women, or rather furies let loose, threw themselves with horrible shrieks upon the wounded, and disputed who should kill them by the most cruel tortures. They stabbed their eyes with knives and scissors, and seemed to exult with ferocious joy at the sight of their blood . . . Meantime [the rest of] the detachment had remained motionless, facing the enemy, to wait for us . . . Not having been able to procure a guide, we took the first path which led off the beaten road . . . and wandered for some time in the fields without knowing where we were. We then saw a man on a mule riding from a farm . . . and, placing him between two of the advanced guard, ordered him . . . to guide us to Ronda . . . We had hardly entered a pretty long valley when we perceived on the heights towards our left a troop of a thousand or fifteen hundred persons watching our march. We distinguished among the number women and even children. They were the inhabitants of Setenil and the neighbouring villages who . . . had set off in pursuit of us. They were running very fast in hopes of cutting off our march at a pass in front of us. We pushed on our horses that they might not succeed and fortunately passed the defile. We were soon after surrounded by a cloud of peasants detached from the main body . . . whose fire just reached our flanks.

They followed us along the rocks without daring to approach nearer than musket-shot for fear of not being able to regain the mountain if charged . . . Such of our wounded as had the misfortune to fall off their horses were stabbed behind us without mercy. One alone escaped, for he had the presence of mind to give the bystanders to understand that he wished to confess before he died, and the priest of Setenil saved him from the fury of his enemies.[240]

Hippolyte d'Espinchal, meanwhile, found himself in charge of a convoy travelling from Madrid to Seville:

About four o'clock in the morning, hardly had the first ten wagons entered a defile . . . than we were suddenly attacked by a mass of infantry and cavalry who fell upon us uttering the most terrifying war cries and peppering the convoy with bullets. As a result, the convoy was immediately flung into the greatest confusion . . . However, I got together some of the infantry, along with our two cannon . . . and at first this was enough to make them fall back . . . Yet they soon got over their first fear, and, with extraordinary sagacity, were soon edging round the convoy by its left-hand side for in this fashion they could keep out of the way of the fire of the two guns. In the midst of all this I ordered the convoy to get moving while the infantry gave covering fire, but horses and mules kept being shot in their traces and this soon brought all movement to a halt. The situation was now becoming critical: a good number of my men had already been hit . . . while the approach of night only threatened the onset of fresh disasters. I was therefore beginning to consider abandoning the vehicles whose teams had been shot, and pressing on with the rest, when I suddenly realised that the Spaniards seemed to be in the grip of panic. For this I was unable to discern the reason, but it seemed a good idea to take advantage of the moment, a couple of rounds of canister serving to speed them on their way. With the rabble who had attacked us in a state of complete rout, fifty lancers then appeared at full gallop, and they were soon cutting down our opponents right and left. From this moment the convoy was saved.[241]

The extent of popular resistance in Andalucía is open to serious question. No forces appeared in the style of those commanded by El Empecinado or Espoz y Mina, and it is hard to see the scattered guerrilla bands that did emerge as anything but brigands. Yet, brigands or not, they still killed many French soldiers and presented the invaders with a problem that could not be ignored. Among the men fighting the insurgents was Sergeant Lavaux:

We set off from Seville on 10 April. Our orders were that the first village that fired a shot at us should be burned to the ground and put to the sword down to the last baby and the last lamb. At the second village, a place on the Guadalquivir called Boetis [*sic*: the place referred to appears to be Brenes], we found five enemy pickets. They tried to put up a fight, and so the place was immediately . . . ravaged. The next day we took the road for Constantina, where the brigands had their headquarters. A peasant was sent on ahead to tell them that if they laid down their arms they would come to no harm, but they replied that they would never yield to the French . . . Our colonel . . . ordered the *pas de charge* to be beaten, whereupon we all advanced as one, while at the same time keeping the enemy under heavy fire. The brigands very soon took to flight, whereupon the cavalry sounded the charge. Cutting down all those who came within reach, they accounted for nearly 600 men . . . As for us, we quickly entered the town, which was immediately pillaged and reduced to ashes. A number of men got into a convent and its occupants were robbed, raped, murdered and so on . . . The next day we returned to Seville . . . Almost immediately we set off again. This time it was Málaga and Granada, and especially the mountains of Ronda. Arriving at a small village where the brigands had entrenched themselves, we attacked them. In the first assault we lost twenty-four *voltigeurs*. Although we got into the village, we soon had to leave as the brigands had retired into the houses and were keeping up a fierce fire from the side streets. Among the people shooting were a number of women, while others were seen bringing ammunition to their husbands. Placing us in the gardens on the outskirts of the village, the general ordered us not to spare a single person, even the women and children. At length we got into the village. The horrible carnage that followed had to be seen to be believed. All the houses were set on fire. Moving forward, I came across several women and young girls. Acting out of pity, I spared their lives, but some other *voltigeurs* came up after me and ran them all through with their bayonets . . . 'These brigands should be shown no mercy', my comrades told me. 'They make out as if they're begging for their lives, and then cut your throat as soon as your back is turned.' A little further on . . . I entered a windmill. There were eighteen people lying dead in the courtyard. Among them was a poor little child of three or four years of age. He was cradled in the arms of his mother, but she had suffered a number of bayonet wounds and was quite dead . . . The leader of the brigands had fled to a large house on the main square. It was decided to storm the place, but nobody could get near it without being killed or wounded: it was a single mass of gun smoke. As a result it was set on fire. Our general had a lot of tow and dry wood brought up. Keeping close to the walls . . . some soldiers managed to fling all this material on to the balconies and set it on fire . . . Forty brigands were inside. Once it became clear that they would otherwise perish in the flames, they began to throw themselves from the windows and balconies, but no sooner had they done so than they were shot down . . . Running out on to the main balcony, the daughter of the brigands' commander waved a white handkerchief as a sign of surrender. This was accepted, but then her mother appeared beside her, and killed a soldier who was sheltering in the same house as me with a carbine. Immediately, one of the soldiers posted on the roofs of the nearby houses shot her down: falling from the balcony, she was run through again and again by the troops below.[242]

Kill Frenchmen though some irregulars did, what really counted in the south were the assorted forces of regular troops that the Allies could send against the invaders. Operating from a variety of bases on the coast or simply disembarked from the sea, these often struck deep into French-occupied territory, and on occasion went so far as to threaten Seville. The most famous of these operations was the ambitious raid launched on the rear of the French siege lines outside Cádiz in March 1811. On the fifth of that month this produced a bitter battle around a lonely Moorish watchtower called the Torre de Barosa. In this fight, which ended in the rout of the French, the brunt of the action was borne by troops drawn from the Anglo-Portuguese forces that had been sent to Cádiz under Sir Thomas Graham. First in action was a composite battalion of flank companies which found itself taking on an entire division that had seized a prominent hill overlooking the Allied rear. Fighting with the unit concerned was the Irishman Robert Blakeney:

> All being now ready, Colonel Browne rode to the front of the battalion, and said in a voice to be heard by all, 'Gentlemen . . . General Graham has done you the honour of being the first to attack those fellows. Now follow me, you rascals!' He pointed to the enemy, and [gave] the order to advance . . . As soon as we crossed the ravine close to the base of the hill . . . a most tremendous roar of cannon and musketry was all at once opened . . . Nearly 200 of our men and more than half the officers went down by this first volley . . . In closing on the centre and endeavouring to form a second line, upwards of fifty more men were levelled with the earth; and . . . the remainder of the battalion now scattered. The men commenced firing from behind trees, mounds or any cover which presented, and could not be got together.[243]

The light battalion was badly hit in this action – indeed, Blakeney himself was slightly wounded by a musket ball – but it had won valuable time for the rest of Graham's forces to deploy (the story is too long to be told here, but, in brief, the Allies had been taken by surprise and caught in an awkward position with their backs to the sea). The story of what happened next is picked up by another officer of the Twenty-Eighth, Charles Cadell:

> We had not long left the heights, and were proceeding through a thick pine wood, when a Spaniard galloped up to Sir Thomas at the head of the column, his horse covered with foam, and reported that the French were advancing . . . The admirable decision of our gallant chief was the means of our gaining the day: he did not take time to counter-march the column, but went at once to the right about, the men getting into their places on the march. As soon as we cleared the wood, we saw Colonel Browne's little band of heroes hard at it, keeping the enemy's left wing in check; the guards were in front, and they pushed forward . . . to his support. As we disengaged ourselves from the wood, we formed line under cover of the Ninety-Fifth, and advanced to meet their right wing, which was then coming down in close column. This gave us a great advantage, and here the coolness of Colonel Belson was conspicuous: we being the left regiment, he moved us up without firing a shot close to their right battalion, which . . . began to deploy. Colonel Belson then gave orders to fire by platoons . . . at the same time [shouting] 'to be sure to fire at their legs and spoil their dancing'. This order was observed for a short time with dreadful effect. The action now became general: twice did we attempt to charge the enemy

who, being double our strength . . . only retired a little. Giving three cheers, we charged a third time and succeeded: the enemy gave way and fled in every direction: in less than two hours they had been beaten in every part of the field . . . We collected on top of the hill, from which we had beaten the enemy, and saw the French retreating in great confusion towards Chiclana, dismayed and crestfallen: we gave them three hearty British cheers at parting.[244]

Also taking part in this battle, albeit somewhat further to the right, were two companies of the Twentieth Portuguese commanded by Lieutenant Colonel Bushe; with them was Thomas Bunbury, who had recently transferred from the Third Foot in the hope of advancing his career. Sent to cover the deployment of the Twenty-Eighth and the rest of Graham's infantry with a battalion of the Ninety-Fifth Rifles from a useful defensive position afforded by a sunken road, this force soon found itself in severe trouble:

The advance of the French was a most imposing spectacle, and there was a much more ostentatious display of plumes and martial music than we could have shown under similar circumstances. The fire of their invisible enemies (the Rifles), must, however, have proved very deadly, as it served to arrest their march and caused them to open a desultory fire from their whole line in return . . . The object of gaining time to protect the formation of our troops having been attained, the Rifles withdrew. Lieutenant Colonel Bushe being very short-sighted, I pointed out to him . . . that, the Rifles having been withdrawn, our present position between the two armies could only obstruct the fire of our line . . . He, however, chose to remain and told me to mind my own business . . . The French seemed suspicious of an ambuscade, halting, vacillating, then marching again, but, as Bushe and his horse were the only objects visible to them, they were soon placed *hors de combat.* The lieutenant colonel contrived to get out of his . . . saddle, and I was in hopes that his wounds were not serious, but almost immediately after he fell backwards apparently dead. . . . The detachment seemed greatly disheartened, and, to make matters worse, the senior captain . . . harangued his men, saying, 'Boys, I always told you that these mad Englishmen would get us into some such scrape as this. Let us be off: what are we doing here!' I was now as desirous that they should remain as I was before anxious for their withdrawal when it could be done without loss. But that time was now past, so, pointing out to them [that] our line was formed and ready to advance, and showing them that we yet had good cover, I begged they would stay, as, if they attempted to move while the enemy was so near, they would be shot down like mosquitoes. My representations were of no avail, the old captain saying, 'I will take my company away at all events.' Off they went, taking with them half the other company, to which I had been attached. As I had foreseen, the enemy made dreadful havoc among them . . . My fellows in the same manner went away in twos and threes. I seized one man in order to drag him back, but he was shot dead while I held him. On looking back to my . . . post, I saw two French soldiers rifling my old colonel, and then thought it high time to vanish with the others . . . The line now advanced, but without firing a shot. The French formation was already broken by their irregular attack on the Portuguese. The Eighty-Seventh gave them a . . . most unearthly howl. This was more than the French could stand and they put about. The Eighty-Seventh then poured a volley into them and the whole line charged. It was here that I saw Sir Thomas Graham on foot, his horse having been shot under him, waving his cocked hat and cheering on the Guards to the charge.[245]

After the battle, Cadell and his fellow officers of the Twenty-Eighth wearily took stock:

We [had] suffered much, both in officers and men. Lieutenant Bennet of the Light Company was killed, Lieutenant Light of the grenadiers mortally wounded, Captains Mullins and Bradbey [and] Lieutenants Wilkinson, Moore and Anderson . . . severely wounded, and Lieutenant Blakeney slightly [wounded] . . . Lieutenant Blakeney was rather astonished to find, on examination, that the musket ball that had wounded him had almost spent itself in going through a ration loaf and a roast fowl. I recollect also [that] . . . Captain Bowles . . . [had gone] into action with a canteen of brandy over his shoulder, made fast under his sash . . . On untying the canteen, he found that a shot had gone through it, and not a drop of the brandy was left.[246]

Torres Vedras

With the French bogged down before Cádiz, the chief focus of operations shifted to Portugal. Here Wellington now had some 36,000 British troops. Taking their place alongside them in the front line for the first time would also be a completely remodelled Portuguese army. This was just as well. Throughout the spring and summer fresh troops had been pouring into Old Castile under Marshal André Masséna. Once in Spain they encountered the usual misery and discomfort. Among the many camp followers was General Junot's wife, Laure:

We left Salamanca for Ledesma . . . in the midst of a heat such as I have never experienced. For some way the road passed through woodland, but there was no relief to be had among the trees while . . . the terrain became ever more arid and desert-like. To try to give an idea of the life I lived during the two months I spent in Ledesma would be so wearisome as to do a disservice to the reader. I will only say that Ledesma is a large town surrounded by Moorish and even Roman walls that otherwise offers not a single resource in respect of social life. I lived in the best house in the place, but in France it would not have been fit to be a gardener's cottage on a country estate in one of the poorest of her provinces. I was suffering from being big with child, and the misery that came with that was all the more alarming in view of the illness that had struck my husband's *corps d'armée*, for large numbers of unfortunates were dying of the malady known as *nostalgie*: nothing could save them, and as they expired they turned their faces towards France and begged her to send them her protection. I, too, was suffering from the same disorder – I kept being seized by floods of tears – but what kept me alive was the fact that I had access to a special medicine in the form of my pregnancy. This fought hard against the evil, and the fact is that my baby kept me from harm. Nature is truly admirable! Unlike us, she does not create in order to destroy. Only one other thing marks out my stay in Ledesma in my memory . . . As my saint's day was approaching, Junot decided to mark it in a suitably martial fashion. We had never seen a bullfight, for they had been prohibited at the time that we had first visited Spain, and very soon he had improvised a pretty good bull-ring in the main square of the town. On 10 August, then – the feast of St Lawrence – there was held the best *corrida* that could possibly be organised in the circumstances. It cost a lot of money, for if procuring the men was bad enough – in the end the *corregidor* told us that an assistant of the famous Pepe Hillo was living in retirement quite close by and bestirred himself to send for him – bulls had generally been sent up from Madrid for all the best fights. But in the end everything was arranged and the fight went ahead. Only three or four bulls, but that was quite enough for me. It is without doubt a curious spectacle, but for a woman it is quite revolting, say what you will.[247]

With some difficulty, Junot could organise a bullfight, but there was little he could do to meet the needs of his men, while his wife remained miserable and despondent:

Junot received orders to leave Ledesma and travel to San Felices el Grande. I followed him, but my position had become very difficult: I was in a great deal of discomfort, and I had no means of either returning to France or getting to Madrid. Both journeys would have required a stronger escort than Junot could have spared from his *corps d'armée*, and, as he always said, 'Duty comes first.' And in any case we both believed that we would be in Lisbon within a few weeks: indeed, such was our vanity that we even thought we would be there within a few days. By now it was autumn: always recalcitrant in respect of matters of diet, the soldiers had remained deaf to the orders that had been issued prohibiting them from eating grapes and melons. Eating too much fruit is bad everywhere, but especially so in Spain, and the soldiers of the Eighth Corps had in consequence nearly all been attacked by the worst sort of dysentery. Pretty soon the hospitals of Salamanca, Zamora and the towns round about no longer sufficed to hold the sick, and it became necessary to billet them in private houses. Junot became gloomy, morose even, and so our stay at San Felices only served to increase the depression that had taken possession of my soul. Conjure up the most melancholic images that you can, and you will have a fitting picture of San Felices. Ledesma was a positive paradise by comparison with this place which had gone through the very worst that insurrection and war can offer, and looked as if the entire place had been struck by a gigantic bolt of lightning. Situated in the midst of rocky mountains that were devoid of all vegetation, it was not as sombre as some places I have been in in the Alps and the Pyrenees . . . but even so imagine . . . half-ruined buildings with walls blackened by the smoke of the bivouac fires that had at one time or another been set everywhere by the thoughtless soldiery; a house whose doors and shutters had been stripped of all their metal fittings and could now only be closed by means of some rough wooden bars; a village distant some leagues from anywhere from one which one might attain some assistance: such was the retreat in which I spent a month, lying on a sick bed and thinking of the death that I was sure was coming for myself and my unborn baby . . . My condition became ever more alarming, and I could not get up. Fortunately my travelling bed and some other items of portable furniture had been brought in one of the wagons, and these sufficed to render any room habitable in an instant. But the one I had in San Felices was small and dank, and only got the sun through a small window barely two feet square high up in the wall; as for the floor, it was nothing but beaten earth.[248]

Eventually, however, the campaign got under way. After first taking the Spanish strongholds of Astorga and Ciudad Rodrigo, on 21 July the French crossed the frontier and headed for Almeida, only to find the way blocked by General Craufurd's famous Light Division. Good soldiers though they were, the men of the Light Division found themselves in a difficult position: immediately behind them ran the River Côa, which flows in a deep gorge and was only crossed by a single narrow bridge. Fighting began with a general advance that was fiercely contested by Craufurd's men; with them was a 19-year-old lieutenant of the Ninety-Fifth Rifles from Beverley named George Simmons, who had originally qualified as a doctor:

> The whole plain in our front was covered with horse and foot advancing towards us. The enemy's infantry formed line and, with an innumerable multitude of skirmishers, attacked us fiercely; we repulsed them; they came on again, yelling, with drums beating, frequently the drummers leading . . . French officers like mountebanks running forward and placing their hats upon their swords and capering about like madmen, saying as they turned to their men, 'Come on, children of our country. The first that advances, Napoleon will recompense him!'[249]

Quickly turned out of their initial position, the troops were soon scrambling for the bridge, and for a moment catastrophe threatened. The bridge became blocked by Craufurd's guns and transport, while French cavalry charged in among the retreating infantry and began to cut them down. The Forty-Third Foot, indeed, were soon in real trouble:

> Our line was . . . contracted, and brought under the edge of the ravine. In an instant 4,000 hostile cavalry swept the plain, and our regiment was unaccountably placed within an enclosure of solid masonry at least ten feet high . . . with but one narrow outlet . . . A few moments later and we should have been surrounded, but . . . we contrived to loosen some large stones, when by a powerful exertion we burst the enclosure . . . There was no room to array the line, no time for anything but battle; every captain carried off his company as an independent body, the whole presenting a mass of skirmishers, acting in small parties and under no regular command . . . Having the advantage of ground and number, the enemy broke over the edge of the ravine . . . and their hussars . . . poured down the road, sabreing everything in their way.[250]

Another soldier caught up in the chaos was Edward Costello, a 22-year-old private in the Ninety-Fifth Rifles. Initially apprenticed to a cobbler in Dublin, in 1806 he had been persuaded to enlist in the militia by the tales of an old soldier working for the same master, and then in 1808 volunteered for active service:

> While [we were] hotly engaged with the enemy in our front, one or two troops of their hussars which, from the similarity of their uniform we had taken for German hussars, whipped on our left flank between our company and the [right] wing of the Fifty-Second ... Taken thus unprepared, we could oppose but little or no resistance, and our men were trampled down and sabred on every side. A French dragoon had seized me by the collar, while others, as they passed me, cut at me with their swords. The man who had collared me had his sabre's point at my breast when a volley was fired from our rear by the Fifty-Second ... which tumbled the horse of my captor. He fell heavily with the animal on his leg ... and, dealing him a severe blow on the head with the butt of my rifle, I rushed up to the wall [held by] the Fifty-Second, which I was in the act of clearing at a jump, when I received a shot under the cap of my right knee and instantly fell. In this emergency there seemed a speedy prospect of my again falling into the hands of the French, as the division was in rapid retreat, but a comrade by the name of Little instantly took me on his back, and was proceeding as quick as possible with me towards the bridge of the Côa, over which our men were fast pouring, when he, poor fellow, also received a shot which, passing through his arm, smashed the bone and finally lodged itself in my thigh. In this extremity Little was obliged to abandon me, but, urged by a strong desire to [escape] imprisonment, I made another desperate effort and managed to get over the bridge.[251]

It was a desperate moment. However, grouping his British infantry on a knoll above the crossing, Craufurd managed to hold out long enough for the rest of his forces to get across and then to disengage his rearguard as well. But his casualties were severe. Among those who fell was George Simmons:

> The enemy ... kept up a terrible fire ... Lieutenant Harry Smith, Lieutenant Thomas Smith and Lieutenant Pratt were wounded, and I was shot through the thigh ... Captain Napier took off his neckerchief and gave it to a sergeant, who put it round my thigh and twisted it tight with a ramrod, to stop the bleeding. The firing was so severe that the sergeant, on finishing the job for me, fell with a shot in the head. Captain Napier was also about the same time wounded in the side.[252]

Foolishly several French battalions now assaulted the bridge, but in three separate charges they were shot to pieces, the battle eventually being ended by a heavy thunderstorm. Under cover of the rain, Craufurd and his men slipped away to join the rest of the Anglo-Portuguese army, while the French settled down to besiege Almeida. Though very well fortified and provided for, that fortress did not hold out for very long. In the evening of 26 August a 33-year-old officer on the staff of Marshal Masséna named Jean-Jacques Pelet was reading peacefully on the glacis of the abandoned fort of La Concepción several miles to the east:

Suddenly I felt the earth tremble strongly under my feet. I heard a vast and deep noise. It was an awful explosion. My first thought was for our powder, but the concussion was too great. 'It is the fortress,' I shouted with a feeling of horror and joy. 'It is certainly ours!' My thoughts passed quickly to our army. Now it would be able to concentrate against Wellington's army, which was scattered weakly in cantonments . . . Meanwhile, I ran in all haste towards the fortress, where everyone was in great suspense. Soon an officer arrived from the trenches and announced that he had seen an awful explosion in the middle of the fortress followed by a violent fire, and that a rain of huge stones and debris together with a small piece of artillery had fallen on our approaches.[253]

Now ensconced in Ciudad Rodrigo, Laure Junot was still further away:

One evening just after sunset, the house was shaken by a violent shock. Full of fear, I cried out, 'Is it an earthquake? Is there no danger that we do not have to brave in this wretched country?' There then came a second shock: this time I thought the house was going to come down. 'It is the fortress,' cried all the men, and Junot set off at top speed for an old tower that . . . overhung the town. Reaching it, he shouted, 'It is an extraordinary sight. Laure, you must come and see it: I'll have some men carry you. Almeida is on fire!' So some soldiers duly carried me to the tower, and there I saw a most frightful marvel. A horizon full of flames bordered a sky the colour of slate, and against that sombre background there kept shooting up trails of fire . . . while across the interval that separated us from the fortress there came what sounded like one continuous cry of despair. Truly, there was something in the sight that gave pause to the very bravest.[254]

The explosion at Almeida was beyond doubt one of the greatest ever to have been witnessed in the history of the world up till that point. A day or two afterwards the town was visited by the artilleryman Hulot:

The detonation was terrible and the spectacle truly terrifying . . . Fortunately for them, most of the population that was able to work were to be found at the furthest points from the explosion, as were the majority of the garrison, but the bulk of the women, children and old people were killed, while a number even of our own soldiers were wounded by stones that were hurled more than 300 fathoms through the air . . . On the twenty-eighth I entered the city and visited its bloody ruins. Hardly a house remained inhabitable. Where the powder magazine had stood one saw nothing but a deep pit that was nothing but a jumble of corpses, limbs, missiles and debris of every sort. Further away the disaster had followed a sliding scale in accordance with . . . a series of concentric circles. In the first and smallest, there was trace of neither life nor edifice. Further out there had survived a few stubs of buildings, albeit no more than a few feet of the ground-floor walls heaped with piles of debris, and further out again the damage gradually decreased until one came to the very last buildings of the town, these having generally survived apart from the fact that their roofs had been blown off. Finally one came to the walls and even these had visibly been shaken. Walking along them, I came upon Portuguese gunners who had been maimed and crushed when the pieces they had been serving had been pushed against the parapet by the blast, while, astonishing though it may seem, in one place a heavy gun . . . had been flung over the parapet into the ditch. One of my comrades . . . was later given the task of digging out such items as could be salvaged for the artillery and he assured me that several weeks later he was still coming across severed limbs.[255]

Initially, the French could be said to have enjoyed some success. But, pressing on, the invaders discovered that their progress was going to get a lot harder. The first major town they reached in the sparsely populated frontier district they had to cross was Viseu. What they found there is graphically recounted in the memoirs of André Delagrave, the 45-year-old son of a notary from Argentan who had been one of the famous 'volunteers of 1792', and was now one of Junot's *aides-de-camp*:

On reaching Viseu, the army was astounded to find hardly a single person. The town, a place of from 8,000 to 10,000 souls, was absolutely deserted. The rich had fled to Oporto or Lisbon, while the common folk had hidden themselves in the woods and mountains at some distance from the town. The old, the women, the children, all had gone. The sight of this pretty and picturesquely sited settlement filled the hardest hearts with pity and sadness when we thought of its unfortunate inhabitants wandering amidst the trees and rocks. There are few peoples among whom the resolve to flee at the approach of an enemy is so general. It is a custom that has characterised the Portuguese since the earliest centuries . . . On this occasion, however, the disposition of the nation was somewhat changed. Having had the opportunity to become familiar with them on a number of occasions, many of the inhabitants did not feel any great alarm at the arrival of the French. They knew that, while there was some reason to fear the French soldier in the heat of the first moments of conquest, the latter soon resumed his naturally humane and sociable character so long as he was not exasperated by resistance or unnecessary privations. In consequence, there was no urge to flee the foreign yoke . . . and so . . . a great number of people, and certainly the most sensible elements of the populace, would have been quite happy tranquilly to await the result in their homes. But these sentiments did not suit the English, who had conceived of the idea of turning the whole country . . . into a desert. The most rigorous orders laid down that the inhabitants should abandon anywhere that seemed likely to be occupied by the French after having first destroyed everything that they could not carry away. Secret emissaries of the Junta [*sic*: Delagrave means the Lisbon Regency] supervised their execution with a fury that recalled the conduct of the Inquisition in days gone by. Breaking into people's homes, at the slightest sign that these tyrannical measures were not being obeyed, they would immediately arrest the entire family and confiscate their goods; often enough, meanwhile, one person or another would be handed over to the daggers of the mob, which was always ready to look for scapegoats. Still worse, more than one of the barbarous tortures which Lord

Wellington had used on the soldiers of Tippu Tib during his campaigns in India were used on those Portuguese who wished to remain neutral and tried to remain in their homes by barricading themselves in. Fires were lit to smoke them out, and when they came out their noses or big toes were cut off. Inaccessible to all sentiments of pity, the English general excused his atrocities with the words 'the needs of war'. To escape this horrible persecution, the only thing that each family could do was to go with the flow willy-nilly.[256]

Much of this is wildly exaggerated, though it does seem clear enough that the 'scorched-earth' policy had in many places to be imposed by force, that the evacuation was accompanied by a degree of looting and other lawlessness, and that real suffering was felt among the populace. Another British observer was William Warre, the scion of an English family with deep roots in the port trade, who was serving on the staff of the commander of the Portuguese army, General Beresford:

> Poor things, I could not but pity them. It was most distressing to see them abandoning their habitations and flying away . . . loaded with what little they could carry . . . crying and lamenting [and] followed by their helpless children, while the men drove away their cattle, and all uncertain where they might find a place of safety . . . I pitied them from my heart: to relieve them was not in my power.[257]

Whatever the impact on the civilian population may have been, the impact on the French army was enormous. Jean Noël was a captain in the First Regiment of Horse Artillery from Saint-Dié who had joined the army in 1796 and had since fought mostly in Italy:

> In their retreat, the English had laid waste the countryside, seizing and burning as the population fled before them; they cut the bridges and destroyed everything that might have been of use to us, furnaces and mills, food and forage . . . Being forced to get supplies by any means it could find, and obeying the sad law of warfare, the army resorted to pillage, and, since circumstances did not restrict looting to taking only what was necessary, the inhabitants suffered far more than would have been the case if they had stayed at home. Discipline in the army slackened because the soldiers acquired the habit of looting. Unfortunately the officers, even those on the staff, presented a bad example. The effects on obedience and respect were evident.[258]

In the face of mounting difficulties, the French struggled on along roads reputed to be some of the worst in Portugal. In front of them Wellington's forces at first continued to retreat. Among the wounded travelling ahead of the main army was George Simmons:

> In the evening I was put upon a car drawn by bullocks – the most clumsy machine possible. Here now commenced my misfortunes. The car proceeded, with me upon it, to Pinhel; [I suffered] the most severe torture from the jolting motion to my poor limb sustained at almost every movement. I was lodged in the bishop's house, and . . . I now became anxious to know the nature of my wounds. My trousers and drawers were cut up the side: the latter article of dress was literally glued to my thigh, [and] in fact I had bled so profusely that it had steeped my shirt which stuck

to my skin most unpleasantly. I found the ball had passed . . . directly through my thigh, directly injuring the bone . . . My thigh and leg were frightfully swollen and also the lower part of my body. My ration bread I directed my faithful servant, Henry Short, to make into a large poultice, which was soon done . . . At daylight we proceeded to Celorico, which place we reached in the evening after suffering indescribable torture . . . Several of our poor fellows died from the rough usage they suffered, and several soldiers who had neglected to cover their wounds [found they] now became one frightful mass of maggots . . . The flies and mosquitoes followed us in myriads. We had no means of keeping off the swarms of insects, and the slow pace the bullocks went [at] made us feel the vertical rays of the sun with redoubled force. We had some salt meat as rations, [but] in the feverish state of our existence, we turned from [it] with disgust . . . The driver did not pay attention to the road, so that I was jolted over large stones, which made me suffer extremely. My man, Short, observed his carelessness and gave him a good drubbing, which had a very good effect, and we jogged on afterwards quietly.[259]

Eventually placed on a boat on the River Mondego, Simmons was evacuated by water to Lisbon. Thirty miles to the south-west of Viseu, meanwhile, the army had suddenly turned at bay at the Serra do Buçaco. It was certainly a good place to fight. An undulating granite ridge some 9 miles long covered with outcrops of rock that straddled the French line of march at right angles, the *serra* was extremely steep and rose high above the river valley along which the French were advancing. Yet rather than immediately looking for a way round, Masséna chose to attack head on. On the morning of 27 September, two massive columns of infantry drawn from the corps of Reynier and Ney assailed the Allied centre-left. Despite a thick mist that cloaked their advance, Reynier's men were attacked on all sides at the summit and after some sharp fighting were forced to retreat in disorder. For a good account we may turn to William Grattan, an Anglo-Irish ensign in the Eighty-Eighth Foot who had enlisted the previous year:

Wallace and his regiment, standing alone without orders, had to act for themselves . . . The colonel sent his captain of grenadiers (Dunne) to the right where the rocks were highest to ascertain how matters stood . . . In a few moments Dunne returned almost breathless; he said the rocks were filling fast with Frenchmen, [and] that a heavy column was coming up the hill beyond . . . Wallace, with a steady but cheerful countenance turned to his men, and . . . said, 'Now Connaught Rangers . . . when I bring you face to face with those French rascals . . . don't give the false touch, but push home to the muzzle! I have nothing more to say, and if I had it would be of no use, for in a minute there'll be such an infernal noise . . . you won't be able to hear yourselves.' This address went home to the hearts of us all, but there was no cheering: a steady and determined calm had taken the place of any lighter feeling . . . Wallace then threw the battalion from line into column . . . and moved on . . . at a quick pace. On reaching the rocks, he . . . threw himself from his horse and . . . ran forward . . . into the midst of the terrible flame in his front. All was now confusion and uproar, smoke, fire and bullets; officers and soldiers . . . knocked down in every direction; British, French and Portuguese mixed together; while in the midst of all was Wallace fighting . . . at the head of his devoted followers and calling out to his soldiers to press forward.[260]

Present in the ranks of the French forces was Jean-Baptiste Lemonnier-Delafosse, a captain in the Thirty-First Line. Advancing up the hillside some distance to the south of the spot occupied by Grattan and the Connaught Rangers, he and his men were checked by heavy fire before they even reached the summit:

The task facing us was a full-scale assault, an escalade even, while we could not expect any artillery support, as the only positions available for the cannon were the spurs at the foot of the mountain, from which the only thing they could do was to fire blindly into the air in the hope that they might hit something . . . I still wonder even today how, laden down with their packs and muskets, our poor soldiers could have pulled themselves up through the broom that cloaked the hillside: even though I was wearing gaiters and carrying nothing but my sabre, I found it a constant struggle to make progress . . . At length, overcoming every obstacle, the ardent courage of the soldiers allowed the heads of each column to reach a point half-way up the mountain in musket range of the enemy. At this point an accident of the terrain allowed the Thirty-First to make an attempt at forming line, but there was no escape from the terrible plunging fire with which the enemy assailed us and struck men down with every shot. Several other regiments also tried to form line, and succeeded in doing so, but in the Thirty-First only a part of the first battalion managed to execute the command: in so far as the company which I myself led is concerned, I never managed to get more than four files together, all the other soldiers being shot down as they came up . . . Nevertheless, we eventually got into some sort of order, and, deployed anyhow though we were, resolved to endure the fire of the English line. Indeed, little by little we assumed the form of a two-deep line just like theirs and began to fight in the same fashion: I swear that in all my life I have never seen troops fire with such speed and precision . . . As for me, some minutes after I had begun trying to get my company into line, I was struck by a bullet just above my right eye. The wound wasn't serious, but I was none the less thrown to the ground . . . Though both stunned by the blow and blinded by the blood that was running from my wound, I picked myself up and began to look for my lieutenant, Gay, with a view to handing over the command. No sooner had I got to my feet, however, than on all sides the soldiers began to retreat. Had any such order been given? I do not believe so, but, for all that, the movement was complied with no less readily.[261]

Lemonnier-Delafosse escaped the slaughter, and was later awarded the Legion of Honour for his courage. But his regiment had lost 296 men killed and wounded. To the right, meanwhile, things went even worse for the French. Ney's men moved forward in fine style, but they were much harassed by skirmishers from the Light Division. Waiting in hiding for them, meanwhile, were the rest of Craufurd's men, who proceeded to give them short shrift:

With a division of his corps [formed] in column of mass, [Marshal Ney] advanced against the height occupied by our . . . division . . . During his advance the enemy experienced little opposition, and without difficulty gained possession of a village situated on the brow of the ascent, but no sooner did he crown the height than he found us drawn up to receive him, and his column became exposed to a most destructive fire, both of musketry and artillery. This . . . was but of short duration, yet . . . the leading regiments of the assailants were almost totally annihilated. A charge of bayonets followed: the whole column was routed and driven down the hill with prodigious slaughter. We pursued them into the village, when we were stopped by some artillery which they had there in reserve. While endeavouring to regain the hill, I ran into a house . . . to avoid their fire, and . . . observed the end of a sword hanging from the chimney just below the jamb. Thinking there must be an owner to it, I looked up the chimney and discovered a French officer, who had hidden there to escape pursuit. I immediately pulled him down and told him that he was my prisoner, upon which he took out a gold watch and offered it to me if I would release him. I immediately took the watch, and was leaving in a hurry, when, unfortunately for the Frenchman, I met another soldier at the door, who, however, consented to let him go upon his giving him his gold epaulettes.[262]

Despite the considerable victory that Buçaco amounted to, the position could not be held: the French found a way around the north end of the *serra*, and were soon bearing down on Coimbra once more. At this Wellington fell back yet again. With him went thousands of refugees. With the autumn rain falling in torrents, it was a miserable scene. Present with the Thirty-Fourth Foot was Joseph Sherer, a 21-year-old lieutenant who had been serving in the army since January 1807:

My pen altogether fails me: I feel that no powers of description can convey . . . the cheerless desolation we daily witnessed on our march from the Mondego . . . Wherever we moved, the mandate which enjoined the wretched inhabitants . . . to forsake their homes had gone before us. The villages were deserted; the churches . . . were empty; the mountain cottages stood open and untenanted . . . The flanks of our line of march were literally covered with the flying population of the country. In Portugal there are at no time many facilities for travelling, and these few the exigencies of the army had very greatly diminished. Rich indeed were those . . . who still retained . . . any mode of transporting their families and property . . . for respectable men and delicate women . . . might on every side be seen walking slowly and painfully on foot, encumbered by heavy burdens of clothes, bedding and food.[263]

As for the troops, they were little better off. John Douglas was a private in the First Regiment of Foot from Lurgan, who had enlisted at the age of 20 early in 1809, and since served at Walcheren:

We . . . encamped in a beautiful field of grapes, but in the course of the night it commenced to rain with a gale of wind, and we were awakened in the morning . . . [by] the water running over us in the trench as we lay between the bushes. To attempt a description of our misery would be a task too hard for my old pen . . . All the resource we had was to stand upright and let the water run off as well as possible.[264]

But for the soldiers, at least, help was at hand. For the past year British engineers had at Wellington's direction been masterminding the creation of a series of defensive lines across the peninsula on which Lisbon is built. Encompassed by the Atlantic ocean on the one hand and the immensely broad river Tagus on the other, this could only be reached via a narrow neck of land that was entirely blocked by a range of rugged hills centred on the towns of Torres Vedras and Sintra. Reaching the northern fringes of these hills, the French were stunned by what they saw. Let us here turn to Jean-Jacques Pelet:

> The Lines were of such an extraordinary nature that I daresay there was no other position in the world that could be compared to them . . . The right extended from Alhandra; the centre was at Monte Agraço . . . facing Sobral, and the left reached through Torres Vedras to the sea. There was a very narrow defile in front of Sobral, and, beyond, the mountain rose up again suddenly like a gigantic wall of rocks extending on both flanks. On both sides of the passage two deep valleys full of ravines opened out and extended all the way to the sea and the Tagus. They served as the first obstacle of the primary defence line . . . Every part of the mountain not covered by rocks or absolutely inaccessible, all the avenues and all the small detached abutments useful for observation had been carefully entrenched . . . The enemy had . . . conceived a perfect defence for this country and had executed it completely to their advantage . . . It was very difficult, if not impossible, to force the Lines without losing a dreadful number of soldiers.[265]

To be faced by such an obstacle came as a terrible shock, and all the more so as the French had believed that the Anglo-Portuguese forces were in such a state of disorder that a decisive victory was literally just a few short miles ahead. The mood at French headquarters, indeed, was very bleak. As Marbot, who had been assigned to Masséna as one of his *aides-de-camp*, recounts:

> Neither Ney, who had just spent a year at Salamanca, nor Masséna, who for six months had been making ready to invade Portugal, had the least inkling of these gigantic works. Reynier and Junot were equally ignorant. Most surprising of all – incredible, indeed, if the fact were not absolutely certain – the French government itself did not know that the hills of Sintra had been fortified. It is inconceivable that the emperor, who had agents in every country, could have omitted to send some to Lisbon. At that time . . . thousands of ships were daily bringing into the Tagus stores for Wellington's army, and it would have been perfectly easy to have introduced some spies among the numerous sailors and clerks employed on these vessels. Knowledge of all kinds can be obtained by money; it was by this means that the emperor kept himself informed of all that went on in England and among the great powers of Europe. Nevertheless, he never gave Masséna any information as to the defences of Lisbon.[266]

In the circumstances, it would have been entirely understandable if Masséna had ordered an immediate retreat. However, this was not a course he would contemplate. Instead the marshal resolved to hold his position in the hope that something might turn up. With a situation of live and let live established at the outposts, the business of the moment became that of survival. At first, it seems, things were not too bad, the countryside having been stripped by no means as thoroughly as Wellington had wished. As witness to this, we have Jean-Baptiste Barrès, a young man from Blesle in the Auvergne who had volunteered for the *vélites* of the Guard in 1804 and been appointed to a commission in the Sixteenth Light Infantry in 1809:

> On the eighth of October, before Leiria, in a torrential rain, the company could find no other shelter . . . than the church, of which it gladly took possession. There was corn and wood in plenty, so we had soon established a bivouac so comfortable that we had no cause to regret the houses, which were crammed with troops. We found excellent wine there, and, as there was plenty of sugar in the bags and baggage, we made a lot of mulled wine, which restored our bodies, worn out with exertion and soaked to the bones . . . On the following day, the morning being delightfully fine, I went for a walk with several officers along the neighbouring slopes, covered with vines not yet stripped of their grapes, and fig trees bending under the weight of their fruit.[267]

Such plenty did not last long, however. Very soon, the army was having to survive by pillage. As the artillery officer Noël recounts, the price was terrible:

> When we arrived there were still some supplies to be had in the countryside. These were quickly exhausted, and, in order to live, recourse was had to marauding. Each corps, each branch, organised itself in its own way. Detachments, at first sent out into the immediate neighbourhood, were forced to go further and further away. The parties, commanded by officers of various ranks, split up as they fanned out. The result was that the men, separated from their leaders, gave themselves up to every sort of pillage, and even to the practice of cruelty on the miserable peasants who had thought that their wretched poverty would protect them from such violence. This was done not so much to force the peasants to reveal hoards of grain, or the hiding place of cattle, as to compel them to hand over money . . . Wretchedness became so widespread that discipline suffered to the point where even the most basic military duties were neglected. One day . . . we came upon a bivouac that had been established to protect Sobral . . . All the detachment's weapons had been stacked and not a single man, not even a sentinel, was on guard . . . Hunger had driven all of them to go out pillaging although they were only a couple of paces away from the enemy's advanced posts.[268]

As the French troops grew more desperate, so ever grimmer scenes were enacted. In this respect, we have a particularly graphic account from the pen of Lemonnier-Delafosse:

> The French army entered Portugal with six days' worth of supplies in each soldier's

haversack, and on top of that a few wagons. It was, therefore, without any proper magazines, and soon it found itself without food of any sort. Nevertheless, it was necessary to live. Once the initial resources had run out . . . a regular system of marauding was organised . . . Woe betide the peasant who was caught by such an expedition! The poor unfortunate was stripped of all he had and often . . . put to death by men whom hunger . . . had rendered cruel and savage. When the troops were operating in places they did not know, guides were needed. If no one came forward at their call, someone would be seized at random. Having got such a person, he would be ordered to take them to a village . . . and, once he had got there, to point out where all the food had been hidden . . . The poor devil would not know where it was any more than those who were searching for it, and the confusion into which he was necessarily thrown was taken as proof of bad faith by the soldiers. Threats were then quickly followed by actions: a rope would be put round his neck, and the unfortunate man would hear the words, 'Up you go until you tell us where the grain is!' As he could give no answer, he would be strung up until he began to turn blue, whereupon he would be taken down and given another chance to speak. Alas! Worse than barbarous as they were, these atrocious means sometimes succeeded, but this was only when fate had pitched upon an inhabitant of the village that was being raided. Unless that was the case, such men could reveal nothing, and so the soldiers said to them in their ferocity, 'Oh, you don't want to tell us where the grain is, do you? You are a brigand: hanged you were and hanged you will remain!'[269]

As the winter wore on and real starvation set in, so the bonds of military discipline began to break down altogether as desperate men began to strike out for themselves. There is, for example, the tale of 'Marshal Stock-Pot':

A French sergeant, wearied of the misery in which the army was living, resolved to decamp and live in comfort. To this end he persuaded about a hundred of the worst characters in the army, and, going with them to the rear, took up his quarters in a vast convent, deserted by the monks, but still full of furniture and provisions. He increased his store largely by carrying off everything in the neighbourhood that suited him . . . and the leader received the expressive if contemptuous name of 'Marshal Stock-Pot'. The scoundrel had also carried off numbers of women, and, being joined before long by the scum of three armies attracted by the prospect of unrestrained debauchery, he formed a band of some 300 English, French and Portuguese deserters who lived as a happy family in one unbroken orgy. This brigandage had been going on for some months, when . . . three battalions . . . were told off to attack the convent. That den having been carried after a brief resistance, Masséna had 'Marshal Stock-Pot' shot.[270]

To add to the general horror, the civilians who had remained beyond the protection of the Lines responded to the brutality with which they were treated in kind. From the very beginning of the campaign the existence of both a substantial force of local militia and the irregular home-guard known as the *Ordenança* ensured that the French encountered much irregular resistance. But the straits to which the inhabitants of such towns as Santarem were driven ensured that the French were assailed by a genuine 'people's war':

> In front of an isolated house we found . . . four bodies hanging from a tree. On going inside a hideous spectacle confronted us. On a wall was nailed up the newly flayed skin of a man. Underneath was written in Portuguese, 'French dragoon skinned alive for hanging our brothers.'[271]

One man who experienced the depredations of the *Ordenança* at first hand was the artillery officer Hulot, who had fallen sick and been left behind at Ciudad Rodrigo, but now found himself struggling to reach Masséna with a column of reinforcements commanded by General Foy:

> On the thirtieth [of January], some two hours after we set out we found ourselves at the mouth of a defile whose entrance was masked by a small village. The general and I were chatting to one another with nothing ahead of us but a few *voltigeurs*, when all of a sudden we were assailed by a volley of musketry that struck down several of our soldiers. Immediately, the entire force dashed forward, and, in an instant, the few inhabitants of the village who were still in residence had been put to the sword, and the entire place set alight. With some difficulty I managed to hold back my own men, however, and, taking charge of the baggage, I led them to a nearby hillside. Very visible as it was, this covering force served a very useful purpose . . . for it was clear that the firing had not come from the inhabitants, but rather a party of guerrillas who had hidden in the unhappy place and then slipped away. If everyone had followed their first instincts, they would assuredly have had good sport with us! General Foy praised me for my foresight, and then placarded the ruins of the village as a warning against further attacks . . . On the thirty-first, from the crack of dawn onwards we tramped through countryside infested with partisan bands commanded by British officers between the rivers Zezere and Moncul . . . and eventually made camp in a village on the right bank of the latter stream. The next day, 1 February, turning sharply to the right . . . we followed a narrow path that was very difficult for horses along the gorge though which flowed the river . . . while our progress was followed on the other bank by large masses of enemy troops. From time to time they came down to the water's edge to shoot at us, but, while we fired back, we did not stop. At eight o'clock we arrived at the foot of the highest and most redoubtable of the chains of mountains that run across Beira in the form of the Serra da Estrella . . . Still pursued and harassed by Portuguese snipers, our column made its way up the mountain. At the summit, we ceased to be pursued by musket shots, but it now looked as if our assailants had simply been trying to deliver us into the hands of an opponent who was even more cruel . . . Thus, with nightfall such a storm as you can only get at the sort of height at which we found ourselves descended upon us. So great was its violence that even the strongest men had to make great efforts to stand before the wind, while, lashing down at high speed, the rain fell in torrents. At first we did our best to support and

protect the weaker soldiers . . . but by eleven o'clock everyone was thinking only of themselves . . . and exhausted men were collapsing on the ground without the strength to get up again . . . At last at four o'clock in the morning we reached a miserable village . . . We had been longing to reach the shelter it represented, but, alas, it could not hold all our men, and in the morning we found numbers of unfortunates strewn lifelessly along the main street.[272]

Nor were things much better back at Ciudad Rodrigo, where Madame Junot was enduring a thoroughly miserable confinement:

I suppose I ought to speak of Ciudad Rodrigo, but nothing can possibly give an idea of that mountain of ruins in the midst of which a few houses that were still intact stood up like milestones. Even these, however, were held up by enormous wooden buttresses which gave a sinister aspect to the narrow streets. No sooner had I entered than my heart was seized with anguish, and I had to close my eyes. General Cacault, who was the governor of the place, had been warned that I was coming, and had informed me that he had prepared me a comfortable lodging, but all 'comfortable' turned out to mean was that I would be kept dry from the rain, which at that season of the year fell in torrents . . . [The] house had belonged to a canon and was the best in the town . . . but it lacked for everything, while its windows looked out on nothing but the sick and wounded soldiers left behind by Masséna who wandered the streets . . . Of all the places in the peninsula, Ciudad Rodrigo is the most wild and the most savage. There is not a tree to be found around its old walls, and it truly feels as if it has been anathematised by nature . . . But the desolate countryside was not the only misfortune that we experienced during our stay: we had literally no food, and even golden daggers could not have got us any: all the peasants had fled, and the countryside had become a desert. Because the lower floors were too dark, I chose a room in the upper part of the house, and there got on with preparing my baby's layette. Yet the sight of its little garments often filled my eyes with tears. A month went by before I got any letters from France while I heard nothing at all from Junot or the rest of the army: it is beyond doubt the first time in history that an army of 60,000 men has marched across a little river to invade a country and the next day left behind nothing but the most profound silence . . . It was as if they had all been struck down by death. Meanwhile, General Cacault talked to me far more than he should . . . of the dangers that I was running in Ciudad Rodrigo on account of Don Julían [Sánchez] knowing that I was here . . . while assailing me with talk of the malignant fever that was establishing itself in the town on account of the multitude of corpses that had been buried in shallow graves during the siege, not to mention the manner in which dogs were every day digging up arms and legs, this being something that I myself saw the first time I went out for a walk along the battlements.[273]

Safely delivered of a son whom she named Alfred, Madame Junot was eventually able to make her way back to France. Thousands of her compatriots were not so lucky, however. By the close of the year dozens of men were dying every week in the French cantonments.

Yet at Masséna's headquarters at Santarem, Pelet found time to attend to the literary needs of his fellow staff officers and even to revel in the superiority of French culture and the esteem in which it had seemingly been held in Portugal:

> We formed a small and very incomplete library . . . On our trips . . . we had found most of the good French books. In Spain the mere possession of a great number of them would have carried us into the arms of the Inquisition: Voltaire, Rousseau, Helvetius, Condorcet, Dupuis, Raynal, our classic novels, even the works of Restif de la Bretonne. Specifically, there were many works on the Revolution, books in which its principles were praised and developed, and finally some military works, among which I had Puységur. What was interesting was that our literature was much more abundant than that of any other people: although [the Portuguese] had lived for such a long time under the influence of the English, the works of the latter were infinitely less numerous in the libraries where I had been. There were a great many of them, and only a few large villages where we could not find the *Encyclopédie*.[274]

What, meanwhile, of the situation inside the Lines? During the retreat from Almeida, there had been much grumbling and discontent in the army, but all such feelings were now swept away. From Wellington's headquarters the *aide-de-camp* Alexander Gordon wrote to his brother Lord Aberdeen:

> We have now been three or four days under cover of the forts which have been erected across the country for the defence of Lisbon, and our army is all assembled to be able to take up any position on which the battle will be fought at the shortest notice. Lord Wellington has chosen his ground for fighting in whatever way [the enemy] may come . . . They must have suffered uncommonly from the weather – we have lately had six days of incessant rain. Our troops have been under cover while theirs are exposed to it. Our army is in high spirits and no one fears the approaching termination of the campaign. I really think Masséna never before was in such a scrape . . . Nothing can equal the conduct of Lord Wellington . . . I hope to be able very soon to tell you of a most brilliant victory.[275]

In so far as the officers and men of the British army were concerned, it was a time that was remembered as one of relaxation and laughter. John Cowell Stepney, an ensign in the Third Foot Guards who had enlisted the previous year, recalled:

> Among others of my comrades, I was a sportsman: woodcocks were numerous, and snipes were to be found on the low marshy grounds. We had at this time no dogs, but Lord Wellington kindly allowed officers of his acquaintance to take his, and we frequently did so to our pleasure and profit, as not only the sport, but the result of it when a good bag was made, was most acceptable . . . In preparation for a day's sport, two of us were seated one fine morning at breakfast in my quarters . . . We were in a hurry to proceed to our day's sport, but found our servants dilatory in making the necessary preparations for us. After sundry hailings and ejaculations symptomatic of our impatience, one of our people at last came to us with a face in

which was depicted surprise, risibility and disgust. On our inquiring what had happened, he replied, 'Oh, we have got him out!' 'Got whom out?', we asked. 'Why, Sir, in drawing water I had the misfortune to drop the camp kettle into the well, and in trying to fish it out with a hook, I pulled up by the collar of his great-coat a dead French infantry soldier.' We had been drinking the water for a month![276]

In another part of the British cantonments, alas, a rather different 'bag' was the subject of discussion. At the centre of the incident was the Dorset soldier William Lawrence:

We were cantoned in a large cellar, but it was unfortunately empty, or at least there was no wine in it . . . The owner of our cellar generally visited us every day, and we could not help thinking after a time that he seemed to take particular notice of a large . . . bin that two of our men were using to sleep in, so we moved it one morning, and found that the ground underneath had been disturbed. Of course, we thought that there must be some treasure concealed there, so we went to work with our bayonets, having no other tools at hand, and soon we came across a large jar which we found contained bags of dollars, about 250 in each bag, which treasure we distributed privately among the cellar company, carefully . . . returning the earth to its proper place with the chest on top of it, so that a minute eye could not have told that it had been disturbed. Next morning as usual the owner came, bringing with him two labourers . . . That night he must have dreamt of our manoeuvre, for he now . . . moved the chest, and . . . found the bird had flown. I shall never forget the rage the man was in . . . He cried, 'Ladrón! Ladrón!', which was his way of expressing 'Thief! Thief!', but, finding that we did not take much notice of him, he reported his loss to the colonel . . . but as the colonel did not understand his language, I was sent for, as by that time I was pretty well acquainted with it, and on my replying . . . that he required a corporal and three privates to guard a stack of wood, the colonel told me to let him know that he had nothing to do with it.[277]

Such behaviour, unfortunately, was by no means uncommon, though the booty – most often animals, food and wine – was rarely as great as the 7,000 dollars netted by Lawrence and his colleagues. Indeed, British accounts are often positively cheerful in their admission of what went on. One such comes from the pen of a rifle officer named John Kincaid:

We certainly lived in clover while we remained here: everything we saw was our own, seeing no one there who had a more legitimate claim, and every field was a vineyard. Ultimately it was considered too much trouble to pluck the grapes, as there were a number of poor native thieves in the habit of coming . . . every day to steal some, so that a soldier had nothing to do but to watch one until he was making off with his basketful, when he would very deliberately relieve him of his load without wasting any words about the bargain. The poor wretch would follow the soldier to the camp in the hope of having his basket returned, as it generally was, when emptied.[278]

For another account let us turn to Edward Costello, who had survived the wound he had received at the river Côa and now recovered sufficiently to rejoin his battalion at a small village called Arruda:

Arruda . . . presented a picture of most wanton desolation. Furniture of a most splendid description in many instances was laid open to the spoliation of the soldiery. Elegant looking glasses wrenched from the mantelpieces were wantonly broken to obtain bits to shave by, and their [frames] with chairs, tables, etc., etc., used as common firewood . . . Tom Crawley was particularly pre-eminent in this havoc: his enormous strength and length fitting him especially for the pulling down and breaking up department. Our company was one night on picket at Arruda. We had, as usual, made a blazing fire close to the stable of a large house, which in the morning we had noticed contained a very handsome carriage (the only one, by the by, that I had ever seen in Portugal). Rather late in the evening we missed Tom, who, by the way, had a great love of exploring the houses in the village, and whom we imagined to be employed in his favourite amusement, looking for wine. After having consumed sundry chairs to keep alive our fire, we found it necessary to obtain fresh fuel, and, while consulting where it was to come from, one man, with an oath, proposed to burn the Portuguese coach. The novelty of the thing . . . was received with acclamations, and . . . several started up on their legs for the purpose. The stable doors were immediately opened, and the coach wheeled backwards into the blazing fire. 'This will make a jolly roast!', exclaimed several of the men as the paint and panelling began to crack under the influence of the heat. Our scamps were laughing and enjoying what they called a capital joke, but, just as the flames were beginning to curl up round the . . . vehicle, a roar like that of a bull came from its interior . . . Immediately afterwards, one of the windows was dashed out, and Tom Crawley's big head was thrust through [it] amid shouts of laughter from the men . . . We had some trouble ere we could extricate the poor fellow, and then not before he was severely scorched. It afterwards appeared he had gone half-tipsy into the carriage, and was taking a snooze when he was so warmly woke. After this occurrence Crawley used to boast of going to sleep with one eye open.[279]

What made such behaviour still worse was that even within the Lines, the civilian population suffered terribly. A particularly compassionate observer was the rifle officer John Leach, in which respect it is but fair to note that the redcoats were by no means all of them thieving brutes:

Thousands of the unfortunate inhabitants of the provinces through which our army had recently retreated . . . were endeavouring to exist between Lisbon and the Lines. There was, therefore, an immense population hemmed up in a small space of country, hundreds of them without a house to cover them or food to eat, except what was afforded by the bounty of the rich at Lisbon, and by the liberal subscriptions raised for them in England. In the course of the winter the number of Portuguese who actually died of want was quite dreadful. It was not unusual to see hordes of these poor wretches, old and young, male and female in rags, the very picture of death, round a miserable fire, on which was placed an earthen vessel, full of such herbs as could be gathered in the fields and hedges. Thousands contrived to drag on a miserable existence on this vile sustenance. Their death-like, emaciated faces were sufficient to have touched the heart of the most callous and unfeeling. The British soldiers assisted them by every means in their power, and in the Light Division (as well as, I conclude, in every other) soup was made from the heads and offal of the cattle killed for the troops, and distributed among the starving inhabitants.[280]

Back in the French lines, by the beginning of March all was in ruins. Masséna had done well – extraordinarily well, indeed – but the game was up, and on 5 March 1811 his forces evacuated their cantonments and set off for the Spanish border. As they went, however, they exacted a terrible revenge. Wounded at the Côa, George Simmons was back with the Ninety-Fifth Rifles:

The Light Division . . . entered Santarem, where we remained about an hour. How different this town now appeared . . . The houses were torn and dilapidated, and the few miserable inhabitants moving skeletons; the streets strewn with every description of household furniture, half-burnt and destroyed, and many . . . quite impassable with filth and rubbish, with an occasional man, mule or donkey rotting and corrupting and filling the air with pestilential vapours . . . Two young ladies had been brutally violated in a house that I entered, and were unable to rise from a mattress of straw . . . Kincaid and I went into a house where an old man was seated: he had been lame in the legs for many years. A French soldier . . . had given him two deep sabre wounds on the head and another on the arm . . . It is beyond everything horrid the way these European savages have treated the unfortunate Portuguese. Almost every man they get hold of they murder. The women they use too brutally for me to describe. They even cut the throats of infants. The towns are mostly on fire – in short, they are guilty of every species of cruelty. I have seen such sights as have made me shudder with horror, and which I really could not have believed unless an eyewitness of them.[281]

Another eyewitness was Commissary Schaumann:

Never during the whole of the war did I again see such a horrible sight . . . Murdered peasants lay in all directions. At one place I halted at a door to beg water of a man who was sitting on the threshold . . . He proved to be dead, and had . . . been placed there . . . for a joke. The inside of the house was ghastly to behold. All its inmates had been murdered in their beds . . . The corpse of another . . . peasant had been placed in a ludicrous position in a hole in a garden wall . . . to make fun of us when we came along.[282]

What French bayonets had spared, French-induced hunger had not. Time and again, the British came across the most distressing scenes. As an example, we have the sight witnessed by an anonymous sergeant of the Light Division:

A large house . . . was discovered near the line of our route. Prompted by curiosity, several men turned aside to inspect the interior, where they found a number of famished wretches crowded together . . . Thirty women and children had perished for want of food, and lay dead upon the floor, while about half that number of survivors sat watching the remains of those who had fallen. The soldiers offered some refreshment to these unfortunate persons, but one man only had sufficient strength to eat.[283]

Still more touching was the little group of victims encountered by Joseph Donaldson of the Ninety-Fourth Foot:

On the top of a hill . . . we found three children lying, two already dead but the other . . . still breathing. There were pieces of biscuit lying beside them, which our soldiers had brought, but it was too late . . . One of them had expired with [a] bit in his mouth.[284]

Many British soldiers were not so compassionate, however. Costello and a friend called Wilkie were among the many men scouring the countryside for whatever they could find:

We stumbled at last on a small cottage into which we entered in full hopes of having made a substantial discovery. An emaciated half-starved looking hag squatted by some extinguished embers like the last survivor of a universal wreck. She was, indeed, the only living inhabitant we had seen in the village, and remained squatting by the embers as if permitted that privilege only to recount her tale. The old soul remained a fixture until Wilkie, suspecting something, pressed her to move. 'Non hai nada!' screamed the old lady. 'Non hai nada!' ('There is nothing.') 'Oh, but there is,' replied my comrade, until, growing furious, he upset the old woman from her position and out rolled a loaf of bread from under her, as natural as if it had been an egg from under a hen. Wilkie pounced at it instantly, and the miserable old creature burst into tears and screamed herself almost into fits. Her cries in a few seconds brought in her daughter, who, unable to keep herself concealed at this agonising appeal of her parent rushed forward to her assistance. Never before did I see such a pitiful pair: both were almost cadaverous with want and begged hard for the loaf . . . and at last Wilkie and I willingly shared it with them.[285]

The French, however, did not escape scot-free. Indeed, with discipline and comradeship in a state of collapse, they were by now at the last extremity:

When men became so fatigued with marching and want of food that they could not go further, they were left to perish on the roadside. Disease raged freely in their ranks, but the men . . . would not even lift their comrades to the side of a wall to die in peace, but allowed them to . . . be trodden to death under the feet of the baggage mules . . . Those French soldiers who were lying on the roads in a still sensible state soon suffered retribution at the hands of the Portuguese peasantry. Wherever they were found . . . the first step was to strip the victims of all clothing and leave them in a state of nudity. Those still living were summarily dispatched by having their brains . . . dashed out . . . or [being] stabbed, and when all else failed suffered the death of stoning . . . The very bodies of the dead were kicked about as if they had been footballs, and every indignity that could be heaped upon the inanimate frame was resorted to.[286]

By now, then, the French were little more than a horde of fugitives. The last fight of the campaign came at the border town of Sabugal. Following a desperate attempt on the part of Masséna to maintain at least some small lodgement within the borders of Portugal, the full force of Wellington's army descended on him. Thanks to the incompetence of the temporary commander of the Light Division, Sir William Erskine, however, the plan of action miscarried, and a single brigade of his men found itself fighting the entire French army. There followed a bitter struggle:

> Two guns opened on us and fired several discharges of round and grape. The guns were repeatedly charged, but the enemy were so strong that we were obliged to retire a little. Three columns of the enemy moved forward with drums beating and the officers dancing like madmen with their hats frequently hoisted upon their swords. Our men kept up a terrible fire. They went back a little and we followed . . . Lieutenant Arbuthnot was killed, Lieutenant Haggup wounded [and] Colonel Beckwith wounded and his horse shot.[287]

In the nick of time the beleaguered 'light-bobs' were rescued by the second brigade of the Light Division. A veteran of this part of the fight was John Dobbs, a 19-year-old Dubliner who had served in the Armagh militia before securing a commission in the Second Battalion of the Fifty-Second Foot:

> Hearing the First Brigade under Sir Sidney Beckwith engaged, our brigade returned to their support. The First Battalion [of the Fifty-Second Foot: unusually, both battalions of this regiment were serving in the same brigade] arrived just in time to save them and capture a howitzer. It was taken by my brother's company from the enemy. The enemy made several desperate attempts to retake it from my brother who, with two other companies of the Fifty-Second held [his] ground and the howitzer by lining a walk in [its] rear. We came up on the right of the First Battalion . . . in line, being received by a heavy cannonade and volleys of musketry which we returned with interest . . . A heavy downfall of rain occurring in the middle of our advance, the firing on both sides ceased on the instant – not a musket would go off.[288]

In the opposing ranks once more was the infantry officer Jean-Baptiste Lemonnier-Delafosse:

> The battle . . . cost my regiment in particular many casualties. Without the support of a single gun, it had to bear the full fire of the enemy for the entire day, and lost 120 men, of whom fifty were killed. On the field I saw what the effect of a ball could be even at the end of its course. Arrayed with his men in square, the captain of the *voltigeur* company . . . saw a cannon ball rolling towards him in just the same manner

as if it had been tossed by a child. Despite our cries of warning, he refused to open his ranks to let it pass, and was in the very act of shouting out, 'There's no danger: it is spent!', when it suddenly struck a stone. Notwithstanding its apparent lack of momentum, it bounced up and took him full in the chest; smashed to pieces, he fell dead in an instant . . . That same day of battle I also saw something so extraordinary that it almost defies belief. It was like black magic. One of our officers was advancing on the enemy when he had his head taken off by a cannon shot, and yet his body remained on its feet, and, with sabre held aloft, took a couple more paces before collapsing. How is one to explain such a thing? Had the man's innate will survived? Or was it simply a reflex action of nerve and muscle? The matter will have to be resolved by someone more learned than me. All I know is that I know of nothing more hideous than the sight of that corpse marching on, intent on dealing the death blow which it had already suffered.[289]

Badly battered, at length the French gave way. Caught up in the general retreat across the frontier was a weary and disillusioned Jean Noël, whose last act in the campaign had ironically been to fire a 101-gun salute at the miserable Portuguese village of Alfayates in honour of the arrival of the birth of Napoleon's son, the King of Rome.

When we had crossed into Portugal on 15 September 1810, the artillery train of the Eighth Corps possessed 142 wagons . . . and 891 horses. When we returned to Spain we had only 49 wagons and 182 horses . . . I had no idea of what we were to do . . . It was quite certain that for the time being our army was in no state to undertake even the smallest offensive action. Our supply situation was deplorable; we lacked everything: food, ammunition, clothing, boots, money and horses . . . Six months of deprivation in a country without any supplies, obtaining no provisions from outside and depending on marauding to live, had not lessened the army's courage, but [it] had exhausted it and destroyed its discipline. Much had been left to the soldier's initiative and the soldier had taken advantage of it. We had left sad memories behind us with the Portuguese, and they would curse the name of France for a long while. Survival had been necessary, it is true, but bad soldiers had behaved like brigands towards the unfortunate peasantry . . . I had seen things so dreadful that they can never be forgotten.[290]

* * *

The retreat of Masséna's army is an excellent place at which to pause for another moment of reflection. In the eighteen months that had passed between Ocaña and Sabugal, much had happened. The French had over-run Andalucía, and taken the key fortresses of Ciudad Rodrigo, Almeida and Badajoz, the latter having been seized by an expeditionary force dispatched from Seville by Marshal Soult. Meanwhile, the heart had been cut from the Spanish cause: Cádiz and a few scattered regions around the periphery of the country might still hold out, but the days of large armies sallying forth to do battle with the invaders were gone for good. All that was left was the guerrilla war. This was by no means devoid of success: while regular troops under commanders such as Villacampa, Ballesteros, Porlier and Sánchez engaged in endless small-scale operations against the French, in the north in particular self-appointed chieftains such as Espoz, Martín, Merino and Longa were building up substantial bands of followers. But in the end, however brave and dedicated, these leaders could not save Spain. With every Spanish fortress that was taken, their ability to operate was undermined and the danger to their survival was increased. In theory, then, a complete French victory was a distinct possibility. The only force now standing in Napoleon's way was the victorious Anglo-Portuguese army, and the war had essentially resolved itself into a race against time. Could Wellington rescue the Spaniards before they were crushed? For a moment, then, everything hung in the balance.

Chapter 5

Race Against Time

It is often forgotten that the Peninsular War was not just limited to the struggle between Wellington and his opponents. Just as fierce fighting had continued to rage while the Anglo-Portuguese army prepared its defences to meet the onslaught of Marshal Masséna in 1810, so the agony of the latter's army before the Lines of Torres Vedras was accompanied by bitter fighting in the rest of the peninsula. As for the shape of this fighting, it had but one aspect. In Portugal Masséna was going nowhere – was besieged and beaten, even – but in Spain the French forces remorselessly over-ran position after position. And, for all his success in Portugal hitherto, Wellington knew that a fresh invasion launched by the sort of forces that could be unleashed against him were the Spaniards to give up the fight would be a very different matter. The defensive victory at Torres Vedras would therefore somehow have to be translated into offensive action, and, at the very least, the frontier secured by the reconquest of the three border fortresses taken by the French. With Almeida, Ciudad Rodrigo and Badajoz in British hands once more, Portugal might yet be held, and the war even carried into the heart of the Bonaparte kingdom of Spain, thereby relieving the pressure on the beleaguered Spaniards, but Sabugal had shown that even beaten French armies could put up a fierce fight. In short, there beckoned a bloody contest, and one it was by no means clear that Wellington could win.

Bloody Albuera

In the wake of the French defeat in Portugal, Wellington was free to take the offensive in Spain. Here the first task was to take the recently captured fortress of Badajoz which was promptly besieged by a detached corps of 18,000 men under Beresford. Poorly planned and supported by the most inefficient of siege trains, however, the attack got nowhere, and Soult was afforded sufficient time to bring up a large army from Andalucía. After some hesitation, Beresford decided to confront the oncoming enemy in an excellent defensive position at a small village some miles south-east of Badajoz called La Albuera. Among the troops gathered to await the French was Charles Leslie:

> We scarcely had time to get a little tea and a morsel of biscuit when the alarm was given . . . We accordingly instantly got under arms, leaving tents and baggage to be disposed of as the quartermaster . . . best could. We moved forward in line to crown the heights . . . which were intended for our position . . . which may shortly be described as follows. The rivulet of Albuera ran nearly parallel at about 600 yards' distance to the front of the heights, which sloped down to it. They were perfectly open for all arms, but beyond our right they swelled into steeper and more detached ones. The village of Albuera was nearly opposite the centre of our line and on the

same side of the water, at which point was the only bridge. The banks of the rivulet were at some places steep and abrupt. On the opposite or French side, they were rather low, and the ground flat and open for some little distance, [but the land] then gradually rose to a gentle height covered with woods.[291]

As Leslie goes on to describe, the battle began with what appeared to be a heavy French attack on Albuera, but this was a mere feint: in fact Soult had made use of the ridge that rose parallel with the southern bank of the screen to switch the bulk of his forces against the Allied right, which was held entirely by Spaniards from the armies of Generals Castaños and Blake. The result was much confusion:

> It was with no small surprise that we heard a sharp fire commence in that quarter. The error our chief had been led into now became evident. We were suddenly thrown into open column, and moved rapidly along the heights to our right flank for nearly a mile under a tremendous cannonade, for the French had already established themselves on some commanding heights [and] raked us as we advanced, Captain Humphrey and several men being killed. They were at the same time attacking the Spaniards with great vigour, having put them into some confusion when in the act of throwing back their right to meet this flank attack.[292]

In choosing to attack the Spaniards, Soult was not only avoiding a suicidal frontal assault on the Anglo-Portuguese infantry, but bearing down on what should have been the weakest troops in the Allied array. Yet, by chance, the men struck were not mere levies but experienced veterans: though badly outnumbered, they fought with great courage, and won enough time for British troops to be brought up from the centre of the Allied line. Commanding the first division to get into action was General Sir William Stewart. Not one of Wellington's better generals, Stewart made the mistake of rushing his men into action too quickly. What happened next was a terrible blow:

> Colborne's brigade . . . [had been] brought up in a hasty manner in column, obliqueing to their right towards the heights now occupied by the enemy . . . Colonel Colborne wished to move to the attack with the two flank regiments in quarter-distance columns, and the two centre ones in . . . line, but Sir William Stewart, anxious to show a large front, was deploying the whole. The Third, Forty-Eighth and Sixty-Sixth regiments were in line and the Thirty-First . . . still in column, when a body of French lancers, taking advantage of the thick weather and heavy showers of rain, got round those regiments which were in line, broke them and swept off the greater part as prisoners into the French lines. The Thirty-First . . . stood firm, and fortunately escaped the disaster, and the Spaniards continued with some difficulty to hold their ground.[293]

Among the victims of this charge was Major William Brooke of the Forty-Eighth Foot, a long-serving officer who had obtained his first commission as long ago as 1782:

> Part of the victorious French cavalry were Polish lancers. From the conduct of this regiment . . . I believe many of them to have been intoxicated, as they rode over the

wounded, barbarously darting their lances into them . . . I was an instance of their inhumanity: after having been most severely wounded in the head, and plundered of everything that I had about me, I was being led as a prisoner between two French . . . soldiers when one of these lancers rode up, and deliberately cut me down. Then, taking the skirts of my regimental coat, he tried to pull it over my head. Not satisfied with this brutality, the wretch tried by every means in his power to make his horse trample on me by dragging me along the ground and wheeling his horse over my body. But the beast, more merciful than the rider, absolutely refused to comply with his master's wishes, and carefully avoided putting his foot on me.[294]

Despite this disaster, Stewart still had two brigades of infantry ready for action under Hoghton and Abercrombie, and these now moved forwards together. It was none too soon, for the outnumbered Spaniards could clearly take no more:

We closed up . . . and deployed, but before the Fifty-Seventh and Forty-Eighth regiments had completed the formation, a body of Spaniards in advance of our left flank gave way, and . . . came rushing back upon us. We called out to them, urging them to rally and maintain their ground, and that we would shortly relieve them. On these assurances, with the exertion of some of the officers and of our adjutant, who rode among them, they did rally and moved up the hill again, but very shortly afterwards down they came again in the utmost confusion, mixed pell-mell with a body of the enemy's lancers who were thrusting and cutting without mercy. Many of the Spaniards threw themselves on the ground [and] others attempted to get through our line, but this could not be permitted, because, we being in line on the slope of a bare green hill, and such a rush of friends and foes coming down upon us, any opening made to let the former pass would have admitted the enemy also. We had no alternative left but to stand firm and in self-defence to fire on both. This shortly decided the business: the lancers brought up and made . . . their way back to their own lines, and the Spaniards were permitted to pass to the rear.[295]

With the Spaniards in retreat, the brigades of Hoghton and Abercrombie now advanced on the enemy. It was a stirring moment. To quote Charles Leslie:

The formation of our brigade being now completed, and [Abercrombie's] brigade having taken place on our left . . . Sir William Stewart rode up . . . and, after a few energetic words, said, 'Now is the time: let us give three cheers!' This was instantly done with heart and soul, every cap waving in the air. We immediately advanced up the hill under a sharp fire from the enemy's light troops which we did not condescend to return . . . On arriving at the crest of the height, we discovered the enemy a little in rear of it, apparently formed in masses, or columns of grand divisions, with light troops and artillery in the intervals between them.[296]

Disordered though they might have been after their long fight with the Spaniards, the French infantry were not cowards, while the front ranks were so hemmed in by the masses of troops behind them that they could scarcely have run even had they wanted to, and there followed a terrible firefight. Fighting as he was in Abercrombie's brigade, Sherer was an eyewitness to the struggle:

> This murderous contest of musketry lasted long. We were the whole time progressively advancing upon the enemy . . . The slaughter was now . . . dreadful: every shot told . . . To describe . . . this wild scene with fidelity would be impossible. At intervals a shriek or a groan told that men were falling around me, but it was not always that the tumult . . . suffered me to catch these sounds. A constant feeling to the centre . . . more truly bespoke the havoc of death.[297]

With matters balanced more-or-less equally between the two sides, the advantage would go to the first side able to deploy fresh troops. As matters worked out, this proved to be the Allies. On the right flank the Fourth Division of Sir Lowry Cole had arrived just in time. Present in the ranks was John Cooper of the Seventh Foot:

> The day was now apparently lost, for large masses of the enemy had gained the highest part of the battlefield, and were compactly ranged in three heavy columns with numerous cavalry and artillery ready to roll up our entire line . . . At this crisis the words 'Fall in Fusiliers!' roused us, and we formed line. Six nine-pounders, supported by two or three squadrons of the Fourth Dragoons, took the right. The Eleventh and Twenty-Third Portuguese regiments, supported by three light companies, occupied the centre. The Fusilier brigade . . . stood on the left. Just in front of the centre were some squadrons of Spanish cavalry. The line in this order approached at quick step the steep position of the enemy under a storm of shot, shell and grape which came crashing through our ranks. At the same time the French cavalry made a charge at the Spanish horse in our front. Immediately a volley from us was poured into the mixed mass of French and Spaniards. This checked the French, but the Spanish heroes galloped round our left flank and we saw them no more. Having arrived at the foot of the hill, we began to climb its slope with bated breath while the roll and thunder of furious battle increased. Under the tremendous fire of the enemy our thin line staggers, [and] men are knocked about like skittles, but not a step backward is taken. Here our colonel and all the field officers of the brigade fell killed and wounded, but no confusion ensued. The orders were 'Close up! Close in! Fire away! Forward!' This is done. We close the enemy's columns; they break and rush down the hill in the greatest mob-like confusion. In a minute or two, our nine-pounders . . . gain the summit, and join in sending a shower of iron and lead into the broken mass. We followed down the slope firing and huzza'ing till recalled by the bugle. The enemy passed over the river in great disorder, and attacked us no more, but cannonading and skirmishing in the centre continued till night.[298]

In the end, then, it was Beresford's army that had won the day, but there was little sense of triumph in its ranks. So great were the casualties suffered by both sides in the fighting that the battle was ever-afterwards known as 'Bloody Albuera'. The aftermath is described by Charles Leslie:

Monitoring the living and recording the dead became afterwards our melancholy duty. On reckoning its numbers, the Twenty-Ninth Regiment had only ninety-six men, two captains and a few subalterns; the Fifty-Seventh Regiment had but a few more, and were commanded by the adjutant; and the . . . Forty-Eighth Regiment had suffered in like manner . . . Major General Hoghton, commanding the brigade, and Lieutenant Colonel Duckworth of the Forty-Eighth Regiment were killed; Lieutenant Colonel White of the Twenty-Ninth Regiment mortally wounded; [and] Colonel Inglis of the Fifty-Seventh [Regiment] and Major Way of the Twenty-Ninth Regiment . . . very severely wounded. In fact, every field officer of the whole brigade was either killed or wounded, so that at the close of the action the brigade remained in command of a captain. Singular enough, that captain was a Frenchman named Cemetière ('Cemetery'). The field afterwards presented a sad spectacle, our men lying generally in rows and the French in large heaps . . . Some days afterwards, I have been told, His Grace [i.e. Wellington], while inspecting the hospitals at Elvas, said to some of our men. 'Old Twenty-Ninth! I am sorry to see so many of you here!' They instantly replied, 'My Lord, if you had only been with us, there would not have been so many of us here.'[299]

Back on the hillsides around Albuera, the victors were in no state to continue fighting. For a graphic account of the night after the battle, let us turn again to John Cooper:

Having returned to the top of the ridge, we piled arms and looked about. What a scene! The dead and wounded [were] lying all around. In some places the dead were in heaps. One of these was nearly three feet high . . . What was now to be done with the wounded that were so thickly strewn on every side? The town of Albuera had been totally unroofed and unfloored for firewood . . . and there was no other town within several miles. Besides, the rain was pouring down, and the poor sufferers were as numerous as the unhurt. To be short, the wounded that could not walk were carried in blankets to the bottom of the bloody hill and laid among the wet grass. Whether they had any orderlies to wait on them, or how many lived or died, I can't tell. But if they were ill off, our case was not enviable. We were wet, weary and dirty [and] without food or shelter . . . We lay down at night among the mire and dead men. I selected a tuft of rushes and coiled myself up like a dog, but sleep I could not on account of hunger and cold. Once I looked up out of my wet blanket, and saw a poor wounded man stark naked, crawling about, I suppose, for shelter. Who had stripped him, or whether he lived till morning I know not.[300]

It is tempting to hope that the sufferings of the naked man seen by Cooper did not last long. Had he lived, he may well have been consigned to a convoy of wounded of the sort encountered soon after the battle by George Farmer, a private with the Eleventh Light Dragoons:

At the village where we halted there arrived on cars about 700 wounded men from Albuera, whose plight was as pitiable . . . as it is easy for the human imagination to conceive. No doubt they had received, when first taken in hand by the surgeons, all the care which the nature of their condition would allow. But they had performed since that period a long journey through a barren country and under a broiling sun, and their wounds, remaining undressed all this while, were now in such a state as to defy description. There was no lack of willingness on our part to assist them. We soon cleared out the best houses in the place, spread straw on the floors, and gave ourselves up to the business of cleaning their hurts, the smell proceeding from which was fearful. Over and over again we were forced to quit the miserable patients in a hurry and run out into the open air in order to save ourselves from fainting, while they, poor fellows, reproached us with a degree of bitterness which none of us cared, even in thought, to resent for a moment.[301]

Nor were things any better on the French side. For the thousands of Soult's men who had been wounded in the course of the battle, there followed an agonising journey of some 100 miles back to the haven provided by Seville. Present with the convoy was the captured William Brooke:

About two o'clock in the morning the main convoy of wounded, amounting to near 4,000 in all, was put in motion. Dreadful were the cries of these poor . . . wretches! Had my heart been made of adamant I must have felt for the pitiable condition to which the ravages of war had brought them . . . Two or three hundred . . . died on the seventeenth, and between 600 and 700 more expired on the road to Seville.[302]

Fuentes de Oñoro

While Beresford had been fighting in Extremadura, the rest of the British army had moved to invest Almeida and Ciudad Rodrigo. However, nothing if not resourceful, Masséna succeeded in rebuilding his army far more quickly than had been expected, and by the end of April, having been reinforced by a small cavalry division brought up by the commander of the Army of the North, Marshal Bessières, the French were on the move. To meet this fresh threat, Wellington took up a defensive position just inside the Spanish frontier. This was very strong: the Allied army was stationed along a line of low hills between a ruined fort and the village of Fuentes de Oñoro, while its centre and left was screened by a deep ravine through which ran the Río Dos Casas. Encountering this position on the morning of 3 May, Masséna quickly decided that the best means of making progress was to seize the village, which, strongly garrisoned, was thrown forward on the slopes which led down to the Dos Casas. Very soon, then, his leading infantry division had charged across the river and into the village's warren of alleys and courtyards. For several hours there followed a bitter fight, which cost the two sides over 900 casualties. Something of the chaos is recorded by one of the defenders, most of whom came from a composite battalion made up of the light companies of a number of different battalions:

The overwhelming force which the French now pushed forward on the village could not be withstood by the small number of troops which defended it [and] they were obliged to give way . . . While retreating through the town, one of our sergeants . . . being pushed hard by the enemy, ran into one of the houses. They were hard on his heels and he just had time to tumble himself into a large chest . . . when they entered and commenced plundering the house . . . They were in the act of opening the lid of his hiding place when the noise of our men cheering as they charged the enemy . . . forced them to take flight.[303]

Another of the soldiers involved in the fighting was the failed actor Thomas Howell:

We stood under arms until three o'clock when a staff officer rode up to our colonel and gave orders for our advance. Colonel Cadogan put himself at our head, saying, 'My lads, you have had no provision these two days. There is plenty in the hollow in front: let us down and divide it.' We advanced as quick as we could run and met the light companies retreating as fast as they could . . . They called to us, 'Seventy-First, you will come back quicker than you advance.' We soon came full in front of the enemy. The colonel cries, 'Here is food, my lads, cut away!' Thrice we waved our bonnets and thrice we cheered; [then we] brought our firelocks to the charge, and forced them back through the town . . . In this affair my life was most wonderfully preserved. In forcing the French through the town . . . a bayonet went through between my side and clothes to my haversack, which stopped its progress. The Frenchman to whom the bayonet belonged fell, pierced by a musket ball . . . [but] a ball took off part of my right shoulder-wing, and killed my rear-rank man, who fell upon me . . . We kept up our fire till long after dark. About one o'clock in the morning, we got four ounces of bread served out to each man . . . on which we feasted heartily, and lay down in our blankets, wearied to death. My shoulder was as black as coal from the recoil of my musket, for this day I had fired 107 rounds of ball cartridge.[304]

Thus baulked, Masséna spent the whole of the next day reconnoitring the Allied position, and at length concluded that the best means of defeating Wellington would be to march around his left flank and force him out of his position by means of a pincer movement. Realising that something of the sort was afoot, Wellington sent out the newly formed Seventh Division to occupy the area of the village of Pozo Bello two miles south of the end of his line, while at the same time supporting this force with the whole of his cavalry. However, when the French thrust came it was much stronger than the British commander had anticipated. No sooner had dawn broken on 5 May than thousands of French troops began to envelop Pozo Bello. Fighting bravely, the Allied cavalry tried to slow them down, but their best efforts were to no avail. William Tomkinson, the 21-year-old son of a Cheshire squire, was serving as a cornet in the Sixteenth Light Dragoons, having enlisted in December 1807:

Our two brigades of cavalry scarcely amounted to 900 men, and these in bad condition . . . On the right . . . Major Myers of the Hussars was in advance with two squadrons – one from the Sixteenth and one from his own regiment . . . and, the enemy having sent forward two or three squadrons . . . he ordered the squadron of the Sixteenth to charge. The enemy's squadron was about twice their strength and awaited their charge. This is the only instance I ever met with of two bodies of cavalry coming in opposition and both standing [their ground], as, invariably as I have observed it, one or the other runs away. Our men rode up and began sabreing, but were so outnumbered that they could do nothing and were obliged to retire . . . in confusion, the enemy having brought up more troops at that point. Captain Belli was wounded . . . and taken; Sergeant Taylor . . . and six men . . . were killed . . . in attempting to rescue him. The enemy cannonaded the cavalry a good deal in retiring, in which we lost Lieutenant Blake of the Sixteenth. He was hit by a four-pound shot in the thigh, and . . . rode with it to Castelo Mendo, where a Portuguese surgeon took it out. Surgeon Robinson of the Sixteenth went in the morning to Castelo Mendo and cut his leg off, and in half an hour afterwards he was dead . . . From the spot where he received his wound to Castelo Mendo is a good six miles, and the large bone [was] shattered all to atoms.[305]

With the French deploying in overwhelming strength, the village's garrison was quickly overwhelmed, and the main body of the Seventh Division was forced to retreat in search of safer ground. Among the ranks of the Fifty-First Foot was William Wheeler, a private soldier who had transferred into the army from the Surrey Militia in April 1809 and had first seen service in the Walcheren campaign:

We retired through the broken ground in our rear . . . and were pretty safe from their cavalry, but they had brought up their guns . . . and were serving out the shot with a liberal hand. We continued retiring and soon came to a . . . rapid stream. This we waded up to our armpits, and from the steepness of the opposite bank we found much difficulty in getting out. This caused some delay [but] the regiment waited until all had crossed, then formed line and continued [its] retreat in quick time. Thanks to Colonel M. we came off safe . . . He dismounted . . . faced us and frequently called the time . . . He would now and then call out, 'That fellow . . . cannot march; mark him for drill, Sergeant Major. I tell you they cannot hurt us if you are steady; if you get out of time, you will be knocked down.' He was leading his horse and a shot passed under the horse's belly, which made him rear up. 'You are a coward,' he said, 'I will stop your corn for three days.'[306]

Stiffened by such gallantry, Houston's men were able to reach a good defensive position some way further back. Here the retreat stopped, for the French horsemen found that they could make no further progress, while the infantry forces that had followed them had swung northwards and were now heading for Wellington's main position. This, however, was now perfectly secure, the British commander having heavily reinforced the area around Fuentes de Oñoro. All that troubled him, indeed, was the situation of the Seventh Division, which was still dangerously isolated. To avoid the possibility of Masséna securing even the partial success that would have been achieved by its destruction, the British commander therefore sent the Light Division (now once more led by Craufurd, who had fortuitously resumed its command only the night before) to bring it in. As the Seventh Division fell back, the 'light bobs' were attacked in their turn, however. Well up with the skirmishers of the Ninety-Fifth Rifles was Edward Costello:

We had no sooner beaten back the enemy than a loud cheering to the right attracted our attention, and we perceived our First Heavy Dragoons charge a French cavalry regiment. As this was the first charge of cavalry most of us had ever seen, we were all naturally much interested on this occasion. The French skirmishers who were extended against us seemed to participate in the same feeling and by general consent both parties agreed to suspend the firing while the affair . . . was going on. The English and French cavalry met in the most gallant manner, and with the greatest show of resolution. The first shock when they came in collision seemed terrific and many men and horses fell on both sides. They had ridden through and past each other, and now they wheeled round again. This was followed by a second charge accompanied by some very pretty sabre practice by which many saddles were emptied, and English and French chargers were soon seen galloping about the field without riders. These immediately occupied the attention of the French skirmishers and ourselves, and we soon engaged in pursuing them, the men of each nation endeavouring to secure the chargers of the opposite one as legal spoil. While engaged in this chase, we frequently became intermixed, when much laughter was indulged in by both parties at the different accidents that occurred in the pursuit. I had secured a very splendid charger when, chancing to turn my head, I perceived that the French were playing a deep game. They had succeeded in moving a regiment of infantry, with some cavalry, through the wood in our rear. The alarm, however, was immediately given, and our company, as foremost, had to run for their lives into a square formed by the Fifty-Second . . . During this sudden movement I was obliged to part with my horse; the cavalry did not pursue us, but their artillery opened upon the Fifty-Second's square and did some execution.[307]

As Costello implies, at this moment the Light Division was almost overwhelmed, but it was saved by the courage and quick-thinking of its commanders. Here the story is taken up by Lieutenant Dobbs of the Fifty-Second:

We were somewhat startled by Sir Sydney Beckwith riding up, exclaiming, 'They're in among you! They're in among you!', and presently we saw the troop of horse artillery, with their guns, surrounded by the enemy, but gallantly fighting their way out. With the most perfect coolness, the three battalions – [the] first of the Forty-Third and [the] first and second of the Fifty-Second – formed an echelon of squares which covered the retreat of the horse artillery. Lord Wellington having determined on a change of position, the Seventh Division was ordered to retire, and we had to do the same over the plain . . . This was done by alternate squares under a heavy cannonade, the balls sometimes hopping in and out of the square. The distance was about three miles, and marching in square a most difficult operation, as, if the correct line is not kept by the front or rear faces, or the sides in file marching not looked up or well covered [i.e. kept well aligned], the square must be broken.[308]

The story is concluded by Kincaid:

The execution of our movement presented a magnificent military spectacle as the plain between us and the right of the army was by this time in possession of the

French cavalry, and, while we were retiring through it with the order and precision of a common field day, they kept dancing around us and every instant threatening a charge, without daring to execute it. We took up our new position at a right angle to the then right of the British line . . . with our right on the [river] Turón. The enemy followed our movement with a heavy column of infantry, but when they came near enough to exchange shots, they did not seem to like our looks, as we occupied a low ridge of broken rocks against which even a rat could scarcely have hoped to advance alive, and they again fell back, and [opened] a tremendous fire of artillery, which was returned by a battery of our guns.[309]

A movement that had started out with great hopes for the French therefore ended in bitter frustration. Practically the only success which they obtained, indeed, was when some light cavalry got in among the skirmishers covering the main line and caused about a hundred casualties. Yet, as Charles Parquin, a 24-year-old lieutenant in the Twentieth Chasseurs who had risen from the ranks and spent some time as a prisoner of war in Russia, recalled, even this minor triumph was dearly bought:

Our brigade was the last unit to engage the enemy. General Fournier had his horse killed under him as he charged an enemy line that was completely broken . . . Captain Lasalle [and] Lieutenants Labassée and Hymonet, as well as several *chasseurs*, were unhorsed by the enemy artillery and infantry fire, and a bullet fired at point-blank range smashed into my face and knocked out six of my teeth. I had to retire to the field hospital for treatment . . . For a week I could eat only soup which my servant poured into my mouth through a funnel.[310]

At this point it should have been clear to Masséna that the battle was lost, for the British position was once again too strong to force. Yet the battle had acquired a life of its own. Thus, as soon as the outflanking move was seen to be making progress, the French had once again charged across into the village. There followed a desperate fight that saw first one side gain the advantage and then the other. On at least two occasions French troops made it to the very last buildings of the village, but each time they were hurled back. The final counter-attack was the work of the Connaught Rangers. In the lead was William Grattan:

It so happened that the command of the company which led this attack devolved upon me. When we came within sight of the French Ninth Regiment, which [was] drawn up at the corner of the chapel waiting for us, I turned round to look at the men of my company: they gave me a cheer that a lapse of many years has not made me forget, and I thought that that moment was the proudest of my life. The soldiers . . . were the picture of everything that a chosen body of troops ought to be. The enemy were not idle spectators of this movement: they witnessed its commencement, and the regularity with which the advance was conducted made them fearful of the result. A [French] battery of eight-pounders advanced at the gallop to an olive grove on the opposite bank of the river, hoping by the effects of its fire to annihilate the Eighty-Eighth . . . or, at all events, embarrass its movements as much as possible, but the battalion continued to press on, joined by its exhausted comrades, and the battery did little execution. On reaching the head of the village, the Eighty-Eighth was vigorously opposed by the Ninth Regiment, aided by some hundred of the Imperial Guard, but it soon closed in with them, and . . . drove the enemy through the different streets at the point of the bayonet, and at length forced them into the river that separated the two armies. Several of our men fell on the French side of the water. About 150 . . . grenadiers . . . in their flight ran down a street that had been barricaded by us the day before, and . . . their disappointment was great, upon arriving at the bottom, to find themselves shut in. Mistakes of this kind will sometimes occur, and when they do the result is easily imagined: troops advancing to assault a town . . . have no great time to deliberate as to what they will do; the thing is generally done in half the time the deliberation would occupy, [and] in the present instance every man was put to death.[311]

With this action the battle closed and the French drew off to Ciudad Rodrigo. But it had been a sanguinary affair. Especially in Fuentes de Oñoro itself, the dead offered mute testimony to the ferocity of the fighting:

Among the dead that covered the streets . . . it was quite a common thing to see an English and a French soldier with their bayonets still in each other's bodies, and their fists convulsively grasping the butt ends of their muskets, lying on top of each other. At one spot I saw seven, and at another five, French officers killed by bayonet wounds.[312]

Failure at Badajoz

Following the French repulse at Fuentes de Oñoro (from which the invaders received some slight compensation in the form of the subsequent escape of their garrison from Almeida), Wellington concentrated his army before Badajoz for a renewed attempt on that fortress. This was not, however, to prove one of Wellington's happier ventures. From the beginning the French put up a furious fight. Among the troops set to dig the first parallel and then to man the front line was the Eighty-Eighth Foot, and with them William Grattan:

Nothing astonished me so much as the noise made by the engineers; I expected that their loud talking would bring the enemy's attention towards the sound of our pickaxes, and that all the cannon in the town would be turned against us, and in short I thought that every moment would be my last. I scarcely ventured to breathe until we had completed a respectable first parallel, and when it was fairly finished, just as morning began to dawn, I felt inexpressibly relieved. As soon as the enemy had a distinct view of what we had been doing, he opened a battery or two against us with, however, but little effect, and I began to think a siege was not that tremendous thing I had been taught to expect, but at this moment a thirty-two-pound shot passed through a mound of earth in front of that part of the parallel in which I was standing . . . and, taking two poor fellows of the Eighty-Third who were carrying a hand-barrow across their bellies, cut them in two, and whirled their remnants through the air. I had never before had so close a view of the execution a round shot was capable of performing, and it was . . . full a week afterwards before I held myself as upright as before. On the second of June our batteries commenced against the castle and San Cristobal . . . but the brass guns were inadequate to the task they had to perform, and, after being a short time at work, became so hot as to be useless. The artillerymen were occupied for several hours throwing buckets of water over their barrels in order the sooner to render them fit for work. The cannon of the enemy were, it is true, of the same description, but their train was more numerous, and besides they could without much trouble disarm such of their batteries as were not opposed to ours, and thus, by a continual interchange of guns, overpower our fire, while we were obliged to continue with the same set . . . The touch holes of several of the cannon melted away and became so large that they were unserviceable . . . and by ten o'clock each morning our line of batteries presented a very disorganised appearance: sandbags, gabions and fascines knocked here and there, guns flung off their carriages, and carriages beaten down under their guns. The boarded platforms of the batteries, damp with the blood of our artillery men, or the headless trunks of our devoted engineers, bore testimony to the murderous fire opposed to us . . . It was on a morning such as I am talking of that Colonel Fletcher, chief officer of engineers, came into the battery where I was employed: he wished to observe some work that had been thrown up by the enemy near the foot of the castle the preceding night. The battery was more than usually full of workmen repairing the effects of the morning's fire, and the efforts of the enemy against this part of our work were excessively animated. A number of men had fallen . . . but Colonel Fletcher, apparently disregarding the circumstance, walked out to the right of the battery, and, taking his stand upon level ground, put his glass to his eye, and commenced his observations with much composure. Shot and shell flew thickly about him, and one of the former tore up the ground by his side and covered him with clay, but, not in the least regarding this, he remained, steadily observing the enemy. When at length he had satisfied himself, he quietly put up his glass, and, turning to a man of my party who was sitting on the outside of an embrasure pegging in a fascine, said, 'My fine fellow, you are too much exposed: get inside the embrasure, and you will do your work nearly as well.' 'I'm almost finished, Colonel,' replied the soldier, 'and it isn't worth while to move now: those fellows can't hit me, for they have been trying it these fifteen minutes.' They were the last words he ever spoke. He had scarcely uttered the last syllable, when a round shot cut him in two, and knocked half of his body across the breech of the gun. The name of this soldier was Edmund Man; he was an Englishman though he belonged to the Eighty-Eighth Regiment . . . One evening while we were occupied in the usual way in the trenches, a number of us stood talking together. Several shells fell in the works, and we were on the alert a good deal in order to escape from them . . . One, however, took us by surprise, and before we could escape fell in the middle of the trench. Everyone made the best of his way to the nearest battery, and the confusion was much increased by some of the sappers passing at that moment with a parcel of gabions on their backs. Colonel Trench of the Seventy-Fourth in getting away ran against one of these men, and not only threw him down, but fell headlong over him, and, sticking fast in one of the gabions, was unable to move. As soon as the shell exploded, we sallied forth from our respective nooks, and relieved Colonel Trench from his awkward position. 'Well,' said Colonel King of the Fifth, 'I often saw a gabion in a trench, but this is the first time I ever saw a trench in a gabion.' Considering the time and place, the pun was not a bad one and made us all laugh heartily.[313]

Inadequate though Wellington's siege artillery was, some damage was eventually done to the walls, but the courage and fortitude of the defenders remained undimmed. When an assault was launched on the outlying fort of San Cristobal on 6 June, it was beaten off with heavy losses. Much the same fate, meanwhile, met a second attack that was made three days later. A participant in both attacks, Wheeler gives a graphic description of the scene:

> We advanced up the glacis . . . Not a head was to be seen above the walls, and we began to think the enemy had retired . . . when sudden as a flash of lightning the whole place was in a blaze. It will be impossible for me to describe to you what followed. You can better conceive it by figuring . . . a deep trench or ditch filled with men who are endeavouring to mount the wall by means of ladders. The top of this wall [is] crowded with men hurling down shells and hand grenades on the heads of them below, and when all these are expended they each have six or seven loaded firelocks which they discharge . . . as quick as possible. Add to this some half a dozen cannon scouring the trench with grape . . . heaps of brave fellows killed and wounded, [and] ladders shot to pieces, and falling together with the men down upon the living and the dead . . . But in the midst of all these difficulties . . . we should have taken the fort, but for an unforeseen accident that could not be remedied . . . The ladders were too short . . . As soon as this was discovered, all hopes of gaining possession was abandoned, and the order was given to retire.[314]

Given time, Wellington might have starved the city into surrender, but time was not a luxury that he possessed. Determined to save Badajoz, Marmont – Masséna's successor as commander of the Army of Portugal – and Soult combined their field forces and marched on Wellington, who, badly outnumbered, proceeded to raise the siege. Retreating a few miles into Portugal, he took up a defensive position behind the river Caya near Elvas. The result was stalemate. Knowing that the British were near unbeatable in a position of their own choosing, neither marshal would attack. Eventually, indeed, they were left with no option but to retreat, but in the meantime both armies sat it out in the worst heat of an Iberian summer:

> Our life in this camp was by no means pleasant. Every morning between two and three o'clock we had to march out with the whole army as an enemy attack was expected. Only at nine, when the patrols returned, were we allowed to go back to our quarters. During the day the heat was tropical, with no shade anywhere, and we suffered from eternal dust . . . All day long we were infested by snakes, blowflies and other vermin, while our water came from a dirty . . . stream . . . in which the whole

army bathed. At night we were plagued by scorpions, mosquitoes and a piercingly cold wind. If one heard the slightest sound of crawling or wriggling under one's mattress or pillow at night, one called one's servant immediately, and the latter had to get up, strike a light, examine the floor of the tent . . . and proceed to kill the scorpion, which had usually crept in under the skirt of the tent. One morning just as I got up and was on the point of drawing on my nankeen pantaloons, I thought I saw an object in my tent that looked like a leaf . . . I drew back my leg and found that it was a fat scorpion. Even during the day we were not safe, for, on one occasion when several officers were lying on a tarpaulin drinking grog, we found, when they got up to go, that Captain von der Decken had squeezed a scorpion that had crawled under the tarpaulin perfectly flat . . . In addition to all this, the unhealthy nature of the district in which the army was bivouacked began to tell. The banks of the Guadiana that flowed not far away, as also the Caya, were proverbial throughout Spain as plague spots during the hottest part of the summer . . . All kinds of typhus and ague began to break out.[315]

Prisoners

Throughout the Peninsular War many thousands of soldiers were taken prisoner. Generally speaking, the British and French treated one another with reasonable courtesy, but, even so, for the rank and file especially the experience was rarely one to be relished. Among the prisoners taken in one minor skirmish was George Farmer:

> Our sojourn in Badajoz was brief – only four days, at the termination of which we set out on foot for Mérida. We suffered, as may be imagined, horribly during that march, for, besides [the fact] that several of us were wounded, cavalry soldiers are but little accustomed to pedestrian exertions, and the heat was quite overwhelming. Our lieutenant . . . became at last so weak that he fainted. Still, there was neither time given to rest, nor horse, nor mule, nor any vehicle of any kind furnished for his conveyance. The French guard brought him to by shaking, and he was forced, at the bayonet's point, to struggle on . . . till we reached a halting place . . . We were all famishing, for no food had been issued ere we quitted Badajoz . . . The third day brought us to Mérida . . . We were halted in the market-place, where crowds, both of the inhabitants and of French soldiers, immediately surrounded us. The former expressed commiseration for our fate; the latter gloried in saluting us with such epithets as marked a feeling for us both of hatred and contempt. But they did us no serious injury, and, as we were permitted to halt here a day, our jaded limbs gathered a good deal of refreshment from the indulgence . . . As evening closed a quantity of loaves were thrown in at our window by the inhabitants till we soon had enough to last us, not for the day alone, but for a whole week, supposing the means of transport to have been accessible.[316]

For such men, the prospects were grim, with the majority facing a long march to the French frontier and beyond. As was the case with French prisoners, officers were treated rather better, and in many instances were offered parole. Captured at Albuera, for example,

Major William Brooke was hardly kept in close confinement as the army of Marshal Soult made its slow and painful way back to Seville:

> We marched this day [23 May] to Constantina. I was billeted on a carpenter, who received me in a civil manner, made up a bed for me in a corner of the room, and began to prepare food. I was not long seated when two graceful and elegant young Spanish ladies . . . entered the room . . . They addressed me in Spanish, but, finding that I did not well understand their language, made me comprehend in the best way they could that they had brought a surgeon to dress my wounds. He was called in, and was followed by a group of young women, gaping with open mouths like one of Hogarth's caricatures. The doctor unbound my head, dressed it and tied it up again. Some of [these] girls were then called forward with a basket filled with sweetmeats, fruit and cake, and at least a gallon and a half of excellent wine, of which they pressed me to partake. [The two young ladies] . . . seated themselves on my right hand and on my left, and one of them desired a girl to come forward with some cigars: she gave one to her sister, and, having lighted another, put it to her own mouth, and then passed it to me. At first I received it with some reluctance until I understood that this was the highest compliment a Spanish lady could pay a gentleman. They remained with me some time, [and] then, politely wishing me good night, left me to enjoy the rest that wearied nature craved.[317]

Yet even senior officers could face rough treatment at the moment of capture. Taken prisoner in the course of an abortive commando operation at Fuengirola, the British general Andrew Blayney found himself in the hands of some Polish troops:

> I soon . . . observed a column close in from the left, on whose caps I perceived the number 'four' with an eagle, and which proved to be the *quatrième polonais*. The troops with me, after firing a few rounds, charged this column, and a very severe conflict ensued, which unfortunately ended in my being made prisoner, having but nine men remaining of those that advanced with me. Those only who have suffered a similar fate can form any idea of my sensations at being thus obliged to surrender to a ferocious banditti, who loaded me with every vile epithet, but in whose outrageous violence I in great measure found my personal safety, for they crowded so thick on me that they had not room to give force to their blows. They tore my clothes, rifled my pockets and attempted to pull off my epaulets, and the resistance I made to this last indignity procured me several blows from the butt ends of their muskets that covered me with contusions . . . The scene that presented itself at this moment can never be effaced from my memory: both officers and soldiers had all the appearance of . . . desperate banditti, their long moustachios, their faces blackened by smoke and gunpowder, and their bloody and torn clothes giving to their whole appearance a degree of indescribable ferocity.[318]

For captured Allied soldiers, the best hope was rescue at the hands of some patriot. William Brooke was one of those spirited away in this fashion:

Twenty-fifth July: on this morning I was sitting at the iron bars of my window reading the Old Testament, when a Spaniard . . . entered my room, and . . . gave me from his shoulders a Spanish cloak, took from out of his hat another one, and produced from his pocket a . . . paper of paint. . . which, toned in colour with brick-dust from the walls, I . . . rubbed over my face and hands . . . We then passed from my cell through a small room where six British officers were confined . . . Five sentries kept guard here . . . There was also a strong . . . guard at the outer gate. All these posts I had to pass, being several times obliged to put my hand gently against the sentry to make him give way to let me pass. On my arrival in the open street . . . my preserver led me through many by-ways, in which we met French officers and soldiers innumerable, and at last . . . conducted me to his abode, where I found his wife ready to welcome me with a good supper . . . I was extremely anxious to go forward at once, but my preserver alleged that it would take time to fix me a route by learning in what direction the French troops were least numerous . . . Thus two days ran by, during which I learned that the French . . . had offered for my detection 5,000 *reales*.[319]

British soldiers taken by the French, then, faced danger and discomfort, but for Spanish soldiers the situation was infinitely worse. In many instances, they were treated very harshly by the French. In Alcalá de Henares a record of events was being kept by Juan Domingo Palomar, a hospital administrator and member of the French-appointed town council:

On 19 November [1809] there took place the unfortunate battle of Ocaña in which our army lost 12,000 men, almost all of whom were prisoners. Having first been stripped of all they possessed, including their clothes, they were taken to Madrid, where many of them arrived dressed only in a few rags or even draped in sacks or rush matting. In spite of the heavy frosts that now set in, a large number were then imprisoned out in the open air in the bullring, and some of them in consequence died of cold. . . . More than half later escaped while they were being taken to France, but the journey was none the less conducted in the most inhuman manner: the only thing they were given to eat was a few raw turnips, while anyone who could not keep up was shot.[320]

A participant in one of these veritable death marches was Juan Manuel Sarasa, who had been captured at the battle of the river Gebora on 5 March 1811:

It would have been difficult to conduct the journey in a worse manner. It really seemed as if they wanted to starve us to death: when we set out each morning we left behind the bodies of friends and comrades who had died in the night. Meanwhile, from the rear of the column, alas, there would come a constant rattle of shots: it was the French finishing off the poor fellows who could not drag themselves along any further. It would be impossible to come up with a more distressing picture than the sight we presented. Reduced to mere spectres, we did our best to help one another along, for to fall behind meant certain death, but one

The city of Lisbon viewed from the River Tagus. For years this was the hub of the British war effort in the peninsula. (*Philip Haythornthwaite*)

The city of Cádiz viewed from the fort of Santa Catalina. Some idea of its impregnable situation may be judged from the fact that the French siege lines lay on the far horizon. (*Philip Haythornthwaite*)

All that remains of the castle of Almeida. The town still shows the effects of the explosion which consumed 4,000 shells, 150,000 pounds of loose powder and several million musket cartridges. (*Andrew Jackson*)

The ravine through which the River Côa flows near Almeida. The Light Division was deployed on the ridge to the right. (*Richard Tennant*)

The bridge over the River Côa. Only the undoubted fighting qualities of the Light Division avoided disaster at this spot. (*Richard Tennant*)

The battle of Busaco. The scenery is much romanticised, but the hopeless situation faced by Massena's troops is captured well enough. (*Philip Haythornthwaite*)

The remains of the fort of Sâo Vicente in the Lines of Torres Vedras. (*Andrew Jackson*)

Goya's impression of the war in Spain. Such images have been used to create a view of the fighting that is distorted, if not downright erroneous. (*Museo del Prado*)

French troops massacre Spanish civilians armed only with improvised weapons. Such scenes were probably less common than is sometimes implied. (*Museo del Prado*)

The battlefield of Fuentes de Oñoro viewed from Wellington's main position. (*Richard Tennant*)

French light cavalry swirl around a British square at the battle of Fuentes de Oñoro. Wellington had over-extended his right wing and sent out the Light Division to retrieve the situation. (*Taylor Library*)

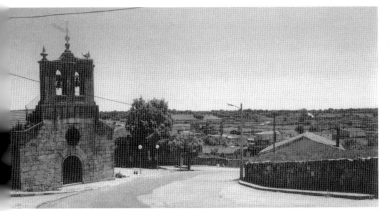

The village of Fuentes de Oñoro showing the ground over which the Eighty-Eighth Foot counter-attacked in the last moments of the battle. (*Richard Tennant*)

The area of the main clash of arms at Albuera. The undulating open ground offered enormous advantages to the French cavalry. *(Richard Tennant)*

The battlefield of Albuera. Beresford's army occupied the ridge in the distance. *(Richard Tennant)*

Polish lancers overwhelm the infantry of Colborne's brigade at Albuera. It was amid such scenes that William Brooke was taken prisoner. *(Taylor Library)*

The ramparts at Ciudad Rodrigo showing the site of the greater breach. The tower of the cathedral remains pockmarked by the shots fired by Wellington's siege guns. (*Richard Tennant*)

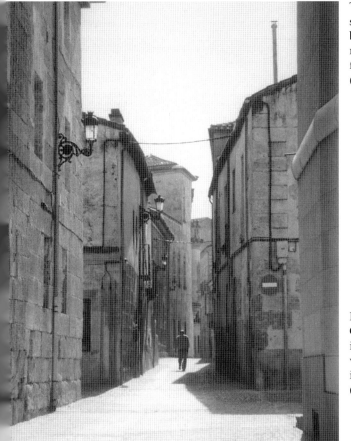

Narrow streets in the old town of Ciudad Rodrigo. Once troops got into such rabbit warrens in the wake of a storm, it was almost impossible to control them. (*Richard Tennant*)

The attack on the breaches at Badajoz. In the confined space shown by this picture 2,200 men were killed or wounded in the space of less than 6 hours. (*Philip Haythornthwaite*)

British soldiers press forward to assault the walls of Badajoz. In the words of George Simmons, 'Our columns moved on under a most dreadful fire ... that mowed down our men like grass'. (*National Army Museum*)

The walls of the castle of Badajoz looking north. There is no trace of the ditch mentioned by Joseph Donaldson. (*Charles J. Esdaile*)

A focal point of the attack on the castle of Badajoz, this tower was the scene of savage fighting. (*Charles J. Esdaile*)

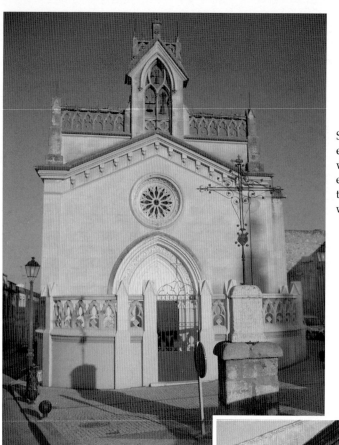

Standing only a few yards from the entrance to the castle, this convent was one of the first buildings to be entered by Picton's troops; according to local tradition, all the nuns inside were raped. (*Charles J. Esdaile*)

The postern gate through which the victorious troops of the Third Division poured from the castle into the town. (*Charles J. Esdaile*)

The battlefield of Salamanca viewed from the Arapil Grande. The Arapil Chico is in the foreground to the right, while the city of Salamanca may just be perceived in the distance. (*Richard Tennant*)

The battlefield of Salamanca looking east from the vicinity of the position occupied by Maucune's division. (*Richard Tennant*)

A well-dressed woman walks past a group of starving beggars with averted eyes. By 1812 large parts of Spain were in the grip of a terrible famine. (*Museo del Prado*)

A resident of Madrid, Goya witnessed the horrors of the year 1812 at first hand and recorded them for posterity. In the capital alone 20,000 people died of starvation. (*Museo del Prado*)

The bridge of Tres Puentes where the Light Division got across the River Zadorra during the battle of Vitoria. (*Richard Tennant*)

The battlefield of Vitoria viewed from the north bank of the River Zadorra looking south-westwards towards Subijana de Alava. (*Richard Tennant*)

The Anglo-Portuguese army falls on the French baggage train in the wake of the battle of Vitoria. (*Philip Haythornthwaite*)

British cavalry attack fleeing French infantry in the last moments of the battle of Vitoria. (*Taylor Library*)

The pass of Maya. The Ninety-Second Foot made its stand across the track seen in the middle distance. William Keep made his dramatic escape down the steep slope to the right. (*Richard Tennant*)

The Puerta de Francia in the north wall of the city of Pamplona. King Joseph's last act as King of Spain was to ride through this gate on his way back to France. (*Charles J. Esdaile*)

This modern painting depicts the Eleventh Foot at the battle of Salamanca. Unfortunately, however, the terrain shown does not resemble Salamanca. Instead, the picture is here used to depict the battle of the River Nivelle, in which the Eleventh also took part. (*Regimental Trustees of the Devonshire and Dorset Regiment*)

'Bury them and be silent.' By 1814 much of the Iberian Peninsula lay in ruins, while losses among the population have been estimated at a minimum of 500,000. (*Museo del Prado*)

by one we were forced to abandon our friends and bid them farewell for ever . . . We were so hungry that, when we were at one place lodged in the cemetery as the best place to keep watch on us, we were overcome by the fragrance of the grass that grew there and fell upon it as if it was the richest delicacy imaginable. In the end even our very tormentors felt pity for us and let us keep the bread that the inhabitants of the villages through which we passed offered us; however, this was so hard that it could not be eaten without first soaking it in water.[321]

Yet the Spaniards were in no position to complain about such treatment. Indeed, for many of the French soldiers in Spanish hands the situation was deteriorating still further. Following the mass escapes in the spring of 1810, the remaining prisoners of Bailén had all been shipped to the tiny Balearic islet of Cabrera. A bare scrap of barren rock, Cabrera did not possess the resources to feed 800 men, let alone 8,000. The prisoners, then, were entirely dependent on food brought over from the mainland, but all too often this failed to arrive. In February 1811, for example, nine days went by without the prisoners receiving any food:

With the food that we had succeeded in putting by completely gone, there was nothing for it but to scramble about among the rocks to see if we could find any plants that might pacify the hunger that was tormenting us. All we could find was a handful of dry thistles and a little clover. Putting all we had got together, we boiled it for some hours in some brackish water, and, as soon as we judged it to be cooked, we sat down to eat. God above, what a meal! How could civilised nations have let soldiers – men, indeed – be treated so cruelly? The ingredients tasted unbearably bitter, while the sharp spines of the thistles made our mouths bleed, and in the end we had to give up . . . One of my friends was a sergeant, and he had made an overcoat out of two or three sheepskins that had come over in a consignment of medical supplies. Having previously burned off all the wool, he had now cooked them. The result was paltry enough, but, when I told him about the meal we had just tried, he offered me a spoonful of the liquid and a couple of small pieces of the skin. This gift I accepted with great gratitude, and I pronounced it excellent, even though it consisted of little more than some traces of glue floating in hot water. Consternation reigned on all sides: it was painted, indeed, on every visage . . . The next day we learned that during the night death had put an end to the sufferings of a large number of the prisoners . . . At dawn on the eighth day that we had gone without food, I got up and wandered mechanically towards the shore, lost in the saddest of reflections. Sitting down on a stone, I cast my gaze upon the waves, but all in vain: nothing offered itself to my eyes, and the latter filled with tears. Just at this moment, my attention was attracted by some voices that I heard nearby. Getting up, I walked a few paces towards the sound, and discovered a small cave. There I was confronted by the most appalling spectacle. Two men in Swiss uniforms were occupied in dismembering the limbs of one of our unfortunate comrades who had died during the night. Absolutely famished, they had already put a thigh to roast over some hot coals. Seized with horror, I could not utter a single word.[322]

In Garrison

Albuera and Fuentes de Oñoro were the two main battles that took place between the Anglo-Portuguese army and the French in 1811. The early autumn witnessed a further flurry of activity when a brief French counter-offensive temporarily drove the British back from the vicinity of Ciudad Rodrigo, and this served to prove that, despite the tactical superiority of his army, Wellington still could not advance into Spain. This was soon to change, but for the time being let us again rather look at the occupied zone of Spain. Here the dominant feature of life very much remained the 'little war'. For one thing, around the periphery of King Joseph's illusory kingdom small forces of Spanish regulars continued to wage war on the French by making sudden dashes at isolated strongholds. To deal with such threats, the French had no option but to concentrate a field force and march against the enemy, but this was a process that invariably wore out the troops, used up valuable supplies and alienated the already resentful populace still further. Having taken service with the commander of the Berg lancer regiment to escape the miseries of imprisonment, George Farmer was a witness to one such expedition:

> Sixteen days of constant marching brought us to Astorga, in and around which the corps proceeded to establish itself. The cavalry had quarters within the walls, the infantry and guns encamped outside, and strange and wild were the scenes which they alike enacted . . . The soldiers received a sort of unspoken licence to plunder, and terrible was the havoc which in their wantonness they occasioned. Moreover, the honour of the women, and here and there the lives of the men, fell a sacrifice not infrequently . . . You might see all manner of rich hangings converted into tents. The soldiers lay or danced and sang among the tents arrayed in priests' robes and ladies' dresses . . . Of course, the town became rapidly thinned of its inhabitants, of whom all capable of bearing arms went to swell the number of the Spanish forces . . . We remained in the vicinity of Astorga but a few days at the expiration of which the order to march was issued, and, without having seen an open enemy, or had any opportunity of taking vengeance on a guerrilla party, we began to retrace our steps towards Toro. There was no deviation in the route, and the consequence was that our sufferings during the retreat were to the full as intolerable as they had been on the advance, and that, when we reached Toro, both men and horses – but especially the latter – were all but unfit for service.[323]

The Spanish troops that hung about the fringes of the French zone of occupation constituted but the first of several prongs of the 'little war' with which the invaders found themselves confronted. More recognisable as guerrillas, but still part of the regular army, were the various independent forces of regular troops that had for one reason or another become detached from their parent bodies and were fighting what amounted to a private war in the interior of the country. Examples include those of Pedro Villacampa, Francisco Ballesteros and Julián Sánchez. Of these, the latter was the figure most well known to British observers, as he regularly cooperated with them in the region of Ciudad Rodrigo and even fought with Wellington at the battle of Fuentes de Oñoro. One man who encountered him was Winchester College-educated Francis Hall, who had given up studying for a degree at Trinity College, Cambridge, to enlist as a cornet in the Fourteenth Light Dragoons in June 1810:

An alarm was given after dinner of a strange body of cavalry. On reconnoitring them from the church tower, they proved to be the detachment under Don Julián Sánchez, an adventurer, who, from a shepherd, had become a corporal in the Spanish army, and, since the [start of the] war a captain of an independent corps who lived by plundering friends and foes, seldom fighting unless when ten to one, but often doing good service both to themselves and [their] country by cutting off straggling detachments and convoys of provisions. They came into Fuente Guinaldo looking as wild and whiskered as freebooters need to be. They were armed with lances, miserably mounted, and dressed more like hussars than any other description of troops.[324]

Very similar to the forces of Julián Sánchez were the troops improvised deep in the zone of French occupation from bands of irregulars by army officers who had become separated from their regiments, representatives of the Old Order, or adventurers who perceived the war against France as a means of rising from obscurity and making their fortunes. And, finally, there were bands of irregulars who possessed little or nothing in the way of military discipline, and were in reality little more than bandits, but none the less exacted a steady toll of French lives and spread terror in their ranks. One such group was encountered in the area of Salamanca by Charles Parquin in February 1811:

On the morning of 1 February 1811, Major de Vérigny . . . instructed me to arrange for one officer and fifty chasseurs to be ready and mounted by noon . . . The strictest secrecy had been maintained about this mission. These were the circumstances which had led up to it. A French merchant, Monsieur Magnan, had wanted to return from Ciudad Rodrigo to Salamanca and had taken advantage of the departure of a detachment of infantry for Salamanca to start out with his young wife. He had already completed the first stage . . . when, urged on by his wife who was anxious to finish the journey, and also thinking that he was out of danger, he whipped up the mules pulling his carriage. He had not gone a league when, at a bend in the road where it ran through a forest, the carriage was attacked by a band of brigands . . . Any resistance would have been useless. Monsieur Magnan, his pretty young wife, his servant, his mules and his carriage were led half a league into the forest. The bandits robbed the prisoners of all their possessions and were preparing to put the men to death and to make the unfortunate woman submit to an even worse fate when the leader of the band, prompted by the thought of obtaining a substantial ransom, offered Monsieur Magnan his life and his wife's honour for 10,000 *francs* in gold. This sum was to be paid by one of Monsieur Magnan's friends in Salamanca. The offer was joyfully accepted and the merchant wrote a note to one of his associates, telling him to pay the bearer the sum demanded. At eight in the morning one of the bandits left with the note . . . If he had not returned by three in the afternoon, the prisoners' fate would be sealed . . . Armed with his letter of credit the messenger arrived at the house of the person who was to pay him . . . The undated letter was so brief that his suspicions were aroused. He questioned the Spaniard, who, not being able to speak French, said nothing but 'dinero' as he rubbed his thumb and forefinger together. The merchant sent for . . . Major de Vérigny, and informed him of his difficulty. The major immediately had the Spaniard arrested and ordered him to speak the truth . . . Thereupon, the bandit confessed everything . . . [and] offered to lead the French to the spot . . . where poor Magnan, his wife and his servant were awaiting their fate . . . When the detachment set out . . . the Spaniard was riding an army horse held by a chasseur on either side. They had orders to kill him if he made the slightest move to escape. They had been riding for some time when . . . they suddenly came upon the band. They were not a moment too soon! The leader had become concerned, and . . . had [just said], 'It is now three o'clock. If within the quarter of an hour which I generously allow you, my messenger has not returned . . . you and your servant may commend your souls to God. As for your charming wife, who is all the more charming for her tears, her fate . . . is decided!' Providence willed this crime should not take place. Before the fatal hour came, Major de Vérigny and his men arrived and opened fire on the brigands without giving them time to reach for their weapons. Many of them were wounded or killed; the remainder flung themselves on their knees, and, wringing their hands, begged for mercy.[325]

Even in the vicinity of large garrisons, the result of this wide mixture of activity was that the invaders could never feel secure. Badly wounded, George Farmer's master travelled to Burgos to recuperate:

The hatred borne by the Spaniards towards the French had become . . . bitter in the extreme . . . In and around Burgos, I soon discovered that this was peculiarly the case. At first, indeed, the manners of the people deceived me quite, for I fancied they were content because of the gentleness and deference with which they appeared to treat . . . every Frenchman with whom they openly came into contact. But the experience of a few days taught me that this air of weakness was put on for the sole purpose of enticing victims into their power. There was scarcely a day passed without bringing in reports of assassinations attempted, if not perpetrated, upon our people. No man could walk half a mile beyond the town without being fired at, and even in the grand promenade, which extends along the bank of the river and is shaded on either side by rows of noble trees, the same scenes were constantly enacted. I have ridden over and over with my master to enjoy the refreshing breezes in that shady spot, and been driven out again by showers of bullets which knocked the leaves about us and came we knew not from whence. In a word, the French were, both in camp and in quarters, prisoners at large, with the comfortable assurance continually forced upon them that even within their own lines they could not count on escaping the knife of the assassin.[326]

An equally depressing picture comes from the pen of the artillery officer Jean Noël, who had survived Masséna's invasion of Portugal and in the summer of 1811 was stationed at the Castilian town of Toro:

We missed Italy greatly when we were in Spain. Apart from bread, meat and wine, the country offered us nothing. In the towns we had no acquaintances; there was no theatre, no entertainment, no promenades; and the countryside was barren, devoid of trees and gardens. It was impossible to leave our cantonments. For our necessities, clothes, boots and toilet articles, we had to rely on traders who came from France and exploited us outrageously. It was sad to see how everything combined to take advantage of the needs of the unhappy soldier who risked his life daily, and endured every discomfort for the common good. In our various cantonments around Toro where the countryside was infested with guerrillas, I had to take great care that we were not taken by surprise, for we were isolated from the division. I placed one post in the middle of the village and, during the day, another on the top of the clock tower. By night the roads were blocked with wagons . . . All were aware of a rallying point to be used if there should be an alert.[327]

In these conditions travel was both difficult and dangerous. For many French soldiers their first experience of Spain was a journey along the high road linking Bayonne with Madrid. Among the French soldiers to enter Spain in 1810, for example, was Elzéar Blaze, the elder brother of the prisoner of Bailén, Sébastian Blaze, who had enlisted in the Vélites of the Guard as a private at the age of eighteen in 1805 but by 1809 had transferred into a line-infantry regiment as a lieutenant:

In Spain we never travelled singly: the first tree would have served as a gibbet for the imprudent wight who should have ventured alone upon any road. It was necessary to go in bodies with advanced guard and rear guard always in readiness to fire. The governor of Bayonne stopped the detachments and the officers proceeding singly to Spain, and, when the whole formed a mass capable of resisting, he permitted them to set out for Irun. When I crossed the Bidassoa . . . our convoy consisted of a dozen detachments belonging to different corps, a great number of single officers rejoining their regiments, persons attached to the commissariat, young men going to Madrid to solicit appointments, and administrators of the *droits réunis* proceeding to Spain to organise it in the same manner as France . . . At the moment of our departure from Irun, the commander of the convoy regulated the march of this motley assemblage, a task that was none of the easiest. Sixty carriages drawn by oxen were laden with the baggage and marched in the centre; two wagons with three horses would easily have carried the whole, but the carts of Biscay are so small that four knapsacks would completely fill one of them . . . The mountain of Salinas was frequently celebrated at that period for the ambuscades which [Espoz y] Mina, Longa and El Pastor were incessantly laying for our convoys. Never was a spot more favourable: a mountain which it took four hours to climb, a road bordered by heights and precipices, could not be cleared by the riflemen. The enemy concealed himself behind rocks; you never saw him, but you heard the reports of his musketry, which made some amends . . . We had been ascending for three hours, preceded by our advance guard, when all at once a pistol, discharged close to us, gave the signal to two or three hundred muskets to fire at the same moment. A ravine separated us from the Spaniards: our men immediately set about descending into the valley, but the guerrillas had soon disappeared. We lost fourteen men in this affair; a charming woman, the wife of one of the superior *employés* of the hospitals . . . at Madrid, was wounded by a ball in the breast, and died two days afterwards at Vitoria . . . At each town some portion of the convoy found themselves at the place of their destination; the column, thus weakened, needed fresh reinforcements before it could pursue its route. Half, nay, I may say almost the whole, of the French army was occupied in escorting couriers; we had garrisons in all the towns and villages upon the high roads, and very often midway between them there had been erected little forts . . . each occupied by perhaps 100 soldiers.[328]

Another soldier who experienced a clash with the guerrillas – in this case the forces of Espoz y Mina – was Jean-Baptiste Lemonnier-Delafosse, who had been sent back to France with a convoy of Spanish prisoners following the battle of Sabugal, and in April 1812 once more found himself bound for the peninsular front with a draft of recruits.

At Bayonne we found a convoy formed of a number of pieces of artillery . . . and four vans filled with gold . . . awaiting an escort. Also there was a gig belonging to a Madame C. who was travelling with her daughter to join her husband, who was the chief director of supplies at Vitoria. Initially, this had been denied permission to join the convoy . . . but, as a result of my pleas, the commander of the convoy agreed that it could come with us. Crossing the Bidassoa, we passed through Irun and . . . stopped at Tolosa in order to wait for a regiment of the [Young] Guard that had been sent from Vitoria to pick us up. On the latter's arrival, its commander . . . refused to take charge of the artillery and its slow-moving train of little bullock carts . . . on the grounds that news had just been received . . . that [Espoz y] Mina was planning to attack the convoy . . . He would, then, he said, only take the gold. Our dispositions were therefore made accordingly, and on the morning of 19 April we set off with the treasure and Madame C.'s gig, escorted by the Guard unit, our march-battalion and two pieces of field artillery. Well aware of the danger that threatened us . . . my chief concern was to allay the fears of my *protégés* who were constantly asking if we were going to be attacked. Mounting the gig's running board, I asked the daughter to sing me a love song . . . Hardly had she got through the first couplet when a shot rang out . . . There immediately followed the sound of regular volleys: the advanced guard had found the enemy. I ran to my duty. [Espoz y] Mina had placed the bulk of his forces on a bluff overlooking the road on its left-hand side, while at the same time stationing a strong detachment . . . in a farm that directly blocked our way. This second party were quickly chased away, but the men on the hillside, who were fighting in the style of troops of the line, held their ground bravely . . . Two columns of attack therefore marched out against them, one of them from the front and the other from the flank, and, enduring their fire without letting off a single shot in return, soon had them in a state of complete rout . . . The cost of this affair was six dead and twenty-five wounded. Among the latter were two officers of the Guard, who, when the march resumed, were placed in the gig . . . At length the convoy got back on the road, and at about six o'clock in the evening, it arrived at Villareal . . . The next morning I hastened to search out my poor *protégées* . . . As their vehicle had been requisitioned . . . they had had to walk the two and a half leagues that had remained of the journey, and had ended up barefoot, the road having completely worn out their satin shoes. But that was not the only thing. In floods of tears, the mother begged me to help her daughter. 'My poor girl has gone mad! Her head is quite lost! The whole night has been one long delirium. What are we going to do? What will her father say?' 'Take heart,' I replied, 'I will go and speak to your daughter.' Going into her room, I found her crouched on her bed, babbling to herself with her head in her hands and her elbows on her knees . . . I tried to reason with her . . . but nothing could distract her attention from the sporadic gunshots that could be heard outside, at every one of which she started violently . . . 'We are lost!,' she cried, 'They are here!' 'No, it is only some soldiers cleaning their arms . . . Get up, give me your hand: come with me and you will see.' For two hours I repeated the same words, and at long last I succeeded in reviving her feeble courage a little, and getting her to come out of the house . . . Poor girl! Fancy being barely 16 years old and fresh out of finishing school, and suddenly finding oneself in the middle of a battle . . . with musket and cannon shots echoing all around and wounded men all covered in blood being laid out in front of you . . . Such a loss of wit is only too easy to understand.[329]

Nor was it just a question of the constant danger. Spain was not just a foreign country but one whose standard of living was far below that of France and Germany. There was therefore little in the way of physical comfort. Let us again quote Elzéar Blaze:

The transition from St Jean de Luz to Irun is as great as from Calais to Dover, and yet the Bidassoa is but a rivulet . . . What a difference [from] our quarters in Germany . . . Instead of the most scrupulous cleanliness and the kindness of the people behind the Rhine, we had to encounter the nastiness and sour looks of the Spaniards. Though accustomed to the climate of Poland, we felt cold in Spain. In Biscay and Castile it is impossible to have a fire in winter: nobody has the least notion that a door, a window, is made to shut. A floor [covering], a carpet, are unheard-of luxuries; the trade of chimney sweep is unknown, for there are no chimneys. In the kitchens you see a hole at which the smoke escapes when it can escape at all. In large towns, such as Burgos and Valladolid, you find one or two fireplaces in the houses of the great, and most of these were built by French generals who wished to make their quarters comfortable . . . People everywhere warm themselves with a *bracero*, an iron vase filled with charcoal . . . It is placed in the principal room, where all the inmates of the house meet. There, forming a circle, they scorch their knees, thus making, it is true, due compensation for their backs, which are always chilled cold . . . Of all the people in the world, the Spaniard is certainly the least eater and drinker: with what a hundred [artisans] in Paris consume, you might keep a thousand Spaniards . . . Put into a pot full of water, grey peas, *garbanzos*, cabbage, a plentiful allowance of capsicum and a little piece of bacon . . . boil the whole sufficiently, and you will dine as all Spain dines when it has a good dinner . . . The Spaniard is a stranger to luxury, and to those superfluities which with us are matters of the first necessity. The arts, agriculture, [manufacturing], have not advanced a step since the time of Charles V. Advanced, I say? They have retrograded . . . In Spain the comfortable is unknown, perhaps disdained.[330]

To discomfort was added the most violent clash of cultures. An interesting comment here comes from the pen of the Prussian officer Heinrich von Brandt, who late in 1811 found himself invited to a *soirée* at the headquarters of the Polish divisional commander, General Chlopicki, which was then situated at the Aragonese town of Sádaba. Present at the gathering were a number of Spanish ladies including a marchioness whom Von Brandt suspected of being a spy in the service of Espoz y Mina:

One of our lieutenants was a very talented violin player, and Gulicz, my good friend the surgeon, was quite good on the flute. The general requested they play a mazurka, which they did, and to which the other Poles danced, to the great astonishment of the Spanish ladies, who had never before seen such a dance. After the mazurka came a waltz which caused even more surprise and perhaps not a little scandal. The Spaniards were very keen to know whether the ladies and gentlemen really embraced and held each other so close during a waltz. Meanwhile, as I noticed that most of the ladies were continuing to stare at me as though I was an exotic animal, I managed to draw one of my comrades aside and ask him to explain the meaning of all this. I learned from him that the marchioness had asked the general whether or not it was true that there were heretics among our soldiers and officers and wanted to know if it was possible for her to meet one. It was therefore in my capacity as a Lutheran that I [had been] invited to the party . . . In the Spain of that period many people believed that a Jew or heretic was some kind of devil with horns and a tail to prove it! Many of the quite affluent classes, especially the women, were convinced this was so, and it was therefore with some surprise that they noticed we were in fact just like anybody else. A strange incident a few days later clearly demonstrated that such beliefs also held sway among the lower classes. The Fourteenth Line, which garrisoned Tauste, had a Jew from Alsace called Salomon who provided food and wine for them, and this man was often in contact with the locals, buying victuals and supplies. Now, he paid quite well for the items he bought and so was quite popular with the people and believed he had nothing to fear from them. One day he went off with a detachment on reconnaissance and stayed on in a village against the advice of the commander . . . As he did not reappear, a patrol was sent out, and they found him sprawled naked in the middle of the road, half dead of fear. A band of people had jumped on him as he came out of the village and pulled off his clothes, and as they left they were shouting, 'He is not a Jew: he hasn't got any horns or a tail!' His little cart and his clothes were later found intact, thus proving that these people had not wanted to rob him.[331]

Yet it was not all enmity. Particularly in towns which they held for some time, the French found that it was possible to find both friends and adherents. Let us here quote Fée:

> Throughout the occupation, Seville was as quiet as any French city: she had accepted her new destiny, while Joseph had many adherents there. The inhabitants bore our domination as if they were our compatriots. The resident French population – officers of the general staff and the medical services [and] employees of the civil and military administration – all had friends within the walls, and the women paid no attention to nationality, but rather let themselves go wherever their sympathy took them. Thanks to their victories, the French were frequently able to stage veritable triumphs in Seville, while the fact that they were foreigners, in despite of the patriotic sympathies that ought to have prevailed, made them seem preferable to Spaniards. The *soirées*, balls and dinners given by Marshal Soult were all very much to the taste of the *sevillanos*, and tickets for them were much in demand.[332]

Even if some of his claims are a little questionable – it has, for example, been argued that *afrancesamiento* was strongest among the older generation – Brandt is very interesting on the subject:

> The French were not as universally hated as has since been alleged. The monks and priests, who fought for *aris et focis*, were generally against us, as were the majority of the peasants and, in the towns, the very young, who were still under the influence of the clergy. In the middle classes, older people were exclusively against us, but among those between twenty and thirty there were many *afrancesados* who hoped that the presence of the French might speed up essential reforms in society and in the administration of their country. Although women, especially the mature ones, bitterly rebuked the French for their lack of religion and for their insatiable appetites . . . on occasion during our wanderings we had the agreeable experience of meeting ardent francophiles, especially young brides with old husbands or . . . nuns or novices whose Mother Superiors had set them at liberty on the approach of the French.[333]

Although it is hard to know how far such stories can be trusted, tales of friendship and romance abound. For a good example, let us turn to the memoirs of Charles Parquin, who passed most of the two years he spent in Spain in garrison in Old Castile:

> At Salamanca my duties as adjutant obtained for me excellent quarters in the house of a beautiful Spanish noblewoman, Doña Rosa de la N., whose husband, a colonel in the Spanish army, had died two years previously. Like any widow who still retains a touch of vanity, she had instructed her maid to say she was twenty-five and this was the answer I received when I sought this detail from the maid. But this little lie, if indeed it was one, was not at all necessary for, whatever her age, Doña Rosa was one of the most enchanting women I have ever seen in my life. She was quite small, but her movements were marked by a supple gracefulness . . . She had no children and lived alone with her servants in a house where comfort and even luxury were

clearly in evidence. Mine were clearly very good quarters; I could have had none better. Every evening I would spend an hour or two by the fire with my hostess. I had to avoid politics in our conversation as Doña Rosa, who was as proud as any Spaniard could be, would not tolerate contradiction. In the end I persuaded her to banish politics from our conversation. This was a considerable achievement . . . Later on, as one can imagine, I did not stop there. I made further requests and, in short, I was happy, very happy indeed.[334]

Sadly for Parquin, this relationship did not last. Shot in the mouth at Fuentes de Oñoro, however, he found Spanish companionship of a rather different sort:

I was living with a wealthy Spaniard in a village not far from Salamanca which was occupied by a detachment from our army. After the initial pain, my wound no longer hurt me much, but it condemned me to complete silence. I could not say a word. My host, who was a most worthy man, would come every morning to enquire after my health and to hold forth on the disastrous effects of a war about which no doubt I felt strongly since I had been wounded in it. 'But,' he added, 'whatever evils they have in store for us, they will never do us enough harm to equal the good they have done by destroying the Inquisition.' I took my pencil and wrote, 'And by giving you institutions which you would never have had without our presence.' He nodded in agreement and added, 'Let us hope that we are wise enough to retain them.'[335]

The fact of the matter was that the invaders were never completely isolated. Invited to typical Spanish *tertulias*, many Frenchmen even began to pick up certain local habits and characteristics. One area where this was particularly so was the use of tobacco. In the early nineteenth century smoking was a routine pleasure in most of Europe, but it was in general only men who smoked, while the only means by which the smoker could indulge was by means of the clay pipe. In Spain, however, neither was the case. Not only did large numbers of women smoke and that quite openly without the slightest social stigma, but the method employed was the cigar or even a primitive form of cigarette. Such devices being much less bothersome to use than pipes, many soldiers on both sides began to copy the Spaniards' example, and in this fashion the Peninsular War may be said to have had a considerable influence on the social and cultural history of the world. At all events the sort of scene witnessed at one gathering by Sébastian Blaze was perfectly normal:

A packet of little cigars was handed round . . . and everyone began to smoke. For a foreigner, the sight of a numerous assembly made up of papas and mamas, priests and young men about town, monks and young girls all smoking cigars comes as a great surprise. It is a taste that is peculiar to Spain, which is unknown in Paris to this day . . . Experts in the art of love, Andalusian girls have even introduced coquetterie into the manner in which they smoke . . . It is considered a great favour among them to be allowed to take a light from the cigar which they are smoking, while to be asked for the same service in return is seen a still greater boon. The cigars which women use are called *pajillas* and are very short, and this obliges two smokers who are exchanging lights to approach very close; they share the same smoke, indeed . . . and these little favours multiply and bring greater ones in their turn.[336]

Even where overt tensions existed with the families on whom the French were billeted, some degree of human intercourse survived. In Chiclana, for example, Fée found himself lodged in the house of the mayor, Ambrosio Múñoz:

> The family . . . consisted of the father . . . an exalted patriot, who wished us all to the antipodes and expressed his hatred of foreigners with an energy and freedom of expression that were entirely new to me . . . [and] three daughters. The oldest, Ines, did not live with the family: she had married a captain of the Ninety-Sixth Regiment, and, on the retreat of the army, followed him to France. The second, Maria, had the character of her father and took hatred of the French to a state of exultation . . . She could never manage to give the name of brother to her sister's husband, and rather always called him by his rank (her sister, meanwhile, became *la capitana*). Yet I tamed this fierce apparition, and, without surrendering her patriotism, she in the end became affectionate enough towards me. As for the youngest daughter, who was always surrounded by the strictest surveillance, she was called Josefa . . . If her father spoke of liberty, she did not contradict him, but . . . left to her natural instincts, she had nothing in her heart but the sweetest sentiments . . . One night I came in and found everything ready for a little party. It was . . . my saint's day, and I was very touched by the signs of affection that were lavished upon me. The patio had been illuminated; an elaborate supper, which only the misery of the times prevented from being called sumptuous, was served; and I was presented with bunches of wild flowers . . . two Roman medals . . . [and] a drawing of a view of Chiclana . . . Every face was smiling, even that of the second sister, who for the time being seemed prepared to forget that I was an enemy. Some of my comrades had been invited, while dessert was taken on the terrace. It was a delicious evening.[337]

Service in Spain, then, was not always the terrifying ordeal that it has often been made out to be. That said, there must have been many imperial soldiers who shared the feelings of Captain Noël when the latter was repatriated to France in preparation for the Russian campaign at the end of 1811:

> At last on 25 December we came to Irun, the last Spanish town, where we should have slept. However, with several companions as eager as myself, we continued on our way and on that same Christmas Day crossed the Bidassoa. It would be quite impossible for me to describe the emotion we all felt. When we saw the frontier we all started to run, and, the Bidassoa once crossed, I believe that, if fear of what others would think had not held us back, we should have kissed the soil of our beloved country.[338]

Between the Lines

Thus far, we have mainly looked at the experience of the combatants. What, though, of the experience of the Spanish people of French occupation? In general, it may be said that their sufferings were intense in the extreme. In the first place economic activity was at a standstill. Writing of Extremadura, for example, Noël remarks:

> Throughout our travels, the country through which we passed was uncultivated and all the villages had been abandoned. This was not because the land was barren, but rather because the inhabitants had given up the attempt to cultivate land on which the harvest brought them no profit. In any case, everything they needed for husbandry had been taken from them – horse, carts and seed.[339]

For a more urban picture, we might turn to the city of Málaga. In 1810 this normally thriving port was traversed by Andrew Blayney:

> Though [Málaga] still retains some external appearance of its former prosperity, it is but the insubstantial shadow of departed reality. The total cessation of commerce and the losses consequent on the war have produced innumerable bankruptcies and universal distress; the port . . . has lost all appearance of commercial life, some fishing boats alone being seen in movement, while a few . . . feluccas and other smaller vessels are laid up rotting. What a contrast with the former flourishing commerce of this city, whose annual exports were valued at half a million sterling . . . Such have been the desolating effects of the . . . invasion of the French.[340]

In addition to the economic difficulties Spain was experiencing, the population was also affected very badly by the ever-growing financial demands imposed by the French army and the administration of King Joseph. For some idea of what was involved, let us turn to Juan Domingo Palomar:

> In the month of December 1810 all stocks of colonial products – cocoa, sugar, cinnamon and the like – were confiscated from the merchants of [Alcalá de Henares], the value of the goods that were taken coming to about 500,000 *reales*, and this after they had been brought in at the say-so of the government and had all the proper customs duties paid in their respect. As everything went to Madrid, it was, we agreed, a right royal sacking. At the beginning of [1811], on top of all the burdens that had been inflicted on it in the two years that had gone before, the city found itself faced by the so-called patents licence, what this boiled down to being that everyone who exercised any sort of trade or profession had to obtain a paper that generally cost him more than he could earn in one month, and sometimes more than he could in half a year. On top of this there was the 10 per cent levy on income gained from the rent of houses, and the 6 per cent levy on income from the rent of land, while the city also had to find 1,000 *reales* a day for the maintenance of the garrison, and the 245,000 *reales* that was its share of the 20,000,000 or so that had been levied on New Castile as a whole. And all this at a time when the ordinary taxes had not fallen in the slightest, when there was no commerce, and when industry was at a standstill, all this, of course, being thanks to the war. To add insult to injury, the inhabitants were also prisoners in their own city, for fear of El Empecinado had caused the French to block all the ways out of the city apart from the four main roads and even these were blocked with strong wooden gates that were shut at

nightfall. As all this had been executed by the labour of the inhabitants themselves at the cost of the city, it could even be said that we were the instruments of our own imprisonment, and all so the French could feel safe from the guerrillas . . . At the beginning of September the town council received word of its share of the levy that had been imposed on the harvest. In terms of value, this came to a total of 750,000 *reales*, while the government's order made it clear that the grain was to be seized by force from anyone who had some in their possession . . . On 18 September operations began to collect the levy. Led by the sub-prefect Trammaria, the governor Azlor, and the war commissary Miguel de Belgrano, a party of troops went round the town with fixed bayonets, smashing down the doors of the peasants and other producers and taking whatever they wanted . . . In all, Alcalá's losses came to 11,000 *fanegas* of wheat and barley . . . On 8 October all the grain that they had stockpiled . . . was taken out and loaded into more than a hundred carts ready to be taken off to Madrid. What is more, all this was done in the very sight of the inhabitants, and at a time when one could not get a loaf of bread for 3 *reales* and the poor inhabitants were oppressed with hunger and misery.[341]

Nor was the burden necessarily much lighter in areas controlled by the Anglo-Portuguese army. Here, too, the presence of the soldiery was very burdensome. William Tomkinson, for example, gives a stark account of relations with the local populace on the frontiers of Portugal in the winter of 1811:

The procuring of forage through this winter for the horses was attended with the greatest difficulty . . . The detachments left their quarters soon after daylight, and were absent from six to eight hours generally, and frequently until dark. The peasants hid their straw with the greatest care, being the only chance of keeping what few oxen remained to them for the purpose of agriculture alive until the spring. They hid their straw behind stores of wood laid by for fuel, which two or three dragoons would remove with several hours' work, and possibly not find above three or four days' supply for three or four horses. The carrying it away was always attended with the complaints and lamentations of the women, who followed us out of the place saying . . . their oxen must now die . . . Nothing but this would have induced them to exert themselves as they now did, and on the return home of the party . . . it was amusing to hear the tales of one dragoon to another . . . of the plans of the inhabitants to save their straw. It was frequently found under their beds. The scarcity towards the last was so great we took it out of the beds they lay upon. The dragoons were at last so knowing, . . . that nearly every bit through the country was used, and I do not think we could have stayed another month without half of the horses dying of hunger. When we entered a village most of the men hid themselves from being afraid of our taking them as guides or threatening them in some way to point out where the straw was hidden. The women exerted themselves in doing all they could to mislead us, and on our finding any assailed us with cries and entreaties to leave some for their oxen.[342]

Nor was Tomkinson the only British soldier to comment on the sufferings of the civilian population. Born in 1789 and educated at Harrow and Oxford, John Mills was the son of a country gentleman from Ringwood in Hampshire; he arrived in the Peninsula in 1811 as an ensign in the Coldstream Guards. As he reflected in his diary:

> The articles of life are all enormously dear, full three times as much as they were two years ago. Bread is fully four times as dear as in England and is getting dearer every day. The Portuguese live incredibly hard: they have constantly on the fire an earthen pot into which they put a few leaves and water. Those that can afford it add a little oil to this mess; when it is sufficiently boiled, they put it into a plate, and the family assemble round it, each with a spoon and a small bit of bread. Men, women and children [alike] seem to have no occupation . . . One of the great systems of this war is to eat up a country. The word itself sounds horrid, but the eating up is done to render it useless to an enemy. You can then advance or retire and find some other country to be devoured. This cannibal-like system may suit us, who are sure to find some other place when we have devoured the one we are in, but it does not suit the natives . . . The little money they may have gained will not as in England purchase bread: that is all gone, and, if some little should remain, the owner will not part with it, not knowing where to get more. The people know that they must lose all their grain and cattle . . . and who can then wonder that they should be tired of the war. After all, it makes not the slightest difference to them whether the house of Braganza or Bonaparte is upon the throne. The voice of the people would, if they were to open their mouths, call for peace upon any terms. It is the voice of the grandees you hear, who do not suffer the privations to the same extent and are influenced by different motives.[343]

What makes these passages still more distressing is that the self-same villages described by Tomkinson and Mills had often been in the path of the French forces in 1811. At one point William Warre, for example, found himself at Nave village in the vicinity of Sabugal:

> It is impossible to give you an adequate idea of the misery in every village into which the enemy have entered, as they have destroyed everything that they could not carry away . . . In my present habitation a considerable part of the floor has been torn up, and the windows, doors and furniture burned . . . Hunger and famine surround us in all directions among the unhappy peasantry, and our charity to some few has now completely exhausted our means. Money is of little use where nothing is to be bought.[344]

And, finally, the local inhabitants were in many respects just as vulnerable to guerrillas and bandits as the French. Of the troops commanded by Julián Sánchez on the Portuguese frontier, for example, Schaumann wrote:

> They were very much feared. No Spanish municipal authority would have dared to refuse them anything. Even the inhabitants of small towns submitted to their orders without complaining. Let me give just one example of this. One of my muleteers had a young and extraordinarily pretty girl with him . . . One afternoon . . . a guerrilla dashing past, suddenly halted and . . . peremptorily commanded her to

jump up behind him on the horse's back and galloped away with her. The parted couple did not dare to protest against this treatment by even one syllable of complaint![345]

In respect of men who claimed to be guerrillas, there was at least some hope of recourse to the military authorities in cases of pillage and other forms of misbehaviour. The many bandits, however, were another matter. To quote a Catalan priest from the frontier district of the Ampurdan valley named Antoni Perich y Viader who left behind a chronicle of the war in Catalonia:

> As a result of the sort of thing that goes on in war, the number and daring of the insolent reached such a pitch that it was impossible for anyone to travel the roads for fear of being robbed: little escaped the bandits, while they were not even deterred by the capital sentences passed on five of their number on 1 June 1811 [in Sant Jordi Desvalls] . . . Not only did they rob travellers, but in order to humiliate them they stripped them naked . . . not sparing even the women. In houses, meanwhile, they would hang up the lady of the house and torture her by burning the soles of her feet. Such was the fate of Sra Vidal de Flassá, who was left very badly scarred by her burns. This happened on the morning of 18 October 1811, and that same afternoon the house . . . of Sra Pubilla was robbed, the lady concerned being driven out of the building in nothing but a shift.[346]

Plundered and oppressed by all and sundry, the civilian population was also, as ever, at the mercy of climate and harvest. Let us here quote the journal of Faustino Casamayor for 31 January 1812:

> This month the weather has been a continuous round of cold and ice . . . while foodstuffs have been so scarce and expensive that there is no one who can remember the like . . . Bread has cost just as much as it did last month, and the contributions demanded by the French have been so excessive . . . that they are not to be borne . . . As for the misery of the common people, it has been so great that in the streets one sees nothing but beggars.[347]

In this situation the inhabitants had to shift for themselves as best they could. One obvious means of survival was prostitution, and in some towns and villages in areas that were much transited by the rival armies it seems likely that this became the lot of almost the entire female populace. Of one mountain *pueblo*, for example, Schaumann wrote:

> As regards morals, I must confess that in all my travels I have never come across such a Sodom and Gomorrah as that place was. The girls and women of the higher as well as of the lower classes were practically all disreputable. Pure virgins were rare.[348]

To the horror of conservative churchmen in particular, many people sought salvation in gambling, an occupation that must also have served as an escape from the misery and despair of everyday life:

> All the furies of Hell appeared to be making war on the population of Madrid. One of the means which the French and their supporters introduced as a means of

gaining money was . . . a game called roulette. This was played on tables in the streets in various parts of the city, all of them very busy, as well as in a number of gaming houses that were furnished in the best style and manned by dozens of liveried servants. Naturally, the bankers were French. In brief, the way it worked was that there was a dish that was spun round in the middle of the table. This was divided into numbered compartments, and a little ball was thrown into it. When it came to rest, whoever had bet on the number the ball had landed on got perhaps 35 or 36 *pesetas* for every one that they had placed on the table. This might have been quite fun to watch, but it is not a good idea to play such games. Setting aside the numerous evils which they bring in their train, it is always the bankers who win . . . But unfortunately in so calamitous a time such things are not always obvious, and, at all events, all too many of the inhabitants of Madrid certainly thought otherwise. Deluded by the showmanship of the bankers, the novelty of the game, the large amounts of money being placed in bets, and the sight of the lucky winners scooping up their gains, more and more people began to take up the sport, and, indeed, to become gripped by it in the strangest manner. The basic idea, of course, however foolish, was that the most unfortunate of people could become rich in an instant, and in this fashion the infection spread from one person to the next until even . . . humble artisans and day labourers were taking part . . . So widespread did the habit become that the government's cut easily came to 500,000 *reales* a month, and sometimes even more . . . This reflection alone should have been enough to dissuade Spaniards from betting at the tables, and all the more so as it in general brought them little profit. But neither these obvious facts, nor the denunciations of the game that were from time to time heard in San Isidro and other churches, nor the ruin that afflicted many families, nor the fate that befell many of those who turned to thieving to feed their habit, proved sufficient to stem the tide . . . On the contrary, on all sides one heard of the most trusted servants robbing their masters; of merchants, artisans and men of every class repeatedly staking the very substance of their loved ones on the turn of the wheel; and, finally, of many families who had been not just left with nothing, but also abandoned by husbands and fathers who sought in this fashion to escape from the effects of their stupidity.[349]

Other means of escape were to take service with the French, enlist in forces such as those of El Empecinado or Espoz y Mina, or simply to take up banditry, while, particularly in the larger cities, where service in an officialdom that was now almost entirely unpaid thanks to King Joseph's financial difficulties had traditionally offered much employment, many clerks and other bureaucrats tried to set themselves up as small shopkeepers or even artisans. Yet, no matter what the populace did, the situation continued to deteriorate. By the winter of 1811/12 Madrid presented a picture of the utmost horror:

> Cabbage stalks were being sold at 5 or 6 *cuartos* per pound, and in consequence even the very rubbish tips were searched for them. Just as eagerly sought after, meanwhile, were onion skins, radish leaves and old bones. The poor lay in wait for cats, and anyone who caught one . . . considered that he had got himself a real

banquet. By the end even flour made from vetch and . . . carobs was selling like hot cakes . . . In the Rastro . . . there were so many people trying to sell things that it was impossible to get down the street. 'Everything must go' became one of the most common street cries . . . There were so many unfortunates in the streets . . . that it was impossible to walk them without the stoniest heart being wrung and saddened . . . Some people could be heard complaining that it was three o'clock in the afternoon and they had still not broken their fast; others had death clearly written in their faces; others were fainting from want; and still others had just breathed their last . . . At one spot one saw a group of abandoned children crying out for bread; at another a number of tearful widows surrounded by their little ones; and at still a third some young girls assuring passers-by that they were begging so as not to prostitute themselves. On the first corner there would be a cluster of priests humbly asking for alms, and on the second persons of the highest character . . . doing exactly the same. So many were the poor . . . that, however much they wandered the streets . . . they could not get enough to get them through the day . . . Going back to their homes . . . they therefore quietly lay down to die.[350]

In short, the situation had now become one of genuine famine. Nor was Madrid the only place to be affected. As an official of Valladolid's high court named Francisco Gallardo remembered:

In the month of June [1812] things reached such a pass in this city that wagon-loads of wheat and barley were being sold . . . at 1,700-1,800 *reales* and 900-1,000 *reales* respectively. Since the very beginning of the world such prices have almost certainly never been known either in Castile or the rest of the Kingdom, this being all the more extraordinary in view of the proximity not just of the harvest, but also of a harvest that promised to be one of the greatest imaginable. Such was the shortage of bread and other staples that misery and want could not but be general: on all sides one saw haggard paupers who appeared more dead than alive and could get no more help than the inadequate alms offered them by a few pious souls. Unable to find anything else, they were to be seen gnawing on thistle stalks . . . and onion skins that they had gathered from rubbish heaps and had even been rejected by the animals. In this fashion many fell ill and died . . . On the roads, as was inevitable, there were many robberies and worse.[351]

Of all the accounts that we have of the state to which large parts of the populace were now reduced, however, the most graphic by far is that provided by Juan Domingo Palomar:

Today, 29 March [1812], a loaf of bread costs 46 *cuartos*, a pound of good-quality chick peas 38 *cuartos*; a pound of rice 1 *peseta*; a pound of potatos 9 *cuartos*; a pound of meat 24, a pound of vetch flour 26; and a pound of dried cod 28. With prices at such a height, the poor have to subsist on such plants as they can gather in the countryside . . .

Today, 4 April, bread has reached 54 *cuartos*, though in fact it cannot be found at all . . . The inevitable consequence of so much hunger, of so much overwhelming misery, is the infinite number of thieves to be found on road and city alike. Merely leaving the bounds of a village is so dangerous that it is very difficult to find a wagoner who has not been robbed . . . Nor is this surprising: neither labourer nor artisan can find any work, or anyone to help them, and just to eat badly costs a fortune . . . So bad is the hunger that it has also led a number of young men to enlist beneath the banners of our enemies . . .

18 April: today a consignment of bread was publicly burned . . . by the town hangman on account of it being of such poor quality that it could jeopardise the health of the public, and especially that of the poor, who had been buying it because it was going cheap . . .

30 April: the price of bread continues to be above 6 *reales*, and the poor are preventing the inhabitants from getting about the streets, pursuing them determinedly in the hope of obtaining a little aid. It is not enough to tell them three or four times over that one cannot help them: they set up a tremendous clamour and follow at one's heels insisting that one can, and this only adds to the torment . . . Many people are dying of hunger, and yesterday alone there were four such cases. One of them was a day labourer who had spent the entire day hoeing weeds in the fields . . . His name was Tío Paulino and he was very hard-working . . .

3 May: today bread is at 7 *reales*; rice at 38 or 40 *cuartos* . . . lentils at 24; beans at 18; and dried cod at 28. With prices so high, and not a wage to be had in any occupation, misery is increasing, misfortune multiplying, and many people are dying for no other reason than hunger . . .

4 May: a convoy of wheat came in today from Guadalajara. It was composed of seven carts and more than 400 fully laden mules . . . At the very time that it was coming in, I saw two young girls of about 8 or 10 dying of hunger. One was lying at the door of the merchant Gallo, and the other was at the Puerta de Landa . . . The poor are eating the rotting meat of dead animals in an attempt to stay alive. For example, some beggars cut some steaks from the rump of a dead mule . . . and then cooked and ate them . . . Could misery arrive at any worse a pitch? I can testify to this incident, and so can every person in my house, as we lent them the pan in which they cooked the meat . . .

12 May: Soup kitchens have been established to feed the poor, and these are being directed by a junta composed of the leaders of the clergy and representatives of the municipality . . .

20 May: bread continues at a price of 7¹/₂ or 8 *reales*, and so many of the poor continue to die of hunger. The soup kitchens are helping many people, but one still sees the bodies of miserable wretches who have died of hunger scattered round the streets, especially young children and the outsiders who have fled in abundance from Madrid and neighbouring towns in search of work and bread, only to find that neither one nor the other is to be had. He who does not, from generation to

generation, from century to century, hate, detest and abominate the execrable Emperor Napoleon and the whole of the proud French nation . . . can be considered neither a good man, nor a Spaniard, nor a Christian.[352]

Winter Quarters

Back on the frontiers of Portugal the retreat of the French following their unsuccessful foray in the direction of Almeida afforded the British army a period of repose that was afterwards remembered with a mixture of fondness and distaste by William Grattan:

> Fuente Guinaldo was occupied by our Light Division, who made that town agreeable both to themselves and also to their brothers in arms, not only by their hospitality, but by the attraction of their theatrical performances, which were got up in a style quite astonishing considering the place and the difficulties which they must have found in supplying themselves with suitable costume, but the Light Division had an *espirit de corps* among them, whether in the field or quarters, that must be seen to be understood. Their *dramatis personae* were admirable, and Captain Kent of the Rifles, by his great abilities, rendered every performance in which he took a part doubly attractive. The Third Division, although unable to cope with the Light in this species of amusement, got up races, which, though inferior to those of the former year at Torres Vedras, were far from bad. Among the jockeys was . . . an officer in the Portuguese service, who, though an excellent horseman, was, without exception, the ugliest man in the division, or perhaps in the army. Major Leckie of the Forty-Fifth took the greatest dislike to him on this account, and gave him the name of 'Ugly Mug', by which cognomen he was after known . . . As there was no likelihood of any active operations taking place, we began to make ourselves as comfortable as the wretched village of Aldea-de-Ponte would admit of. Any person acquainted with a Portuguese cottage will readily acknowledge that a good chimney is not its forte: we therefore turned all the skill our masons possessed to the construction of fireplaces that would not smoke, and it required all their knowledge . . . to succeed even in part. However . . . we made up for the badness of [the] fireplaces by stocking them abundantly with wood. Of this article there was no lack, but we had barely sufficient straw to keep our horses and mules alive, much less afford ourselves a bed. In the entire village, I believe, there were not a dozen mattresses. Provisions were but ill supplied us, and we were reduced to subsist upon [a] half allowance of bad biscuit. As to money, we had scarcely a *sou*, for, although there was plenty of specie in Lisbon for our use, the want of animals to convey it to the army left us as ill-off as if there had not been a dollar in the chest of the paymaster-general, so that between smoky houses, no beds, little to eat and less money, we were in anything but what might be termed 'good winter quarters'.[353]

The same village housed Wellington's headquarters, and the humble surroundings seemed to sit well with the lack of pretension he was inclined to affect. Another visitor was the commissary Schaumann:

Had it not been known for a fact, no one would have suspected that [Lord Wellington] was quartered in the town. There was no throng of scented staff officers with plumed hats, orders and stars, no main guard, no crowd of contractors, actors, valets, cooks, mistresses, equipages, horses, dogs, forage and baggage wagons . . . Just a few *aides-de-camp*, who went about the streets alone and in their overcoats, a few guides and a small staff guard: that was all! About a dozen bullock carts were to be seen in the large square . . . which were used for bringing up straw to headquarters, but, apart from these, no . . . baggage trains were visible.[354]

For a brief vignette of life at Wellington's headquarters at this time, it is worth turning to the memoirs of Thomas Browne, the son of a Liverpool merchant; commissioned as a lieutenant in the Twenty-Third Foot, he was currently attached to the staff of the Judge Advocate General:

At headquarters Lord Wellington had a pack of foxhounds, and we all occasionally joined in the chase. Game was also in tolerable abundance, and those who were fond of fishing found trout in the Agueda and the Côa . . . The officers of the Adjutant and Quartermaster General's staff were . . . invited to join very frequently with Lord Wellington, and at his table drank of the best French wines, which were from time to time sent to him by the different guerrilla chiefs who had been successful in capturing French convoys. The cheerfulness or gloom of our commander's table depended much on news which he received from England, or reports from the different divisions of his army. I have dined there at times when scarce anyone dare open his mouth except to take in his dinner, and at other times when the conversation was constant and general, and Lord Wellington himself the most playful of the party. He would sit after dinner a long or short time, according to circumstances, and when he wished us to retire would call for coffee. After finishing his cup . . . he would leave the room, and it was then expected that we should all go to our quarters. He had a small iron bedstead covered with Russia leather with one pillow of the same material, and, whenever anything was passing at the outposts which led to the supposition that a movement was intended on the part of the enemy . . . he used to lie down . . . in his clothes with his boots near him, ready to put on, and his cloak thrown round him. His horse, and that of his orderly dragoon, were always ready saddled.[355]

As the autumn wore on so hunger and boredom began to take their toll. One regiment that was particularly known for its plundering was the Eighty-Eighth, a unit known throughout the army as the 'Devil's Own'. As William Grattan somewhat ruefully recalled:

The men of my corps . . . were much perplexed as to what they would do. Several desertions had taken place in the army, but our fellows did not like that at all. 'Why then, by my soul,' said Owen Maguigan of the Grenadiers, 'I think Mr Strahan, the commissary, is greatly to blame for keeping us poor boys without meat to eat, when these *paisanos* have plenty of good sheep and goats . . . If they'd eat them themselves, a man wouldn't say anything, but they'll neither eat them, nor give us leave to do so, and, sure at any rate, *bacalao* and *aceite* is good enough for them.' I need scarcely remark that an argument so full of sound sense was not likely to be thrown away upon the hearers of Owen Maguigan. From this moment our fellows determined to be their own commissaries . . . One night in November 1811 three of the boys walked out of their quarters with . . . their bayonets; Maguigan headed them. For some weeks there had been a general defalcation among the different neighbouring flocks, and the Portuguese shepherds, confounded to know what had become of them, [had] armed themselves, and [were keeping] watch with a degree of vigilance they were hitherto unaccustomed to . . . The sheep-fold [Maguigan] assailed was defended by five armed Portuguese, but what did the boys care for that? After nearly sending the unfortunate men to the other world, they . . . tied their arms and legs together . . . and then, performing the same office to three sheep, they left their owners to look after the remainder. As may be supposed, this affair made a great noise: the provost-marshal was directed to search . . . the quarters and premises of all the regiments, but the fellow instinctively, I believe, turned towards those of my corps, and here, I am sorry to say . . . he found the three sheep, part of them in a camp kettle on the fire and the remainder in an outhouse. This was enough. The men were identified by the Portuguese, tried, flogged, and made to pay for the sheep, which (the worst of it!) they had not even had the pleasure of tasting, but this example by no means put a stop to the evil. The sheepfolds were plundered, the shepherds pummelled and our fellows flogged without mercy. General Picton at length issued orders directing the rolls of the regiment to be called over by an officer of each company at different periods during the night, and by this measure the evil was remedied.[356]

Other members of Wellington's forces found somewhat less objectionable ways to while away their time. Many officers were given periods of leave and took the opportunity to visit Lisbon. One of them, it appears, had a fondness for practical jokes, and the result was one of the funniest stories of the entire war. Witness to the scene was Ensign James Hope, a young man of Scottish origin who had enlisted as a gentleman-volunteer in the Ninety-Second Foot in July 1809 and in September 1811 had been sent out to Portugal in charge of a batch of recruits:

On the second inst. [i.e. 2 December 1811] handbills printed in the British and Portuguese languages were posted and distributed through every part of the metropolis intimating to the inhabitants that a British officer, accoutred in cork boots, was, for a considerable bet, to start at Fort Belem and walk across the Tagus on the following day at one o'clock. As early as nine o'clock in the morning, the streets leading to Belem were crowded with people of all nations, hastening to the starting post as fast as their respective modes of conveyance would allow them. A considerable number were in carriages, many on mules and asses, and thousands of men, women and children [were] running as far as their legs would carry them. A company of Portuguese militia . . . kept a clear passage for the hero to get to the river. About half-past twelve, the beach was completely covered; I counted at one time of coaches and other vehicles upwards of three lines drawn up [upon it]. The river was literally covered in boats, in which [could be seen] the naval and military uniforms of Great Britain and her Allies, [and] the castle and the fort were entirely occupied by the principal nobility and gentry at that time in Lisbon. In the latter, with much difficulty, I got a place. Some 6, 8, or even 10 dollars were given for the use of small boats, the ordinary fare does not exceed 1s 6d or 2s. About one o'clock the scene was at its height. As the clock announced the hour, one jostled another to get closer to the spot where the cork-accoutred hero was to make his appearance previous to starting on his pedestrian voyage. A few minutes after one, a voice from the crowd announced his approach . . . He was not there. Two o'clock struck: still he was absent. The hour of three was announced: there was no appearance of an officer in cork boots. About this time the people . . . began to slip away, fully satisfied that they had been completely hoaxed. Before four o'clock the greater part had retired to their respective places of abode, all the way home vowing vengeance on the British officer and his cork boots. The number of all ranks assembled on this occasion on shore and in the boats on the river has been variously estimated at from 40,000 to 50,000.[357]

*   *   *

With the Iberian peninsula in the depths of winter, let us again pause to consider the situation. On the Portuguese frontier, throughout 1811 the situation had been finely balanced. Although it was unbeatable in the open field on even terms, the Anglo-Portuguese army had been held in check and even repeatedly thrust back by the ability of France's generals to mass their forces and achieve such a superiority in numbers that Wellington could not but retreat to formidable defensive positions inside the frontiers of Portugal. To do so they had been forced to take risks in the territories they occupied, for the much-battered Spanish armies – now supplemented by a number of guerrilla bands that had acquired the status of regular divisions – continued to lurk in the wings from where they emerged from time to time to make damaging forays into the French zone of occupation. But the doings of these forces in the end mattered little: with Wellington out of the way, the French would again and again return to hunt them down. Nor was this the limit of the invaders' success. In the east, neither Wellington nor the guerrillas could prevent the French from over-running more and more of Patriot Spain or, for that matter, establishing the beginnings of a *modus vivendi* with a civilian population increasingly traumatised by the horrors of war. It is not going too far to say, indeed, that the Allies were losing the war, for, had Spanish resistance finally been brought to its knees, could even Wellington have maintained his position in Portugal? Mercifully for the Allied cause, however, that question never required an answer, for in the autumn of 1811 Napoleon resolved on war with Russia. With his soldiers now flowing not south but east, the emperor's ability to maintain control of the territory he had occupied in Spain was placed in increasing jeopardy. With Wellington newly possessed of a proper siege train that had been specially sent over from Britain, it was to prove a dangerous error.

Chapter 6

The Turn of the Tide

In January 1812, in the Iberian peninsula as much as in the rest of Europe, Napoleon was at the height of his power. Thus far, Wellington had successfully defended Portugal from French attack, but in Spain the French had steadily pushed back the Spanish regular army and undermined its capacity to engage in conventional warfare. The Patriots were not yet overcome, true – indeed, in parts of the interior resistance was not only on the increase but gaining in efficacy – but it is difficult to see how even the most determined commanders could have continued to hold out indefinitely in the face of the loss of almost all Spain's main cities, the defeat of her last armies and the apparent inability of the Anglo-Portuguese army to advance across the frontier. By December, however, the situation was very different. Just as Napoleon had sustained a shattering defeat in Russia, so Joseph Bonaparte had sustained a shattering defeat in Spain. As we shall see, with the onset of winter the Allied advance was checked, but even so at the close of the year the French had still lost much ground. It was a dramatic transformation, and one from which the cause of *el rey intruso* never recovered. As to the reasons for the catastrophe, nothing could be clearer. With Napoleon committed to a new war in the east, the autumn of 1811 saw the flow of replacements and reinforcements that had hitherto sustained the tide of French conquest dwindle to a mere trickle, and, still worse, many veteran troops were recalled for service in the *grande armée*. Had the French commanders been permitted to go over to the defensive, disaster might yet have been averted but far away in Paris the emperor was unwilling to call a halt: fearful for his prestige, he also continued to regard Wellington as a mere 'sepoy general', underestimating the number of British troops he had available and discounting the Portuguese as mere levies. Truly, it was a fatal error.

The Keys of the Kingdom
On the frontiers of Old Castile it was a harsh winter. Heavy autumnal rain had been followed by a period of bitter cold, and on New Year's Day there was a terrible blizzard that left the countryside deep in snow. On both sides of the border, the men of the rival armies huddled in their billets, and for the time being all seemed quiet. But the ranks of the French forces were much thinner than normal. Marmont's Army of Portugal had lost relatively few troops to the forthcoming invasion of Russia, but Napoleon's insistence on occupying still more territory had resulted in many units being pulled east and north. In addition to the 2,000 men holding Ciudad Rodrigo, all that was left to cover the Kingdom of León was two infantry divisions. This, however, was hardly wise. Only a few miles to the west, Wellington was ready to pounce with plenty of men, food and – at last – heavy guns. No sooner had news come in that the French forces were weaker than normal, then, than the whole army

was in motion. Among the first troops to cross the Spanish frontier was William Wheeler of the Seventh Division:

> We were quartered in the village of El Payo . . . The country all round was covered with snow. To shelter ourselves from the keen frosty air . . . we dug a large hole in the snow. In the centre, we kept a good fire, round which sat the men on duty. Our fuel consisted of furze and fern. Of this we had abundance from places where the snow had drifted, but in collecting it we wanted snow pattens, for often we would sink in over our heads into some hole or burrow where we had expected firm footing . . . We were on duty every other night, our clothes worn thin and wrecked by the fatigues of the former campaign. It was difficult to tell to what regiment we belonged, for each man's coat was, like Joseph's, 'a coat of many colours'.[358]

Nor were things much better in the trenches around the town. As Joseph Donaldson of the Ninety-Fourth Foot recalled, however, it was not just snow and ice that the troops had to contend with:

> The weather was so severe and the cold so intense that the army could not encamp, but the divisions employed at the siege marched from their different quarters and relieved each other alternately for the space of twenty-four hours. Our division took its turn of duty on the eleventh and the frost was so excessive that we were almost completely benumbed, and nothing but hard working, I believe, kept us from perishing from the cold; indeed, it was said that some Portuguese soldiers actually died of its effects . . . The French kept up a very destructive fire on us during the whole of our operations, and, while [we were] forming the second parallel, they threw out some fire-balls to enable them to see where we were working that they might send some shot in that direction. One of them fell very near where a party was working, and by its light completely exposed the men to the view of the enemy. A sergeant belonging to our regiment of the name of Fraser, seeing the danger to which they were exposed, seized a spade and, jumping out of the trench regardless of the enemy's fire, ran forward to where it was burning, and, having dug a hole, tumbled it in and covered it with earth.[359]

With Wellington well aware that taking the fortress was a race against time, operations were pushed on at a furious pace. Another participant in the siege of Ciudad Rodrigo was Private Anthony Hamilton of the Forty-Third Foot:

> It was considered of importance to gain possession of the convent of San Francisco, by which the approaches were enfiladed on the left. Batteries were accordingly erected against it which speedily destroyed the defences, and on the night of the fourteenth it was carried by assault. The second parallel was then completed, and progress made by sap towards the crest of the glacis . . . On the nineteenth two practicable breaches were completed . . . and preparations immediately made for storming them though the sap had not been brought to the crest of the glacis and the counterscarp of the ditch was still entire.[360]

No sooner had the walls been breached than the assault went in. Crouching in a convent that had been used by the French as an outlying fort, Edward Costello was a member of the forlorn hope:

> Calling out, 'Now lads, for the breach!', General Craufurd led the way. We started off in double-quick time, and got under fire in turning the left corner of the [convent] wall. As we neared the breach, canister, grape, round-shot and shell, with fire-balls to show our ground, came pouring . . . around us, with a regular hailstorm of bullets. General Craufurd fell almost immediately, mortally wounded. Without a pause, however, we dashed onwards to the town, and precipitated ourselves into the ditch before the walls, never waiting for the ladders, which were carried by the Portuguese and never made their appearance until their use had been superceded by a series of jumps made by our men into a trench some 16 feet deep. At length, one or two ladders having been procured, they were instantly placed against the scarp of the trench, and up we mounted to attack the breach. The fire kept up there was most deadly, and our men, for some minutes, as they appeared in small bodies, were swept away. However, they still persevered, and gradually formed a lodgement . . . I had got up with the first, and was struggling with a crowd of our fellows to push over the splintered and broken wall that [blocked off] the breach when Major Napier, who was by my side encouraging on the men, received a shot, and staggering back, would in all probability have fallen into the trench, had I not caught him. To my brief enquiry if he were badly hurt, he squeezed my hand . . . saying, 'Never mind me: push on, my lads, the town is ours.' And so, indeed, it was, our men entering it pell-mell . . . Among the first I saw . . . was my own captain, Uniacke, rushing along with a few men to the right of the breach . . . This was the last time he was doomed to be at our head: a few moments afterwards the French sprang a mine, by which the whole party were killed or maimed. With a few others I had taken a direction to the left . . . While running forward, I came up against a howitzer . . . with such force that it actually tumbled me over . . . I found myself across the body of a wounded French officer, beside [whom] was a cannonier . . . in the act of assisting him. The latter instantly seized me and a fearful struggle ensued till . . . I began to think that after all my escapes my game was over. At this crisis a few of our men came rushing up, one of which was my old chum, Wilkie. The cannonier was in his turn fastened on and tripped instantaneously by the side of his master. But poor Wilkie the next minute himself staggered against the howitzer mortally wounded! I flew to his support, but, seizing me hastily by the hand . . . he fell back and expired.[361]

Facing the other breach, meanwhile, was Joseph Donaldson:

> Some time after it was dark, we . . . advanced rank entire under a heavy fire . . . to the brink of . . . the ditch. After descending, we moved along towards the breach. Our orders were to remain there and protect the right brigade, but, our colonel finding no obstacles in the way, pushed up the breach . . . In mounting the breach, we found great difficulty in ascending from the loose earth slipping under our feet at every step . . . the enemy at the same time pouring their shot among us from above.[362]

Despite gallant resistance, the assault was successful, while the loss of Robert Craufurd, notwithstanding, Allied casualties were relatively low. Not for the last time, there followed scenes of great disorder. A town taken by storm was traditionally regarded as the legitimate prize of the men concerned, and, while the events that took place were by no means as terrible as those that were to follow elsewhere, they were still distressing enough. William Swabey was an officer in the Royal Horse Artillery:

> Our troops, as soon as the breach was gained, more eager for plunder than their duty, broke and ran in defiance of their officers . . . and committed shameful excesses disgraceful to the whole army. [There was] not a soul that was not rifled, and the dead were scarcely cold when they were inhumanly stripped . . . No intentional murders were committed, though some men were so drunk that they fired promiscuously in the streets and killed many of their comrades.[363]

Even more dramatic is the version given by Grattan of the Eighty-Eighth:

> Scenes of the greatest outrage now took place, and it was pitiable to see groups of the inhabitants half-naked in the streets . . . while their houses were undergoing the strictest scrutiny. Some of the soldiers turned to the wine and spirit houses, where, having drunk sufficiently, they again sallied out in quest of more plunder; others got so intoxicated that they lay in a helpless state in different parts of the town, and lost what they had previously gained.[364]

According to John Kincaid of the Ninety-Fifth Rifles, order was only restored thanks to the personal intervention of the redoubtable commander of the Third Division, General Picton:

> Finding the current of soldiers setting towards the centre of the town, I followed the stream which conducted me into the great square, on one side of which the late garrison were drawn up as prisoners, and the rest of it was filled with British and Portuguese intermixed without any order or regularity. I had been there but a very short time, when they all commenced firing without any ostensible cause. Some fired in at the doors and windows, some at the roofs of houses, and others at the clouds, and at last some heads began to be blown from their shoulders in the general hurricane, when the voice of Sir Thomas Picton, with the power of twenty trumpets, began to proclaim damnation to everybody, while Colonel Barnard, Colonel Cameron and some other active officers were carrying it into effect with a strong hand, for, seizing the broken barrels of muskets, which were lying about in great abundance, they belaboured every fellow most unmercifully about the head who attempted either to load or fire, and finally succeeded in reducing them to order. In the midst of the scuffle, however, three of the houses in the square were set on fire, and the confusion was such that nothing could be done to save them.[365]

With order restored, the troops who had taken the city were pulled back, and a garrison installed from the unblooded Fifth Division. Among the men who entered the town was James Hale of the Ninth Foot:

> When we entered the garrison, it was a most miserable place to behold, for the

enemy's dead were lying about in all directions, and the buildings beat to pieces by our cannon shot in a frightful manner . . . Several houses were . . . on fire, in consequence of which we were immediately set to work to extinguish the fire, and fortunately, by a great exertion, we got the upper hand of it in a short time. The next thing that was thought most necessary for us to do was to put the dead bodies under the ground and clear the streets, that the market people might be able to come in with their goods as soon as posible, for at that time there was not a thing of any description to be got in the town except a few bags of French biscuits, and those our commissary seized.[366]

Hale and his fellows had their work cut out. Not only did the dead have to be laid to rest and the fires put out, but the much-battered walls also had to be got into some sort of state of defence. For the men who had stormed the breaches, however, it was a case of to the victor the spoils:

There is nothing in this life half so enviable as the feelings of a soldier after a victory . . . It had ever been the summit of my ambition to attain a post at the head of a storming party. My wish had now been accomplished, and . . . after all was over, and our men laid asleep on the ramparts . . . I strutted about [as] important a personage . . . as ever trod the face of the earth . . . Lord Wellington happened to be riding in at the gate at the time that we were marching out, and had the curiosity to ask the officer of the leading company what regiment it was, for there was scarcely a vestige of uniform among the men, some of whom were dressed in Frenchmen's coats, some in white breeches and huge jackboots, some with cocked hats and queues. Most of their swords were fixed on the rifles, and stuck full of hams, tongues and loaves of bread, and not a few were carrying bird cages.[367]

With the fall of Ciudad Rodrigo, the next target was the even more important fortress of Badajoz. Very soon, the troops who had fought in León were moving south. Among them was 19-year-old Charles Boutflower, a surgeon attached to the Fortieth Foot:

We quitted Villa de Ciervo on the twenty-seventh [of February], having received a route to proceed to Castelo Branco: we reached Alemanda that day and halted there. On the twenty-eighth we halted at Vila Mayor; on the twenty-ninth at Vila Boa; and on the first we crossed the Côa at Sabugal . . . We remained for the night at Pedregão and this day came to Sao Miguel, only two leagues and a good road . . . On the fourth we halted at Escalhas de Cima, and the following day reached Castelo Branco . . . On the seventh we remained at a most wretched place called Requisa which scarcely afforded covering for one fourth of the men. On the eighth we had a most fatiguing march to Nisa, a distance of five leagues and a half over the worst roads in Portugal, added to which we had the dragging of the nine pounders up two most tremendous hills: the men came in so exhausted in the evening that we . . . had much *accesión* to our sick list . . . in consequence. On the ninth we halted at Alpalhão, [and] on the tenth we reached Portalegre, where we still remain, though it is probable we shall march in the direction of Badajoz in a day or two . . . Everything is said to be ready for the siege.[368]

And so it was. In so far as the available evidence suggested, meanwhile, the French, in the short term at least, were in no position to intervene. At headquarters, then, there was a general air of good humour. Among the officers who came into contact with Wellington was an anonymous officer of the Foot Guards:

> I was . . . asked to dine at headquarters. I have a lively remembrance . . . of passing a pleasant evening in one of the best houses the town of Elvas afforded. The assembled party amounted to some eighteen, among whom were the authorities of the town, some ladies, two commanding officers of the regiments of the Guards [and] other younger and livelier characters belonging to Lord Wellington's personal staff . . . Lord Wellington was in high spirits and very attentive to two pretty Portuguese young ladies . . . With great liveliness they possessed good manners, spoke French well, and of course formed the centre of attention. During dinner there was a man . . . whose appetite exceeded everything but our astonishment at it, and his own surprise at finding himself surrounded by so many dainties . . . His youthful passion for pastry made *pâté* after *pâté* disappear, for to the rapidity of a conjuror he added the swallow of a cormorant . . . Like the camel at the spring in the desert, he seemed determined to lay in a stock which should bear him harmless against all common privation. After [he had] unconsciously occasioned us considerable amusement, in which our great chief participated with as much mirth as the youngest among us . . . we all rose together with the ladies from the table . . . Thus concluded an agreeable evening, and, as we returned to our . . . life in the fields, we thought with regret of those pleasant hours that had but too speedily passed.[369]

Very soon, then, the army was in action. Badajoz was invested on 16 March, and a variety of troops were soon digging the first trenches and batteries. As at Ciudad Rodrigo, operations were pushed forward with the greatest haste possible, despite the dreadful weather:

> On the seventeenth the weather, which had hitherto been remarkably fine, became cold and tempestuous. During the afternoon and throughout the night the rain fell in torrents, and, taking advantage of the obscurity, ground was broken within 160 yards of Fort Picurina . . . During the eighteenth, in spite of the elements, the troops persevered in their labours in the trenches . . . On the nineteenth the rain continued with increased violence. The troops were without shelter of any kind and the duties of the siege were uncommonly severe. In the evening a spirited sortie was made by the garrison, in which Colonel Fletcher, the commanding engineer, was wounded . . . The loss on this occasion amounted to nearly 120 men . . . During the night of the twenty-first, the bridge across the Guadiana was carried away by a sudden swell of the river. The only communication was by a flying bridge, which could only be worked with the greatest difficulty, and the quantity of powder thus procured was found so utterly inadequate to the demand that the most serious consequences were apprehended. There were likewise other impediments to be overcome. The trenches on the low ground were flooded, and the earth became saturated with moisture. To palliate the evil, double working parties were employed . . . some with buckets bailing out the water, while others pushed forward the works.[370]

In one respect the rain came as a blessing, for many French shells failed to explode. Yet the enemy fire was still fierce enough. Captain James Macarthy of the Fiftieth Foot was serving with the Third Division as a volunteer engineer:

> Several of the guns . . . were injured by the enemy: two or three were dismounted, and in [the case of] another a twenty-four-pound shot entered the muzzle of a gun so precisely as to split it equally on both sides like the spout of a tea-kettle as far as the band and remained there without disturbing the gun in its position . . . Number Seven Battery . . . commenced its tremendous fire about six o'clock in the morning of 31 March, which the enemy answered with showers of shot and shells so effectually as to explode the magazine three hours afterwards, and by noon a considerable part of the battery was in ruins . . . I was proceeding . . . in the trenches, and met two artillerymen carrying in a blanket a wounded gunner from this battery, the left side of whose head had been struck by a cannon ball . . . His brains in the unbroken membrane (like a bag) hung on his shoulder. I remonstrated on the uselessness of dragging this poor expiring man to the camp, the half of his head having been shot away. They laid him down to rest themselves and consider, at which moment he expired . . . Judging that the men had no objection to be employed out of the battery, I recommended them to bury their comrade on the spot and [then] return immediately . . . Soon after, I met some more artillery men, conveying (also in a blanket) from the same battery an artillery officer . . . very severely wounded. He was a heavy man, and his left arm [was] dreadfully shattered, the shirt and coat torn to rags . . . I then passed on . . . to my duty at the construction of No. 8 breaching battery, where a shell passed over . . . me, and sank into the soft earth of the glacis. Having watched it for some time, [I] remarked to a man standing by my side that I thought it would not explode, [whereupon] it immediately exploded. Hearing the twirling of a fragment coming towards me, I said to the man, 'Here comes a piece of that shell: take care!' I then stepped a short distance to my left. The man did the same, but this placed him, unfortunately, nearly in my former position. The fragment passed, and entered deep into the wall of sandbags near us, and then the soldier very calmly said, 'That struck me, Sir.' Lifting up his right arm, he showed me that his hand was torn in strings. He said, 'What shall I do?' I replied, 'Set off to your camp, to be sure.'[371]

By 6 April it was decided that all was ready for an assault. This, in fact, was questionable – the three breaches that had by now been blown in the walls were still very steep – but Soult was on the march, while it was still unknown whether or not Marmont would join him. Waiting two or three more days would doubtless have made more sense, but in the circumstances the best thing seemed to be to go in straight away. What followed was a terrible affair. The breaches had been booby-trapped and barricaded, and the men defending them provided with hand grenades, incendiary bombs and extra muskets. Unknown to the British, meanwhile, they were also protected by a deep canal that had been cut in the bottom of the ditch. Set to attack these grim defences at ten o'clock in the evening, the men of the Fourth and Light divisions set to with a will, but they became hopelessly entangled with one another and quickly suffered appalling casualties. In the lead was William Lawrence:

> I was one of the ladder party . . . On our arriving at . . . the wall . . . a shower of shot,

canister and grape, together with fire-balls, was hurled . . . among us. Poor Pig [Harding] received his death wound immediately . . . while I myself received two small . . . shots in my left knee, and a musket shot in my side . . . Still, I stuck to my ladder and got into the [ditch]. Numbers had by this time fallen, but . . . we hastened to the breach. There, to our great . . . discouragement, we found a *cheval de frise* had been fixed . . . Vain attempts were made to remove this fearful obstacle, during which my left hand was fearfully cut by one of the blades, but, finding no success in that quarter, we were forced to retire for a time . . . My wounds were still bleeding, and I began to feel very weak. My comrades persuaded me to go to the rear, but this proved a task of great difficulty, for on arriving at the ladders, I found them filled with the dead and wounded, hanging . . . just as they had fallen . . . so I crawled on my hands and knees till I got out of the reach of the enemy's musketry.[372]

Also to the fore, meanwhile, was Anthony Hamilton, who had volunteered for the forlorn hope:

On reaching the glacis we were discovered by the garrison, and instantly a tremendous fire opened. Though the carnage in our ranks was very great, we continued our advance . . . Owing to the darkness of the night . . . we came unexpectedly upon the counterscarp, and nearly half our party, myself among the number, were precipitated into the ditch below. Much bruised by the fall I lay a few minutes insensible, till on the arrival of the main body, the ladders were fixed . . . and the descent into the ditch quickly effected. Though the formation of the troops was necessarily broken in these operations, they immediately advanced against the breaches . . . but such were the obstacles prepared by the enemy that it was found impossible to surmount them . . . To overcome these obstacles many gallant . . . attempts were made by our troops, but . . . we were at length compelled to retire . . . Twenty-one officers of the regiment were either killed or wounded, and of the ten men of our company who volunteered for the forlorn hope only myself and a man by the name of Cummings came back alive, both wounded.[373]

Fighting alongside Hamilton in the Light Division was George Simmons:

Our columns moved on under a most dreadful fire . . . that mowed down our men like grass . . . Ladders were resting against the counterscarp . . . Down these we hurried and . . . rushed forward to the breaches, where a most frightful scene of carnage was going on. Fifty times they were stormed, and as often without effect, the French cannon sweeping the breaches with a most destructive fire. Lights were thrown among us . . . that burned most brilliantly, and made us easier to be shot at . . . I had seen some fighting, but nothing like this.[374]

An anonymous Irishman fighting in the ranks of the Forty-Third Foot left similar recollections of the scene:

For my own part, my mind had been unhesitatingly made up from the first shot that was fired that, so long as life and consciousness continued, I would fulfill my commission to the best of my ability. As the battle grew hot, I caught the contagion that burned all around, and in this desperate and murderous mood advanced to the breach of Trinidad. My pride, perhaps, wanted to be repressed, and, while in the act of marching, I was wounded in the left thigh by a musket shot, which remains unextracted to this day and will probably go with me to the grave. At first, not disposed to heed the casualty, I affected to despise such a trifle and continued to fight on. Nature, however, refused her support, and after firing a few rounds I felt myself getting weak and feverish . . . In this condition, faint with loss of blood, I contrived to descend into the ditch with the help of my musket. Meanwhile, the depth of water by some added inundation had been increased, and no ladder was to be discovered for my ascent on the opposite side. Unwilling to die there, I made another effort, and at length observed a ladder standing in front of the ditch. Unable to get up with my musket, I reluctantly left it behind and scrambled up with extreme difficulty. Numerous shots were fired at me while ascending and I perceived bullets whistling through the rungs of the ladder, but not one of them struck me. But I was sadly grieved at the loss of my musket: it had been a faithful friend to me. I seldom knew it to fail in our hour of need: the number on it was seventy-seven.[375]

For two hours the fighting continued, but around midnight Wellington decided that he could not ask any more of his men and ordered them to fall back. The troops involved having suffered some 2,000 casualties, it looked as though the assault had failed. However, at the last minute Wellington had agreed to the idea of secondary assaults on the castle and the bastion of San Vicente, both of which were points far removed from the breaches. At the castle the assailants suffered heavy casualties. As Donaldson recalled:

At last the order was given, and with palpitating hearts we commenced our march . . . Being apprised of our intentions, they threw out fire-balls in every direction . . . By this means they were enabled to see . . . our columns, and they opened a fire of round and grape shot which raked through them, killing and wounding whole sections . . . We still advanced as before . . . and got down into the ditch. The ladders were not yet brought up, and the men were huddled on one another in such a manner that we could not move . . . When we first entered the [ditch] we considered ourselves comparatively safe, thinking that we were out of range of their shot, but . . . they opened several guns . . . and poured in grape shot upon us from each side . . . Our situation at this time was truly appalling . . . When the ladders were placed, each eager to mount, [the soldiers] crowded them in such a way that many of them broke, and the poor fellows who had nearly reached the top were precipitated a height of thirty to forty feet and impaled on the bayonets of their comrades below. Other ladders were pushed aside by the enemy on the walls, and fell with a crash on those in the ditch, while [men] who got to the top without accident were shot on reaching the parapet, and, tumbling headlong, brought down those beneath them. This continued for some time, until at length, a few having made a landing . . . [they] enabled others to follow.[376]

By these means, the castle was taken, as was the bastion of San Vicente. The town soon followed and Badajoz at last belonged to Wellington, or, to be more precise, to his army. Let us quote, for example, Robert Blakeney:

There was no safety for women even in the churches, and any who interfered or offered resistance were sure to get shot. Every house presented a scene of plunder, debauchery and bloodshed committed with wanton cruelty . . . by our soldiery, and in many instances I saw the savages tear the rings from the ears of beautiful women . . . When the savages came to a door which had been locked or barricaded, they applied . . . the muzzles of a dozen firelocks . . . against that part of the door where the lock was fastened, and . . . fired [them] off together into the house and rooms, regardless of those inside . . . Men, women and children were shot . . . for no other . . . reason than pastime; every species of outrage was publicly committed . . . and in a manner so brutal that a faithful recital would be . . . shocking to humanity. Not the slightest shadow of discipline was maintained . . . The infuriated soldiery resembled rather a pack of hell-hounds vomited up from the infernal regions for the extirpation of mankind than . . . a well-organised, brave, disciplined and obedient British army.[377]

Much the same scenes are recorded by John Patterson:

On all sides drunkenness and tumult appeared amidst the badly lighted streets, while soldiers and followers of the camp, together with hordes of reckless villains, revelling in plunder, were mingled in parties, shouting and hallooing with clamorous tongues. Such of the ill-fated and miserable inhabitants who had escaped the perils of the siege were running to and fro, seeking protection from the brutal attacks of an infuriated and savage multitude. Women and children were huddled together in groups, wildly staring as they crouched into holes and corners and cried loudly in despair for that assistance which it was impossible to render.[378]

One of the few accounts we have from someone who participated in the sack comes from Edward Costello. Shot in the knee at the main breach, he was rescued by a comrade named O'Brien who helped him down into the town:

We proceeded in the direction of the market-place. It was a dark night, and the confusion and uproar that prevailed in the town may be better imagined than described. The shouts and oaths of drunken soldiers in quest of more liquor [and] the reports of firearms and the crashing in of doors, together with the appalling shrieks of hapless women, might have induced anyone to have believed himself in the regions of the damned. When we arrived at the market-place we found a number of Spanish prisoners rushing out of the gaol: they appeared like a set of savages suddenly let loose, many still bearing the chains they had not had time to free themselves from . . . We then turned down a street which was opposite the foregoing scene, and entered a house which was occupied by a number of men of the Third Division. One of them immediately, on perceiving me wounded, struck off the neck of a bottle of wine with his bayonet, and presented it to me, which relieved me for a time from the faintness I had previously felt . . . I had not long been seated at the fire which was blazing up the chimney, fed by mahogany chairs broken up for the purpose, when I heard screams for mercy from an adjoining room. On hobbling in, I found an old man, the proprietor of the house, imploring mercy of a soldier who had levelled his piece at him. I with difficulty prevented the man from shooting him, as he complained that the Spaniard would not give up his money. I immediately informed the wretched [man] in Spanish, as well as I was able, that he could only save his life by surrendering his cash. Upon this he brought out with trembling hands a large bag of dollars from under the mattress of the bed. These by common consent were immediately divided among us . . . according to the number of men present . . . I must confess that I participated in the plunder, and received about 26 dollars for my own share. As soon as I had resumed my seat at the fire, a number of Portuguese soldiers entered . . . and a regular scuffle ensued between our men and the Portuguese, until, one of the latter being stabbed by a bayonet, the rest retired . . . After thus ejecting the Portuguese, the victors, who had now got tolerably drunk, proceeded to ransack the house. Unhappily they discovered the two daughters of the old *patrón*, who had concealed themselves upstairs. They were both young and very pretty. The mother, too, was shortly afterwards dragged from her hiding place. Without dwelling on the frightful scene that followed, it may be sufficient to add that our men, more infuriated by drink than before, again seized the old man, and insisted on a fresh supply of liquor. And his protestations that he possessed no more were as vain as were all attempts to restrain them from ill-using him.[379]

Badajoz, then, is not a pretty story. By the end of the sack, indeed, as many as 250 Spanish civilians lay dead. It is, then, pleasant to record that for one officer it brought a happy postscript. The 24-year-old son of a surgeon from Whittlesea, Harry Smith had been commissioned into the Ninety-Fifth Rifles in 1805, and had recently been promoted to the rank of captain. Returning to the camp the morning after the storm, he encountered a young Spanish girl who had fled the city. Very soon, the two were married and the result was perhaps the greatest love story of the Peninsular War:

The atrocities committed by our soldiers on the poor, innocent and defenceless inhabitants of the city, no words suffice to depict . . . Yet this scene of debauchery, however cruel to many, to me has been the solace and whole happiness of my life for thirty-three years . . . If any reward is due to a soldier, never was one so honoured and distinguished as I have been by the possession of this dear child (for she was little more than a child at this moment) . . . Thus, as good may come out of evil, this scene of devastation and spoil yielded to me a treasure invaluable . . . to me, a wild youth not meriting such reward, and, however desirous, never able to express half his gratitude to God Almighty for such signal marks of His blessing . . . From that day to this she has been my guardian angel. She has shared with me the dangers and privations, the hardships and fatigues, of a restless life of war in every quarter of the globe. No murmur has ever escaped her . . . Every day was an increase of joy. Although both of us were of the quickest tempers, we were both ready to forgive and both intoxicated in happiness.[380]

If Harry Smith was a happy man that morning, his joy was not shared by many of the inhabitants of the city. Dazed and traumatised, they looked around them at a city laid waste. Laureano Sánchez Magro, for example, was the prior of the friary of Santo Domingo:

The friary . . . has suffered the most terrible ruin as a result of the four sieges which Badajoz has suffered since the beginning of last year, not to mention the damage caused to its fabric by the soldiery. Its roofs have gone; its doors, its panelling and its furniture have all been stripped from it; its walls have fallen in in many places; and the flagstones of its church are buried in rubble. And, on top of all this, following the British and Portuguese troops' glorious recapture of the city . . . many members of the community were stripped of all they possessed and left without even a shirt to clothe their nakedness.[381]

In Hospital

For most soldiers in the Napoleonic Wars, the worst horror that they faced was not death but rather sickness and wounds. A variety of diseases stalked the peninsular armies incessantly, while the number of men who died in battle was always far outstripped by the number of those who were wounded. For those afflicted the result was, at the very least, weeks of misery. After major actions, men might lie on the battlefield for more than a day before they were rescued, and then they invariably faced agonising journeys by mule or wagon to improvised hospitals. Among the 2,210 officers and men wounded at Badajoz was the volunteer engineer James MacCarthy. Shot in the leg during the attack on the castle, he was dragged clear by two soldiers, only to be abandoned by them amidst a pile of other wounded men at the foot of the mound on which the castle stood:

> During the night the moans, prayers, cries and exclamations of the wounded fully expressed . . . their agonies in varieties of acuteness and cadence of tone from the highest pitch in the treble to the lowest note in bass. Some . . . were undoubtedly raving mad, violently vociferating dreadful imprecations and denunciations; others singing; and many calling the numbers of their regiments . . . to attract attention . . . One man sat on my left side, rocking to and fro with his hands across his stomach. In the morning he was dead, stretched on his back . . . The dead and wounded were as close as a regiment laying down to repose . . . and, this part becoming the readiest road for the soldiers from the town to the camp, the cravings for water and bearers were reiterated by all to those who . . . passed, but they were too intent on their own sports except an artillery man who . . . kindly administered his [water] bottle . . . to my mouth . . . Late in the afternoon an officer with bearers came to take up a man of his regiment who laid at my side with eleven shots in him, and, as he was apparently expiring and could not be moved, I prevailed on the officer to allow his men to convey me to my tent, but they were unwilling and, though obliged to carry me, jostled [me] and . . . laid me down . . . at the end of the second parallel . . . and joined the sports in the town. I found myself in a very remote situation, and in danger of remaining undiscovered. In despair, I reached [for] one of the strewn sandbags, and, placing it under my head, resigned myself to my fate. Some time afterwards four Spaniards strolled near and examined me, and I requested them to carry me to the camp; they . . . refused, but, as they were taking off, a surgeon . . . most providentially approached and, seeing me, compelled the

fellows to carry me . . . and I arrived at my tent where surgeon Fitzpatrick . . . immediately attended me. On the third day I was removed to the town, and, dreading [being] placed among upwards of 500 on the stone floor in the church, where the difficulty of supplying all their necessities and administering tender care increased the sufferings of the wounded patients beyond the means in the power of the surgeons to avert . . . I preferred a place alone and was put into a house pointed out by a surgeon in the street, who recognised me and expressed his happiness at being able to attend me, but I did not see him again for three days, when he dropped in for a gossip, without examining or touching my limb. In this manner he at his leisure paid me a few visits, and I remained until the middle of May . . . when he called in . . . to tell me that he expected his promotion by the next gazette. I never more saw him. He was succeeded by a truly worthy man . . . who immediately . . . set my limb with an eighteen-tail bandage.[382]

Among the many soldiers wounded in the storming of Badajoz was the anonymous Irish sergeant of the Forty-Third who was shot in the thigh while storming the main breach. Helped to a field hospital by a private soldier, he arrived to find the surgeons over-run with casualties:

With so large an influx of patients it will be supposed that the hospital attendants were not very prompt: I was placed on the ground with many others in a worse condition than myself to await my turn for surgical assistance. After some hours I found that unless my wound ceased bleeding I should not long survive: this with a little contrivance I managed to effect. But the most intolerable sensation was that of raging thirst: all my worldly substance, ten times valued, would have been no price at all for a draught of water. Meantime, the frost was so severe that my limbs appeared to be deprived of flexibility and motion. In the course of the night, hearing a deep moan at a little distance, I called out, 'Who is there?', and was answered, 'It's me, Tom.' The voice was familiar, and I found it was that of Patrick Murphy, an old comrade and countryman . . . He had been miserably burnt while endeavouring to force the breach and suffered extremely. In the course of a day or two we were placed in military spring wagons and conveyed to Elvas . . . On alighting from our vehicles at Elvas, we were at first placed in a dark, uncomfortable apartment adjoining the fortifications. The roof was of arched masonry and so damp on the inner side that water fell on us in large drops. Our attendants were also nothing to boast of, for, under pretence of bringing our haversacks with provisions, they walked away with them altogether, an evil against which we knew no remedy, being unable, through weakness, to search for the depredators or procure more food. The confusion in this unhappy lazar house was extreme. Every man naturally thought his own case the more serious, and that it demanded care before all others. We were not, however, destined to remain long in these unsuitable quarters: orders were received directing our removal to Estremoz, and our journey thither was commenced the same night. The procession was rather melancholy: several times we had to halt in order to bury some poor creature, who, exhausted by suffering, had fled away. On our arrival at Estremoz, we found accommodation more suited to the exigencies of the invalided guests: a convent, sufficiently spacious, had been fitted up as a military hospital and was well adapted for the purpose . . . Having an excellent constitution, I soon recovered my health and in the course of a few weeks was pronounced convalescent.[383]

Typical of the many sick were the experiences of Joseph Donaldson, who, having fallen ill with ague in the wake of the storming of Badajoz, was abandoned to the care of a widow in a remote Portuguese village, and, after spending some days lying on the floor covered only by a greatcoat, was eventually taken by mule with several other sufferers to a convent that had been converted into a hospital at Castelo Branco:

> We were placed . . . on the floor without mattress or covering. Night came and a burning fever raged through my veins: I called for drink, but there was no one to give it me. In the course of the night I became delirious: the last thing I remember was strange and fantastic shapes flitting around me, which now and then catched me up and flew with me like lightning through every obstacle . . . For some days I was unconscious of what was passing, and when I recovered my senses I found myself in a small apartment with others who had bad fevers, but I was now provided with mattress and bedclothes. A poor fellow, a musician of the Forty-Third Regiment, was [in the] next berth to me, [and was] sitting up in his bed in a fit of delirium, addressing himself to some young females whom he supposed to be spinning under the superintendance of an old woman in the corner of the ceiling; he kept up a constant conversation with his supposed neighbours, whom he seemed to think were much in awe of the old dame, and he frequently rose up out of his bed to throw up his handkerchief as a signal . . . There was a great want of proper attendants in the hospital, and many a time I . . . heard the sick crying for drink and assistance the whole night without receiving it . . . Those medical men we had were . . . chiefly, I believe, composed of apothecaries' boys, who, having studied a session or two, were thrust into the army as a huge dissecting room where they might mangle with impunity . . . The extent of their medical knowledge in most disorders was to 'blister, bleed and purge'.[384]

Yet not all those involved in the care of the wounded were lackadaisical and ignorant. For a very different perspective we might turn to Lieutenant Dobbs of the Fifty-Second Foot:

> On the eighth of April I was ordered on command with all the wounded that could be moved to Elvas. On going to take charge I found the surgeon still busily employed in cutting off legs and arms, of which there was an immense heap close to the hospital tents. Surgeon Malling was a man of first-class abilities in his profession: he was rather rough in his manner, but very prompt to act. I found him on this occasion with his coat off, his sleeves tucked up, his patient stretched upon a table, and the knife in his hand. After a sweeping cut around the limb, he would take the knife between his teeth that he might have his hands free to tie up the arteries. When a case of emergency arose, he would throw off his coat and tuck up his sleeves, which action gave him the nickname of 'Short Sleeves'. One look was sufficient to tell him when a man was shamming.[385]

Equally, life in hospital was not always quite so terrible. Also hit at Badajoz was William Lawrence of the Fortieth Foot:

> A day or two after these events [i.e. the storm] the wounded were all conveyed to hospital, some to Elvas and some to Estremoz. I was among the latter . . . On our arrival at hospital, we were allowed to take in no spirits or wine, which, as we had lately had so much of them, seemed to be more of a hardship to us than our wounds, but we were not long in working out a system by which we were enabled to procure something to drink. The window of our ward looked out on to . . . a wine shop, which for some time tormented us horribly: it was something like the fable of the fox and the grapes. The man of the house was often at his door on the look-out . . . [and] we soon devised a plan to gain our desired end. There was in the ward a tin kettle holding nearly two gallons, and, having procured a long string, we put our money into this and lowered it to the Portuguese, who . . . would put the money's value in the shape of wine into the kettle and tie it to the string so that we could hoist it up to the window again. After that we arranged for our ward to be pretty well supplied with grog too in the same way . . . Thus I passed about six weeks before I recovered sufficiently to get out of the hospital.[386]

The Battle of Salamanca

With Ciudad Rodrigo and Badajoz both in the hands of the Anglo-Portuguese army, the way was at last open for a blow at the heart of the Bonaparte Kingdom of Spain. The ground having been prepared by a variety of diversionary operations, on 13 June 1812 the Anglo-Portuguese army duly invaded León. Very soon the army had reached Salamanca. For men who had been there in 1808 it was a sad return:

> It was melancholy to view the destruction which had taken place in this fine town from the time I had been in it before. The French had thrown a great part of it into one heap of ruins. The fine convents and churches that I had admired before . . . I did not know . . . again the alteration was so great . . . I went one day to buy a loaf of bread, thinking I would have purchased it for the old price, fourpence or a little more. But to my surprise I was asked . . . about four shillings and sixpence . . . This shows the distressed state of a country in which the seat of war is pitched by choice or necessity.[387]

Battered or not, the city gave the Anglo-Portuguse army a warm welcome. Riding with Anson's brigade of light cavalry was William Tomkinson:

> We were received with shouts and *vivas* in the town. The inhabitants were out of their senses at having got rid of the French, and nearly pulled Lord Wellington off his horse. The scene in the Plaza [Mayor] was the most interesting I ever saw. The troops (Sixth Division) were there formed, supposed preparatory to an immediate attack. The place was filled with inhabitants, expressing their joy in the most violent manner. The women were the most violent, many coming up to Lord Wellington and embracing him. He was writing orders on his sabretache and was interrupted three or four times by them.[388]

Moreover, relations with the populace continued to be good. As John Mills recorded:

> Nothing could exceed the generosity of the Spaniards during the whole of our stay at Salamanca . . . While we were on the position they supplied us with food and water, though they had to carry both not less than three miles. They would accept, too, of no remuneration. Lord Wellington begged for a convent for the use of the sick. His wish was no sooner made known than linen, beds and everything that could possibly be wanted was brought in by the inhabitants. There certainly is in this part of Spain a great desire to assist us. It arises in great measure in the novelty [of] the sight of English troops, none having been here since Sir John Moore's army passed through. The long residence and numerous contributions which the French have levied have rendered any change of situation desirable for them.[389]

In fact, however, the enemy were not yet fully gone. Ensconced in a complex of fortified convents on some high bluffs overlooking the bridge across the river Tormes, a small French garrison was still holding out:

> We threw up a battery . . . and mounted the four eighteen-pounders we brought with us. They soon battered the wall of the convent and then left off, finding, I fancy, that they could do but little good . . . Our people are beginning to find out that these . . . forts are stronger than they at first gave them credit for . . . The fire . . . is incessant, but their men are so well covered it is almost impossible to hit them. We have already lost fifty or sixty men . . . Several townspeople have been hit in the streets, and some shots have been fired into the steeple of the cathedral. I went down to a house out of which our men were firing. I tried, but could not perceive that I did any execution. All the men but one in one of the batteries were either killed or wounded by a shell . . . A corporal and a private of the German rifle corps lay all day wounded without the possibility of their being carried off as they were so far advanced.[390]

Eventually the convents fell to a bombardment of red-hot shot that set them afire. Eager to pursue the French army, Wellington marched north-eastwards with his army to the line of the river Duero. Here the French and Anglo-Portuguese faced one another across the river for some days, and there was an outbreak of the fraternisation that was a common feature of relations between the French and British. Having recovered from his attack of ague, for example, Joseph Donaldson had caught up with his regiment at the village of Pollos:

> In this place . . . there was an understanding, I believe, between both armies that each should have the use of the river without molestation, and our men and the French used to swim in it promiscuously, mixing together, and at times bringing brandy and wine with them for the purpose of treating each other . . . This friendly feeling between our soldiers and the French was remarkably displayed during the whole war whenever we were brought in position close to each other, and it could only be accounted for by the bravery of each nation and a similar generosity of sentiment, for in this the French were not deficient. How different were our feelings in this respect from many of our countrymen at home, whose ideas of the French

character were drawn from servile newspapers and pamphlets or even from so low a source as the caricatures in print shops, but I myself must confess, in common with many others, that I was astonished when I came in contact with French soldiers to find them, instead of pigmy spider-shanked wretches who fed on nothing but frogs . . . stout, handsome looking fellows who understood the principles of good living as well as any Englishmen among us, and, whatever may be said to the contrary, remarkably brave soldiers.[391]

The advance to the Duero took place in the midst of blazing summer heat which exhausted man and beast alike:

We are here bivouacked on a wild heath with nothing but shrubs and without a single tree. In the shade of my hut the thermometer was for two days at 94. In the sun (in which we have been sufficiently exposed of late), it could not be less than from 110 to 120 . . . The whole atmosphere was black with heat and a distressing scirocco wind prevailed, which . . . felt to the hand . . . like burning steam. The hilt of my sword became so hot that I literally could not grasp it for any length of time, and the heat of the stirrup irons was not less annoying. Such weather, you may well conceive, is ill adapted to taking or keeping the field, and the scarcity of water completes the quantum of suffering.[392]

The lull in the fighting did not last long, for the French suddenly mounted a counter-attack which soon had Wellington's army falling back on Salamanca. In the ranks of the First Division there marched John Mills:

At daybreak we were formed in two lines in the plain. Soon after, the enemy were seen moving to their left. We remained as we were and offered them battle, which, however, they declined accepting. We were then obliged to move too. It was a fine sight to see the two armies in motion at the same time. They moved parallel to each other, and at no time were more than two miles distant. They passed along a hill and we along the bottom. We described the string of the bow and consequently got ahead. It was in fact a race. Their object is to get between us and Portugal, thereby obliging us to move as they do and eventually it must end in us being obliged to quit Spain or fight . . . At one time during the march our division came within range of the hill on which they were moving. They fired at us for some time, but without doing any harm. The villages through which we passed were all deserted, the inhabitants having carried off all the valuables they were possessed of. A squadron of the enemy's cavalry took most of the baggage of the German hussars at Canizal . . . I had dismounted in the morning thinking that we were going into action, and I was consequently obliged to walk. I was not very well and the heat of the sun and the depth of the sand through which we passed quite knocked me up. I believe I should have lain down and been taken prisoner had I not found a beast I had with me loaded with baggage on which I mounted and thus got to the end of my journey. The want of water in this part of the country is dreadful: the men run to the most stagnant pool of water as thick as mud and drink it with the greatest avidity.[393]

There followed further manoeuvring that saw Marmont seek to edge round the southern flank of the Anglo-Portuguese army in an effort to force it to retreat to Portugal. By the late morning of 22 July both armies were in an area of rolling hills south of Salamanca. With Marmont on the very brink of success, however, he committed a fatal error: convinced that Wellington was in full retreat, he pushed his leading troops still further west. The events of the next few hours were to prove a bitter awakening for the French. Far from being set on retreat, the British commander was actually looking for an opportunity to counter-attack. Perceiving that the enemy forces were becoming ever more strung out, he rode to the right-hand end of his line to find the Third Division commanded by his brother-in-law, Sir Edward Pakenham. Alerted by Wellington, Pakenham led his men to the westernmost end of the ridge along which the French were advancing and attacked the leading French division (that of Thomières). There followed a sharp clash in which one participant was Stephen Morley of the Fifth Foot, who had now been promoted to the rank of sergeant:

> We were going up an ascent on whose crest masses of the enemy were stationed. Their fire seemed capable of sweeping all before it . . . Truth compels me to say . . . that we retired before this overwhelming fire, but . . . General Pakenham approached and very good-naturedly said, 'Reform', and in . . . a moment, 'Advance . . . There they are my lads; just let them feel the temper of your bayonets.' We advanced, everyone making up his mind for mischief. At last . . . the bugles along the line sounded the charge. Forward we rushed . . . and awful was the retribution we exacted for our former repulse. Immediately before the charge I received a slight flesh wound in the left side . . . which I have often thought was prevented from being mortal by the situation of my pocket knife. Just after, Ensign Hamilton was wounded [while] we had lost Sergeant Watson and another, so, to prevent the colours falling, [many] officers being wounded at nearly the same instant, Sergeant Green and myself had the honour of bearing both colours for upwards of an hour, a circumstance which served as a good pretext for throwing away my pike, a useless piece of military furniture.[394]

A long way from its nearest fellow and supported only by some light cavalry, Thomière's division was overwhelmed with the loss of almost half its strength, Pakenham then pursuing its remnants eastwards. Yet the advance was not without loss. Another infantryman fighting with Pakenham was Joseph Donaldson of the Ninety-Fourth:

> The Fifth Regiment, in attacking a body of infantry posted on a small height, were furiously charged by some of the enemy's cavalry and thrown into some confusion, but ours coming up in time not only routed them, but cut off the retreat of their infantry, who were taken prisoners, many of them dreadfully wounded by our dragoons, some having their arms and legs hanging by a shred of flesh and skin and others with hideous gashes in their faces. In this manner driving in their left, we came in front of where our artillery was playing on the enemy, but no time was lost: we marched past in open column, while they continued to fire without interruption, sending their shot through the intervals between each company without doing us any injury, although it created rather unpleasant sensations to hear it whistling past

us. The enemy's shot and shell were now making dreadful havoc. A Portuguese cadet who was attached to our regiment received a shell in the centre of his body, which, bursting at the same instant, literally blew him to pieces. Another poor fellow receiving a grape shot across his belly, his bowels protruded, and he was obliged to apply both his hands to the wound to keep them in: I shall never forget the expression of agony depicted in his countenance.[395]

The advance of the Third Division naturally posed a serious threat to the flank of the next French division, which was that of General Maucune. But it was not just the Third Division that was threatening Maucune. After setting Pakenham in motion, Wellington had ridden back to his main position and ordered the troops there to attack in echelon from the right. First off were the Fifth Division of General Leith, and the cavalry brigade of General Le Marchant. Among the former's men was John Douglas:

> The enemy . . . commenced extending their left to outflank us, at which Sir James Leith advanced our division in double-quick time to check them . . . Down we lay on the slope for the purpose of letting the roundshot pass over us as quickly as possible. In this position we loaded . . . On the Second Brigade forming, a man of the Forty-Fourth was killed and lay for a few minutes, when a shell fell under him and, exploding, drove him into the air. His knapsack, coat, shirt, body and all flew in every direction. A Dublin lad lying on my right looks up and exclaims with the greatest gravity, 'There's an inspection of necessaries.' The Spaniards seemed to have a great curiosity in viewing the combat. You would really imagine that the town of Salamanca was emptied of its inhabitants. The hill to the rear of our lines was as densely crowded as . . . the Park on . . . the anniversary of Waterloo, which did not escape the attention of the French, who, being busy as they were, took time to spare them a few rounds . . . General Leith rode up about two o'clock. The cannonading at this time was terrible. Addressing the regiment, he says, 'Royals . . . This shall be a glorious day for Old England. If these bragadoccian rascals . . . stand their ground, we will display the . . . British bayonet, and where it is properly displayed no power is able to withstand it. All I request of you is to be steady and obey your officers. Stand up men!' A few paces brought us to the crest of the hill when we became exposed to the fire of all the guns they could bring to bear on us. I think the advance of the British at Salamanca never was exceeded in any field. Captain Stewart of our company, stepping out of the ranks to the front, lays hold of Captain Glover and cries, 'Glover! Did you ever see such a line?'[396]

In Maucune's ranks, meanwhile, all was confusion. Seeing the British cavalry, Maucune ordered his men to form in squares, only for the troops that hit home to turn out to be Leith's infantry. If this was bad, to the left of Maucune the situation was even worse. In this area a confused mass of fugitives from Thomières's division was attempting to reform their ranks. Into these men plunged Le Marchant's three regiments of heavy cavalry. Smashing through the broken infantry, the redcoated horse then swung left and took Maucune in the rear. Riding with the Third Dragoons was William Bragge:

The cavalry advanced upon the backs of the infantry. Our brigade literally rode over the regiments in their front and dashed through the wood at a gallop, the infantry cheering us in all directions. We quickly came up with the French columns and charged their rear. Hundreds threw down their arms, their cavalry ran away, and most of the artillery jumped upon their horses and followed the cavalry. One or two charges mixed up the whole brigade, it being impossible to see for dust and smoke.[397]

In an attempt to halt the rot, the squadron of French light cavalry that was serving as Marmont's personal escort was sent forward into the mêlée. Among them was Charles Parquin. His account, however, begins a little earlier in the battle:

The marshal had just had his artillery sited on the hill . . . and had gone up the slope again with his staff. He told Major Denys to station the escort where he saw fit. The major put us into the line on the right of the Fifth Hussars where for an hour we were subjected to the enemy's fire. We moved from this trying position to charge a regiment of heavy cavalry which was wearing red uniforms. As we returned, I saw a *chasseur* of the Twentieth who was being closely pursued by two English horsemen. 'Turn and face them!' I cried, going to his help. But he did not stop, and one of the Englishmen whose horse was obviously out of control cannoned into me and we both went down. Then the second Englishman galloped up and shouted, 'You are my prisoner!' With his sabre he gestured to me to walk ahead of him . . . Instead, I parried the blows which he aimed at me with his sabre, for I had quickly risen from beneath my horse, which made off towards the escort. I endeavoured to strike the legs of his horse so as to unhorse him. When my horse returned without me, the other members of the escort became alarmed, and two of them came to look for me and to bring me my horse. As soon as they saw me they rode towards us at full speed and the Englishman, when he saw them, retired immediately. In this unequal fight I had received a blow on my wrist. My gauntlet had deadened the blow, which had been aimed at my head: otherwise I would certainly have had my wrist cut through. In the heat of battle I had not felt the blow, although I had lost much blood. I noticed it only when I tried to put my hand on the saddle to remount . . . We left at the gallop . . . as large numbers of enemy cavalry were threatening our left flank. I lost so much blood as I rode with my sabre hanging by its knot from my wrist that I would surely have fallen from my horse if the *chasseurs* had not observed my state and helped me.[398]

Thus far, thus good, but Salamanca was no walkover. On the British left flank matters were going by no means so smoothly. Advancing in echelon with Leith's division was the Fourth Division of General Cole, but its two British brigades had both suffered heavily at Badajoz and were badly understrength. Advancing across the valley that separated the two armies, they succeeded in reaching the crest of the French ridge and driving off part of the division of General Clausel. Their commander, however, was badly wounded, and they were then hit by a sudden French counter-attack. Present with Cole's staff was a future field marshal (and the son of the General Burgoyne defeated at Saratoga), John Burgoyne:

The French regiment came up the hill with a brisk and regular step and their drums beating the *pas-de-charge*. Our men fired wildly . . . among them; the French never returned a shot but continued their steady advance. The English fired again, but . . . men in such confusion had no chance against the perfect order of the enemy, and when the French were close upon them, they wavered and gave way. The officers all advanced in a line in front, waving their swords and cheering their men to come on, but the confusion became a panic, and there was a regular *sauve qui peut* down the hill.[399]

Still further to the left, the buttel known as the Arapil Grande that dominated the entire battlefield saw another French success when the Portuguese brigade of General Pack was checked at its very summit and routed with heavy losses. However, reserve formations soon plugged the gap in the British line, and, as evening started to draw on, Wellington's men were soon sweeping forwards once more. Among the units leading the advance was the Thirty-Second Foot, whose ranks included Henry Ross-Lewin:

It was half-past seven when the Sixth Division, under General Clinton, was ordered to advance a second time and attack the enemy's line in front, supported by the Third and Fifth Divisions. The ground over which we had to pass was a remarkably clear slope, like the glacis of a fortification – most favourable for the defensive fire of the enemy and disadvantageous to the assailants – but the division advanced towards the position with perfect steadiness and confidence. A craggy ridge on which the French infantry were drawn up rose so abruptly that they could fire four or five deep . . . The fire of musketry . . . was by far the heaviest I have ever experienced, and was accompanied by constant discharges of grape. An uninterrupted blaze was then maintained so that the crest of the hill seemed to be one long streak of flame . . . At the very first volley that we received, about eighty men of the right rear of my regiment fell to the rear in one group. The commanding officer immediately rode up to know the cause, and found that they were all wounded.[400]

The troops faced by Ross-Lewin, who was himself wounded shortly afterwards, belonged to a reserve division commanded by General Ferey. Threatened with envelopment, this fell back in good order to a thick swathe of ilex trees that formed the eastern border of the battlefield. Here Ferey turned at bay, only to be badly wounded by a cannon ball. Among his men was Lemonnier-Delafosse:

Formed up on the edge of the wood, the . . . division saw the enemy advance upon it in two lines, of which the first was formed of Portuguese troops and the second of British. Quite alone, its ranks much diminished by combat and deprived of its artillery, its position was critical, but it nevertheless awaited the shock. This came soon enough. The two lines bore down on the division, their order being so regular that we could see through the gaps between the files, and perceive the Portuguese officers keeping their men in position with their swords or canes. We opened fire on the enemy as soon as they came within range, and, arrayed in two ranks as we were, our volleys were so well nourished that, in the space of time that it took for the first line to halt and attempt to return our fire, it had melted away completely . . . The second line, meanwhile, was still coming on, and, although it was composed of British troops, everything suggested that they would be met in the same way, for the division was standing firm: indeed, it had not moved an inch, and that despite the fact that it was being swept by the fire of the enemy artillery. However, all of a sudden our left wing ceased fire and broke and ran. The Seventieth Line had been enveloped by cavalry and swept away the Twenty-Sixth and Forty-Seventh Line in its flight. Yet the Thirty-First Léger, for all that it mustered only two battalions and was now all on its own, stood firm and checked the enemy . . . So fierce was our fire that they did not dare to press home their assault, thinking, perhaps, that the wood sheltered fresh troops. Only when the sun had finally set did our gallant [commander] . . . evacuate the position . . . At roll-call, it was found that 360 men were missing, of whom 80 were dead. In my own company alone, ten men had been struck down by the artillery that had done us so much damage . . . Yet, though you might not believe it, in the very midst of this carnage there was a sudden burst of wild laughter. A man had been cut in two by a roundshot, and his neighbours had all got covered from head to foot in the flour that he had in his haversack.[401]

With the defeat of Ferey's rearguard, the battle of Salamanca came to an end. Two days after the battle, a weary John Mills looked back on the fighting in a letter that is redolent of the turmoil felt by many soldiers in the aftermath of victory:

We are delighted, as you may well imagine, at the result of our labours, which I assure you have been great. Day and night have we been marching. Our division was ordered to attack a height nearly inaccessible before the general attack. We were, however, counter-ordered and sent to the left. Colonel Pack's brigade attacked the height and were cut to pieces. The darkness of the night alone saved what is left of their army . . . They are absolutely running, have nothing to eat and do not know what commands them . . . Their eagles are in our hands. You will hardly be able to make head or tail of this, but I am so distressed I know not what to do. The weather is dreadfully hot and [there is] hardly any water. At the sight of a little stagnant water we run like ducks. The whole business has been most truly lucky. Lord Wellington did not mean to fight but to retire into Portugal. Luckily for us they bullied and that brought it on. They fought very ill and seem at last to have been panic struck . . . Yesterday I saw them running through cornfields like a pack of hounds.[402]

If Mills was exhausted, it was hardly surprising. Even troops who had been in reserve and scarcely fired a shot, such as the Seventh Division, could take little more by the end of the day. William Wheeler, for example, saw out the battle with the Fifty-First Foot:

In the afternoon we broke into open column of divisions . . . and marched upon the rear of our enemy. This was not a very agreeable job as the enemy were cannonading the whole length of their line, and our route lay within range of their guns. The fire at length became so furious that it was expedient to form grand division, thus leaving an interval of double the space for their shot to pass through. Our support being required on the right of the line, we now moved on in double-quick time. This raised such a dust that, together with the heat of the day, we were almost suffocated. The want of water now began to be severely felt, [and] those who had some in their canteens were as badly off as those that had none, for, what with the heat of the day and the shaking it got, it was completely spoiled. Those who drank of it immediately threw it up. As we proceeded the fire increased. We were [as] wet with sweat as if we had been in the Tormes, and so great was the quantity of dust that settled on our faces and clothes that we scarce knew each other. In fact we more resembled an army of sweeps or dustmen than any [other] thing I can conceive. Almost fagged to death, we arrived at our position on the right of our line . . . We found some water near us, but it was so bad we could not drink it. However, it served to rinse our mouths and wash the dust off our faces, [and] this refreshed us much. Lord Wellington rode up to us and entered into conversation with Colonel Mitchell . . . We afterwards learned that . . . the whole of the enemy was in full retreat. We kept advancing but could not come up with them. About nine we halted for the night . . . Having examined a few dead Frenchmen for money, etc., we collected what dead bodies were near and made a kind of wall with them. We did this to break the wind, which was very cutting as we were damp with sweat. Under this shelter we slept very sound until morning.[403]

As usual, meanwhile, the aftermath of battle witnessed terrible scenes. Of these, Beresford's *aide-de-camp* William Warre left a stark record:

Owing to the army having advanced and the few means of transport, many of the wounded, particularly of the French, have suffered horribly, for, three days after, I saw a great many still lying who had received no assistance nor were likely to till next day, and had lain scorching in the sun without a drop of water or the least shade. It was a most dreadful sight. These are the horrid miseries of war. No person who has not witnessed them can possibly form any idea of what they are. Humanity shudders at the very idea, and we turn with detestation and disgust to the sole author of such miseries. What punishment can be sufficient for him! Many of the poor wretches have crawled to this place [i.e. the city of Salamanca]. Many made crutches of the barrels of their firelocks and their shoes. Cruel and villainous as they are themselves . . . one cannot help feeling for them and longing to be able to assist them. But our own people have suffered almost as much, and they are our first care.[404]

Again, however, the British army found help from among the populace. Among those who remembered them with gratitude was John Aitchison:

Having thus noticed the battle of Salamanca, I must not pass over the behaviour of its inhabitants, who in every respect have showed themselves as sincerely attached to us as from the behaviour of the French to them and their own professions we had reason to expect. During the three days that we were on the heights of Villanes where there was no water and we were so much exposed that we could not get a bush to make a fire, they cheerfully obeyed Lord Wellington's order, and men and women, young and old, visited us, bringing with them loads of fresh water and dry wood. After we returned to Salamanca on the twenty-first, apparently being driven back by the enemy . . . they manifested no desire to upbraid us with having deserted them; on the contrary, most seemed to place full reliance that we would do our utmost to protect them, and all those who had little hope of our exertions being successful yet were resigned to their fate and treated us to the last moment with as much civility as when we first entered. After [our] driving off their enemy after the battle, when their assistance was most wanted, they came forward both high and low as became them, and even ladies of birth went to the field of battle and lent all their delicate assistance at removing the wounded into their houses and administering every comfort in their power.[405]

From Salamanca to Madrid

As the Anglo-Portuguese army advanced, it was at every turn presented with scenes of misery among the populace. Near Salamanca, for example, stood the village of Santa Marta:

This wretched place was in a sad condition, for it had been occupied alternately by the French and English several times in the course of the spring and summer, and its resources were completely exhausted. Provisions were dear and scarce, and, on every side, poverty and want assailed you with imploring prayers. It was really heart-breaking to look upon the squalid appearance of the children, which is always more affecting than that of grown beggars, for childhood is the season of careless and playful joy, and to see the roses on their young cheeks blighted by the icy touch of famine is peculiarly distressing.[406]

Hunger and want, meanwhile, were augmented by further depredations on the part of the enemy. Present with the Fortieth Foot was the surgeon Charles Boutflower:

The country we pass through is highly fertile, but the corn is everywhere lamentably destroyed. The villages have been systematically plundered by the enemy, the churches destroyed and vast numbers of houses burned to the ground; indeed the same scenes present themselves that we witnessed in Portugal on the retreat of Masséna. It would really appear from these horrible devastations that they have little hope or expectation of speedily returning to this part of the country.[407]

Little better than the French were the swarms of self-professed guerrillas who infested the countryside. Attached to the two most important commanders in León as a liaison officer, for example, Tomkinson very soon smelt a rat:

I this day, with one dragoon, marched to Santibañez, where I joined Colonel Saornil . . . El Príncipe Borbón, the other attached to the brigade, was in Quintanilla de Abajo . . . At the time the enemy entered Valladolid [in 1808] Saornil was in prison. Released by them, [he] has ever since been organising [his] corps. They are complete banditti, two-thirds clothed in things taken from the enemy. The only pay they receive is from plunder . . . The country provides them with regular rations . . . The French call them brigands.[408]

Very soon, similar doubts were also being voiced in the rest of the army, as witness, for example, this comment by John Mills:

I wish we could transfer the seat of war to the Continent. This country is getting worse and worse every day . . . It may suit the ideas of interested persons to keep the idea alive and harp on Spanish patriotism, but where is it to be found? Certainly not among brigands who obey no law, and whose sole object is plunder . . . The guerrillas say they will not have Ferdinand VII for their king, but will choose one of their own. They are right to keep the thing up, for, should affairs become quiet, these gentry would be out of employment and could never turn their hands to anything like honest work.[409]

Amidst the ravaged landscape of Spain at war, Wellington's soldiers could find little to cheer them. However, one feature that did arouse their interest was the many nunneries they encountered:

With the fair inmates of the [convent], we had a deal of chit-chat, although the close iron gratings which separated us from our inamoratas obscured them in great measure from view. That they were all blessed with sparkling black eyes, I am ready to swear; the rest was left to the imagination. By means of the whirligig concern in which various matters find their way out of and into the convent, these fair ladies presented us with preserved fruits, nose-gays and all sorts of fine things, in return for which certain little notes or love-letters . . . were transmitted by the same mode of conveyance to them. They appeared much interested as to the result of the campaign . . . and two of them who were heartily tired of their unnatural prison declared to myself and a brother officer that they were ready and willing to make their escape with our assistance . . . When one considers that by so doing they would have brought down on them the vengeance of monks, friars, padres and mother-abbesses, and that those black-eyed damsels must have calculated on being buried alive or baked on a gridiron had they been detected in such an adventure, we must admit they were heroines of the first class.[410]

There is, of course, a considerable degree of fantasy here, and on occasion this gave rise to comic results. At Trujillo, for example, Ulsterman George Bell, a 17-year-old ensign in the Thirty-Fourth Foot, was witness to a particularly farcical scene:

Our doctor . . . got up a . . . dinner with a few friends [and] took the chair . . . until he got so merry [that] he bolted off to a convent to release the nuns like a gallant knight! Many of the fair *señoritas*, he knew, were there pining for liberty, but the watchful and wily priests came to the rescue. There was a shindy, of course, [and] a few officers of the baggage guard, who had shared in the toasts, collected their forces and joined the *médico*. They assailed the convent again, and had nearly forced an entrance when the second-in-command received a wound on the head and tumbled down the stairs. The doctor called off his troops to see after the wounded . . . and the holy priests made their escape, satisfied in preserving the dark-eyed maidens from the hands of such heretics.[411]

Meanwhile, the campaign continued. Having first occupied Valladolid, Wellington's troops turned south and headed for Madrid. Among the leading troops was William Grattan of the Connaught Rangers:

In less than two hours we reached the heights which command Madrid: the soldiers ran forward to catch a glimpse of the countless steeples that were distinguishable through the haze, and their joy was at its height when they beheld a city that had cost them so much toil and hard fighting to gain the possession of. Ten thousand voices at one and the same moment vociferated, 'Madrid! Madrid!' The enthusiasm of the army was still further increased by the thousands upon thousands of Spaniards that came from the town to accompany us in our entry: for miles leading to the capital the roads were crowded almost to suffocation with people of all ranks who seemed to be actuated by one simultaneous burst of patriotism, and it was with difficulty that the march was conducted with that order which we were in the habit of observing. The nearer we approached the city, the greater was the difficulty of getting on, for the people forced themselves into our ranks, and joined hand in hand with the soldiers . . . At length we entered that part of the town near which the palace stands, but the obstacles which impeded our march, great as they were before, now became ten-fold greater. Nothing could stop the populace, which at this period nearly embraced half that which Madrid contained, from mixing themselves with us. The officers were nearly forced from their horses in the embraces of the females, and some there were who actually lost their seats, if not their hearts. Old or young, ugly or well-looking, shared the same fate, and one, in particular, an old friend of my own, and a remarkably plain-looking personage, was nearly suffocated in the embraces of half a dozen fair Castilians. When he recovered himself and was able to speak, he turned to me and said, 'How infernally fond these Madrid women must be of kissing, when they have hugged nearly to death such an ill-looking fellow as me.' We soon reached the convent of Santo Domingo near the Plaza Mayor, which was destined for our quarters, and for a time took leave of these people who had so cordially welcomed us to their capital.[412]

For a Spanish view, let us turn to the priest José Clemente Carnicero Torribio:

When the bells began to announce the entrance of our troops at about ten o'clock, it was wonderful to see the people rushing to . . . the Portillo de San Vicente, which is the one through which they were said to be coming. A new town council was formed, and this immediately set forth to greet . . . the immortal Wellington . . . To the accompaniment of a crescendo of bells, the people massed in ever greater numbers round the Plaza de la Villa. When a portrait of our Don Fernando [i.e. Ferdinand VII] was placed in the window of the town hall, they simply went mad.

The cheering was incessant; hats and caps were thrown in the air; on all sides people were giving thanks to God; and everyone was filled with the greatest joy and happiness. Another of the incidents that made the day shine out was the behaviour of the women and the children of the poorer quarters. Joseph . . . had made a new avenue from the palace to the Casa de Campo [i.e. the royal hunting park] . . . This had been lined with fruit trees . . . but the crowd . . . fell upon them and ripped them up . . . When Lord Wellington arrived, many of the people who greeted him were therefore carrying branches and sprigs of greenery which they waved in time with their cheers and happy shouts of greeting. In this manner he was accompanied to the town hall. When he got there the cheering redoubled, and all the more so when . . . he came out on to one of the balconies accompanied by El Empecinado. Amidst thunderous applause everyone flung their arms around one another, and gave themselves over to congratulating their neighbours in the most unreserved fashion.[413]

As John Mills wrote, the rest of the day was taken up with rejoicing:

The inhabitants seem delighted to see us – they call us their deliverers. I never thought the Spaniards in earnest before but they really seem overjoyed. During the day tapestry, silks, curtains, etc., are hung out of the windows. The whole town seems mad. Groups of English officers and guerrillas [are] parading up and down the streets dressed in the most grotesque manner. Whenever Lord Wellington appears he is followed by an immense crowd eager to get a glimpse of him . . . The men and women (particularly the latter) hug us in the streets . . . The women . . . wear large veils which they put on most gracefully . . . You will begin to think I am likely to fall in love with them. I could do such a thing to be sure as I think there are a great number of pretty women here. But I am in one respect too much of an Englishman to be pleased easily for they consume a great deal of garlic. In other respects they are delightful, and you may meet with those who do not use that . . . vegetable. There is a naivety about them that is very pleasing and none of the reserve so peculiar to Englishwomen. Entering their capital, as we have done, with flying colours and our enemies flying before us, you may imagine, is a great advantage. They make much of us, and all mortals, you know, are tickled by flattery.[414]

But it was not just in Madrid that the Spaniards were delighted. A few miles east stood the town of Alcalá de Henares, its reaction to liberation being recorded for us by the unwilling town councillor, Juan Domingo Palomar:

The twelfth of August was a . . . day of the greatest joy in [Alcalá]. At half past one in the afternoon the worthy José Mondedeu, the lieutenant colonel of the [Voluntarios de] Guadalajara light cavalry regiment rode into town shouting that the Allied army commanded by the Duke of Wellington had occupied the capital that morning accompanied by the troops of El Empecinado, and that the only Frenchmen left in the capital were about 1,000 men who had been left behind in the Retiro to guard the wounded. This news caused such joy that it is impossible to describe it . . . No sooner had the news spread than the populace came out on to the streets and the church bells began to ring. Cheers rang out on all sides, and the gravest and most serious of men were seen . . . capering about in the most public of places. Some people were in floods of tears, others were shouting their heads off: the fact is that quite simply we all went mad . . . After that first outburst of joy, we all went to give thanks to the Almighty in the church of Santa María . . . In the midst of many tears, a most solemn Te Deum was sung, but after that the rejoicing began again. The most perfect illuminations were organised for that same night (and most perfectly did they shine out too); there was dancing in the Plaza Mayor; there were bands of musicians in every street; and there were scenes that it is simply impossible to describe without having seen them. In just three hours, too, a cart appeared with a young girl dressed up as Spain; beautifully clothed and armed with a sword in one hand and some broken chains in the other, she represented the freedom of the nation, and was proceeded by a guard of soldiers carrying swords and axes and a choir singing patriotic hymns . . . On 13 August we saw for the first time General Juan Martín Díez, El Empecinado. Such was the anticipation created by his arrival in the city that there was not a single person who did not go out into the streets . . . to look upon him and celebrate him as one of the saviours of the Fatherland. Not excluding the leading ladies of the town, people of every class seized hold of him, embraced him, even kissed him, while calling down blessings upon him and loading him with praise, while he gazed round him with tears in his eyes.[415]

In Madrid Wellington's victorious troops soon settled into their new quarters. After the rigours of the past few months, many of them were clearly all too glad to relax for a week or two, and see the sights. One first impression of the city comes from the pen of Charles Boutflower:

The principal curiosities of Madrid are the royal palace (which in point of magnificence is said to be unrivalled in Europe), the museum and the public walk called the Prado . . . The Prado is said to be the finest public walk in Europe. The churches . . . have nothing extraordinary in them; the principal one is dedicated to San Isidro, but it is very inferior to the cathedral at Salamanca. There are two theatres tolerably good, but the performers are very indifferent, the principal actors having gone off with the intrusive king. The two great inconveniences we sustained . . . were the excessive heat (far greater than I have ever before experienced it) and the hardness of the pavement, so much so that there was a general complaint of sore feet. What particularly strikes a stranger in Madrid is the elegance of the women, the beauty of their dress and their inimitable walk.[416]

For a somewhat livelier account, we might turn to William Grattan:

Madrid stands in a flat, uninteresting country, devoid of scenery . . . and the rivulet that meanders round it is in summer so insignificant as to be barely able to supply the few baths on its banks with a sufficiency of water; nevertheless, this side of the town, which is next to the grand park . . . called the Casa de Campo, is far from uninteresting, and as the park, which abounds with game of all sorts, was open to the British officers, we had abundance of sport when we wished to avail ourselves of it. The streets are wide, and the principal ones, generally speaking, clean, but the part of the town possessing the greatest interest is the great street called the Puerta del Sol . . . Half a dozen of the principal streets empty . . . their population into this gangway, where the Exchange is held and all public business carried on, so that anyone desirous of hearing the news of the day, the price of the funds or any other topic discussed has but to station himself here, and his curiosity will be satisfied, as almost the entire . . . population of Madrid pass and repass under his eye . . . Merchants, dealers, higglers, charcoal vendors, fellows with lemonade on their backs, girls with panellas [*sic*] of water incessantly crying out 'Quien quiere agua?', all congregate to this focus where everything is to be known. Next to the Puerta del Sol must be placed the Prado, or public walk, which is decidedly the most agreeable lounge that Madrid can boast of . . . By five o'clock . . . it begins to be frequented, the great heat by this time having subsided, and the siesta [ended]. At seven it is crowded almost to suffocation, and groups of singers with guitars slung across their shoulder enliven the scene. At each side of the walk are tables at which sit groups of people enjoying the scene, but you rarely see men and women seated at the table; indeed, it would seem as if the men totally shunned the company of the fairer sex, and engrossed themselves more with the news of the day than with the gaiety of the Prado.[417]

Another soldier eager to wander the city was Joseph Donaldson:

We were now peaceably quartered in the town, having time to look about us and recover from our former fatigues. No place could have been better adapted for this than Madrid: the air was pure and healthy; wine, fruit and provisions good and cheap. Here we had food for observation in the buildings, institutions and manners of the inhabitants, and we ranged about in the environs, and from one street to another, as if we had been in a new world. Madrid has so often been described by writers of ability that it would be presumption in me to attempt it . . . but the delightful walks of the Prado, the gardens breathing perfume, the beautiful fountains, the extensive and picturesque view from the Segovia gate, the cool and delicious shades on the banks of the Manzanares, the women, the music and nightly serenades, gave it to my mind the charm of romance. During the time we remained at Madrid, our troops were allowed free access to the museum in the street [called] Alcalá, nearly opposite our barracks. In it there was a very valuable collection of natural history, particularly a lump of native gold brought from South America which weighed many pounds, some enormous boa constrictors and the entire skeleton of a mammoth . . . Several times during our stay in Madrid we were admitted gratis to see the bullfights, the great national amusement of the Spaniards . . . I do not believe that many of our men were much captivated with this amusement; it was rather considered a cruel and disgusting one. I cannot understand how it is so much encouraged in Spain unless it be to serve the same purpose that we pay boxers to murder each other, namely to keep up the national courage.[418]

Donaldson was not the only member of Wellington's forces who found that he disliked bullfighting. Another attendant at a *corrida* was Charles Boutflower:

> I had yesterday an opportunity of witnessing a bullfight, a spectacle the most delightful there can be to the people of this nation, but one which to a mind tinctured with the smallest degree of humanity cannot be witnessed without horror. On these occasions ten or twelve bulls and nearly as many horses are sacrificed amid every species of cruelty and the applauding shouts of an immense multitude. So concordant is this spectacle with the Spaniards of both sexes that many a poor family, who know not where to get money to purchase a bit of bread to eat, will sell the clothes they wear or the bed they lie on in order to procure the wherewithal to pay for their admittance. The shouts of applause are in an exact ratio with the degrees of cruelty that are practised, and if the unfortunate bulls are killed without at least one of the fighters being also victims the disappointment is extreme . . . Though the number of bulls for yesterday's amusement was ten, I could not witness the sufferings of more than one: I had a presentiment of the disgust I should experience, and I can with truth assert that my feeling was never before so completely horrified. The endurance of this barbarous amusement, and the protection afforded to it by the government, I consider as a stain upon the national character [and] the applause and joy manifested by the people at the sufferings of the poor animals has given me an idea of their hearts as bad as it is possible to conceive.[419]

Yet even in this summer of pleasure and relaxation, there were disturbing undercurrents. In an interesting passage, Grattan makes it clear that there was little real intercourse with the population:

> In some instances we experienced much hospitality from the people, but those occurrences were rare, for the Spaniards are naturally a lofty and distant people, and most unquestionably our officers did not endeavour by any act on their part to do away with this reserve, and in fact after a sojourn of nearly three months in the Spanish capital, they knew nearly as little of its inhabitants as they did of the citizens of Peking. This is a fatal error, and I fear one that will be difficult to counteract for it is not easy to correct national habits and national prejudices, but if the officers of the British nation were to reflect upon the effect their conduct must have on the people of a different nation, and if they could be made to understand, how different, how far different, their reception in foreign countries would be if they unbent themselves a little and conformed themselves to the modes of those nations among whom they were sent by their sovereign, they would at once come to the resolution of changing their tone, and they would by so doing get themselves not only respected and regarded, but the British nation as much beloved as it is respected. It is a singular fact, and I look upon it as a degrading one, that the French officers while at Madrid made in the ratio of five to one more conquests than we did! How is this to be accounted for? The British officer has the advantage of appearance: his exterior is far before that of a Frenchman; his fortune, generally speaking, ten times as great, but what of all this if the one accommodates himself to the manners, the whims, of those

he is thrown among, while the other, disregarding all forms, sticks to his national habits, struts about and not only despises, but lets it be seen that he despises, all he meets save those of his own nation. What a fatal error! The British armies under Lord Wellington have immortalised themselves in Portugal and Spain . . . but . . . have made few friends in either.[420]

Still more disturbingly, few British officers appear to have been moved by the scenes of famine around them. One of the few to make mention of the matter was George Hennell, the son of a ribbon manufacturer from Coventry, who had recently joined the Forty-Third Foot as a gentleman-volunteer:

The poor are very numerous here, and many are the most wretched objects. In the great streets, you are stopped every five or six yards, and frequently by six or seven at once . . . I have seen children five or six years of age lying on the pavement with scarcely one ounce of flesh on their bones and making a piteous moaning. After dark they lie down against a door doubled almost together . . . some sleeping, others crying.[421]

Another officer who recalled such sights was John Patterson:

Notwithstanding the unsettled state of things, the inhabitants of Madrid seem to enjoy life to the fullest extent, and in the constant pursuit of gaiety endeavour to dispel that gloom which would otherwise pervade their city . . . The number of poor, however, is very great, many dying in the streets of starvation. We met several persons, male and female, who had formerly been possessed of wealth and distinction, endeavouring to obtain a livelihood by selling . . . different articles of their dress and household furniture. Others, particularly women, whose looks bespoke their having lived in better days, were reduced to the miserable situation of vending pamphlets or small wares, or keeping stalls, or even hawking salt fish or vegetables through the city.[422]

Nor was the suffering restricted to the starving inhabitants of Madrid and other cities. The battle of Salamanca had left the French with no option but to evacuate first central Spain and then the whole of Andalucía. With them went the many Spaniards who had collaborated with King Joseph's government. From both Madrid and Seville, then, long columns of troops and civilians set out to make the long journey to Valencia, where safety awaited in the form of the army of Marshal Suchet. Among the soldiers who made the trek in the south was the pharmacist Antoine Fée:

We set out on 26 August . . . Our convoy covered the road for a very great distance, and was so big that a great deal of trouble would have been required to keep it in order . . . Hardly had we set out than a large number of sick and wounded soldiers appeared among us. The fear of being taken prisoner had raised them from their beds of suffering, and they were begging us to let them ride on our wagons and carriages. Poor souls: they promised not to be any trouble, but a deaf ear was turned to their appeals, and it looked very likely that they would be left behind. At length, however, an order came from Marshal Soult directing that their demands be satisfied. Indeed, he was the first to give the example, and gave several of the invalids spaces among his baggage. But no sooner had the order been issued than selfishness mobilised its every resource to show that it could not be carried out. All of a sudden, wagons were found to be full to capacity or to have developed problems with their axles. Horses that were full of vigour were suddenly announced by their masters . . . to be barely able to stand . . . In the end force had to be used to put an end to such lies, and little by little all was arranged. For a brief moment, then, joy lit up the faces of our poor sufferers . . . That night we had to reach Marchena, and I am sure that we could not possibly have made the journey any slower than we did, stopped, as we were, at every instant by breakdowns that disrupted the movement of the wagons. The harvest had been brought in, and, being devoid of trees, the countryside was heartbreakingly sad and monotonous. The sun flooded us with light, and I have never felt its power so strongly. There was not a scrap of shade in which to rest even for an instant, nor any breeze to temper the violence of its rays. The burning air dried out one's lungs, and it was necessary to fight at one and the same time against a devouring thirst and an overwhelming desire to go to sleep. We had a number of men who were actually asphyxiated by the heat; horses that refused to go a step further and then dropped dead; dogs that died of thirst in agony from paws that had been burned by the fiery ground. In short, we experienced all the sufferings of a caravan crossing the desert. When the sun finally went down and we made camp by a pool whose banks offered a little verdure, I lay down with great delight on the grass and was immediately overcome by the deepest sleep.[423]

Watching the French and their supporters flee, meanwhile, was a populace torn between joy and terror. As a young boy named Nicolas Peñalver later recalled, in Granada the populace were ordered to place lights in their windows so as to illuminate the streets a little, while around them the French blew up their fortifications:

I still remember the night of 17 September 1812 with terror . . . Who can forget the fear that reigned in our homes, for all that they were lit up on the outside as if we were celebrating some festivity? Some time around midnight, meanwhile, the peace and silence . . . of the night were ripped apart, the French having chosen this moment as the time that they would set off their mines. Who can forget the terrible sounds made by the ancient towers as they crashed to the ground or the explosions that ripped them apart? The continual crashes that came from the [Alhambra] and the various other places that had bedevilled our existence for so long were the very last expression of the horrible system of cruelty and oppression which had been imposed upon us.[424]

Burgos

The capture of Madrid placed Wellington in an awkward position. Forced to evacuate a great deal of territory, the French were for the first time since 1809 enabled to unite in considerable masses around two main nuclei. In the north the army that had been defeated in Portugal was echeloned between Valladolid and Burgos. Now reorganised under General

Clausel, it numbered 40,000 men, and there was good reason to suppose that it could be increased to as many as 50,000 from the troops stationed in Navarre and the Basque provinces. In the east, meanwhile, not counting the garrison of the Levante and Aragón under Marshal Suchet, King Joseph and Marshal Soult could muster 65,000 men. At Madrid, meanwhile, Wellington had no more than 60,000 Anglo-Portuguese troops. What was required, obviously enough, was a rapid thrust against one or other of the two threats. On 31 August, then, Wellington marched north, but at this point things began to go wrong. For political reasons many men were left in Madrid. Still worse, meanwhile, Clausel got away. At this point, the logical choice would have been to fall back on Madrid and hope that some enemy error would open the way for another Salamanca. Yet Wellington chose rather to attack the improvised citadel which the French had constructed on the basis of Burgos's medieval castle. But taking this was problematic, for the British commander had not been anticipating a siege and in consequence had brought hardly any heavy guns with him. All that he had, in short, was the courage of his men, and this currently seemed in short supply. Indeed, there was much grumbling:

> The weather is now so bad that campaigning is more than a joke. We are never under cover even of a shrub, for this country is not favoured with anything bigger than a vine. The rain comes down in torrents. Headquarters and the staff are always snug in houses, and do not care about the weather, and you must know that our noble marquis is not gifted with much feeling – ambition hardens the heart. He only regards the comforts of the men as far as it is actually necessary to his purposes: all have their faults and this is his.[425]

Arriving before the castle of Burgos on 19 September, the Allies found themselves confronted by a most formidable position. Let us here quote John Aitchison:

> The garrison in the castle and works around it are reported [as being] from 1,200 [to] 1,800 men, and a general officer . . . has undertaken its defence . . . The castle itself is a a high square building of masonry and so solid as to have five twenty-four pounders on the top, and it is fortified so as to form a sort of citadel, and this again is surrounded by all such works as the French in their great experience of such situations in Spain have found best calculated for its defence. The work is irregular but approaching in form a four-sided figure. The first line is of earth . . . but in some places with a stone revetment, and a small convent at one of the angles is so dextrously taken into it as to add greatly to its strength; the parapet is fraised [i.e. palisaded] throughout its extent and all the guns have embrasures. The second line is a *fauss-bray*, being lower than the rampart and at about ten feet from it, which space is intersected by palisades. In front of this again there is a shallow ditch and [a] covered way with palisades.[426]

Covering the main area of fortification was an outlying redoubt called the Hornwork of San Miguel. Believing that this was the key to the position, Wellington had hardly arrived before the castle than he had ordered an assault on it. Among the men who charged forward was an anonymous corporal of the Black Watch:

We were to make the attack in three divisions – a division to each flank [of the hornwork] . . . and one to the front; these divisions were to keep up a constant fire on the top of the walls, while the storming . . . party were placing ladders against the scarp . . . About an hour after dusk we got under arms and marched up to the height, and about ten o'clock we advanced till we were within one hundred yards of the works. The night was very dark, but we were soon perceived by the enemy, and in an instant all the works opened upon us a most tremendous fire of roundshot, shells, grape and musketry. We did not fire . . . till the scaling ladders were placed against the wall: we were to commence by beat of drum and stop by the same. The forlorn hope, having mounted the ladders, found, to their great grief, that they were about two feet too short. We could not succeed . . . and I believe the attack on the right demi-bastion was unsuccessful from the same cause. However, a narrow pass having been found by some of the regiment, the place was carried at the point of the bayonet in the course of fifteen minutes. A few of the enemy made their escape into the castle, but the havoc was great that was made in and about the works.[427]

The hornwork having been taken, albeit at a cost of 421 dead and wounded, a battery was established within it from which to batter the main French line of defence. However, conscious that he needed to return to Madrid, Wellington could not spare the time to wait upon the effects of a bombardment, but rather decided to try to scale the walls. This time the responsibility fell on 400 volunteers from the First Division. Though not a participant in the attack, John Mills was seemingly an eyewitness:

A party of 130 of the Brigade of Guards led the way with the ladders. The enemy opened a tremendous fire, on which the Germans filed off to the right and the Scots followed them. Our men got up the ladders with some difficulty under a heavy fire from the top of the wall, but were unable to get to the top. Hall of the Third Regiment [of Foot Guards] who mounted first was knocked down. Frazer tried and was shot in the knee. During the whole of this time they kept up a constant fire from the top of the wall and threw down bags of gunpowder and large stones. At last, having been twenty-five minutes in the ditch and not seeing anything of the other parties, they retired, having lost half their numbers in killed and wounded . . . Thus ended the attack, which it was almost madness to undertake.[428]

With the repulse of this attack, there was nothing for it but to engage in formal siege operations. With the handful of heavy guns available, an attempt was made to breach the walls, while at another spot a mine was begun. However, trained engineer officers and even picks and shovels were in desperately short supply, and progress was extremely slow. For the troops it was a miserable time. In the first place, it did not help that the weather was worse than ever. Stationed outside the city with some of the troops Wellington had set to watch Clausel was John Green of the Sixty-Eighth Foot:

Our brigade encamped on the side of a hill south of the main road . . . under a few scattered oak trees, where we made wigwams or huts of the boughs, but from the want of proper materials we could not make them waterproof. There were not more than three or four huts that would turn the rain, so that for twenty-four days or more we were exposed to the constant dribbling . . . which had now set in. Some days, indeed, it rained all day without intermission. What rendered our situation most uncomfortable and unpleasant was [the fact that] we were almost naked, for we were nearly out of all the necessaries so essential to our comfort, such as stockings, shoes, shirts, blankets, watchcoats and trousers, and, what was worse than all, it now began to be very cold, for, when the rain ceased, there was a frost almost every night, so that we were nearly perished.[429]

Things were no better in the trenches, but here there was also the danger of shot and shell, not to mention sallies by the garrison. Among the men manning the siege works were the Forty-Second Foot:

There were a few of the company I belonged to collected together in one spot in the trench . . . We were all sitting on the ground: there was an officer of the company and a sergeant too . . . A shell fell right in the midst of us: we all got up . . . except one stupid body who sat still, [with] the shell, I may say, between his feet. He took handfuls of earth and tried to smother the fuse . . . but in an instant he was blown to pieces. I threw myself flat down on the earth where I was about four yards from the . . . shell; the rest . . . were eager to get as far from it as possible . . . but flight was unavailing. The officer was struck with two pieces of the shell . . . on the head and the arm; the sergeant was struck with one piece on the head, which caused his death soon after; my musket was wrested out of my hand by another splinter, and broken into a hundred pieces . . . The enemy sent a great quantity of shells down among us on this day, and opened a heavy fire of roundshot on our battery, which had opened a heavy fire of red-hot shot on a large house they called a convent. It was near to the castle, and about fifty yards from that part of the wall on which I was stationed . . . The enemy made a sally after dusk . . . to endeavour to drive us from the wall. The officer of our party was absent at the time. I lost not a minute in getting my men planted in the most obvious places where the attack was meditated. On us the enemy advanced, but we kept up a very brisk fire on them, and they were forced to retire back to the castle again with loss.[430]

On 19 October all was ready for another assault on the castle. There was a small breach in the northern walls, while the mine was pronounced ready for firing and duly wrecked a small convent that had been turned into an improvised bastion. Once again, then, various parties from the First Division charged forwards, but the results were no better. For a graphic account of the attack, we can do no better than turn to John Mills, who this time actually participated in the attack:

Our party was to escalade the wall in front. Burgess ran forwards with thirty men, [and] Walpole and myself followed with fifty each . . . A most tremendous fire opened upon us from every part which took us in front and rear. They poured down fresh men, and ours kept falling down into the ditch, dragging and knocking down others. We were so close that they fairly put their muskets into our faces, and we pulled one of their men through an embrasure. Burgess was killed and Walpole severely wounded. We had hardly any men left on the top, and at last we gave way. How we got over the palisades I know not. They increased their fire as we retreated, and we came off with the loss of more than half our party. All the badly wounded were left in the ditch. Burgess behaved nobly: he was the first up the ladder, and waved his hat [from] the top. I found him lying there wounded. He begged me to get my men up and in the act of speaking . . . was shot dead. The time we were on the wall was not more than six minutes. The fire was tremendous: shot, shell, grape, musketry, large stones, hand grenades and every missile weapon were used against us. I reckon my escape particularly fortunate.[431]

Retreat

The failure of the assault of 19 October marked the end of the siege. Determined on success though he was, Wellington could not remain before Burgos forever. On the other side of the Ebro, there were signs that a counter-offensive was imminent. With only 24,000 Anglo-Portuguese and 11,000 Spaniards in the area, a stand looked very dangerous, and so on 21 October Wellington raised the siege and set off for Valladolid. Marching with the Black Watch was the anonymous corporal whom we have quoted before:

In the course of the night we marched through the town of Burgos, leaving the castle almost in the same state as when we commenced the siege. We continued our march till day dawned upon us, when we halted for a few hours. We started again, and marched till it was evening, when we were halted and bivouacked in grass fields. Next morning again we started before day, and the retreat went on very rapid . . . The weather now became very bad; the rains fell more copiously . . . and very long marches made it excessively fatiguing. Besides we hardly ever had on this retreat a day's complete ration, and some days we wanted it altogether. Beef, however, we scarcely ever stood in want of, but it was marched alive with the army, and whenever we halted a certain number of bullocks were killed for the brigade by the butchers of the different regiments. When provisions were scanty, the men, in great crowds, attended at the killing of the bullocks with their camp kettles . . . shouldering, pushing, climbing one over another, and tongues going, aye, and fists too sometimes. We cooked [the blood] by boiling it . . . and eating it when cold like cheese . . . Though some disliked this mess, I liked it well enough at that time; it was not the place, was a retreat bivouac, to turn up one's nose at the blood of a bullock . . . The bullocks were killed in the fields . . . and cut upon the ground, and by the time the flesh was served out in messes for the company it was so full of sand and grass that it was impossible to clean it, and, when this was done at night, it was still worse. I have seen the men eating it, and picking the grass and dirt out of it as they ground it between their teeth, and . . . happy to get it.[432]

Though far worse was yet to come, the retreat was not a pleasant experience. There were frequent skirmishes with the French cavalry, while the months of campaigning had taken a heavy toll. Near Valladolid, William Hay, a 20-year-old lieutenant of the Twelfth Light Dragoons who had been on detachment in Portugal, came up with his regiment for the first time in many months:

> On reporting myself . . . to the headquarters of the Twelfth, I [had] found the men in new uniforms and the horse and appointments in the best condition. At that time they had but recently arrived from England, and it was a treat to look upon so neat and clean a corps. But what a difference one campaign had made: the men's clothes were actually in rags, some one colour, some another; some in worn-out helmets, some in none; others in forage caps or with handkerchiefs tied round their heads; the horses in a most woeful state, many quite unfit to carry the weight of the rider and his baggage. The edge was indeed off all but the spirit of his dragoons and the edge of his sabre.[433]

Further south the situation was no better. Just as the French moved forwards in the north, so they also did in the Levante and New Castile. Very soon, indeed, 60,000 men were in motion for Madrid under Marshal Soult and King Joseph. Facing them were just 30,000 men under Rowland Hill, and so he too had no option but to retreat. For a graphic example of what passed in the capital, let us turn to Surgeon Boutflower's diary:

> The events of the last few days have been of the most painful nature, nor were they at all suspected by anyone. On the twenty-ninth rumours were afloat in the morning that the British army was about to retreat for the purpose of concentrating with Lord Wellington. Towards the afternoon an unusual bustle was observed to prevail among the civil authorities and their families and equipages were seen . . . quitting the town. On the morning of the thirtieth the removal of all the sick and wounded and the destruction of the guns in the Retiro left no sort of doubt that we were going to abandon the capital: the shops were nearly all shut, and the greatest agitation prevailed. I quitted Madrid myself in the afternoon of the thirtieth . . . On the night of the thirtieth I remained with a part of the army in Las Rozas about two and a half leagues [along] the road leading to the Escorial . . . Here we learned that there was every reason to believe that the enemy had occupied the strong pass of . . . Guadarrama, and that there was no retreat for us but by the mountains of Avila, by which it was considered our sick, artillery, stores and baggage would be all lost. Lord Wellington was supposed to have been worsted in a general action and to have been compelled to retire beyond the Tormes: in short, nothing could possibly be more gloomy than our prospects . . . It is impossible to calculate the consequences of our being compelled to quit the capital, but it is not unlikely that it will have so great an effect on the minds of the people as to excite a despondency fatal to the liberties of the country. It is certain that they have not availed themselves as they should have done of the much that has been done, and it may, I think, be fairly questioned whether in that time, with two-thirds of their country unoccupied by the French, they have added 10,000 men to their army.[434]

Coming up with the forces deployed to south and east of the city, meanwhile, was Joseph Donaldson:

We supposed at first that we would again occupy Madrid, but when we came in sight of it the Retiro was in flames, and we could hear the report of cannon, which proceeded from the brass guns in the fort being turned on each other for the purpose of rendering them useless to the enemy . . . The staff officers were galloping about giving directions to the different divisions concerning the route; the inhabitants whom we met on the road were in evident consternation; and everything indicated an unexpected and hurried retreat. Instead, therefore, of entering the city, we passed to the left of it. The enemy's cavalry by this time being close on our rear, before ours had exited the town on one side, the French had entered it on the other.[435]

Around Madrid, at least, the initial stages of the retreat were not marked by the same privations as those experienced on the road from Burgos. Yet, angry and frustrated, Hill's troops began to behave in much the same manner as those of Sir John Moore had in 1808, one early casualty being the town of Valdemoro. William Swabey was a 23-year-old lieutenant in the Royal Horse Artillery:

Here a scene of the most disgraceful character ensued. It was at the time of year when the new wine was in open vats and there were many at this place. Numbers of men fell out of the ranks and surrounded them, and I saw with my own eyes many actually drowned in the vats. They were bailing out the liquor with their caps to their comrades till, overcome as much by the fumes of the wine as what they drank, they sank down and expired in their glory.[436]

Left behind in Madrid was a populace that until the last moment had believed Hill's men would fight. Some of the despair that filled the city is communicated to us by the priest Carnicero Torribio:

On the first [of November] the retreat of the British and their allies became known for a certainty, and all the more so when it was noted that in so far as they could they had demolished . . . the china factory in the Retiro, this being the site of the chief French batteries and magazines. In spite of these signs that the retreat was definitive, there were those who said that the French would not come to Madrid. However, they were soon disabused. At four o'clock in the afternoon on this same Feast . . . of All Saints, an *aide-de-camp* of the Intruso's arrived at the Puerta de Toledo with a guard of eighty men. He informed himself as fully as he could of the situation in Madrid and . . . haughtily announced that the king would be back the next day. And so it transpired: the king arrived about three o'clock in the afternoon . . . Over the preceding months the general idea had been that the soldiers of King Joseph had all died of hunger, or that they were at the very least in a state of great misery. However, in the days that followed the people of Madrid not only observed them in great numbers, but saw that they were plump, well dressed and loaded with money. Still worse, they were so puffed up and pleased with themselves that much patience and skill were required . . . to answer them in a manner that did not leave one exposed to their rage. It is easy to imagine the faces of the people of Madrid at this development, whereas the *afrancesados* were going around full of smiles.[437]

Nearby Alcalá de Henares was just as despondent. As Juan Domingo Palomar remembered:

> At nightfall on 5 December the division of . . . General Palombini entered the city . . .
> Among the people there was great consternation and fear . . . All the soldiers were
> laden with large quantities of clothing, furniture and personal effects that they had
> stolen in the towns and villages of Castile, and the next day this stuff was being sold
> in the streets in a regular market . . . From everything that I have seen, the places
> where they have been must be utterly bereft. On 7 December the division remained in
> the city and the troops all day caused a great deal of trouble. Full of terror, the
> inhabitants gathered together at dusk, for in their eyes every single soldier is . . .
> someone who robs, beats up or otherwise mistreats anyone they meet. In those houses
> that were taken over as billets, what labours and misfortunes did we endure! We were
> the slaves of these savages, and not only that but we had to supply them with firewood,
> coal, oil, beds, coverlets, seasoning and anything else in the place that they happened
> to want or need. But the worst thing of all was the impolite, uncouth and barbarous
> behaviour of the officers . . . the patient abnegation with which we attended to their
> needs being repaid . . . with diktats, threats and blows. All of the division being
> composed of Italians, we can only conclude that in Italy humanity and religion have
> been abandoned since its sons took up arms in the service of the tyrant of Europe.[438]

By dint of a combination of good luck and good management, the two halves of
Wellington's forces were reunited without mishap at Salamanca. But there was no chance
of a stand, for the Anglo-Portuguese army was still badly outnumbered. In consequence,
the retreat continued. Trudging along with the Ninety-Fourth Foot was a miserable and
bedraggled Joseph Donaldson:

> I never saw the troops in such bad humour. Retreating before the enemy at any time
> was a grievous business, but in such weather it was doubly so. The rain, now pouring
> down in torrents, drenched us to the skin, and the road, composed of a clay soil,
> stuck to our shoes so fast, that they were torn off our feet. The . . . cold wind blew
> in in heavy gusts, and the roads became gradually worse. After marching in this state
> for several hours, we halted in a field on the roadside, and, having piled our arms,
> were allowed to dispose ourselves to rest as best we could. The moon was now up,
> and, wading through the dense masses of clouds, she sometimes threw a momentary
> gleam on the miserable beings who were huddled together in every variety of
> posture, endeavouring to rest or screen themselves from the cold. Some were lying
> stretched on the wet ground rolled in still wetter blankets; more, having placed their
> knapsack on a stone, had seated themselves on it with their blankets wrapped about
> them, their head reclining on their knees and their teeth chattering with cold, while
> others more resolute and wise, were walking about. Few words were spoken, and, as
> if ashamed to complain of the hardships we suffered, execrating the retreat and
> blaming Lord Wellington for not having sufficient confidence in us to hazard a battle
> with the enemy . . . were the only topics discussed . . . The feeling of hunger was
> very severe. Some beef that had remained with the division was served out, but our

attempts to kindle fires with wet wood were quite abortive. Sometimes, indeed, we managed to raise a smoke, and numbers gathered round in the vain hope of getting themselves warmed, but the fire would extinguish in spite of all their efforts. Our situation was truly distressing: tormented by hunger, wet to the skin and fatigued in the extreme, our reflections were bitter . . . About the same hour as on the previous morning, we again fell in and marched off, but the effects of hunger and fatigue were now more visible. A savage sort of desperation had taken possession of our minds, and those who had lived on the most friendly terms in happier times now quarrelled with each other, using the most frightful imprecations on the slightest offence. All former feeling of friendship was stifled and a misanthropic spirit took possession of every bosom. The streams which fell from the hills were swelled into rivers, which we had to wade, and vast numbers fell out . . . having been . . . reduced to the most abject misery.[439]

For another description of the retreat, we have the words of William Grattan:

The rain fell in torrents, almost without any intermission: the roads . . . were perfect quagmires; the small streams became rivers; and the rivers were scarcely fordable at any point. In some instances the soldiers were obliged to carry their ammunition boxes strapped on their shoulders to preserve them while passing a ford which on our advance was barely ankle deep. The baggage and camp-kettles left us: the former we never saw until we reached [Ciudad] Rodrigo, and the latter rarely reached us till two o'clock in the morning when the men, from fatigue, could make but little use of them. The wretched cattle had to be slaughtered, as our rations seldom arrived at their destinations before the camp-kettles, and when both arrived there was scarcely one fire in our bivouac sufficient to boil a mess. Officers and soldiers had no covering except the canopy of heaven: we had not one tent, and the army never slept in a village. We thus lay in the open country, our clothes saturated with rain, half the men and officers without shoes . . . But this was not the worst . . . The retreat each day generally began at four o'clock in the morning in the dark dead of night . . . Each man obtained his portion of the quivering flesh, but before any fires could be relighted, the order for march arrived, and the men . . . were obliged either to throw away the meat or to put it with their biscuit into their haversacks, which from constant use without any means of cleaning them more resembled a beggarman's wallet than any part of the appointments of a soldier. In a short time the wet meat completely destroyed the bread, which became perfect paste, and the blood which oozed from the undressed beef, little better than carrion, gave so bad a taste to the bread that many could not eat it. Those who did were in general attacked with violent pains in their bowels, and the want of salt brought on dysentery.[440]

Yet another miserable British soldier was John Green of the Sixty-Eighth, whose account begins with the evacuation of Salamanca on 15 November:

It now began to rain very fast, and continued all that day and most of the night. I

... threw [a biscuit-bag] over my shoulders, and every time it was saturated . . . wrung it out. By this means I kept much dryer than could have been expected, but . . . was [still] as wet as though I had been dipped in water. The rain fell in torrents; indeed, part of the country through which we passed was completely inundated. After dark we encamped in a wood, completely drenched and almost lost in mire . . . Here we lay in our wet clothes, exposed to the inclemency of the season, having nothing to partake of but cold water: our rum, which would have been very acceptable, could not be obtained. After all, I got a good sleep on the wet ground until morning, when we recommenced our march. I shall ever remember these days: we marched several miles up to the ankles in water, sometimes, indeed, up to the knees, and continued to move along through mud and mire until night, and then encamped in a place completely flooded . . . A shrubbery being near, we cut down the boughs of the young trees and piled them on the ground until we [had] raised ourselves out of the water, and in this way made the best of our condition . . . In the morning we fell in and recommenced our retreat, but had to leave one of our poor fellows, who had perished from cold and hunger . . . [We] soon had to encounter the worst road I ever saw: the whole of our baggage, and part of the army having passed along had made it like a bog . . . Some of our men sank into the mud and stuck as fast as possible; others went to their rescue and they all stuck fast together! This was frequently the case: hundreds of the men lost their shoes and were obliged to walk barefoot the rest of the retreat.[441]

To add to the confusion, the weary Anglo-Portuguese were pursued by enemy cavalry. Sir Edward Paget was taken prisoner and with him many other officers and men. Among those who narrowly escaped this fate was the Highlander mentioned above:

I was left behind with two men of our company that could not keep up with the regiment, poor fellows. I had not been an hour with them till there were muskets firing at intervals through the wood. We thought it was some of the stragglers shooting pigs . . . But the shooting . . . proved to be the enemy firing at stragglers. The French had taken another road, and had pushed upon the rear of our army. A few shots came flying about our ears; I then thought it was time for me to run, but my two wearied soldiers could not follow . . . I crossed the road and made into the wood, thinking I would have a better chance if the enemy offered to pursue or even to fire. I had hardly dived into the wood, when I saw . . . six of the enemy . . . crossing the road to the two men I had left. I was then sure they would not follow me till they had plundered their prize. They fired a few wanton shots after me, but, thanks to the thickness of the wood . . . I soon got out of their view.[442]

About the only comfort to be attained in all this was the fact that the French were suffering just as badly from the weather. Among the troops who retook Madrid was Antoine Fée:

From two days into the march onwards, rain waged a cruel war on us. For the whole of the campaign, it was to prove the worst thing we had to bear. Freezing cold and mixed with sleet, it gave us a rude welcome as soon as we crossed the [pass of]

Guadarrama . . . Shrouded as it was in thick mist, I could hardly pick out El Escorial off to our left . . . The army had no equipment for camping in winter: there was nothing that could defend it from the cold and wet . . . Tents were unknown among us, and the . . . greatcoat was in consequence shelter and bed alike. Once it had got soaked through, it was just one more burden to lug along. Our shakos weighed down our heads without protecting them in the slightest, and in fact the one thing on us that remained dry was our cartridges . . . To resist the general misery better, we formed . . . clubs and pooled our meagre resources . . . Grouped together in this fashion, we endured our misfortunes cheerfully enough. Our good humour survived intact, and, no sooner had we arrived at our camp-site than we were having a good look round, and making skilful use of all the resources that it offered us.[443]

*   *   *

At the end of 1812, then, the Allied cause appeared to be staggering under a weight of great misfortune. Yet the war was far from lost. In the first place, however battered they may have been left by the retreat from Burgos, Greene, Grattan, Donaldson and the rest were still intact, and needed only a little rest and recuperation to ready them for a fresh campaign. Moreover, Spanish forces had continued to fight the French throughout 1812, and the concentration of so many troops against Wellington had allowed such commanders as Longa, Durán and Espoz y Mina to over-run much of Navarre and Aragón, the invaders in consequence quickly being forced to withdraw many troops from the pursuit of the Anglo-Portuguese army. Without this assistance the latter might have suffered a major disaster: the retreat from Burgos, Wellington confessed, was the worst 'scrape' he was ever in. Though Spain's role in the struggle in part remains a hidden war, there is no reason to see the campaign of 1812 as an affair of Wellington and Wellington alone. And, even if the year had been a question of the proverbial two steps forwards and one step back, the Allied position was still greatly improved. Andalucía, Extremadura, Asturias and Cantabria had been completely cleared of the French, while much of León, New Castile, Aragón and Navarre had in effect slipped from their control. With Napoleon fully engaged in building a new *grande armée* in Germany in the wake of the Russian campaign, there was also no chance of the French getting the sort of reinforcements that they would have needed to reconquer the territory they had lost: from now on, indeed, they would be firmly on the defensive. The outlook for the Allies, then, was very good, but for the civilian population the situation was less rosy: 1812 had seen their position plunge to fresh depths of misery, and there was no sign that 1813 would bring any improvement.

Chapter 7

The Overthrow of Joseph Bonaparte

In 1812, as we have seen, campaigning in the Iberian peninsula appeared to have ended on an upbeat note for the French. The Anglo-Portuguese army had been forced to evacuate its gains in central and northern Spain and pushed back almost to the frontier of Portugal amid scenes of considerable disorder, while Madrid was once more in the hands of the invaders. Yet in reality the situation had changed dramatically in the past twelve months. Up until the end of 1811 the French had been doing most of the attacking, and their troops had in fact been making constant gains, while at the same time repeatedly containing the efforts of Wellington's forces to make progress against the crucial border fortresses of Ciudad Rodrigo and Badajoz. Indeed, it could be said that the invaders were actually winning the war, for every Spanish fortress they took and every Spanish army they defeated represented one more nail in the coffin of the 'little war' that continued to rage in the hinterland of the French zone of occupation. All this, however, had now changed. Enormous swathes of Spanish territory had now passed back into the hands of the Allies, while the diversion of the chief efforts of the Napoleonic Empire first to Russia and then to Germany ensured that King Joseph and his commanders no longer had the strength to regain the initiative. All they could do, indeed, was remain on the defensive, in which respect they no longer had even the security that had been provided by the fortresses of Badajoz and Ciudad Rodrigo. In Portugal, by contrast, the situation was very different. Wellington's army had certainly suffered in the course of its long retreat to the frontier in November 1812, but the damage was more superficial than actual, while heavy reinforcements had been received in the course of the winter. Very soon, then, Wellington was planning a fresh offensive, its chances of success rendered all the greater by the fact that much of the French army guarding the frontier with Portugal had been sucked into an offensive against Espoz y Mina. Exactly what was in Wellington's head is not clear, but the campaign that began in May 1813 was none the less to prove decisive.

Farewell to Portugal

The advance of the Anglo-Portuguese army from the Portuguese frontier is well captured by William Wheeler, who was with the Fifty-First Foot:

> On 4 May the division was inspected by the Earl of Dalhousie in the neighbourhood of Moimento. On the eleventh we began our advance in search of the enemy. Part of the army [marched] by the great road to Salamanca. Our division kept more to the left, [and] crossed the Douro near Vila Nova. The reason of our making this circuitous route was to get round the right flank of the enemy, they having entrenched themselves in a strong position . . . After we had crossed the Douro, the

face of the country altered. We now continued to advance through a pleasant country well studded with large cities, towns and pretty villages without seeing the enemy or meeting with any remarkable occurrence. Having plenty of provisions . . . to beguile our time on the road we were continually starting hares . . . and, being provided with some good greyhounds, the fatigue of marching was much enlivened. So great was the quantity of game . . . that it was no uncommon thing to have half a dozen up at once, some of which would be running through the intervals of our column.[444]

In the face of the Allied advance, the badly outnumbered French troops who had the task of containing Wellington had no choice but to flee, and, with them went Joseph Bonaparte. Among the civilians who observed their departure from Valladolid was a procurator of the Real Chancillería named Francisco Gallardo:

At three o'clock in the afternoon of 23 June, King Joseph left the city accompanied by his suite and part of his baggage . . . The whole of the next day large numbers of troops, together with quantities of baggage and artillery, were constantly coming and going. As for the soldiers who were lodged in the city, they engaged in acts of pillage and robbery, while at the same time insulting the inhabitants in a variety of other ways . . . As the entire population was in a state of great alarm, all the shops and taverns were shut. The result being that food could not be had, the soldiers seized many men and forced them to show them the places where the supplies were kept, while at the same time maltreating them and stripping them of all they had. In consequence, nobody dared venture out, while the whole city presented the most lamentable and melancholic aspect.[445]

For the Allies, the discomfiture of the French came as revenge for the horrors of the previous autumn. William Keep was a 21-year-old ensign with the Twenty-Eighth Foot whose father was a clerk in the War Office, and who had just come out to the peninsula with a batch of reinforcements:

On the fifth of May we marched from Coria, our joyful days of revelry there being suddenly closed by the stern mandates of war . . . Horses saddled, baggage animals laden, we bade adieu to scenes we can never expect to revisit . . . Sad as our departure was from Coria, we had none of the usual sources of regret on this occasion, as we were only like travellers proceeding together to the same destination, and all united besides in one pursuit. With uninterrupted fine weather and all the necessary appurtenances of our march, it was a very agreeable and by no means toilsome task even to those on foot, and to such as were relieved from all fatigue by riding, it was a journey of pleasure, though certainly a very long and rapid one, for we moved constantly forward with little respite, meeting with few obstacles to our progress from the French . . . Along the dusty and well-beaten high roads which we most frequently followed, the thirsty soldiers hailed with delight the sight of a village or town, where we found the people at their doors with jugs in readiness to answer their impatient outcries for water, and the pleasure these good women took in thus offering relief to the soldiers was an agreeable sight, joy beaming [from] their countenances upon the *ingleses* or *buenos amigos* . . . as they called us.[446]

Yet despite the easy conditions, the army was soon up to its old tricks. To quote Kincaid:

We were welcomed into every town or village through which we passed by the peasant girls, who were in the habit of meeting us with garlands of flowers . . . and it not infrequently happened that while they were so employed with one regiment, the preceding one was diligently engaged in pulling down some of the houses for firewood – a measure which we were sometimes obliged to have recourse to where no other fuel could be had, and for which they were, ultimately, paid by the British government, but it was a measure that was more likely to have set the poor souls dancing mad than for joy had they foreseen the consequences of our visit.[447]

Liberation, then, often meant ruin for the peasants who greeted the army, and all the more so as the physical passage of the army caused severe damage to the wheatlands of Old Castile. William Tomkinson, for example, was riding with the Sixteenth Light Dragoons:

From the time of our crossing the Esla . . . we have been marching through one continuous cornfield. The land is of the richest quality and produces the finest crops with the least possible labour . . . The horses fed on green barley nearly the whole march and got fat. The army has trampled down twenty yards of corn on each side of the roads by which the several columns have passed – in many places much more – from the baggage going on the side of the columns and so spreading further into the wheat. But they must not mind their corn if we get the enemy out of their country![448]

Soon, however, the country changed, for, set as he was on constantly outflanking the French, Wellington marched his men through some of the wildest areas in the entire peninsula. For the artillery, especially, it was a difficult business:

We marched to the Ebro, descending to it by a causeway five miles in length made between clefts of stupendous rocks. Lord Wellington [watched] us descend with great anxiety, for it was not quite certain whether artillery could pass. The descent was very sudden and steep, the road very roughly paved, not very wide, and in many places with frightful precipices at the sides. It was the most nervous thing I ever did: we had the good fortune to get down without injury, [but] a slip would have been fatal. The pass is called Puente Arenas. After crossing the river we wound about its course by a most beautiful but most frightful road cut in the side of the rock . . . Night brought us without accident to a camp at Villarcayo.[449]

In theory, the army was fed from mule trains and herds of cattle operated by the commissariat, but in practice so swift was the advance that the men had often to live off the country. In fairness to the British troops, some men were ready to pay for what they took, but so tired were many villagers of the marauders by whom they were constantly plagued that their response was less than friendly. Edward Costello, for example, had a most alarming experience:

On 16 June we passed through the pretty little town of Medina de Pomar, and encamped on the other side of it close to the banks of a large river. On this march we suffered much from a deficiency of supplies . . . Myself and one or two others, having some few pence, determined to start off on the sly, as we were not allowed to move from our camp ground, and purchase bread at a little village we beheld on the other side of the river. Fording the river unobserved, we entered the village. There, however, the alarm of the people became very great upon our appearance, and, not wishing apparently to have any dealings with us, they asked an immense price for the bread. Irritated by this conduct and urged by hunger, every man seized a loaf, and threw down the usual price in the country. Seeing that we were all totally unarmed, for we had not even our side-arms, an immediate outcry was raised against us by the people, and we had to run for safety. This we did, carrying the loaves with us, until we were overtaken by some of the swift-footed peasantry who came up to us with knives and clubs. Our lives being thus in jeopardy . . . our party instantly had recourse to stones for defence . . . 'Kill the English dogs!' was the general cry of the Spaniards as they brandished their long knives. They were evidently about to make a rush in among us . . . when several men of the Forty-Third and Fifty-Second Regiments . . . came running up . . . It was the turn of the Spaniards now to retreat – which they did in a hurry.[450]

Costello and his fellows had at least started out with good intentions, but other men did not have even this excuse. Among those feeling the pinch was William Wheeler:

The country about us is well stocked with pease and all kinds of vegetables. Fortunately for us it is so, for we are getting badly off for rations. Major Roberts commands the regiment, and a better commander we could not have. He allows us to fill our haversacks with what we can get on the roads . . . It is now nine days since we had any bread issued to us, but as a substitute we get wheat or rye. This is but of little service as we have neither time nor inclination to boil it sufficiently. Meat we get every day, but the fatigue of marching has reduced the bullocks to skin and bone . . . On the morning of 21 June we advanced. We had not proceeded far when the company to which I belonged was ordered out to scour a wood on our right flank. We extended [into open order] and marched through without falling in with the enemy, but we [did fall in] with plenty of cattle, sheep and goats. We haversacked a few sheep, and ran against an old shepherd. We soon relieved him of all he had, viz. a four-pound loaf, some cheese and about a quart of wine. The poor old fellow cried. It was no use: we had not seen a bit of bread these eleven days, [while] the old man was not far from home and could get more.[451]

The Battle of Vitoria

Wheeler's reference to the morning of 21 June brings us to the battle of Vitoria. In brief, the situation was as follows. Manoeuvred out of position after position by the rapid advance of Wellington's army, the French had retreated further and further north-eastwards. Crossing the Ebro, they finally came to a halt in a narrow rectangle of land stretching westwards for 10 miles from the city of Vitoria between the river Zadorra on the one hand and a steep ridge of hills known as the heights of La Puebla on the other. Believing that they had a good chance of blocking an attack from the west (the only direction from which the Anglo-Portuguese were deemed likely to come), confident that two divisions which had been chasing Espoz y Mina were on the brink of joining him, anxious to buy time to get his convoys further east and, perhaps above all, desperate not to give up Spain without a fight, King Joseph resolved to stand firm. However, this decision underrated Wellington's willingness to take risks, while also ignoring the fact that there were plenty of tracks through the rugged hills and mountains that ringed the French position on all sides. On the night of 20 June the French troops therefore bivouacked in the firm expectation that the next morning would see Wellington's men obligingly debouch into the valley from the defiles at its western end and dash their heads against their serried ranks, whereas in fact two-thirds of their enemies were feeling their way around their flanks to north and south. What was planned, in fact, was a massive envelopment that had the capacity not only to defeat but totally to destroy the French army. While four divisions moved to threaten the line of the Zadorra from the north, the equivalent of four others were hooking round Joseph's southern flank and moving to occupy the heights of La Puebla, leaving just two divisions to brave the French fire at the western entrance to the battlefield. First into action on the morning of 21 June was the southern flanking force commanded by General Hill. Amazingly, the French had placed only a few companies of light infantry on the heights of La Puebla, and the Allies therefore made good progress. Very soon, however, columns of French troops were advancing up the hill from the other side. With the Spanish troops who had been the first to reach the summit under heavy pressure, Hill ordered the Seventy-First Foot to go to their assistance. As Thomas Howell relates, there followed some fierce fighting:

> Immediately we charged up the hill, the piper playing, 'Hey Johnny Cope'. The French had possession of the top, but we soon forced them back and drew up in column . . . sending out four companies to the left to skirmish . . . Scarce were we upon the height when a heavy column, dressed in greatcoats with white covers on their heads, exactly resembling the Spanish, gave us a volley, which put us to the right about at double-quick time down the hill, the French close behind . . . The four companies . . . likewise thought them Spaniards until they got a volley that killed or wounded almost every one of them. We retired . . . covered by the Fiftieth, who gave the pursuing column a volley which checked their speed. We moved up the remains of our shattered regiment to the height. Being in great want of ammunition, we were again served with sixty rounds a man, and kept up our fire for some time until the bugle sounded to cease firing. We lay on the height some time. Our drought was excessive: there was no water . . . save one small spring, which was rendered useless. One of our men . . . called out he would have a drink, let the world go as it would. He stooped to drink, [but] a ball pierced his head, [and] he fell . . . in the well, which was discoloured by brains and blood. Thirsty as we were, we could not [touch] it.[452]

The firing that Howell describes was directed at a series of French counter-attacks which for a time threatened to wrest back control of the heights. In the end, however, these were driven off, and the Seventy-First, with their accompanying Spaniards, were soon pushing eastwards along the crest of the ridge. In the valley below, meanwhile, other troops from Hill's force had rounded the north-western shoulder of the massif. George Bell was with the Thirty-Fourth Foot:

> We were gaining ground along the side of the mountain when we were met with a biting fire, and the battle here remained stationary for some time until our general sent us more aid. Then . . . we won the village of Subijana de Alava . . . and maintained our ground in spite of all opposition. There was a good deal of fighting in the churchyard, and some open graves were soon filled up with double numbers. Churches and churchyards were always a favourite resort for this particular amusement. They were places of strength, and contended for accordingly . . . I thought that we had killed more of our French neighbours . . . than was needful, but, as they cared little for life in their excitement, they would be killed. As Colonel Brown said, 'If you don't kill them, boys, they'll kill you: fire away!'[453]

Another officer of the 'Cumberland Gentlemen', as the Thirty-Fourth was known, was Joseph Sherer. In command of its light company, he soon found himself engaged in a sharp fight with some French light troops:

> My brigade marched upon the village of Subijana de Alava . . . and had orders to carry it with the bayonet. The enemy opened upon us with fourteen pieces of artillery from their position as we moved down, but with little effect . . . Not a soul was in the village, but a wood a few hundred yards to its left and the ravines above it were filled with French light infantry. I, with my company, was soon engaged in some sharp skirmishing among the ravines, and lost about eleven men killed or wounded. The English do not skirmish as well as the Germans or the French, and it really is hard work to make them preserve their proper extended order, cover themselves, and not throw away their fire, and in the performance of this duty an officer is, I think, far more exposed than in line fighting. I enjoyed, however, from my elevated post, a very fine view of the field.[454]

In all, the Seventy-First Foot lost 54 dead, 272 wounded and 40 missing, while another 76 officers and men fell in the Thirty-Fourth. With Spanish losses amounting to perhaps 200 more, and other regiments such as the Fiftieth also much battered, Hill's men had paid a heavy price. Yet it was well worth it. So exercised were the French at the threat to their left flank that two-thirds of their front line had been pulled into the fighting, and this allowed first the Light Division and then the Third Division to get across the Zadorra unopposed. Seeing this, King Joseph and Marshal Jourdan pulled back the single infantry division they had left in the sector and formed a new line on a ridge crowned by the villages of La Hermandad and Gomecha, this being protected by an outpost that had been left behind in the valley below at Ariñez. As the British came up, they came under heavy fire. On the very left of the line was Vandeleur's brigade of the Light Division, and, with it, George Hennell of the Forty-Third Foot:

We formed line about twenty yards from the [river] bank . . . Here we had a very strong fire from a battery of theirs. The first ball that came was a spent one. It struck the ground about fifty yards from us, and was coming straight for me, but it rebounded about ten yards and went to my left, just over the heads of the men and struck our . . . colonel on the arm. He called out, but was not much hurt . . . Finding the fire heavy, we moved under [the] bank and lay down. At that moment a shell came hopping direct for me, but it was polite enough to halt . . . about six yards from us . . . and in about one minute it burst, doing no harm. In another minute a ball struck the close column of the Seventeenth Portuguese . . . It killed the sergeant and took off the legs of each of the ensigns with the colours.[455]

Kincaid, too, remembers the intensity of the French artillery fire as the Anglo-Portuguese forces advanced through Ariñez, and redeployed ready for the next phase of the battle:

Old Picton rode at the head of the Third Division dressed in a blue coat and a round hat and swore as roundly all the way as if he had been wearing two cocked ones. Our battalion soon cleared the hill [i.e. the ridge that had marked the original French front line] . . . but we were pulled up on the opposite side of it by one of their lines, which occupied a wall at the entrance of a village immediately under us [i.e. Ariñez]. During the few minutes that we stopped there while a brigade of the Third Division was deploying into line, two of our companies lost two officers and thirty men, chiefly from the fire of artillery bearing on the spot from the French position. One of their shells burst immediately under my nose. Part of it struck my boot and stirrup iron, and the rest of it kicked up such a dust about me that my charger refused to obey orders, and, while I was spurring and he capering, I heard a voice behind me which I knew to be Lord Wellington's, calling out in a tone of reproof, 'Look to keeping your men together, sir!', and though, God knows, I had not the remotest idea that he was within a mile of me at the time, yet, so sensible was I that circumstances warranted his supposing that I was a young officer cutting a caper, by way of bravado, before him that worlds would not have tempted me to look round at the moment.[456]

When Wellington's troops attacked, however, there was no stopping them, and all the more so as they had now been reinforced by some units of the Seventh and Fourth Divisions. Having first cleared Ariñez, no fewer than twelve brigades of British and Portuguese infantry swept forward towards La Hermandad and Gomecha. Let us again quote George Wood of the Eighty-Second, which was with Grant's brigade of Lord Dalhousie's Seventh Division:

We advanced through the tumultuous scene with a battery in our front, dealing out dire destruction . . . Men and officers fell in every direction, and their wounds were most dreadful, being all inflicted with cannon balls or shells, except that of our colonel, who received a musket shot in his stomach. Our front was exposed to the full range of this [position], and had to contend with a French regiment on the right of the battery, but, after politely receiving us with a few sharp volleys, which we as politely returned, they . . . retreated into a thicket. Towards this we advanced firing, and drove them furiously before us till they were completely routed.[457]

For another view of the advance let us turn to William Lawrence of the Fortieth Foot:

Once on the other side of the river, we were up and at them in spite of a murderous fire which they kept up from their cannon. We soon neared them, fired, and then charged, and succeeded in driving the centre over the hill. A column . . . appeared on our right, and we immediately wheeled in that direction, but the sight of us, together with the play of our artillery on them, was quite sufficient to make them follow their centre over the hill, whither we pursued them, but were unable to come up with them. I came across a poor wounded Frenchman crying to us English not to leave him, as he was afraid of the bloodthirsty Spaniards. The poor fellow could not at most live more than two hours as a cannon ball had carried off both thighs. He entreated me to stay with him, but I only did so as long as I found it convenient: I saw, too, that he could not last long, and very little sympathy could be expected from me then, so I ransacked his pockets and knapsack and found a piece of pork ready cooked and three or four pounds of bread, which I thought would be very acceptable. The poor fellow asked me to leave him a portion, so I cut off a piece of bread and meat and emptied the beans out of my haversack, which, with the bread and meat, I left by his side. I then asked him if he had any money, to which he replied no, but, not feeling quite satisfied at that, I again went through his pockets. I found . . . seven Spanish dollars and seven shillings, all of which I put into my pocket except one shilling, which I returned to the poor dying man, and continued on my way up the hill.[458]

Outnumbered, badly shaken, harassed by large numbers of skirmishers, and threatened from the south by Hill, the French could take no more. Among the men in at the death was John Green of the Sixty-Eighth Foot:

We continued to advance until we had got through the wood, when the firing from the enemy became dreadful, and our men fell in every direction. I really thought that, if it lasted much longer, there would not have been a man left to relate the circumstance. We now came to plain ground and continued to move forward . . . but were so weakened by their fire that we were obliged to take shelter in a deep ditch, not more than 200 yards from the muzzles of their guns . . . It was now reported . . . that the enemy were advancing, and that we should all be taken prisoners, but, resolving to avoid being taken if possible, I looked up to see whether the enemy were advancing or not. I had scarcely raised my head . . . when a grapeshot struck the top of my cap and carried away the rosette with part of the crown; had it been three inches lower, I should have been no more. 'There, Green,' said one of our men, 'it has only just missed you.' I observed . . . that it was sharp work. 'Aye', said he, 'yet we are well off if we can only keep so.' Scarcely had he offered these words, however, when our company was ordered to the left to skirmish, and such was the quickness of the enemy's fire that we were obliged to get out of the ditch one by one, and run squatting along to our station. We then opened a brisk fire upon the enemy which continued several minutes. It appeared we had advanced about fifteen minutes too soon for the Light Division, which was to have supported us. At length this division came in sight [whereupon] our . . . brigade immediately sprang over the ditch, gave three cheers and charged the enemy, the Light Division breaking their ranks in haste to join us . . . The enemy could not withstand the shock, but were panic-struck, and fled in confusion. We followed them shouting and huzza'ing, and gave them no time to form, but drove them before us like cattle to destruction.[459]

As William Swabey learned to his cost, however, the French artillery continued to give a good account of itself to the end:

We came into action twice in the centre of the enemy's columns, but always, such was the nature of the country, on low ground. At the last place . . . in the act of leading my guns off the road to an eminence where we were to come into action, I received a ball in my knee . . . About the same spot where I was hit we had one man killed and thirteen wounded, twenty-six horses killed and wounded, and a shot cut in two the axle tree of the howitzer limber . . . The moment I was hit I turned my horse around and quietly walked to the village, where I met [my servant] Sutton . . . He helped me off and I got into the first hovel I could find. I found there the doctor with two or three of our men, likewise wounded. As soon as they were dressed, he came to me, and on examination we found the ball had . . . gone directly between my knee-cap and the top of my leg bone, taking in the cloth of my overalls . . . The piece in the wound not being entirely separated from the cloth outside, I vainly thought I could pull the ball out with it. In this I failed. The doctor then probed the wound and said decidedly [that] the ball was not there, so that where it went God only knows. While he was dressing us, a cannon shot, and afterwards a shell, came into the building, doing us fortunately no other injury than that of knocking the tiles about our heads.[460]

Himself caught up in the rout, Joseph could only order a general retreat. To the north-east, meanwhile, Sir Thomas Graham had been advancing on the French right flank and rear with 20,000 men. Had Graham shown a modicum of initiative, Joseph would have found himself completely cut off, for the Scottish general had only to seize the city of Vitoria itself – a relatively easy task given his numerical advantage – to trap almost the whole French army. However, mindful of orders that his prime objective was to cut the Madrid-Bayonne highway, which ran north-eastwards from Vitoria along the Zadorra, Graham struck east rather than south. Getting across the river at Durana, the Spanish division of Francisco Longa duly cut the road on the enemy's extreme right flank, but the bulk of the Allied troops became bogged down around the village of Gamarra Mayor. As Douglas remembered:

We reached the village, which we named Gomorrah as it was a scene of fire and brimstone. The enemy were driven . . . over the river Zadorra . . . The light company entered a house at the end of the bridge, from the windows of which a very destructive fire was kept up, while as many as could pushed across and formed as they arrived close to an old chapel. Here there appeared to be some want. Had the regiments which entered the village been pushed across the bridge . . . the wreck of the French would have been nearly as bad as Waterloo. [But] the enemy seemed to know the value of this spot and poured down a heavy fire on the few that got over and so obliged us to retrace our steps. The day was uncommonly warm, and many ran down to the river for a drink, numbers of whom fell in the water and . . . were carried away by the stream. In advancing across the bridge . . . exposed to a heavy fire which raked it, . . . one of the Fourth regiment and I were close together when he received a ball in the head, and down he went. Contrary to my expectations I cleared it, [but] on turning the corner of the house occupied by our light company, a ball struck a stone close to my head, and, rebounding, lodged in my skull. Well, I really thought all the world was in a blaze around me, and there I stood for some time unconscious of everything, but when I got the use of my eyes, I found I was on my feet and not much the worse.[461]

Thanks to Graham, then, the French had an escape route, for a narrow road led eastwards from Vitoria to Pamplona by way of the pass of Salvatierra. Even as it was, however, things were bad enough, for the French rear was clogged up with Joseph's immense baggage train, every available track soon being jammed with fugitives. Fortunately for the defeated *rey intruso*, though, many of the leading Allied troops abandoned the fight in favour of ransacking the stranded wagons. At the same time, the terrain to the east of the battlefield – a tangle of woods, vineyards, drainage ditches, stone walls and little villages – was scarcely conducive to rounding up large numbers of the enemy, while it must also be admitted that even such troops as remained in hand appear to have been poorly directed. Riding with Anson's brigade, which the collapse of the French army had finally allowed to get across the river from its post with Graham's command, William Hay and his men even experienced a last-minute reverse when they came up against a strong force of cavalry and infantry that had been posted in a gap between two woods:

In this order we . . . soon came in sight of the French cavalry. On seeing our advance, advantage was taken of some broken ground . . . to halt and form for our reception. As we approached this appeared madness, as their numbers did not exceed half ours. Our trumpet sounded the charge when . . . their flanks were thrown back, and there stood, formed in squares, about 3,000 infantry. These opened such a close and well-directed fire on our advance squadrons, that not only were we brought to a standstill, but the . . . leading squadrons went about, and order was not restored till a troop of horse artillery arrived on our flank and . . . opened such a fire of grape that . . . I saw men fall like a pack of cards.[462]

Another participant in this charge was William Tomkinson of the Sixteenth Hussars, from whose account it appears that part of the problem was the lack of order that was a common problem with British cavalry:

My squadron was in advance, and . . . formed immediately and advanced to the charge. All was confusion, all calling 'Go on!' before the men had time to get in their places . . . The enemy had about six squadrons in line, with one a little in advance consisting of their elite companies. This I charged and broke and drove on their line, which, advancing, obliged me to retire, having had a good deal of sabreing with those I charged and with their support. A squadron of the Twelfth was in my rear, and, in place of coming up on my flank, followed me, so that they only added to the confusion by mixing with my men. Captain Wrexon's squadron of the Sixteenth then came to the charge. We were so mixed that I could not get my men out of his way . . . The enemy, seeing the remainder of the brigade coming up, retired through the defile with their cavalry, leaving a square of grenadiers in its mouth. We came close upon them without perceiving they were there, and, on our going about, they fired a running volley which did considerable execution, and then made off through the defile . . . I lost in my squadron Lieutenant the Honourable George Thelluson . . . It was the first time he had ever been engaged, and he was so anxious to distinguish himself that he rode direct into the enemy's ranks.[463]

Still worse was the experience of the staff officer, Browne:

As I was accompanying a squadron of the Eighteenth Hussars in pursuit of the enemy, who were flying as fast as possible, we overtook a line of carriages and baggage, which offered so much temptation to many of the soldiers . . . that they could not resist falling to the work of plunder, while others with their officers continued in pursuit. The squadron was thus considerably weakened in number, a circumstance which was observed by the French rearguard, near which we rapidly approached. They suddenly detached a body of cavalry from it, which, falling on the few of the Eighteenth who were in advance, killed some, wounded others, and took some prisoners. In this last lot I was myself included, my horse having been killed, and my head cut longitudinally with a sabre so as to knock me over.[464]

Protected by the gallant rearguard that had wreaked such havoc among Anson's cavalry, King Joseph and his headquarters staff managed to get away. Among the fugitives was the king's close friend, Miot de Melito:

It was only four o'clock in the afternoon, but the battle was lost. Leaving the field of battle, the King and Marshal Jourdan skirted round the right-hand side of the town of Vitoria, and in this fashion we eventually reached the main road to France. Along with the plain which it crosses to the north of the town, this was obstructed by the army's artillery park, by a collection of caissons of all sorts, by the wagons containing the military chest . . . and finally by the baggage belonging to the royal household, the various generals and the leading figures in the military administration . . . Seeing all these vehicles, we paused to discuss which way they should be directed to retire. The progress of the enemy on our right giving rise to concern that the main road had already been cut, it was resolved that they should take the road to Salvatierra. But where was that road, and how was it to be reached? The fact was that not a single person in the king's entourage had the faintest idea.

One of the great faults that was committed in respect of that day . . . was not to have foreseen that, in the case of defeat, the retreat might have to be made via Salvatierra. Nothing had been done to prepare for such a case. Not only had the road not been prepared for the passage of the army, but it had not even been reconnoitred. The only thing that was known was that Salvatierra lay somewhere to the east of Vitoria. Eventually a guide was found in the person of an employee of the royal household who came from Salvatierra, and under his direction the mass of wagons was set in motion, but just at that moment the enemy suddenly swept around the left-hand side of the town and . . . sent forward a strong force of hussars who rode forward at the gallop . . . This unexpected attack threw the mass of people who accompanied the baggage into a complete panic, and they fled in confusion in all directions . . . In a moment, the disorder had become general. The drivers . . . cut the reins of their teams, and the wagons were simply given up for pillage . . . I was near the king at the moment the rout began. Like everyone else, he was carried along with it, while he was in serious danger of being attacked by the British hussars. I saw one man struck down by a ball at the very feet of his horse. Luckily for the king, the regiment of *chasseurs à cheval* of the guard, which . . . was making its retreat in good order, appeared at just the moment that it was needed. Deploying it into line, its commander, General Jamin, charged the enemy hussars and drove them away, large numbers of soldiers who had become separated from their regiments amidst all the wagons also owing their safety to the good conduct of this unit . . . Making our way anyhow towards the Salvatierra road, we found ourselves in an area of ground that was cut up with impassable marshes and deep drainage ditches. A number of people were drowned in them, and I was very nearly among their number. To get across one of the ditches, the king had to get off his horse and lead it across. Following his example, I had just reached the far side when my foot slipped and I fell with such force that I pulled my horse over as well. It came down on me with all its weight, and I was completely stunned. When I came to myself, my horse was still there, but the king and everybody else in his party had disappeared. Lost among the crowds of fugitives, I then wandered on for four leagues, until, in part guided by them and in part simply drawn along in their wake, about eleven o'clock I arrived before the walls of Salvatierra. By a lucky chance, the king happened to be at the main gate. Having last seen me lying inert in the ditch into which I had fallen, he was very surprised to see me. Entering the town together, we sat down to supper. Along with the king and myself, the party included General O'Farrill and Comte d'Erlon. While we were sitting there, Marshal Jourdan came in. 'Well!', he said. 'You would have a battle and now it's been lost!'[465]

Another French observer who has left us his impressions of the collapse of the French army was the pharmacist Antoine Fée, who was attached to the division of General Sarrut and in consequence was among the men who had been holding back Graham's forces north of Vitoria:

Having got across the Zadorra at various points the enemy had turned our left . . . and very soon we were falling back in disorder . . . Charged in front and flank, the cavalry brigade attached to us tried to resist, while my own horse bolted and carried me into the midst of the fighting. Loud shouts, pistol shots and the clash of sabres rent the air around me and yet there I was with my sword still in my scabbard. But the fight did not last long. Deployed in an area cut up with ditches and hedges marking out a mass of waterlogged gardens and smallholdings, our horsemen could not keep their lines. Many of the horses, indeed, were brought down, while such of the riders who remained able to do so began to swing their horses round and gave them free rein. Along with everyone else, I followed their example, and we were soon in a state of complete rout. With nothing to detain their progress any more, meanwhile, the British hussars pursued us at full speed, throwing themselves on the wagons and cutting down the defenceless multitude at will, the latter's terror being increased still further by the shells that kept bursting in the air above them and showering them with fragments that tore apart anyone whom they hit. It was not without distress that I forced a passage through that terrified crowd, but, once I had done so, it offered me some protection for it had become so thick that it became impossible to penetrate, the enemy therefore contenting themselves with sabring only those men whom they could reach. Little by little, meanwhile, I began to draw ahead of the throng until at length I came to a large ditch that had been turned into a dreadful morass by all the horses . . . Fearing that I would fall and lose my horse, I dismounted and, after first having tied a scarf to my horse's reins, I tried to get him to jump and pull me over with him. After making some difficulties, this he eventually did, but the movement was so violent that I lost my spurs and suffered an injury to my wrist. Despite the balls that still whistled round my ears, I was now out of the thick of the fighting, but how can I possibly recount the scenes that I saw as I crossed the sad plain where so many men had found ruin and death. From the defeated there came cries of despair, from the victors cries of vengeance and from the many Spanish turncoats who could now expect death at the hands of their own compatriots cries of terror, while still worse were the screams of defenceless women and children cut down without mercy or trampled under the hooves of the horses. As for the sights on offer, in one direction one saw transports of madness at the sight of the gold spilling from the treasure wagons, in another unheard of cruelties and in still another acts of the most sublime devotion. In that scene of carnage and desolation, indeed, nothing was lacking. Once I had at last got clear of the mêlée, I cast one last glance back over the field, but could see nothing but a thick pall of smoke . . . All around me, meanwhile, was marching a crowd of our soldiers . . . bent on finding a refuge in the mountains. Infantrymen and cavalrymen, officers and generals, all were pressing on without any order, while there was not a cannon to be seen nor a round of ammunition to be had. Some efforts were made to rally the fugitives, but it was in vain: all authority had broken down . . . With the coming of night, the disorder . . . grew still worse. As for me, meanwhile, all alone and without the slightest idea where I was headed, I was sunk in the bitterness of my thoughts. It was not difficult to see that the theatre of war would very soon be moving to France: our frontiers were entirely open to the enemy.[466]

Nearby was the other pharmacist, Sébastien Blaze:

> The confusion among the embarrassment of wagons, carriages, caissons and mules
> can easily be imagined. In their efforts to get across the narrow bridges that crossed
> the ditches, they got piled up and ended by pitching one another into the water.
> Pursuing us at the gallop, meanwhile, the British cavalry seized the train of artillery,
> and with it . . . more than 2,000 limbers and other vehicles . . . the drivers having
> cut their horses' traces in order to save themselves. Meanwhile, many of the
> baggage wagons had been filled with gold and silver, and many of our men were in
> the act of pillaging them when the enemy cavalry rode up. At first the soldiers of
> the rival armies fought one another for the treasure, but soon it became clear that
> there was enough money to satisfy both sides, whereupon the soldiers decided that
> it was more profitable to collect the coins than it was to exchange blows. Thus it was
> that British and French soldiers were soon to be seen emptying the same sacks side
> by side. As for me, however, I galloped onwards amidst the crowds of fugitives. Of
> these the majority had flung away their arms to lighten their load. Their condition
> was one and the same – it was all too clear that they had all run away rather than
> face the enemy – and yet as they ran they accused each other of being cowards and
> poltroons and sometimes even came to blows . . . In the midst of the turmoil I came
> across several old acquaintances, but our only communication was . . . just a quick
> nod of the head or wave of the hand.[467]

In the end French losses, including prisoners, were no more than 8,000 men. But also gone
were all but one of Joseph's 152 guns; over 500 artillery caissons; huge quantities of
supplies, clothing, footwear and equipment of all sorts; virtually all the transport that the
French possessed; the personal baggage of the king, Marshal Jourdan (both of whom had
come within an ace of being captured themselves) and many other senior officers; and the
whole of Joseph's state papers and treasury, including 5,000,000 francs newly sent from
France. Stranded amidst the turmoil, too, aside from a swarm of camp followers of all
sorts, were many of the *afrancesado* officials who had been the very heart and soul of the
Bonaparte administration. Thanks to the mistakes of Sir Thomas Graham, the British
victory had not been total, but even so for the French there was no way back. As so often
before, however, the glory of victory was marred by the behaviour of Wellington's army.
The captured French baggage train presented an extraordinary sight. As George Bell
recalled:

> Never was a victory so complete, nor an army so very well thrashed . . . I happened
> to be marching along in [King Joseph's] track, and came upon his carriage upset in
> a ditch, and also seven wagons loaded with his personal baggage jammed up in a
> heap. The mules [were] all gone, [and] soldiers excitingly [*sic*] engaged, their
> muzzles black with powder from biting the cartridges . . . [in] stripping the carriage
> even of its lining in search of something portable . . . I never saw such handy
> fellows. So expert were they that the whole contents were laid before the public in
> about fifteen minutes . . . Another party were actively engaged [in] unloading the
> wagons [and] pitching into the whole contents – trunks, boxes, great bundles of

papers . . . charts, pictures of great value . . . wines, brandy . . . portable furniture, a whole library of books, everything in the cuisine department . . . and a multiplication of other things which had belonged to this robber king . . . It was not generally a night of repose. There was a grand general auction in the camp of every brigade . . . The great variety of articles for sale was far beyond anything ever heard of, and, if one was to attempt to enumerate them, would be beyond belief.[468]

Still another eyewitness to the confusion was George Wood, though in his case he did at least seek to ensure that his men did not just concern themselves with drink and doubloons:

We had now taken up our ground, and piled our arms, [and] some of the men went to the rear under various pretences. But [they] soon returned, some with bread, brandy, fowls and all kinds of eatables, others with dollars, doubloons, plate and every article that could be procured from the French baggage . . . Such plenty now prevailed that I do not suppose there was a man in the field who had not a good meal that night from the stores of the enemy, which were copiously supplied with every comfort, and now came to us most seasonably . . . We also got a most seasonable supply of those valuable articles, good shoes . . . Our men had been constantly on the tramp for many weeks together, without having time or opportunity to get their old ones mended; indeed, several of them had marched for the last few days barefooted. Not getting quite enough [from the French magazines] to supply all my men . . . I sent the remainder to exchange theirs with the dead . . . many of whom were found scattered about the field with much better shoes than their living comrades . . . To paint the scene that now ensued . . . among the troops would be far beyond my power. Some were carousing over their spoils, others swearing at their ill luck at not obtaining more; some dancing mad with *eau de vie*, others sharing doubloons, dollars, watches, gold trinkets and other valuable articles . . . Amid this extraordinary scene, with a bottle of French brandy in one hand, some biscuit in the other . . . and two fat fowls under my head, I sank on my pillow to sleep.[469]

By far the best story of the day, however, comes from the pen of John Kincaid, who describes how an attempt to reward those soldiers who had kept together in the fighting and not gone off to rifle Joseph's baggage train came to a sad end:

Sir James Kempt, who commanded our brigade, in passing one of the captured wagons in the evening, saw a soldier loading himself with money, and was about to have him conveyed to the camp as a prisoner, when the fellow begged hard to be released and to be allowed to retain what he had got, telling the general that all the boxes in the wagon were filled with gold. Sir James, with his usual liberality, immediately adopted the idea of securing it as a reward for his brigade for their gallantry, and, getting a fatigue party, he caused the boxes to be removed to his tent, and ordered an officer and some men from each regiment to parade there next morning to receive their proportions of it, but, when they opened the boxes, they found them filled with hammers, nails and horseshoes![470]

The Siege of San Sebastián

In the wake of the battle of Vitoria, the Anglo-Portuguese army had necessarily to cross the Cantabrian mountains and push into the foothills of the Pyrenees. Here, as Hennell ruefully recounted in a letter he wrote home on 6 July, they found themselves in a very different Spain from the scorched plains of León and Old Castile:

> We have driven the main French army out of Spain. I shall now give you some details of their retreat and you will see how delightfully wet, hungry and cold we have been in following up this victory . . . Next morning [i.e. 22 June] we marched three leagues . . . between very high mountains . . . and halted in a beautiful wood at sunset. It there began to rain and blow, and was as cold as England in November. It rained all night and wetted us through. At daylight [we] marched. If it had been fine the road would have been bad, but as it was it was almost impassable. The road was two yards wide with large and small loose stones and mud and water well mixed up by French feet and prevented from settling by the English . . . We soon met parties of three, four, six, ten or twelve prisoners hobbling back quite dejected at being taken so near France . . . The inhabitants told us that the French . . . were completely tired and dejected . . . On their approach [they] always left and carried what they could into the mountains. Every door . . . had been wrenched off for a shed, and the furniture used for firing. We passed a fine village in flames and some of the roofs falling in. It had now rained tremendously and our regiments were allowed to go into the houses not on fire . . . After making a fire and getting dry at half past five, at six o'clock we were ordered to fall in, rain continuing, and moved to the next village . . . We passed on the road four men killed and wounded by the same ball: they lay in the space of two yards. One was shot through the lower part of his body, another had both thighs broke, a third his legs and a fourth his ankles . . . One said, 'Pray kill me', and another asked for some water. I had nothing to give them.[471]

An officer who had even better reason to remember the appalling weather was Charles Cadell:

> An awful accident happened to us on the afternoon of the twenty-fourth as we were getting to our bivouac. At the moment when the adjutants of the brigade were called to take up their ground, a thunderstorm burst over our heads. A fine and gallant fellow, Lieutenant . . . Masterman . . . was coming from the rear . . . when the electric fluid struck him on the head, and, passing down through his body, killed both man and horse. Poor Masterman's body instantly turned as black as if it had been burnt. Four men of No. 4 Company were also struck down and rendered unfit for service, and the shock was so great that two or three of our officers . . . were for a short time deprived of the power of speech.[472]

In the aftermath of Vitoria, meanwhile, the troops were again frequently assailed by hunger, and, with their discipline considerably affected by the scenes of disorder produced by the battle, they were not inclined to be too scrupulous with regard to obtaining the food that they needed. John Green, for example, had become separated from his regiment and found himself being sent forward into the new theatre of combat with a small group of fellow stragglers:

On 29 June a party consisting of men belonging to different regiments left Vitoria under the command of Lieutenant Stockford of our regiment; to this detachment I belonged. During the march we passed several wagons and carriages that had been thrown over and dashed to pieces by the enemy in their hurry to escape, and in the evening halted in a small village . . . The following day, while the party was marching along, one of the men loaded his musket, and shot at a pig that was grazing at the roadside. The officer saw, and would have punished the man, but, the pig not being killed and the man making an ingenious defence, the officer let him off with a severe reprimand. The prize certainly was a very tempting one as we were very destitute of food, and had been for the last twelve or fourteen days, with the exception of the days we were in Vitoria, so that we were ready to lay hold of anything that fell in our way, whether living or dead . . . for, all along the line of towns from Vitoria to Pamplona, the two armies . . . had taken or bought nearly all the provisions in the country; indeed, at this time it resembled a famine, since we could not obtain anything for money even if treble its value had been offered.[473]

The consequences of all this for the new seat of the war can well be imagined:

The beautiful valleys begin to look dull. All the corn is gone, [and] the apple trees [were] stripped long ago. The walnuts were scarce ripe before all were gone, and the chestnuts are going fast. You can have no idea what destruction and waste an army carries with it. We are like locusts: every place we halt at, much more [those] where we stay, bears marks of it; although punishments and orders abound, it is impossible to prevent pillage. If a soldier wants a piece of wood to boil his kettle and there is a beautiful peach or apple by the side of a chestnut or oak, I do not believe he would go a yard to choose. I have seen fellows knock down a peck of unripe plums for the sake of eating five or six. Houses fare no better than orchards: bedsteads, chairs, tables, all are taken for firewood . . . The inhabitants being so rapacious does not lessen the inclination the men have to destroy. If you attempt to reason with them, their answer is, 'It is the fortunes of war. Besides, who are for the damned Spaniards? They rob you when they can.' I hope Englishmen will never know . . . what it is to see their property so treated.[474]

Not surprisingly, then, the inhabitants were in many instances less than friendly, and all the more so as officers and men alike began to make free with the local women. Auguste Schaumann, the commissary, was now attached to the Eighteenth Hussars (a unit that had behaved particularly badly at Vitoria):

The inhabitants [were] gloomy and ill-natured. This was particularly true of the agricultural labourers, who used to walk through the streets in gangs and carried carbines under their cloaks. They were so jealous that no hussar was safe whom they saw joking with a girl. They actually killed two men of the Tenth Hussars close to the gate of the town and tore their eyes out. The eyes were found afterwards about twenty feet away from the bodies. When . . . the officers of the brigade were returning home at night after a grog party . . . they frequently had to fight their way through . . . with their swords.[475]

With the French forces still in the area in full retreat, the Anglo-Portuguese forces were soon able to move against the fortress of San Sebastián. Yet this was a tough nut to crack. William Dent, a young surgeon of yeoman stock from the village of Mickleton-in-Teesdale, had joined the Ninth Foot at Gibraltar in late 1810 and spent two years there before being posted with his regiment to join the Fifth Division:

It is necessary that you should have some idea of the situation of the place, which is the strongest fortification I ever saw, Gibraltar excepted: it is nearly surrounded by the sea. On the sea side is an immense high mountain with a strong castle on the top. At the bottom of this mount is situated the town, both sides of which are washed by inlets of the sea; the front of the town, consequently, is very narrow and amazingly strong: it consists of two lines of defence and a regular glacis.[476]

Situated on a narrow promontory that jutted out into the sea between the waters of the Bay of Biscay and the broad estuary of the river Urumea, the town was hard to get at and well fortified, while the governor, General Louis-Emmanuel Rey, was a hardened veteran who was very much out to make his name. Supported by a garrison of 3,000 veteran infantry and gunners, he now put up a spirited defence. In the trenches the troops had a very difficult time. John Douglas, for example, was with the First Foot:

We were completely deluged with shot from the half-moon battery. Lieutenant Armstrong commanded the working party, who did their utmost to dig a hole for shelter from this incessant fire but to no purpose as the earth was battered down as soon as raised, and scarcely a man left unhurt . . . Those who escaped . . . were assembled in the shelter of the walls [of the suburb of San Martín], yet here was no safety as the shot flew through the windows and doors, and, rebounding off the walls, hurt many, while stones and mortar falling in every direction bruised some and blinded others . . . We had scarcely got in shelter when a large shell dropped in the floor, rolling about, the fuse blazing. Armstrong stood looking at it, when I laid hold of him and dragged him to the rear of a broken wall at nearly the instant it exploded.[477]

To compound the problem posed by Rey's belligerence, Wellington made a serious misjudgement. Two fronts of the town could be attacked: the bastioned enceinte that blocked the neck of the peninsula on which it stood, and the old medieval wall that rose above the Urumea on its eastern side. Of these, there was no doubt that the latter was easier to breach, and it was in consequence of this that Wellington selected it as his target. If the garrison's morale collapsed (as the British commander appears to have expected), this was all very well, but if it stood firm, then trouble was certain. Thus, the river wall could only be approached at low tide and even then only by wading the Urumea or dashing northwards along its western shore under deadly flanking fire from the bastions that guarded the land approach to the city. Still worse, whichever route was adopted, the nearest trenches would necessarily be over half a mile away. When the assault came on 25 July, it was therefore a complete disaster. Few men even reached the breaches, while those that did were for the most part quickly killed or wounded:

> Waiting for the tide to be sufficiently low to admit men to reach the breach, it was daylight ere we moved out of the trenches, and, having to keep close to the wall to be as clear of the sea as possible, beams of timber, shells, hand grenades and every missile that could annoy or destroy life were hurled from the ramparts on the heads of the men . . . Those who scrambled on to the breach found it was wide and sufficient enough at the bottom, but at the top . . . from thence to the street was at least twenty feet . . . Some little idea may be formed of the destructive fire of the enemy when [I say that] on the beach were left by the tide more [men] than would have loaded a wagon of fish, killed in the water by the shot of the garrison . . . And it not being sufficiently low at the time of the attack those who fell wounded and might have recovered were swept away by the current which runs here very rapid. Nor was it an easy matter for any man to keep his feet as the stones were so slippery.[478]

Another participant in this doomed attack was James Hale of the Ninth Foot:

> On 25 July we commenced the attack, but unfortunately without success, for the breach was small and so steep that we found great difficulty in getting up, and the enemy continued pouring down their small shot and hand grenades from all quarters . . . In spite of all, we forced our way in, but, what was still more aggravating, when we had got possession of the breach, to our surprise the enemy had thrown a large fire across the passage that led into the town, so that there was no possibility of getting any further. Therefore, all we could do then was to get back as well as we could, which we did, but not without the loss of a great number of brave British soldiers.[479]

Watching from the trenches was Surgeon Dent, who also provides an explanation in respect of the delay in launching the attack that was probably the final nail in its coffin:

> On the morning of 24 July the troops were in the trenches by three o'clock ready to storm, but the enemy had made so large a fire inside the breach it was thought impossible to enter, and they accordingly returned to their camp. They were in the trenches [again] by four o'clock on the morning of the twenty-fifth, and, the signal being given, they moved on towards the breach, but, from some fatality or other, the troops that advanced first were not well supported, and they were cut to pieces. The remainder retired into the trenches, and the business was finished by a furious cannonade. Our loss was from four to five hundred killed and wounded; the next morning the enemy made a successful sortie and took some prisoners.[480]

The failed assault on San Sebastián coincided with a major French counter-offensive. At the very time that Douglas and his colleagues of the Fifth Division were braving the fire poured on them by the defenders of the fortress, the army that had escaped from Vitoria was stealthily ascending the Pyrenean passes of Maya and Roncesvalles in an attempt to turn Wellington's flank and relieve the city of Pamplona, which had been blockaded by a force of Spanish troops. At the summit of the passes they crashed into a screen of troops from the Second, Fourth and Seventh Divisions. At Roncesvalles the defenders were not too hard pressed for the French could only approach the Allied positions along two narrow ridges, but at Maya it was a different matter as the attackers had much more room to manoeuvre. Still worse, meanwhile, there were very few Allied troops actually at the summit. Among the men trying to hold the line was Joseph Sherer of the Thirty-Fourth Foot:

> In less than two hours, my picket and the light companies were heavily engaged with the enemy's advance, which was composed entirely of *voltigeur* companies, unencumbered by knapsacks and led by a chosen officer. These fellows fought with ardour, but we disputed our ground with them handsomely, and caused them severe loss . . . The enemy's numbers, however, increased every moment: they covered the ground immediately in front of, and around, us. The sinuosities of the mountains, the ravines, the watercourses, were filled with their advancing and overwhelming force. The contest now . . . was very unequal, and, of course, short and bloody. I saw two-thirds of my picket, and numbers, both of the light companies and my own regiment, destroyed . . . and, surviving this carnage, was myself made prisoner. I owe the preservation of a life about which I felt, in that irritating moment, regardless to the interference of a French officer who beat up the muskets of his leading section, already levelled for my destruction. This noble fellow, with some speech about 'un francais sait respecter les braves', embraced me, and bade an orderly conduct me to Count d'Erlon.[481]

Also present was George Bell of the same regiment, whose men were sent scrambling up the hillside to attack the French forces which had quickly crowned the top:

> It was death to go on against such a host, but it was the order, and on we went to destruction. The colonel . . . was first knocked over, very badly wounded. The captain of grenadiers (Wyatt) . . . was shot through the head . . . My little messmate, Phillips, was also killed . . . Seven more of the officers were wounded . . . Different regiments scrambled up the hill to our relief as fast as they could. The old Half-Hundred [i.e. the Fiftieth Foot] and [the] Thirty-Ninth got a severe mauling . . . The Ninety-Second were in line, pitching into the French like blazes and tossing them over. They stood there like a stone wall, overmatched by twenty to one . . . When they retired their dead bodies lay as a barrier to the advancing foe.[482]

As Bell implies, however, the chief heroes in this grim struggle were the Highlanders of the Ninety-Second Foot. Among their officers was James Hope:

> The right wing of the Ninety-Second Regiment had now for some time to sustain the brunt of the combat. Their numbers did not exceed 370 men, while their enemies could not be fewer than 3,000 veterans. Colonel Cameron, on seeing the

enemy, withdrew his little band about thirty paces in order to draw them forward, that he might have an opportunity of charging them. They greedily swallowed the bait – they advanced – but, as soon as the Ninety-Second halted, the enemy did the same. The French now opened a terrible fire of musketry on the Highlanders, which they returned with admirable effect. For a quarter of an hour the French officers used every means in their power to induce their men to charge us, but their utmost efforts were unavailing. Not one of them could they prevail on to advance in front of their line of slain, which in a few minutes not only covered the field, but in many places lay piled in heaps. The Highlanders continued to resist the attacks of their numerous and enraged opponents till their numbers were reduced to 120 and all their officers were wounded and borne from the field, except two young lieutenants. The senior of these [i.e. Hope himself], seeing no support at hand and finding that the ammunition of those with him was nearly exhausted, conceived that a retreat was the most advisable measure he could adopt. With this handful of men, he retired from the bloody field, on which he left thirty-three that had been killed or mortally wounded during the action.[483]

Fighting on the slopes to the south of the Ninety-Second was William Keep of the Twenty-Eighth Foot:

As soon as the French appeared . . . our fire opened, though at first in a very slanting direction and with difficulty, friends and foes were so mingled . . . To fire with greater precision, some of our men had descended to a ledge running along the edge of the ravine. Here I stood at the station of the company I belonged to . . . with Colonel Belson and . . . Major Mullins by the side of me, in a state of inactivity and merely looking on. Captain Meacham was wounded, having been firing from the ledge (very few officers make use of the musket) and . . . actively retreated between our legs to the rear. At this moment Mr Bridgeland's voice called for me to the colours, and I proceeded directly there and found that poor [Ensign] Delmar had been shot through the heart . . . I now took the fatal colour and entered into conversation with Ensign Tatlow, bearing the other . . . The French were checked in their progress at the foot of the hill . . . but as the numbers of the enemy increased, they made another effort to advance. A very gallant French officer was leading them, but he was struck to the ground where he [lay] still waving his cocked hat. I became very much interested in the result, and my attention [was] so absorbed in it that I did not observe what was passing behind me. The enemy had been busy surrounding us, and the regiment had been forced instantly to flight and had left me there. A young French conscript levelled his piece at me within twenty paces with a smiling countenance, intimating that I must surrender. A violent zeal seized me to preserve the colours, and, not caring for my life, I turned immediately and pitched myself headlong down the ravine, grasping most tightly the staff. Through bushes and briars I rolled and scrambled, hearing shots after me . . . Rough stones rattled down with me, and it was some time before I put my feet to the ground.[484]

Driven back though Hope and his men were, in the end the pass was recaptured thanks to the arrival of fresh troops from the Seventh Division. However, the British commander at Roncesvalles, Sir Lowrie Cole, had lost his nerve, and with the coming of darkness ordered his men to fall back on Pamplona, leaving the troops at Maya no option but to follow suit. With them was George Wood of the Eighty-Second Foot:

On quitting this position, the most dismal sensations took possession of our breasts. Not a voice, not a sound was heard, save the slow step and casual murmur of the dejected soldiers, intermingled with the moans and groans of the wounded. To add to these horrors, I . . . trod in the dark directly upon, and fell over, a dead body, cold and naked as the clay it was stretched on. In this state we kept moving on the whole of this sad and sorrowful night amidst the mountains, the woods and the rain, the ways being so deluged with mire owing to the great number of cattle and baggage passing before us that it was only with difficulty we could wade through it . . . So entangled were we among carts, horses, vicious mules, baggage and artillery . . . that we could not extricate ourselves from these impediments. Some lighted sticks and candles which the muleteers had with them only added to the confusion, for we were not able to see one yard beyond the light owing to the thick haze, which seemed to render even darkness more dark . . . In this bewildered spot, many who could not stand were obliged from fatigue to sit down in the mire: to attempt going on was impossible except by climbing over the different vehicles that lined the road. In this miserable plight, I seated myself against a tree, where weariness caused me, even amidst the bustle, mud and riot, to fall asleep. My servant, coming up, disturbed my repose by presenting me with his cap full of tea, having trod in a box of it on the way, but he might as well have given me some of the mire that we were in to eat, as at this time there were no fires to make it, or . . . utensils to have boiled it in.[485]

Another man caught up in the retreat was John Cooper, who had been promoted to the rank of sergeant in the wake of the siege of Badajoz, but had since then spent long periods in hospital with fever:

This night march was horrible, for our path lay among rocks and bushes, and was so narrow that only one man could pass at a time; consequently, our progress was exceedingly tedious, stopping, as we did, for five or ten minutes every two or three yards. This was made much worse by the pitchy darkness. Many were swearing, grumbling, stumbling and tumbling. No wonder: we were worn out with fatigue and ravenous with hunger. However, I kept up, though my gaiter straps and one of my shoe ties were broken.[486]

The retreat continued for four days. Pushing on into Spain, the Roncesvalles wing of Soult's army, which was led by the marshal himself, had by 27 July got to within 10 miles of Pamplona, only to find its way blocked by a substantial Allied force that had taken post on a high ridge in between the villages of Sorauren and Zabáldica. In command was Wellington himself, who had just reached the field from his headquarters at Lesaca (much to the delight of the troops, who, buoyed up by their faith in his leadership, greeted his sudden appearance in their midst with deafening cheers), while further south still more Allied forces, most of them Spanish, waited in reserve. Forced to attack head-on on 28 July without the support of the three divisions that had forced the pass of Maya (commanded by the singularly lack-lustre Drouet, these forces had been delayed in their march by a combination of bad weather and excessive caution), Soult tried hard to counter the usual Anglo-Portuguese advantage in such combats by making use of a very thick skirmish screen. For a good description of the scene we may turn to Browne, who was riding with Wellington's staff:

> At daybreak the French columns were observed, formed in columns of attack and ready for battle. These columns were very deep and . . . moved steadily onwards in the most imposing masses I ever beheld . . . The enemy's grenadiers in their bear-skin caps with red feathers and blue frockcoats appeared the most warlike body of troops possible. As they moved on they threw out their skirmishers, which were met by the British light troops, and thus the work of this bloody day began . . . I never remember to have witnessed so tremendous an onset.[487]

There followed ferocious fighting. Very much in the thick of things was William Lawrence of the Fortieth:

> Orders had been issued by our officers not to fire till we could do good work, but this soon came to pass, for the French quickly sallied up, and fired first, and we returned it . . . I never saw a single volley do so much execution in all my campaigning days, almost every man of their first two ranks falling, and then we instantly charged and chased them down the mountain, doing still further and more fearful havoc. When we had done, we returned to our old summit again, where the captain cheered and praised us for our gallantry . . . Our likewise brave enemy tried again two hours later to shift us . . . but they were again . . . sent down the hill. We were again praised by our commander, who said, 'I think they . . . won't make a third attack in a hurry', but . . . four hours had not passed before they were up again. Some of our men then seemed to despair . . . but we reloaded and were then ready to meet them . . . pouring another of our deadly volleys into their ranks and then going at them . . . with our bayonets like enraged bulldogs.[488]

Also in action at Sorauren was John Cooper:

> Early in the morning of 28 July we were under arms. The French covered the opposite heights . . . First, they sent forward a column . . . on our left along the high road to Pamplona. To prevent them passing we descended and attacked them in flank. At the same time other heavy bodies were launched against our right and centre, and the firing became heavier and closer. The leading column of the enemy succeeded in passing us, and marched boldly forward to the brow of the hill 300 yards beyond our flank, when, to their surprise a concealed division of ours rose up, and, rushing upon them, poured a storm of fire into the loose mass which sent them back in disorder. Our fire was now redoubled . . . and men fell fast on both sides . . . All our officers were at this time wounded. I helped one of them whose leg was

broken out of the fray a few yards. A brother sergeant, a morose fellow and no friend of mine, I helped upon the adjutant's horse. He was shot in the loins or spine. I think he died . . . In the midst of all this, Major Crowder, who commanded the left wing of our regiment, now came and . . . ordered me to go and tell the colonel our case . . . I found the colonel on foot close to the enemy. While [I was] speaking to him, the senior major's horse was killed close by . . . and some men . . . wounded just behind me. Without giving any answer to my request for officers, the colonel . . . said, 'Sergeant Cooper, go up the hill and tell the brigade-major to send down ammunition immediately, or we must retire.' This was necessary, as our men were taking cartridges out of the wounded men's pouches. I scrambled up the steep hill with difficulty . . . [and] dragged a Spaniard with [a] mule laden with ball cartridges down to my company. The poor fellow was terribly frightened at the whizzing of the balls about him, and kept exclaiming 'Jesus, María! Jesus, María!' However, I pushed him forward to my former station . . . smashed the casks, and served the cartridges as fast as possible while my comrades blazed away.[489]

Faced by resistance of this order, Soult could make no progress, and by the end of the day the French were back at their starting positions. With food running out, perhaps 4,000 of Soult's men laid low and more Anglo-Portuguese troops coming up to join the action, the offensive was clearly in ruins. In consequence, the marshal would have been well advised to fall back immediately, but just at the crucial moment he heard that Drouet's men were at last coming up in his right rear, and this persuaded him to strike north-westwards in an attempt to cut Wellington's army in two and reach San Sebastián. At best a risky proposition, set in motion on the night of 29/30 July, this plan led to disaster. The only possible chance of success rested on disengaging at Sorauren in secrecy, but Wellington quickly realised what was going on. No sooner had dawn broken on 30 July, then, than his men were streaming down from their positions on the heights. Caught at a hopeless disadvantage, short of food, demoralised by defeat and deprived of their commander, who had ridden on ahead to join Drouet, the French were utterly routed. To quote William Wheeler:

Fifty buglers were sounding the charge, and the drums . . . were beating time to the music. A general rush was made by the whole brigade, accompanied by three British cheers. The concert was too powerful for the nerves of Monsieur . . . and off they danced, the devil take the hindmost, down the hill to our right, the only way they had to escape. We followed them close to their heels and soon got them on a small level, [where] they soon got huddled together like a flock of sheep. This place was well studded with thick bushes of underwood, and here and there a cork tree. As we were galling them with a sharp fire, they summed up resolution to turn on us and threatened us with a taste of steel . . . Now the tug of war began . . . As they could only get away a few at a time . . . many were the skulls fractured by the butts of firelocks . . . The enemy was soon thinned by some getting away and by their loss in killed and wounded, [and] the remainder we made prisoners.[490]

Here and there, however, the fighting was fierce enough: a large force held out in Sorauren itself for two hours, for example, while the Eighty-Second Foot suffered very heavily. As George Wood remembered:

> The fight was already begun, and it was our turn to come in contact with the formidable foe. They were posted on a great height, and to that spot we hastened to dislodge them . . . till the shot flew as thick as a shower of hail about us with a noise like the buzzing of bees. This was severe fighting . . . In less than ten minutes one half my company were killed or wounded. My brother subaltern and the sergeant [having] gone to support the colours, the ensign . . . shot, my corporal knocked down, and [I] myself severely wounded by a musket ball, my men were now . . . left without even a non-commissioned officer to command them, but the brave fellows went on in line with the regiment, and in about five minutes more I had the satisfaction of seeing them carry the hill.[491]

The Invasion of France

With Soult's forces in full retreat, the French counter-offensive was now at an end, and this, of course, left Wellington free to resume the siege of San Sebastián. A further attempt was made to relieve the city on 31 August, but this merely cost the French another bloody nose, while, even had victory been achieved in the field, it would have come too late, for that same day the besieging forces launched a successful assault on the city. A witness to the scene was the 36-year-old commander of Wellington's horse artillery, Major Augustus Frazer, who moments before the attack went in scribbled these words on a note pad:

> The assault is momentarily expected to take place. Sir Thomas Graham is here; he waits at this battery to see the event, and will give his directions from hence. It is curious at such moments to watch the countenances and endeavour to read the minds of men. Hope, solicitude and anxiety are to be seen; frequently apathy and indifference, the effects of a continuance of scenes of danger; and now and then, though rarely, open fear. But most have the address to conceal this last acquaintance of whom all are ashamed.[492]

Great gaps having been torn in the walls by several days of bombardment, low tide saw thousands of British and Portuguese troops hurl themselves upon the defenders. This time there was no mistake. James Hale, for example, was with a party from the Ninth Foot:

> On 31 August 1813, about ten o'clock in the morning, we began the grand attack, and, having some knowledge of the mine that the enemy had prepared inside the breach . . . false attempts were made in order to banter the enemy [into] springing that mine. The first two . . . were without effect, but the third we made more vigorous, as if we were determined to enter, by which we sprung their mine, but fortunately, instead of catching us in the trap, they blew up a number of their own men . . . Immediately after the mine exploded, we made a grand push, and got full possession of the breach in a few minutes, and it was astonishing to see what quantity of the enemy lay sprawling by the explosion of their mine. But we yet found something to do before we could get possession of the town, for the enemy

had so blockaded the streets, that we found great difficulty in making our way through. They had formed a sort of breastwork with barrels of sand across the streets in several places, which was a great disadvantage to us, for, when we had [driven] them from one place, there was another before us, and they continued pouring small shot on us from all quarters . . . However, in spite of all their exertions, in about one hour we got full possession of the town, driving the enemy to the castle where they were obliged to flee for refuge. By some means or other in this attack some part of the town caught fire, in consequence of which a great part of it was burned to ashes before it could be extinguished.[493]

The failure of 25 July, then, had been avenged. Nevertheless, at 2,376 dead, wounded and missing, Allied losses had been severe, as witness, for example, the memoirs of John Douglas:

I was coming away making use of my firelock as a crutch, having received a grapeshot in the right leg . . . The scene before me was truly awful. Here you might observe . . . legs and arms sticking up, some their clothes in flames, [and] numbers not dead, but so jammed as not to be able to extricate themselves. I never expected to reach my trench with my life, for, not content with depriving me of my limb, the fire shot away my crutch also . . . Contrary to my expectations, I gained the trench which was a dreadful sight. It was literally filled . . . with the dead and dying. 'Twas lamentable to see the poor fellows here. One was making the best of his way minus an arm; another his face so disfigured . . . as to leave no trace of the features of a human being; others creeping along with the leg dangling to a piece of skin; and, worse than all, some endeavouring to keep in the bowels.[494]

In the wake of such heavy losses, the troops were completely maddened, while, as at Badajoz, their fury was increased by stories that San Sebastián had shown itself to be pro-French (a claim for which there was some justification). Notwithstanding the presence of parties of provost-marshals who roamed the streets dealing out summary floggings, the result was inevitable. As a lieutenant of the newly arrived 85th Foot named George Gleig wrote:

As soon as the fighting began to wax faint, the horrors of plunder and rapine succeeded. Fortunately there were few females in the place, but of the fate of the few which were there I cannot even now think without a shudder. The houses were everywhere ransacked, the furniture wantonly broken, the churches profaned, the images dashed to pieces; wine and spirit cellars were broken open, and the troops, heated already with angry passions, became absolutely mad by intoxication. All good order and discipline were abandoned. The officers no longer had the slightest control over their men, who, on the contrary, controlled the officers, nor is it by any means certain that several of the latter did not fall by the hands of the former, when they vainly attempted to bring them back to a state of subordination.[495]

Among those who visited San Sebastián in the aftermath of the action was Augustus Frazer:

I have been in the town, and over that part of it in which the flames or the enemy will permit to be visited. The scene is dreadful: no words can convey half the horrors which strike the eye at every step. Nothing, I think, can prevent the almost total destruction of the unhappy town. Heaps of dead in every corner; English, French and Portuguese, lying wounded on each other . . . The town is not plundered, it is sacked. Rapine has done her work: nothing is left. Women have been shot while opening their doors to admit our merciless soldiery, who were the first night so drunk that I am assured the enemy might have retaken . . . the whole town. The inhabitants who have come out look pale and squalid; many women, but . . . few children. I had occasion . . . to go into several houses . . . All was ruin, women's clothing, children's clothes, all scattered in utter confusion. The very few inhabitants I saw said nothing. They were fixed in stupid horror, and seemed to gaze with indifference at all around them, hardly moving when the crash of a falling house made our men run away.[496]

As well as the capture of San Sebastián, as we have seen, 31 August was marked by the last French counter-offensive of the Peninsular War. This was in large part turned back by Spanish troops in an action known as the battle of San Marcial, but various British troops were also involved in the fighting, including Private Wheeler of the Fifty-First:

We remained in the apple orchard enjoying ourselves under the cooling shade of the trees until 30 August, then marched and encamped near the town of Lezaca . . . In the morning we marched through the town . . . At Lezaca we were joined by Lieutenant Dodd and fifty men from England. The men were distributed through the regiment. One of them was ordered to fall in on my right, [but] this separated me from a man who had stood next to me in many fights, and was not relished by either of us. The man saw we did not wish to be separated, [and] offered to change places. This I accepted, and he took my left. We then advanced. The enemy had crossed the river Bidassoa in three divisions . . . to relieve San Sebastián. We soon came under their fire. They outnumbered us greatly: the nature of the ground prevented us from bringing many men into action, [and] only a few companies could engage . . . Before we had sent out our skirmishers, and by the first fire of the enemy, the stranger on my left was struck in the forehead and fell dead. He, having just arrived from England, had a full kit. Exchange is no robbery, so I slung off my light knapsack and took possession of his. The enemy kept reinforcing their skirmishers, so that the fire that was at first slack now began to be very brisk, and in a short time they began to advance on our line, but not with that firmness one should expect from superiority of numbers. Our skirmishers stood firm, but, the fire being too hot for their liking, they rushed forward on the enemy, who gave way, and in a few minutes our line had possession of their ground. This charge drove the enemy into a forest in their reserve. Their fire was now tremendous, and our line fell back to draw them out on open ground. The hill now swarmed again with the enemy, and a stationary fire was kept up a long time. General English had now ridden forwards to become better acquainted with the ground, when by some unforeseen accident he became separated from his men, and would have been made prisoner but for the little band who at a great disadvantage rescued him. Captain Frederick saw the danger his general was in [and] ordered his bugler to sound the charge . . . and off his company went accompanied by Lieutenant Bayly's company and one company of the [Chasseurs Britanniques] regiment. In a moment they were mixed with the enemy, and down the hill they went together, pell mell, into the wood . . . I never remember [being] under so sharp a fire in an affair of this kind before. My comrade Brown was wounded in the right leg near the knee and obliged to go the rear. Shortly after, a ball clanked the inside of my [own] right knee: it deadened the leg for while and caused some pain.[497]

Another participant in this action was John Green of the Sixty-Eighth Regiment:

Our regiment was now ordered forwards, and extended all along the front of the brigade. We loaded our pieces and waited for the enemy, who were advancing . . . When they came within 200 yards, we began to fire upon them, every man being directed to take deliberate aim. The enemy having approached within 100 yards of us, we retreated deliberately, keeping up a most destructive fire . . . till they arrived within twenty yards. We then fired a volley, gave three cheers and rushed upon them with fixed bayonets. This caused them to give way, and we pursued them exultingly to the bottom of the hill . . . The enemy having obtained a strong reinforcement, [they] now advanced in close column, their drums beating in order to keep them together. We again retreated and I narrowly escaped being taken prisoner, for I was almost exhausted with running . . . We kept up a constant fire as we retired, and took up a position on a hill, at the extremity of which I and about twenty men were stationed. There being several trees, each man posted himself behind one and began to discharge his piece . . . but [I] had only fired one shot when a ball struck me, entering my left side a little below my heart. At first I felt nothing; in about ten seconds, however, I fell to the ground, turned sick and faint, and expected every moment to expire, having an intolerable burning pain in my left side . . . I lay on the ground around five minutes, when the sergeant major, who was on the spot, ordered two of the men to take me to the rear. They attempted to lift me up, but I begged them to let me alone, saying, 'For God's sake let me die in peace!' The men then let me drop on the ground again, no doubt thinking that I was actually dying. The sergeant major, seeing what they had done, said in a loud tone, 'Take him away to the rear, for he is not dead.' They then raised me up . . . and took off my belts. I opened up my coat and waistcoat and, putting my hand against my side, found a lump . . . nearly as large as a hen's egg. My shirt and trousers were drenched with this blood. In this condition I started to the rear, assisted by the men above mentioned . . . The shots from the enemy at this period flew so exceedingly fast that . . . I often wonder I was not wounded a second time . . . At length a surgeon began to examine me: he took off my shirt and ran his probe into the wound. In the meantime the colonel of the Chasseurs Britanniques was brought to this spot, wounded in the head, and the surgeon left me in my naked state to attend on him.

In a few seconds, however, Mr Reid, our regimental surgeon, came to me and ran his little finger into my side to clear it of any substance that might be lodged in the wound. I cried aloud by reason of the pain it occasioned. 'Silence!', said the surgeon. 'It is for your good.' The ball could not be extracted. A little dry lint was put over the wound . . . a bandage [was] bound tight round my body, my clothes were put on, and I was laid on the ground, but [I] was so full of pain that I could not rest more than two minutes in any one posture.[498]

Fierce though the fighting was, 31 August in the end brought complete success. More than that, indeed, with the fall of San Sebastián and the defeat of the French army, the way was clear for an invasion of France. At first, a variety of considerations including concern at his worsening relations with the Spaniards and the intentions of Austria, Russia and Prussia made Wellington stay his hand, but in the end the need for Britain to prove her credentials as a partner in a continental war won the day, and on 7 October 1813 thousands of British, Portuguese and Spanish troops crossed the frontier. While the Fifth Division took the French by surprise by wading the estuary of the Bidassoa, the Light Division and powerful elements of the Spanish Fourth Army scaled the heights that overlooked the river further inland. In the coastal sector of the front, success was immediate, for there were few French troops in the vicinity. Among the troops who waded the river was 18-year-old Ensign Howell Gronow of the First Regiment of Foot Guards, for whom it was his baptism of fire:

> We commenced the passage of the Bidassoa about five in the morning and in a short time infantry, cavalry and artillery found themselves upon French ground. The stream at the point we forded was nearly four feet deep, and had Soult been aware of what we were about, we should have found the passage of the river a very arduous undertaking. Three miles above we discovered the French army and ere long found ourselves under fire. The sensation of being made a target . . . is at first not particularly pleasant, but 'in a trice, the ear becomes . . . less nice' . . . The French army, not long after we began to return their fire, was in full retreat, and after a little . . . fighting, in which our division met with some loss, we took possession of the camp . . . of Soult's army. We found the soldiers' huts very comfortable: they were built of branches of trees and furze and formed . . . streets which had names placarded up, such as Rue de Paris, Rue de Versailles, etc.[499]

The mountains to the east having been fortified by a chain of redoubts, there was some sharp fighting before the defenders were put to flight. Drawn from the élite Light Division, however, the attackers were not to be checked. As John Leach of the Ninety-Fifth wrote:

> The business commenced by our third battalion climbing a small mountain on which the French had a small advanced post. After a sharp conflict the enemy was driven from it . . . and General Kempt's brigade was enabled, by a movement to its right and a flank fire on their engagement, to dislodge a strong force of French infantry, who must have been made prisoners if they had not bolted like smoked foxes from their earths. During these operations Colonel Colbourne's brigade had a much more arduous task to perform. His opponents could not be taken in flank and

he was therefore obliged to advance straight against them, entrenched up to their chins . . . A succession of redoubts . . . were carried by the bayonet, and those who defended them were either shot, bayoneted or driven off the mountain.[500]

Having thus secured a bridgehead inside France, and thereby done his duty by British diplomacy, Wellington once more imposed a check on active operations. With the troops exposed to the onset of winter, the decision was not good for morale. Thus, every day that the Anglo-Portuguese army waited was another in which it had to endure the rigours of the Pyrenean climate, while every moment's delay allowed the French to get further forwards with the field fortifications which they were erecting in an effort to stop Wellington. The month that followed, then, was a trying time:

> Encamped on the face of La Rhune [a dominant massif that had been partly occupied on 7 October], we remained a whole month idle spectators of [the enemy's] preparations, and dearly longing for the day that should afford us the opportunity of penetrating into the more hospitable-looking low country beyond them, for the weather had become excessively cold, and our camp stood exposed to the fury of the almost nightly tempest. Oft have I, in the middle of the night, awoke from a sound sleep, and found my tent on the point of disappearing into the air like a balloon, and, leaving my warm blankets, been obliged to snatch the mallet, and rush out in the midst of a hailstorm to peg it down . . . By way of contributing to the warmth of my tent, I dug a hole inside, which I arranged as a fire-place, carrying the smoke underneath the walls and building a turf chimney outside. I was not long in proving the experiment, and, finding that it went exceedingly well, I was not a little vain of the invention. However, it came on to rain very hard while I was dining at a neighbouring tent, and, on my return to my own, I found the fire not only extinguished, but a fountain playing from the same place up to the roof, watering my bed and baggage and all the sides of it most refreshingly.[501]

Very soon, the constant rain had been succeeded by heavy snow. One of those caught in the blizzard was James Hope:

> There was a prodigious fall of snow here on 28 October. In the valley where we were encamped, it lay eighteen inches deep, and on the mountains, where it drifted, it was fully twelve feet. One of our pickets on the right of the position was almost lost: several men were dug out of the snow, some of whom have lost the use of their legs. In the night the weight of the snow broke my tent pole in two, by which accident I had nearly been suffocated. With considerable difficulty I got myself extricated from beneath the load . . . but where to go I knew not. I groped about for some time without being able to find a place of shelter. At length, however, I poked my foot on the lower part of a tent, which, after some conversation with its inhabitants, I entered and remained there till daylight.[502]

As for the delay in pressing the attack on the French positions, for the men in the front line it was inexplicable. In a letter to his father, John Aitchison of the Third Guards expressed the general sentiment:

There seems now no strong reason against our invasion of France. The principle of reaction which was so much dwelt upon against it has been found to be more in idea than reality . . . Instead of the invasion of France being the signal for every man uniting in her defence, they are deserting to the rear and to us, not for the sake of joining our service, but to avoid being pressed into their own. I have within the last two months had opportunities of conversation with many French officers and men from different quarters and have been truly surprised to find so general a disgust at the war: all are for peace.[503]

In these conditions the morale of the army could not but begin to sag a little, and there were a number of desertions to the enemy. Indeed, such was the concern that this development provoked that a number of those concerned were publicly executed:

A general court martial was lately assembled at Roncesvalles for the trial of a private soldier of this division for deserting to the enemy. The court having found him guilty, sentenced him to death . . . The inlying picket of our brigade being ordered to attend, I, as the officer on duty, was compelled to witness the awful ceremony. The troops being formed, the criminal, attended by Mr Frith, the chaplain to this division, was brought to the place of execution. The rain was then falling copiously, under which the clergyman and the criminal kneeled down on a spot several inches deep with mud and water. They had prayed some time, when an *aide-de-camp* touched the poor fellow on his shoulder and desired him to rise . . . No doubt supposing that mercy had been extended to him, his countenance brightened, and his eyes, before dim, now sparkled with joy. But, alas, it was a dream! He was only raised to have the proceedings and sentence of the court martial read to him, which having been done, he again kneeled down, and in few minutes finished his religious duties. The cap being drawn over his face and the party having taken post a few paces in front of the culprit, the provost-marshal gave the fatal signal, and in a moment he fell, pierced by many balls.[504]

In early November, however, there arrived the news that Wellington had been waiting for: Napoleon had been massively defeated at the battle of Leipzig. It being clearly the moment for another major effort, on 10 November 1813 the Allied army surged forwards once again. The battle that followed – that of the river Nivelle – was a hard-fought affair. Robert Blakeney, who had since Badajoz transferred into the Thirty-Sixth Foot and attained the rank of captain, was with the Sixth Division:

On the evening of the ninth the Sixth Division descended through the pass of Maya . . . and, marching the whole of that night we found ourselves on the memorable morning of 10 November close in front of the enemy's position . . . It was still dark, and here we halted in columns, awaiting the progress of our left and left centre . . . At length the . . . dawn appeared, cheering and renovating after a harassing night march over deep and slobbery roads. Although in our present position we appeared to be well sheltered by trees, as soon as the misty haze of dawn was dispelled by clearer light, our columns were discovered by the enemy's redoubts, which frowningly looked down from the heights above. After a short cannonade . . . their range became so accurate that their shells were falling among us rather rapidly, causing many casualties. I saw one shell drop in the midst of a Portuguese regiment drawn up in our rear: it blew up twelve men, who became so scorched and blackened on their fall that they resembled a group of mutilated chimney sweeps . . . The order at length arrived . . . for the Sixth Division to advance. Wrought up to the highest excitement from being so many hours without moving exposed to a fire of shot and shell . . . we now eagerly rushed forwards. Proceeding rapidly, we soon waded the Nivelle immersed above our middle, the men carrying their pouches above their heads, and immediately drove back all the enemy's pickets . . . without deigning to fire a shot. Some few who were too obstinate to get out of our way we bayoneted . . . Having crossed the Nivelle, we rapidly advanced towards the forts and redoubts above Ainhoa . . . The hill which we . . . faced was the steepest I ever climbed. The ground over which we had to pass had been intersected for months with incessant labour and French resource . . . [and] the brambles . . . were so high and so thickly interwoven . . . as to prevent those . . . not ten yards asunder from seeing each other . . . Under such circumstances but little order could be preserved, and, as must be expected where all were anxious to advance, the strongest and most active gained the front. In this disordered order of battle the regiment advanced against the . . . principal redoubt . . . Between us and the base of this battery, to which we at length drew near, a small and rather clear space intervened . . . I shot forwards alone with all the velocity I could command after so rapid an ascent, and, arriving immediately under the fort, I perceived the enemy regularly drawn up behind trees cut down to the height of about five feet, [with] the branches pointing forward forming an abattis. I immediately turned about, and, after receiving an appropriate salute, retraced my steps with redoubled speed. I seized the King's Colour carried by Ensign Montgomery, and called for the regimental-colour ensign, McPherson . . . Having halted both colours in front of the foremost men, I prevented any from going forwards. By these means we shortly presented a tolerably good front, and gave the men a few minutes' breathing time. The whole operation did not take above ten minutes, but . . . my gallant comrades, Lieutenant Vincent and L'Estrange . . . remarked that if I did not allow the regiment to advance, the Sixty-First Regiment would arrive at the redoubt as soon as we should. I immediately placed my cap on the point of my sword and passing to the front of the colours gave the word, 'Quick march! Charge!' We all rushed forwards, excited by the old British cheer, but my personal advance was momentary: being struck by a shot which shattered both bones of my left leg, I came down. Vincent instantly asked what was the matter. I told him that my leg was broken, and that was all. I asked him to put the limb into a straight position and to place me against a tree which stood close by. In this position I asked for my cap and sword, which had been struck from my hand in the fall, and then I cheered on the regiment as they gallantly charged into the redoubt.[505]

Also downed was William Wheeler, who had been promoted to the rank of corporal following the fighting of 31 August:

The attack was made along the whole line of the enemy's works . . . As we advanced [Tom] Hooker had been relating to me some part of the unpleasant history of his family affairs; it seemed to weigh heavy on his mind. On the contrary my spirits were as light as a feather, [and] I did all I could to enliven him . . . After passing Sarre, we entered a field of Indian corn, [and] I remarked to him . . . that I had never seen [the French] fire so low, and that if they continued the practice some of us would get broken shins, [but] he made no reply [and] seemed full of thought. We now arrived at a wall that ran across our front. We halted here to collect our stragglers and get into order, for we had become much scattered owing to the irregularity of the ground. A fat pig running down our front was soon shot and in a minute several of us began cutting him up, one of the men thus employed [receiving] a shot through his hand. I had got a nice piece of pork and wished Tom to have part. 'It will be of no use to me,' said he. 'Look at poor Webster there: that is the way I shall have my wind knocked out of me directly.' At that moment Sergeant Webster was shot dead by a ball entering about an inch below his breast [bone]. Had I not known Tom Hooker I should have taken him for the greatest coward in the army, but Tom was no coward: he was as brave a soldier as ever drew a trigger. As soon as our stragglers had formed we advanced, drove the enemy from behind a hedge and were soon over after them, and they, by being reinforced, tried to drive us back again. In this they were deceived: we allowed them to come within a very short distance of us, and then we poured a volley into their faces and, before they had well got over their surprise . . . were upon them with our bayonets. Here was a fearful slaughter on the part of the enemy: nearly every shot told and their dead and wounded covered the place. All that could scampered back, and we after them. On the top of the hill, they had a reserve: these came forwards and gave us a crack . . . As I was in the act of pulling my trigger, I received a wound in both legs. The ball . . . scraped the skin just above the outside ankle of the left foot and passed through the gristle behind the ankle of the right, just missing the bone, [and] down I fell. I endeavoured to rise, but found I could not stand and that my shoe was full of blood. 'The devil's luck to you for a fool', said Ned Eagan. 'Now can't you be easy and lie quiet for a minute or so till we . . . send them in double-quick over the hill?' At this moment, Hooker came to me and said, 'I hope . . . you are not much hurt. Take some of this rum.'. . . Hooker was employed in emptying some of the rum into my canteen . . . when down [Eagan] came on top of us . . . shot through the body. Hooker shook my hand, saying, 'Cover yourself behind Ned: I must set to work . . . I know I shall not see this day out: as soon as you get intelligence of my death, write to my mother.' Now the battle raged with double fury. Fresh troops poured up to reinforce each side, and soon our men moved forwards, but it was not many paces before our bugler sounded the retreat and the enemy advanced . . . I soon became in the rear of the enemy's line, and exposed to the fire of our men . . . A French soldier came and took what money I had in my pockets, and was in the act of taking my knapsack when our men cheered and charged. I caught fire at the noise, and, as soon as the enemy had passed me, I put my hand on poor Ned's firelock . . . took a deadly aim at him and down he fell. I was so overjoyed at seeing the rascal fall and so animated . . . at the thought of being released from so perilous a situation, that, forgetting the danger I exposed myself to, I sat up with my cap on the muzzle of my firelock and cheered my colleagues as they passed me. Hooker was in the throng: he smiled and said something to me as he rushed by, but I could not catch the words.[506]

Sadly, Tom Hooker was shot dead a few minutes later. Yet reserves of the sort encountered by Wheeler were few and far between, while many of their defenders found that their flanks had been turned before they had a chance to fire a shot. For a good impression of the fighting, one has only to turn to Donaldson of the Ninety-Fourth:

> The enemy having been driven from the redoubts in front of Sarre, we advanced . . . to the attack of the enemy's main position on the heights behind it, on which a line of strong redoubts was formed with abattis in front . . . Colonel Lloyd, having pushed his horse forwards before the regiment, advanced cheering with the most undaunted bravery, but before he reached the summit he received a mortal wound in the breast, and was only saved from falling off his horse by some of the men springing forwards to his assistance. When this was perceived by the regiment . . . regardless of everything, they broke through all obstacles, and driving the enemy from their position, they . . . charged through their burning huts without mercy.[507]

In short, the French were heavily defeated, only the onset of night saving them from a major disaster. Even as it was, indeed, at 4,300 men, their casualties far outweighed the approximately 3,000 suffered by the Allies, while they also lost fifty-nine guns. Though a much reduced French force continued to cling on in Catalonia till the end of the war in April 1814, in retrospect the battle of the river Nivelle can be seen to mark the close of the Peninsular War. With Wellington's forces firmly established on the soil of France, the *grande armée* worsted at the battle of Leipzig, and the Allies firmly bent on invasion, there was no longer any hope of a French counter-offensive that would take Joseph Bonaparte back to Madrid. Indeed, recognising the imperative need to put an end to the 'Spanish ulcer', Napoleon had embarked upon a plan to neutralise the Iberian front by releasing the captive Ferdinand VII. For the soldiers of the Allied army, however, the victory brought no sense of triumph. Not only did much bitter fighting lie ahead of them, but the conditions which they were enduring were as bad as any that they had confronted hitherto. For a final word, then, let us turn to George Wood, who had recovered from the bullet wound he suffered at Sorauren and returned to duty:

> A general engagement took place, and a very sharply contested one it was. It was the battle of the Nivelle, in which my brigade bore no very active part, being in the reserve. We were ordered to deploy on our right in order to counter a movement of the French troops which threatened this point. This manoeuvre was quickly performed, and the enemy, seeing their designs frustrated, did not come on to the attack, but . . . drew off their forces, leaving us, as usual, masters of the field. After being on the alert the whole day and night, we piled our arms and lighted fires on the ground where we stood. This was most dreadful campaigning – lying out in the

open fields in this cold and wintry weather without any covering but our blankets and cloaks. In this bleak situation we remained, wishing most heartily for morning, preferring a contest with the enemy to perishing in the cold and damp of the night. Daylight at length came, and we waited the whole of the day, expecting the French at every moment to attack us again, but they thought better of it, so we lighted our fires, and set ourselves to work, broiling our rations on the wood-ashes, having no baggage or cooking utensils with us. At night we again cringed together round the fires: some fell asleep, some were telling stories to drown care, but most were grumbling and swearing till a thick and drenching rain coming on pretty well quieted us and made us huddle more closely together, waiting in silent and sullen expectation the approach of light. For my part, being never of a very strong constitution, and having at this time a severe dysentery which weakened me much, I fell fast asleep with my feet close to the fire for warmth. I was awakened by the heat, and, to my sorrow, on examination I found I had scorched the soles of my shoes in such a manner that one of them literally fell from its upper leather. In this situation we stood to our arms, but it would have required the pencil of Hogarth to paint the figure I here cut . . . with my cap, which had served me for both pillow and nightcap, crushed into different forms, my beard somewhat grown, my eyes sunk in, my cheeks quite hollow, my frame diseased and filthy, my countenance woeful, my shoes without a sole, my sword . . . covered with rust, my belt of a deep brown, my epaulette very blue, my shirt very black, and my coat any colour but red, and in the most wet and miry condition. Had I been transported from this unhappy spot by some magic hand and placed on the centre arch of London Bridge, I should have filled more hearts with pity and compassion than any mendicant of [the] great metropolis.[508]

If things were bad for Wellington's army, the situation of the populace was infinitely worse, and it is fitting that this book should end by remembering their plight:

On one of my excursions to Pasages I rode, in company with several brother officers, over to the fortress of San Sebastián . . . The traces of General Sir Thomas Graham's siege were visible everywhere. All the roofs were off the convents . . . and other buildings. The doors, windows, staircases and floors of the houses had been used as fuel, the walls were perforated by cannon-balls . . . the gardens were devastated, and the whole place was deserted. A stillness as of death reigned everywhere. From a distance the fortifications did not seem to have suffered much. But when we reached the gate of the town things looked different. The drawbridge had fallen into the moat and it was not safe to cross it. The massive gates of the fortress had been torn from their supports and one half lay flat on the ground while the other stood leaning against the wall. In the town itself, nothing but the debris right and left showed where the high street had been, while, of the fine houses, five storeys high, both stately and massive in style, only the walls and fronts remained, and they were all blackened by dust and smoke. The roads were blocked by débris, broken furniture, heaps of rags, crushed shakoes, bandoliers, cartridge boxes, broken weapons, shells, fragments of bombs, and corpses already in an advanced state of decomposition, and a pestilential stench hung about the ruins. Apart from a few survivors among the inhabitants, who, with faces grown wild and haggard from hunger, anxiety and sorrow, were groping about the ruins of their former homes, there was nobody to be seen. At the breaches the sight was even worse, for they were literally covered with decomposed carcasses, the smell of which poisoned the air.[509]

* * *

So ended the Peninsular War. Wellington's army was yet to face much hard fighting in France, most notably round Bayonne, and at Orthez and Toulouse, but these operations do not really belong to the history of the struggle in Iberia, but rather to the entirely separate campaign represented by the general invasion of France in 1814. And, while it is true that a French garrison continued to cling to Barcelona and a number of other towns and cities in Catalonia and the Levante, serious military campaigning had come to an end on this front too, the only activity that transpired after the autumn of 1813 being a series of blockades. The importance of the Peninsular War having been discussed by the current author at great length elsewhere, there is little else to say, except once again to stress the horror of what had occurred since 1808. For the combatants of every army the struggle had clearly been a grim affair that, if it did not quite plumb the depths endured during Napoleon's invasion of Russia, was worse than almost anything that the emperor's armies and their opponents had experienced anywhere else: if French soldiers were universally glad to see the back of Spain and Portugal, so were Wellington's Englishmen and Germans. Thus, losses on all sides had been very great – estimates of the French dead alone begin at 250,000 and extend to as many as twice that figure – while none of those who participated in the fighting would ever forget the scorching heat of the summer sun, the piercing cold of the Iberian winter, the endless marches across the length and breadth of the *meseta*, or the misery of campaigning in a poor and backward land that could barely feed its own population, let alone the hundreds of thousands of foreign soldiers who descended upon it. When the veterans of Waterloo all received a medal for their efforts in 1815, it was hardly surprising that there was much discontent among the many Peninsular veterans who missed out on that battle because they had been sent to North America or elsewhere. But if the soldiers had suffered, this was as nothing to the misery endured by the civilian population. Their voices, true, have remained harder to track, but their suffering shines through even the accounts of the many soldiers who seemingly remained utterly indifferent to their plight, and it is therefore but fitting that this book should be dedicated to their memory.

Epilogue

Some Endings

John Aitchison served in the invasion of France in 1814, and thereafter enjoyed a distinguished military career, eventually retiring as a major general; he died in May 1875. Antonio Alcalá Galiano became a leading figure in liberal politics, and was forced to flee into exile following the collapse of the Revolutionary Triennio in 1823. Enabled to return to Spain by the thaw that followed the death of Fernando VII in 1833, he became a leader of the so-called *moderados* and died as Minister of Industry in 1865.

Jean-Baptiste Barrès fought at Lutzen, Bautzen, Dresden and Leipzig, and ended the war besieged in Mainz; in 1815 he joined Napoleon, but served in the west rather than at Waterloo. George Bell fought at the battles of the rivers Nivelle and Nive and at Toulouse, but missed Waterloo and was thereafter placed on half-pay. In 1825, however, he returned to active duty, and by the time of the Crimean War he had become a major general, seeing service at both Alma and Inkerman; he died on 10 July 1877. Auguste Bigarré left Spain in 1813 and for the next year served as a divisional commander. Having rallied to Napoleon in 1815, he was proscribed by the Bourbons, but resumed his military career under the July Monarchy which he served until his death in 1838. Robert Blakeney retired from the army in 1814. Increasingly disillusioned with Catholicism, José María Blanco y Crespo fled into exile in Britain in 1810 and, as Joseph Blanco White, remained there until his death in 1841, gaining an ever-increasing reputation as a writer and free-thinker. Elzéar Blaze survived the Napoleonic Wars and remained in the army till 1830. Sébastien Blaze fought in the campaign of 1814, and returned home to Avignon. Andrew Blayney was imprisoned in France for the remainder of the war; forced to retire due to ill-health in 1814, he died in Dublin in April 1834. Charles Boutflower fell sick and was invalided home in 1813. Transferred to Russia with the rest of the Legion of the Vistula, Heinrich von Brandt survived the retreat from Moscow, but was wounded and captured at the battle of Leipzig. After 1815 he served in the Prussian army, and wrote an influential pamphlet on the Spanish guerrillas, eventually becoming a general; he died in 1868. Robert Brindle escaped Valladolid in 1809 by walking all the way to Oporto with a group of his fellow seminarians; he became a parish priest in Lancashire. William Brooke got back to the army, and fought at Badajoz, where he was again wounded, following which he was discharged with a pension of £300 per year. Thomas Browne ended the Peninsular War as a captain, but, having been detached to the British embassy in Vienna, missed the battle of Waterloo. In 1816 he left the army and settled at his family home near St Asaph, and thereafter lived the life of a country gentleman until his death in 1858. Thomas Bugeaud saw out the Peninsular War in eastern Spain and ended up as part of the garrison of Barcelona. A supporter of Napoleon in 1815, for the next fifteen years he lived in retirement, but in 1830 he was rehabilitated and went on to win fame as the conqueror of Algeria, dying in 1849 as Duke of Isly. Thomas Bunbury transferred back into the British army at the end of the war, and served in Australia, New Zealand and India. Toribio Bustamente was killed in action in 1810. John Burgoyne served at Bayonne and New Orleans, and thereafter enjoyed a long and successful career in the Royal Engineers, including a year in the Crimea. Eventually appointed Constable of the Tower of London, he retired with the rank of field marshal in 1868, and died three years later.

Charles Cadell fought at Maya, the Nivelle, the Nive, Orthez, Toulouse and Waterloo, and continued to serve with the Twenty-Eighth Foot until the early 1830s. José Clemente Carnicero Torribio remained a priest for the rest of his life and acquired a name for himself as a vigorous defender of the Spanish Inquisition, in respect of which he published a number of pamphlets. A classic example of the eternal functionary – as an official of the Audiencia he survived no fewer than six changes of political régime – Faustino Casamayor remained in Zaragoza for the rest of his life, continued to chronicle its experiences and died of cholera in October 1834. Recalled from the peninsula, Dezydery Chlapowski fought at Aspern-Essling, Wagram, Borodino, Lutzen and Bautzen. Increasingly disillusioned with Napoleon, he resigned his commission in the summer of 1813 and went home to Poland, where he became an officer in the new army being raised under the aegis of Alexander I. Now a general, he fought in the rebellion of 1830-31, and died in 1879. John Cooper served in the remaining campaigns of 1813 and 1814 and was then sent to North America where he took part in the battle of New Orleans. Discharged from the army on medical grounds immediately afterwards, he spent many years trying to obtain a pension, but did not finally do so until 1865; he is believed to have died in the early 1870s. Edward Costello invaded France with Wellington in 1814, and was wounded at the battle of Quatre Bras in 1815. Discharged from the army in 1818, he lived for many years in poverty, and in 1835 was therefore glad to put his service as a soldier to good use by enlisting in the so-called British Legion then being raised to support the cause of Spanish liberalism against the ultra-traditionalist rebels known as the Carlists. Again wounded, he was decorated with the Cross of San Fernando – then and now Spain's highest decoration for valour – and was repatriated to become a yeoman warder in the Tower of London, where he died, aged 80, in July 1869. Gaspard de Clermont-Tonnerre left Joseph Bonaparte's service in 1811, commanded the National Guard of the Department of the Eure in 1814, and then rallied to the Bourbons, eventually becoming Minister of War. Devoted to Charles X, he refused to serve Louis Phillippe and thereafter lived in retirement until his death in January 1865. Jean-Roche Coignet served in the campaigns of 1812-15 and ended the wars as a captain; placed on half-pay by Louis XVIII, he was rehabilitated in 1831, and died at Auxerre in December 1869 at the age of 89.

Andrzej Daleki was taken prisoner at Motril and transferred to Portchester Castle; released in 1814, he returned to his home village, where he married and had children. Returning to France with his master General Junot, André Delagrave fought at Borodino, but was taken prisoner by the Russians and did not get back to France till September 1814. Placed on half-pay by Louis XVIII, he rallied to Napoleon in 1815, but did not see active service and thereafter lived in retirement until his death in 1849. Jean-Pierre Dellard became a baron of the empire in 1809 and served in the campaigns of 1812-14 in Russia and Germany, but played no role in the Hundred Days and went on to serve the monarchy in a variety of positions until his death in 1832. After the end of the Napoleonic Wars William Dent continued to serve with his regiment and was stationed in France and, later, the West Indies; on his way home to England, he was lost at sea in 1824. John Dobbs transferred into the Portuguese Fifth Regiment of Caçadores in 1813 and was badly wounded at Bayonne in April 1814. After the war he remained in the army and was given the post of Barrack-Master at Nenagh until he retired in 1841 to take up the post of governor of the Waterford lunatic asylum. A fervent Protestant full of hopes of extirpating Catholicism from Ireland for ever, he fathered eleven children and was still alive in 1863. Joseph Donaldson fought at the battles of the Nivelle, the Nive and Toulouse, and in 1814 was sent to Ireland. He obtained his discharge in 1819 and died in Paris in 1830. John Douglas recovered from the wound he received at San Sebastián, fought at Quatre Bras and Waterloo, and, promoted to the rank of sergeant, thereafter served in the Army of Occupation in France. When his unit was disbanded in 1818, he was sent to a Veterans'

Battalion, and, having at some point got married and fathered a large family, may conceivably have ended up in South Africa; the date of his death is not known, but, as he received the Military General Service Medal, he was still alive in 1848. Charles Doyle achieved the rank of general in the Spanish army, and spent the latter part of the war running a training depot for recruits in the environs of Cádiz; returning home in 1813, he was appointed as one of the Prince Regent's *aides-de-camp*, and remained in the army till 1839; he died in 1842. Benjamin D'Urban became Quartermaster-General (i.e. chief of staff) of the Portuguse army under Beresford, and had a distinguished military career after 1815, serving in a variety of positions, including as governor of the Cape Colony, where the town of Durban was named after him; ending his career as commander of the British forces in Canada, he died in 1849.

Hippolyte d'Espinchal served in Italy in 1814 and after that survived for another forty years.

George Farmer travelled to Germany with the German colonel he had taken service with, and eventually made it back to Britain where he rejoined his regiment just in time for the Waterloo campaign. After Waterloo he served in the Army of Occupation in France, and was then sent to India, remaining there until his discharge on the grounds of ill-health in 1836. Antoine Fée settled in Strasbourg and became a professor of medicine. After his escape from captivity, Charles François returned to France to fight in Russia and Germany. Besieged in Hamburg, he missed the campaign of 1814, but, by now a captain, he fought at Ligny and Wavre in June 1815. Allowed to stay in the army by Louis XVIII, he did not retire until 1823, and thereafter survived until 1853. Augustus Frazer fought at the Nivelle, the Nive and Toulouse, as well as at Waterloo. After 1815 he was employed in a variety of senior positions in the Board of Ordnance till his death in 1837.

Francisco Gallardo remained an official of the Chancillería of Granada until the 1830s. José García de León y Pizarro served both the regency and Ferdinand VII as Foreign Minister, but fell from royal favour in 1818 and thereafter became involved in radical politics. A supporter of the revolution of 1820, he spent the period from 1823 to 1832 in exile, and died in 1835. Louis François Gille was transferred from Cabrera to Portchester Castle in England in July 1810, repatriated to France in May 1814 and found employment as clerk to the board of administration of the military school of St Cyr, eventually dying in his native Paris on 2 December 1863. Pedro Agustín Girón served under Wellington in the campaigns of 1813-14, and in 1820 was appointed Minister of War following the restoration of the constitution of 1812. Very soon, however, he fell out with the new régime and fled into exile in Gibraltar. From 1823 onwards a pillar of the Bourbon monarchy, he died in 1842. George Gleig fought in the campaign in France in 1814, and was then sent to America, where he was wounded three times. Leaving the army, he then studied at Oxford, took Holy Orders and eventually became a close friend and confidant of the Duke of Wellington. In 1844 he became Chaplain-General of the British armed forces and retained this post until 1875, while at the same time becoming noted as a prolific author. Surviving to the age of 92, he finally passed away on 9 July 1888. Alexander Gordon, the *aide-de-camp*, was killed at Waterloo, while his namesake from the Fifteenth Light Dragoons sold his commission in 1811, got married and returned to his estates in Scotland, dying in 1872. William Grattan was invalided home following the retreat from Burgos, retired from the army in 1816 and thereafter lived in Dublin and Paris. Jean Grivel returned to France and fought in the campaigns of 1813-14, in the course of which he was wounded at Dresden. After the fall of Napoleon he enjoyed a long and distinguished career in the French navy, and in the Second Empire served as a senator before dying in Brest at the age of 91 in 1869. Howell Rhys Gronow served as *aide-de-camp* to Sir Thomas Picton at the battle of Waterloo, remained in the army until 1821 and made a name for himself as a Regency dandy. In 1832 he was elected to Parliament as Liberal MP for Stafford, but was almost immediately disbarred following accusations of bribery.

Some years later he retired to Paris, where he died in 1865. Wounded at the battle of San Marcial in 1813, John Green was invalided out of the army the following year, and thereafter made his way as a shopkeeper. Francisco de Paula Guervos fought in eastern Spain and Catalonia throughout the war and died of want in 1814.

Discharged from the army in 1814, James Hale obtained an 'out pension' from the Royal Hospital, and returned to his native Gloucestershire. Basil Hall remained in the navy till 1824, seeing extensive service in the squadron Britain maintained off the coast of South America; on retiring from the service in 1824 he married the daughter of a British diplomat whom he had met in Spain in 1809. After serving at Vitoria, Anthony Hamilton was captured in a skirmish near San Sebastián, but managed to escape from detention in France and reached safety with the Prussian army. Having got back to England, he volunteered for service with a foreign unit called the York Rangers and was sent to the West Indies. Discharged in 1819 he drifted to the United States and worked as a labourer, eventually marrying a girl from up-state New York and ending his life as a temperance campaigner. Sent to Walcheren in 1809, John Harris developed malaria, and thereafter saw service only in England. In 1814 he was discharged from the army altogether with a small pension, thereafter gaining his living in Soho as a shoemaker. Peter Hawker recovered from the wounds he received at Talavera and by 1812 had risen to the rank of colonel; it is not clear, however, whether he ever returned to Spain. William Hay fought in the invasion of France and at Waterloo; having retired from the army in 1828, he eventually became Commissioner of the Metropolitan Police. George Hennell was slightly wounded at the battle of the river Nivelle and was sent back to England at the end of 1813; the following year he transferred into the Thirty-Ninth Foot, but in 1816 his battalion was disbanded and he spent the rest of his life on half-pay. James Hope was wounded at Waterloo and spent long periods thereafter on half-pay though he did not sell his commission – still only a lieutenancy – until the time of the Crimean War, some five years before his death in 1860. Thomas Howell fought at Waterloo and immediately afterwards obtained his discharge, only to disappear into poverty thereafter. Following his experiences at Avila, Abel Hugo was in 1813 made governor of Thionville, and defended that city with great courage when it was attacked by the Allies. Allowed to retain his position by Louis XVIII, he supported Napoleon in the Hundred Days and was one of the very last commanders to surrender to the Allies. Placed on the retired list thereafter, until his death in 1828 he sought to make ends meet as a writer, but is not nearly so well remembered as his son, the famous novelist Victor Hugo. Jacques Hulot became a general and a baron of the empire and went on to see service at the battles of Leipzig, Hanau, where he was wounded, and Ligny.

William Jacob returned to Britain in late 1810, and resumed his seat in the House of Commons. Renowned for his strong interest in matters pertaining to the Corn Laws, he died in 1851. After returning from Spain, George Jackson served in the West Kent militia from 1809 to 1812, and then accompanied Sir Charles Stewart to Germany for the campaign of 1813. There followed a long and distinguished diplomatic career – he retired in 1859 with fifty-seven years' service – and died in May 1861. Ever more estranged from her husband, Laure Junot returned to France, engaged in numerous affairs, and after the Restoration survived on the margins of polite society by, among other things, selling many items of the loot that had been acquired by Junot in Portugal; becoming friendly with the writer Balzac, she was encouraged by him to write her memoirs, and by the time of her death in 1838 had become extremely wealthy.

William Keep fought at Sorauren, the Nivelle and the Nive, where he was badly wounded. Invalided home, he retired from the service and in 1819 caused a great scandal by eloping with the maid of the girl he was supposed to marry; after this, one can only hope that he lived happily ever after, and all the more so as he survived till 1884, and as such was one of the very last of Britain's Peninsular War veterans to pass away. John Kincaid fought at Waterloo, and continued to serve in the Ninety-Fifth Rifles until 1831. In 1852 he was knighted and appointed to a senior post in the Yeoman of the Guard. He died in 1862.

François Lavaux left Spain in 1813 and fought in the campaigns of Saxony and France; after being demobilised in 1814, he returned to his native village and spent the rest of his life as a peasant. Pierre de Lagarde returned to France in 1811, and was posted to head the French police in Tuscany. Another political survivor, he rallied to the Bourbons in 1814, supported Napoleon in 1815, and then inveigled his way back into the favour of the Bourbons, eventually ending as a member of the Council of State; he died in 1848. Louis Lagneau returned to France, served in the campaigns of 1812-15, and following the battle of Waterloo, in which he fought in the Old Guard, enjoyed a long career as a doctor and surgeon; eventually elected as a Fellow of the French Academy of Medicine, he died in 1868. William Lawrence served at both New Orleans and Waterloo, and after the latter battle married a French girl. Having been discharged from the army, he settled in Studland in Dorset and was eventually able to become the landlord of a tavern. He died in 1867. John Leach fought at Waterloo and remained in the army until at least 1818. Charles Leslie returned home on leave after the battle of Albuera, and thereafter, though he returned to Spain, saw no front-line action. After 1815 he transferred into the Sixtieth Foot and served in Canada; he died in 1870. Louis Lejeune returned to France to fight in the campaign of 1809 against Austria. Sent back to Spain with dispatches from the emperor, he was captured by some guerrillas near Toledo and sent to England as a prisoner, only to escape and return to France in time for the campaign of 1812 and in consequence fought in both Russia and Germany. After 1815 he continued to serve as a staff officer, while at the same time painting a number of works that have become classics of their kind. Finally retiring in 1837, he became mayor of Toulouse and died in 1848. Jean-Baptiste Lemonnier-Delafosse fought at Toulouse and Waterloo and lived until at least the early 1850s. Robert Long was recalled from the peninsula in 1813 after criticism of his performance and spent the rest of his life engaged in increasingly bitter controversies with Beresford and other officers; he died in 1825.

Having recovered from the severe wound that he suffered at Badajoz, James Macarthy was posted to a garrison battalion, and in 1819 was placed on the half-pay list, on which he remained until his death in 1846. Marcellin de Marbot survived his two periods of service in Spain and Portugal to fight in the campaigns of 1812–15, and by the end of the wars had been wounded ten times. Banished by Louis XVIII, he lived in Germany for several years, but was eventually allowed to rejoin the army, and went on to win fresh glory in Algeria. Finally retiring in 1848 as a peer of France, he spent the six years left to him writing the memoirs that have immortalised his name. After the battle of La Coruña Benjamin Miller never saw active duty again, rather serving in a series of garrisons in Britain. Eventually promoted to sergeant, he married a Canterbury girl named Sarah Butcher and in 1815 was discharged from the army following a bad fall. John Mills retired from the army in 1814, and thereafter lived the life of, first, a regency dandy and then a country gentleman. Elected to parliament as a Whig in 1831, he also served as a Verderer of the New Forest, his home being at Bisterne near Ringwood. He died in 1871. On his return to France in 1813 André Miot de Melito was appointed to the Council of State and assisted in the defence of Paris in 1814. A supporter of Napoleon in the Hundred Days, he retired from public life in 1815 and died in 1841. Stephen Morley developed typhus after the retreat from Burgos and was invalided home early in 1813. Though he recovered, he never saw active service again, but was thereafter employed as a recruiting sergeant. In the course of these duties, he met a girl from Sheffield whom he married and by whom he had eighteen children. He finally obtained his discharge in 1824. Jozef Mrozinski served in Spain until the beginning of 1812, when all the Polish troops in the peninsula were recalled to fight in Russia. After 1815 he continued to pursue a military career in the army of 'Congress Poland', and became a general. Deported to Siberia for two years for his part in the insurrection of 1831, he died in 1839.

Adam Neale travelled in Europe extensively after returning to Britain in 1809 and eventually became physician to the British embassy in Constantinople. Coming home in 1814, he thereafter pursued a career in medicine in Exeter, Cheltenham and London; he died at Dunkirk in 1832. Jean Noël left Spain at the end of 1811 and fought in the campaigns of Russia, Germany and France. In 1815 he took part in the defence of southern France, and suffered a brief period of proscription, but three years later was rehabilitated and eventually became governor of Neuf-Brisach. Retiring from the army in 1831, he retired to Nancy and died in the 1850s.

A captain by the end of the Napoleonic Wars, Charles Parquin fought in the campaigns of 1813 and 1814, but missed the battle of Waterloo. Despite having rallied to Napoleon in 1815, he was allowed to carry on serving in the French army until his regiment was disbanded in 1819. Living in exile in Switzerland thereafter, he became a favourite of Hortense de Beauharnais and, in time, one of the chief mentors of her son Louis-Napoléon. A fervent Bonapartist, he took part in the latter's abortive rising at Boulogne in August 1840; sentenced to twenty years in prison in consequence, he died in confinement at Doullens in 1845. John Patterson was wounded at Maya and repatriated to England; however, he rejoined the Fiftieth when it returned from France and thereafter served in garrison in the West Indies. Andrew Pearson deserted after the battle of Salamanca, after having been court-martialled for an offence he claimed not to have committed. Getting back to his native Northumberland safely, he went into service as a gardener, had eleven children and survived until 1872; he was remembered as a kindly and entertaining man who never drank or smoked. Jean-Jacques Pelet returned to France with Masséna in 1811, fought with great skill and courage in the campaigns of 1812-14, and commanded the Young Guard at Waterloo. Proscribed by the Bourbons, he was rehabilitated in 1830 and ended his career as director of the army's general staff academy, finally dying in 1858. Robert Porter married a Russian princess in 1814, spent some years travelling in Persia and Mesopotamia, and in 1826 was appointed British consul in Caracas. He died suddenly on a visit to St Petersburg in May 1842. A convinced Jansenist, Juan Antonio Posse became a supporter of the liberals and wrote a number of pamphlets in support of the constitution of 1812. Persecuted by Fernando VII, he spent some years in prison, but was freed by the revolution of 1820; thereafter, however, he seems to have taken no part in politics.

Badly wounded in a skirmish near Ronda, Albert de Rocca was repatriated to France and returned to his native Geneva, where he met, fell in love with and married the renowned lady of letters Germaine de Staël, despite the fact that she was over twenty years his senior. His new wife being a bitter opponent of Napoleon, he spent the rest of the wars in exile, and died of tuberculosis in Italy in 1818.

Released from imprisonment in the fortress of Maubeuge in 1814, Juan Manuel Sarasa rejoined the army and did not return to civilian life until 1819. Very much a traditionalist, he took part in the revolt of 1822-23, played a leading role in the organisation of the so-called 'Royal Volunteers' in Navarre, and fought for the Carlists in the war of 1833-39. By 1839 a major general in the Carlist army, he fled into exile following the Convention of Vergara, and lived in France until 1848, finally dying in Pamplona in 1856. Auguste Schaumann retired on half-pay in 1814 and returned to Hanover, where he died in 1840. Andreas von Schepeler remained in Spain throughout the Peninsular War and in 1813 became Prussian consul in Madrid; after the war he returned to Germany and wrote a major history of the conflict. Robert Semple reached Gibraltar safely and sailed for England. However, he continued to travel extensively in Napoleonic Europe and was on one occasion arrested as a spy. In 1815 he was appointed governor of the Hudson Bay Company's dependencies in Canada, but the following year was killed in a fracas involving agents of the rival North-West Company. Joseph Sherer remained in the army after 1815, but also established a considerable name for himself as a writer; he retired on half-pay in 1832 and died in 1868. Wounded at Waterloo, George Simmons remained in the Ninety-Fifth Rifles till 1845, when he retired as a major, eventually dying in 1858. Harriet Slessor fled to England in 1809, and lived there till her death in 1834. Harry Smith eventually rose to command the Ninety-Fifth (now renamed the Rifle brigade), and fought in the Kaffir, Sikh and Crimean Wars; between 1847 and 1852 he served as governor of Cape Colony, and in this capacity commemorated the girl he rescued from Badajoz in the name he gave to the town of Ladysmith. William Swabey was evacuated to England following the battle of Vitoria. The ball in his leg was never successfully extracted, but, despite this, not to mention being shipwrecked on his return to France, he recovered sufficiently to take part in the battles of Waterloo and Toulouse. In 1825 he retired from the army, and fifteen years later emigrated to Prince Edward Island. A keen sportsman, he was still shooting at the age of 80; he died in 1872.

Captured at Bailén, Maurice de Tascher was repatriated to France with a number of other officers, but died of want in January 1813 in the wake of the retreat from Moscow. William Tomkinson fought at Waterloo, and retired from the army in 1821, thereafter living the life of a Cheshire squire until his death in 1872.

Charles Vaughan formally entered the diplomatic service in 1809 and served in the British embassy there until 1816. Postings thereafter included Paris, Switzerland, the United States and Constantinople, where he died in 1849.

William Warre resigned from the Portuguese army to rejoin the British service in 1813, and thereafter held a variety of staff appointments in England and the colonies, eventually dying in York in July 1853. Having served at Waterloo and, later on, in the Mediterranean, William Wheeler was invalided out of the army in 1824 and was still alive in 1847. Samuel Whittingham continued to serve as a liaison officer with the Spaniards until 1810, when he was given the command of a Spanish division. At the head of this unit he took part in the campaigns in the Levante, and in May 1814 played a leading role in the military coup that overthrew the constitution of 1812. After 1814 he served as governor of Dominica, as Quartermaster-General in India, as commander of the British forces in the Windward and Leeward Islands, and as commander-in-chief at Madras, dying suddenly at his headquarters there in January 1841. George Wood's regiment was demobilised in 1815, whereupon he returned to civilian life.

Notes

1. A. Blayney, *Narrative of a Forced Journey through Spain and France as a Prisoner of War in the Years 1810 to 1814* (London, 1814), I, p. 280.
2. *Cit.* T.H. McGuffie, *Peninsular Cavalry General, 1811-13: the Life and Correspondence of Lieutenant General Robert Ballard Long* (London, 1951), p. 225.
3. For details of Utebo and its losses, cf. J. Latas Fuertes, *La Guerra de la Independencia en Utebo, Monzalbarba, Sobradiel y Casetas* (Zaragoza, 2006), pp. 114-19.
4. L.F. Gille, *Les prisonniers de Cabrera: mémoires d'un conscript de 1808*, ed. P. Gille (Paris, 1892), pp. 42-3.
5. *Ibid.*, pp. 44–5.
6. R. Brindle, 'Memoirs: a Brief Account of Travels, etc., in Spain' (MS: Colegio de San Albano, Valladolid), f. 10.
7. S. Blaze, *Mémoires d'un apothecaire sur le guerre d'Espagne pendant les années 1808 à 1814* (Paris, 1828), I, p. 11.
8. J.C. Carnicero Torribio, *Historia razonada de los principales sucesos de la gloriosa revolución de España* (Madrid, 1814), I, pp. 47-53.
9. L.F. Lejeune, *Memoirs of Baron Lejeune, Aide-de-Camp to Marshals Berthier, Davout and Oudinot*, ed. A. Bell (London, 1897), I, pp. 72-4.
10. *Cit.* F. Iscar-Peyra (ed.), *Ecos de la francesada: las memorias de Zahonero y Alegría* (Salamanca, 1927), pp. 101-2.
11. J. Blanco White, *Letters from Spain* (London, 1828), pp. 402-4.
12. A. Alcalá Galiano (ed.), *Memorias de Don Antonio Alcalá Galiano* (Madrid, 1886), I, p. 160.
13. Lejeune, *Memoirs*, I, pp. 74-5.
14. Blanco White, *Letters from Spain*, p. 408.
15. Alcalá Galiano, *Memorias*, I, pp. 167-8.
16. J. Grivel, *Mémoires du Vice-Amiral Baron Grivel*, ed. M.G. Lacour-Gayet (Paris, 1914), pp. 146-8.
17. Blanco White, *Letters from Spain*, pp. 411-14.
18. Carnicero Torribio, *Historia razonada*, I, pp. 99-103.
19. Marbot, M. de, *The Memoirs of Baron Marbot, late Lieutenant-General in the French Army*, ed. A.J. Butler (London, 1892), I, pp. 314-16.
20. Blanco White, *Letters from Spain*, pp. 415-19.
21. Marbot, *Memoirs*, I, pp. 318-20.
22. C. Leslie, *Military Journal of Colonel Leslie, K.H., of Balquhain, whilst serving with the Twenty-Ninth Regiment in the Peninsula and the Sixtieth Rifles in Canada, etc., 1807-1832* (Aberdeen, 1887), pp. 25-6.
23. Anon., 'Manifiesto de las ocurriencias mas principales de la plaza de Ciudad Rodrigo desde la causa formada en el real sitio del Escorial al Serenísimo Señor Príncipe de Asturias, hoy nuestro amado soberano, hasta la evacuación de la plaza de Almeida en el reino de Portugal en el dia primero de octubre de 1808' (ms.), Archivo Histórico Nacional, Sección de Estado (hereafter AHN. Est.), leg. 65-G, no. 264.
24. Brindle, 'Memoirs', p. 18.
25. Petition of the Marqués de Usategui, 27 March 1809, AHN. Est. 83-N, no. 395.
26. Blanco White, *Letters from Spain*, pp. 426-7.
27. *Ibid.*, pp. 429-32.
28. Leslie, *Military Journal*, pp. 29-30.
29. A. Berazaluce (ed.), *Recuerdos de la vida de Don Pedro Agustín Girón* (Pamplona, 1978), I, pp. 204-5.
30. *Ibid.*, pp. 206-7.
31. Baste's memoirs were originally published in A. de Beauchamp, *Collection des mémoires relatifs aux revolutions d'Espagne* (Paris, 1824). This translation, however, is that provided by T. Mahon as 'Recollections of Capitaine de Frégate Pierre Baste' at <http://napoleon-series.org/military/battles/baste/c_baste1.htm>
32. Berazaluce, *Recuerdos de la vida de Don Pedro Agustín Girón*, I, pp. 208-9.
33. 'Recollections of Capitaine de Frégate Pierre Baste'.
34. R. Douglas (ed.), *From Valmy to Waterloo: Extracts from the Diary of Captain Charles François, a Soldier of the Revolution and the Empire* (London, 1906), pp. 185-6.
35. *Cit.* Anon., *Témoignages sur les campagnes d'Espagne et de Portugal extraits du 'Carnets de la Sabretache', années 1899, 1902, 1908, 1920* (Paris, 1999), p. 14.
36. Gille, *Prisonniers de Cabrera*, pp. 77-9.
37. *Ibid.*, pp. 79-80.
38. *Cit.* J. de Haro Malpensa (ed.), *Guerra de la Independencia: La Mancha, 1808 – Diarios, Memorias y Cartas* (Alcazar de San Juan, 2000), p. 166.
39. Grivel, *Mémoires*, pp. 158-9, 162.

40. 'Recollections of Capitaine de Frégate Pierre Baste'.
41. Douglas, *From Valmy to Waterloo*, pp. 188-9.
42. *Ibid.*, pp. 191-2.
43. *Cit. Témoignages sur la campagne d'Espagne et de Portugal*, pp. 16-17.
44. F. Whittingham (ed.), *A Memoir of the Services of Lieutenant-General Sir Samuel Ford Whittingham* (London, 1868), pp. 44-5.
45. Alcalá Galiano, *Memorias*, I, pp. 201-3.
46. Blaze, *Mémoires*, I, pp. 71-2.
47. Brindle, 'Memoirs', ff. 22-3.
48. *Cit.* F. Presa González, G. Bak, A. Matyjaszczyk Grenda and R. Monforte Dupret (eds), *Soldados polacos en España durante la Guerra de la Independencia Española, 1808-1814* (Madrid, 2004), pp. 157-9.
49. A. Alcaide Ibieca, *Historia de los dos sitios que pusieron a Zaragoza en los años de 1808 y 1809 las tropas de Napoleón* (Madrid, 1830), I, pp. 58-9.
50. F. Casamayor, *Diario de los sitios de Zaragoza, 1808-1809*, ed. H. Lafoz Rabaza (Zaragoza, 2000), pp. 41-3.
51. *Ibid.*, pp. 56-7.
52. *Ibid.*, pp. 60-1.
53. *Cit. ibid.*, pp. 170-1.
54. C.R. Vaughan, *Narrative of the Siege of Zaragoza* (London, 1809), pp. 14-16.
55. Alcaide Ibieca, *Historia*, I, pp. 200-7.
56. *Cit.* Presa González *et al*, *Soldados polacos en España*, pp. 179-80.
57. *Cit. ibid.*, pp. 180-1.
58. Casamayor, *Diario de los sitios*, p. 95.
59. Alcaide Ibieca, *Historia*, I, pp. 248-52.
60. Leslie, *Military Journal*, pp. 31-2.
61. C. Hibbert (ed.), *A Soldier of the Seventy-First: the Journal of a Soldier in the Peninsular War* (London, 1975), p. 15.
62. C. Hibbert (ed.), *The Recollections of Rifleman Harris as told to Henry Curling* (London, 1970), pp. 26-7.
63. J. Leach, *Rough Sketches of the Life of an Old Soldier during a Service in the East Indies, at the Siege of Copenhagen in 1807, in the Peninsula and the South of France in the Campaigns from 1808 to 1814 with the Light Division, in the Netherlands in 1815, including the Battles of Quatre Bras and Waterloo, with a Slight Sketch of the Three Years passed by the Army of Occupation in France* (London, 1831), pp. 50-1.
64. S. Morley, *Memoirs of a Sergeant of the Fifth Regiment of Foot containing an Account of his Service in Hanover, South America and the Peninsula* (London, 1842), p. 49.
65. A. Hamilton, *Hamilton's Campaign with Moore and Wellington during the Peninsular War* (Troy, New York, 1847), p. 14.
66. J.L. Hulot, *Souvenirs militaires du Baron Hulot, général d'artillerie, 1773-1843* (Paris, 1886), pp. 234-5.
67. Leslie, *Military Journal*, p. 50. This account of Brennier's attack is very different from that given by Oman, but William Lawrence, who was fighting in the same brigade, also speaks of the French using skirmishing tactics in the fashion described by Leslie.
68. Hibbert (ed.), *A Soldier of the Seventy-First*, pp. 17-18.
69. G.N. Bankes (ed.), *The Autobiography of Sergeant William Lawrence, a Hero of the Peninsular and Waterloo Campaigns* (London, 1886), p. 45. There are a couple of errors of detail here. The British advance was commanded by General Ronald Ferguson while the British captured only three guns at this spot.
70. G. Wood, *The Subaltern Officer: a Narrative* (London, 1826), pp. 54-6. The piper was one George Clark. Wounded in the groin, he is supposed to have shouted, 'De'il ha' my saul, if ye shall want music', and to have continued to play throughout the action. His heroism is commemorated in a well-known print that has appeared in numerous books on the British army in the Napoleonic Wars. Happily, Clark survived his wound and eventually returned home to Scotland where he was presented with a commemorative set of pipes by the Royal Highland Society.
71. P. Catley (ed.), *The Journal of James Hale, late Sergeant in the Ninth Regiment of Foot* (Windsor, 1997), p. 22.
72. Hibbert, *A Soldier of the Seventy-First*, p. 18.
73. Leslie, *Military Journal*, p. 52.
74. A. Neale, *Letters from Portugal and Spain comprising an Account of the Operations of the Armies under their Excellencies Sir Arthur Wellesley and Sir John Moore from the Landing of the Troops in Mondego Bay to the Battle of Corunna* (London, 1809), pp. 16-21.
75. J. Ormsby, *An Account of the Operations of the British Army and of the State and Sentiments of the People of Portugal and Spain during the Campaigns of the Years 1808 and 1809* (London, 1809), I, pp. 30-2.

76. J. Sturgis (ed.), *A Boy in the Peninsular War: the Services, Adventures and Experiences of Robert Blakeney, Subaltern in the Twenty-Eighth Regiment* (London, 1899), pp. 18-19.
77. R.K. Porter, *Letters from Portugal and Spain written during the March of the British Troops under Sir John Moore* (London, 1809), pp. 6-10.
78. Ormsby, *Operations of the British Army*, I, p. 85.
79. F. Lavaux, *Mémoires de campagne, 1793-1814*, ed. C. Bourachot (Paris, 2004), pp. 133-4.
80. J. Fortescue (ed.), *The Notebooks of Captain Coignet* (London, 1989), p. 165.
81. *Cit.* Lady Jackson (ed.), *The Diaries and Letters of Sir George Jackson, KCH, from the Peace of Amiens to the Battle of Talavera* (London, 1872), II, pp. 274-9.
82. Whittingham, *Memoir*, pp. 48-50.
83. J.M. Sarasa, *Vida y hechos militares del Mariscal del Campo, Don Juan Manuel Sarasa, narrados por el mismo*, ed. J. del Burgo (Pamplona, 1952), pp. 10-11.
84. L. de Villaba, *Zaragoza en su segundo sitio* (Palma de Mallorca, 1811), pp. 18-22.
85. A. Ludovici (ed.), *On the Road with Wellington: the Diary of a War Commissary in the Peninsular Campaigns* (New York, 1925), pp. 79-80.
86. Neale, *Letters from Portugal and Spain*, pp. 219-20.
87. Letter of Francisco de Paula Guervos, 18 November 1808, Real Academia de Historia (hereafter RAE) 11:9003.
88. T. Simmons (ed.), *Memoirs of a Polish Lancer: the Pamietniki of Dezydery Chlapowski* (Chicago, 1992), p. 43.
89. A. Miot de Melito, *Mémoires du Comte Miot de Melito, ancien ministre, ambassadeur, conseiller d'état et member de l'institut* (Paris, 1858), III, p. 22.
90. Fortescue (ed.), *Notebooks of Captain Coignet*, pp. 165-6.
91. Sarasa, *Vida y hechos*, p. 11.
92. J.P. Dellard, *Mémoires militaires du Général Baron Dellard sur les guerres de la République et l'Empire* (Paris, 1892), pp. 266-7.
93. Sarasa, *Vida y hechos*, p. 12.
94. *Cit.* 'Diario de operaciones del Ejército de la Izquierda al mando del Tenente General Don Joaquín Blake', Instituto de Historia y Cultura Militar (hereafter IHCM). CDB. 3/4/28.
95. A. de Rocca, *Memoirs of the War of the French in Spain*, ed. P. Haythornthwaite (London, 1990), pp. 32-3.
96. Marbot, *Memoirs*, I, pp. 332-3.
97. Simmons (ed.), *Memoirs of a Polish Lancer*, p. 43.
98. J. North (ed.), *In the Legions of Napoleon: the Memoirs of a Polish Officer in Spain and Russia, 1808-1823* (London, 1999), p. 46.
99. Whittingham, *Memoir*, pp. 52-4.
100. Lejeune, *Memoirs*, I, pp. 85-6.
101. Brindle, 'Memoirs', p. 24.
102. Lejeune, *Memoirs*, I, pp. 87-90.
103. Simmons (ed.), *Memoirs of a Polish Lancer*, p. 45.
104. Jackson (ed.), *Diaries and Letters*, II, pp. 308-9.
105. J. García de León y Pizarro, *Memorias de la Vida del Excmo. Sr. D. José García de León y Pizarro escritas por el mismo*, ed. A. Alonso Castrillo (Madrid, 1894), I, pp. 251-2.
106. *Ibid.*, pp. 255-9.
107. Duque de Infantado, *Manifiesto de las operaciones del Ejército del Centro* (Seville, 1809), p. 16.
108. A. von Schepeler, *Histoire de la révolution d'Espagne et de Portugal ainsi que de la guerre qui en resulta* (Liège, 1829), II, p. 93.
109. F.J. de Castaños to M. de Garay, 21 December 1808, *cit.* F.J. de Castaños, *Reales Ordenes de la Junta Suprema Central de Gobierno del Reino y representaciones de la de Sevilla y del General Castaños acerca de su separación del mando del Ejército de Operaciones del Centro* (Seville, 1809), pp. 15-18.
110. Jackson (ed.), *Diaries and Letters*, II, pp. 323-4.
111. Alcalá Galiano, *Memorias*, I, pp. 217-20.
112. *Cit.* Iscar-Peyra, *Ecos de la francesada*, pp. 122-3.
113. Porter, *Letters from Portugal and Spain*, pp. 100-5.
114. J. Patterson, *The Adventures of Captain John Patterson, with Notices of the Officers, etc., of the Fiftieth or Queen's Regiment from 1807 to 1821* (London, 1837), p. 73.
115. H. Wylly (ed.), *A Cavalry Officer in the Corunna Campaign: the Journal of Captain Gordon of the Fifteenth Hussars* (London, 1913), pp. 101-16.
116. Marbot, *Memoirs*, I, p. 352.

117. Simmons (ed.), *Memoirs of a Polish Lancer*, pp. 47-9.
118. Wylly (ed.), *A Cavalry Officer in the Corunna Campaign*, pp. 146-7.
119. Sturgis (ed.), *Boy in the Peninsular War*, pp. 49-50.
120. Hibbert (ed.), *A Soldier of the Seventy-First*, pp. 28-32.
121. J.J. de Naylies, *Mémoires sur la guerre d'Espagne pendant les années 1808, 1809, 1810 et 1811* (Paris, 1817), pp. 37-8.
122. Morley, *Memoirs of a Sergeant*, pp. 61-4.
123. Marqués de la Romana to A. Cornel, 18 January 1809, AHN. Est. 18-8, ff. 32-4.
124. Wylly (ed.), *A Cavalry Officer in the Corunna Campaign*, pp. 145-7.
125. Ludovici (ed.), *On the Road with Wellington*, pp. 127-8.
126. R. Herr (ed.), *Memorias del cura liberal Don Juan Antonio Posse con su discurso sobre la Constución de 1812* (Madrid, 1984), pp. 118-19.
127. Ludovici (ed.), *On the Road with Wellington*, pp. 108-11.
128. M. Dacombe and B. Rowe (eds), *The Adventures of Sergeant Benjamin Miller whilst serving in the Fourth Battalion of the Royal Regiment of Artillery, 1796-1815* (London, 1999), pp. 33-4.
129. Wylly (ed.), *A Cavalry Officer in the Corunna Campaign*, pp. 197-9.
130. Dacombe and Rowe, *Adventures of Sergeant Benjamin Miller*, p. 35.
131. P.M. le Noble, *Mémoires sur les opérations militaires des français en Galice, Portugal et la vallée du Tage en 1809 sous le commandement du Maréchal Soult* (Paris, 1821), pp. 38-9.
132. Anon., *The Personal Narrative of a Private Soldier who served in the Forty-Second Highlanders for Twelve Years during the Late War* (London, 1821), pp. 83-7.
133. Sturgis (ed.), *Boy in the Peninsular War*, pp. 114-17.
134. *Cit.* J.C. Moore, *A Narrative of the Campaign of the British Army in Spain commanded by His Excellency, Sir John Moore* (London, 1809), pp. 359-60.
135. Hibbert, *Recollections of Rifleman Harris*, pp. 60-1.
136. C. Doyle to W. Cooke, 30 November 1808, National Archives (hereafter NA), WO.1/227, f. 567.
137. Villaba, *Zaragoza en su segundo sitio*, p. 20.
138. Alcaide Ibieca, *Historia*, II, pp. 114-16.
139. Lejeune, *Memoirs*, II, p. 159.
140. North (ed.), *In the Legions of Napoleon*, pp. 56-7.
141. Casamayor, *Diario de los sitios*, pp. 165-6.
142. Alcaide Ibieca, *Historia*, III, pp. 134-44.
143. *Cit.* Presa González *et al*, *Soldados polacos en España*, p. 226.
144. Marbot, *Memoirs*, I, pp. 360-1.
145. Lejeune, *Memoirs*, I, pp. 167-9.
146. Casamayor, *Diario de los sitios*, p. 166.
147. *Cit.* Presa González *et al*, *Soldados polacos en España*, pp. 239-40.
148. H. d'Ideville (ed.), *Memoirs of Colonel Bugeaud from his Private Correspondence and Original Documents* (London, 1884), pp. 100-1.
149. Marbot, *Memoirs*, I, pp. 363-4.
150. Casamayor, *Diario de los sitios*, pp. 171-2.
151. *Ibid.*, p. 174.
152. Lejeune, *Memoirs*, I, pp. 189-90.
153. Alcaide Ibieca, *Historia*, III, pp. 214-17.
154. *Ibid.*, pp. 63-4.
155. *Semanario Político, Histórico y Literario de La Coruña*, no. 5, pp. 109-11.
156. Villaba, *Zaragoza en su segundo sitio*, p. 77.
157. T. Bustamente to M. de Garay, 7 May 1809, AHN. Est. 41-E, no. 146.
158. Brindle, 'Memoirs', pp. 46-7.
159. H. d'Espinchal, *Souvenirs militaires, 1792-1814*, ed. F. Masson and E. Boyer (Paris, 1901), I, pp. 379-80.
160. L. Lagneau, *Journal d'un chirurgien de la Grande Armée, 1803-1815*, ed. C. Bourachot (Paris, 2000), p. 109.
161. Marbot, *Memoirs*, I, pp. 337-8.
162. A. de Gonneville, *Recollections of Colonel de Gonneville*, ed. C. Yonge (London, 1875), I, pp. 239-44.
163. L. Guimbaud (ed.), *Mémoires du Général Hugo* (Paris, 1934), pp. 144-8.
164. Lavaux, *Mémoires*, pp. 136-7.
165. B. Hall, *Corcubión*, ed. J. Alberich (Exeter, 1976), p. 26.
166. *Cit.* Presa González *et al*, *Soldados polacos en España*, pp. 44-5.

167. North (ed.), *In the Legions of Napoleon*, pp. 72-3.

168. P. Lagarde to Napoleon, 4 May 1809, *cit.* N. Gotteri (ed.), *La mission de Lagarde, policier de l'empereur, pendant la Guerre d'Espagne, 1809-1811* (Paris, 1991), pp. 98-100.

169. G. de Clermont-Tonnerre, *L'expedition d'Espagne, 1808-1810* (Paris, 1983), pp. 259-60.

170. A.L.A. Fée, *Souvenirs de la Guerre d'Espagne, dite de l'Independance, 1809-1813* (Paris, 1856), p. 3.

171. I. Rousseau (ed.), *The Peninsular Journal of Major General Sir Benjamin Urban, 1808-1817* (London, 1930), p. 45.

172. Jackson (ed.), *Diaries and Letters*, II, pp. 409-10.

173. A. Rocca, *Memoirs of the War of the French in Spain*, ed. P. Haythornthwaite (London, 1990), pp. 78-80.

174. G. García de la Cuesta to A. Cornel, 7 April 1809, *cit.* G. García de la Cuesta, *Manifiesto que presenta a la Europa el Capitán General de los Reales Ejércitos, Don Gregorio García de la Cuesta sobre sus operaciones militares y políticas desde el mes de junio de 1808 hasta el 12 de agosto de 1809 en que dejó el mando del Ejército de Extremadura* (Valencia, 1811), pp. 41-5.

175. R. Semple, *A Second Journey in Spain in the Spring of 1809 from Lisbon through the Western Skirts of the Sierra Morena to Sevilla, Córdoba, Granada, Málaga and Gibraltar, and thence to Tetuan and Tangiers* (London, 1809), pp. 103-5.

176. *Ibid.*, pp. 136-9.

177. Le Noble, *Mémoires*, pp. 76-9.

178. Naylies, *Mémoires*, pp. 63-7.

179. *Cit.* A. Haytor (ed.), *The Backbone: Diaries of a Military Family in the Napoleonic Wars* (Bishop Auckland, 1993), pp. 210-11.

180. Semple, *Second Journey in Spain*, pp. 6-7.

181. A. Bigarré, *Mémoires du Général Bigarré, aide-de-camp du Roi Joseph, 1775-1813* (Paris, 1903), pp. 241-2.

182. Naylies, *Mémoires*, pp. 99-100.

183. Wood, *The Subaltern Officer*, p. 78.

184. T. Bunbury, *Reminiscences of a Veteran, being Personal and Military Adventures in Portugal, Spain, France, Malta, New South Wales, Norfolk Island, New Zealand, the Andaman Islands and India* (London, 1861), I, pp. 31-4.

185. W. Stothert, *A Narrative of the Principal Events of the Campaigns of 1809, 1810 and 1811 in Spain and Portugal interspersed with Remarks on the Local Scenery and Manners* (London, 1812), pp. 40-1.

186. Leslie, *Military Journal*, pp. 112-13.

187. P. Hawker, *Journal of a Regimental Officer during the Recent Campaigns in Portugal and Spain under Viscount Wellesley* (London, 1810), pp. 53-6, 58.

188. Le Noble, *Mémoires*, p. 249.

189. Ludovici (ed.), *On the Road with Wellington*, pp. 155-6.

190. Hawker, *Journal*, pp. 60-2.

191. J.S. Cooper, *Rough Notes of Seven Campaigns in Portugal, Spain, France and America during the Years 1809-10 -11-12-13-14-15* (London, 1869), pp. 8-9, 12-13.

192. Naylies, *Mémoires*, pp. 130-3.

193. A. Haley (ed.), *The Soldier who Walked Away: Autobiography of Andrew Pearson, a Peninsular War Veteran* (Liverpool, n.d.), p. 65.

194. Stothert, *Narrative*, pp. 76, 80-1.

195. Wood, *The Subaltern Officer*, pp. 84-5.

196. Bankes (ed.), *Autobiography of Sergeant William Lawrence*, p. 56.

197. Leslie, *Military Journal*, p. 147.

198. Haley (ed.), *The Soldier who Walked Away*, pp. 67-8.

199. Leslie, *Military Journal*, pp. 147-9.

200. Ludovici (ed.), *On the Road with Wellington*, pp. 185-9.

201. Haley (ed.), *The Soldier who Walked Away*, p. 69.

202. Hamilton, *Hamilton's Campaign*, pp. 79-82.

203. Bunbury, *Reminiscences of a Veteran*, I, pp. 42-3.

204. Cooper, *Rough Notes*, pp. 21-3.

205. Wood, *The Subaltern Officer*, pp. 88-91.

206. Haley (ed.), *The Soldier who Walked Away*, pp. 71-2.

207. Clermont-Tonnerre, *Expedition d'Espagne*, pp. 289-90.

208. Carnicero Torribio, *Historia razonada*, II, pp. 78-80.

209. *Ibid.*, pp. 93-4.

210. Naylies, *Mémoires*, pp. 172-7.
211. Berazaluce, *Recuerdos de la vida de Don Pedro Agustín Girón*, I, pp. 319-22.
212. R. Muir (ed.), *At Wellington's Right Hand: the Letters of Lieutenant-Colonel Sir Alexander Girdon, 1808-1815* (London, 2003), pp. 49-50.
213. Leach, *Rough Sketches*, pp. 90-6.
214. Cooper, *Rough Notes*, pp. 28-30.
215. Leslie, *Military Journal*, pp. 160-3.
216. Hawker, *Journal*, pp. 117-18.
217. *Cit.* W. Thompson (ed.), *An Ensign in the Peninsular War: the Letters of John Aitchison* (London, 1981), pp. 62-4.
218. Naylies, *Mémoires*, pp. 183-5.
219. *Ibid.*, pp. 205-8.
220. P. Roche to Wellington, 15 September 1809, US. WP.1/277.
221. Lavaux, *Mémoires*, pp. 142-3.
222. *Cit.* Presa González *et al*, *Soldados polacos en España*, pp. 50-4.
223. Haythornthwaite, *In the Peninsula with a French Hussar*, pp. 107-112.
224. *Ibid.*, pp. 18-20.
225. L. Junot, *Mémoires de Madame la Duchesse d'Abrantès, ou souvenirs historiques sur Napoléon, la Révolution, le Directoire, le Consulat, l'Empire et la Révolution* (Brussels 1837), II, p. 579.
226. Fée, *Souvenirs*, pp. 43, 47.
227. *Cit.* G. Babst (ed.), *Souvenirs d'un canonnier de l'Armée d'Espagne, 1808-1814* (Paris, 1892), pp. 12-13.
228. Fée, *Souvenirs*, pp. 49-50.
229. W. Jacob, *Travels in the South of Spain in Letters written A.D. 1809 and 1810* (London, 1811), pp. 8-12.
230. Fée, *Souvenirs*, p. 65.
231. Douglas, *From Valmy to Waterloo*, pp. 201-3.
232. Blaze, *Mémoires*, I, pp. 216-18.
233. Grivel, *Mémoires*, pp. 219-22.
234. Blaze, *Mémoires*, I, pp. 272-90.
235. J. Donaldson, *Recollections of the Eventful Life of a Soldier* (Edinburgh, 1852), pp. 71-7.
236. Alcalá Galiano, *Memorias*, I, p. 292.
237. Fée, *Souvenirs*, pp. 71-2.
238. *Ibid.*, pp. 74-5.
239. Jacob, *Travels in the South of Spain*, pp. 14-20.
240. Haythornthwaite, *In the Peninsula with a French Hussar*, pp. 133-5.
241. D'Espinchal, *Souvenirs militaires*, I, pp. 376-7.
242. Lavaux, *Mémoires*, pp. 150-7.
243. Sturgis (ed.), *Boy in the Peninsular War*, p. 190.
244. C. Cadell, *Narrative of the Campaigns of the Twenty-Eighth Regiment since their Return from Egypt in 1802* (London, 1835), pp. 94-7.
245. Bunbury, *Reminiscences of a Veteran*, pp. 75-8.
246. Cadell, *Narrative*, pp. 103-4.
247. Junot, *Mémoires*, III, pp. 39-40.
248. *Ibid.*, III, pp. 42-3.
249. W. Verner (ed.), *A British Rifleman: Journals and Correspondence during the Peninsular War and the Campaign of Waterloo* (London, 1899), p. 77.
250. Anon., *Memoirs of a Sergeant late in the Forty-Third Light Infantry Regiment previously to and during the Peninsular War* (London, 1835), p. 93.
251. E. Costello, *Adventures of a Soldier, or Memoirs of Edward Costello, KSF, formerly a Non-Commissioned Officer in the Rifle Brigade and Late Captain in the British Legion comprising Narratives of the Campaigns in the Peninsular War under the Duke of Wellington and the recent Civil Wars in Spain* (London, 1841), pp. 56-8.
252. Verner (ed.), *British Rifleman*, pp. 78-9.
253. D. Horward, *The French Campaign in Portugal, 1810-1811: an account by Jean-Jacques Pelet* (Minneapolis, 1973), pp. 120-1.
254. Junot, *Mémoires*, III, pp. 43-4.
255. Hulot, *Souvenirs militaires*, pp. 316-17.
256. E. Gachot (ed.), *Mémoires du Colonel Delagrave sur la campagne de Portugal, 1810-1811* (Paris, 1902), pp. 55-7.

257. E. Warre (ed.), *Letters from the Peninsula, 1808-1812, by Lieutenant General Sir William Warre* (London, 1909), p. 145.
258. R. Brindle (ed.), *With Napoleon's Guns: the Military Memoirs of an Officer of the First Empire* (London, 2005), pp. 96-7.
259. Verner (ed.), *British Rifleman*, pp. 80-5.
260. W. Grattan, *Adventures of the Connaught Rangers from 1808 to 1814* (London, 1847), I, pp. 52-3.
261. C. Bourachot (ed.), *Souvenirs militaires du Captaine Jean-Baptiste Lemonnier-Delafosse* (Paris, n.d.), pp. 44-5.
262. Hamilton, *Hamilton's Campaign*, pp. 88-9.
263. J. Sherer, *Recollections of the Peninsula* (London, 1823), pp. 115-17.
264. S. Monick (ed.), *Douglas's Tale of the Peninsula and Waterloo, 1808-1815* (London, 1997), pp. 21-2.
265. Horward, *French Campaign in Portugal*, p. 234.
266. Marbot, *Memoirs*, II, pp. 125-6.
267. M. Barrès (ed.), *Memoirs of a French Napoleonic Officer: Jean-Baptiste Barrès* (London, 1925), pp. 144-5.
268. Brindle (ed.), *With Napoleon's Guns*, pp. 105-6.
269. Bourachot (ed.), *Souvenirs militaires du Captaine Jean-Baptiste Lemonnier-Delafosse*, pp. 57-8.
270. Marbot, *Memoirs*, II, pp. 133-4.
271. Bourachot (ed.), *Souvenirs militaires du Captaine Jean-Baptiste Lemonnier-Delafosse*, p. 59.
272. Hulot, *Souvenirs militaires*, pp. 326-9.
273. Junot, *Mémoires*, III, pp. 46-7.
274. Horward, *French Campaign in Portugal*, p. 248.
275. *Cit.* Muir, *At Wellington's Right Hand*, p. 119.
276. J.C. Stepney, *Leaves from the Diary of an Officer of the Guards* (London, 1854), pp. 46-8.
277. Bankes (ed.), *Autobiography of Sergeant William Lawrence*, pp. 71-2.
278. J. Kincaid, *Adventures in the Rifle Brigade in the Peninsula, France and the Netherlands from 1809 to 1815* (London, 1830), pp. 28-9.
279. Costello, *Adventures of a Soldier*, pp. 73-4.
280. Leach, *Rough Sketches*, pp. 175-6.
281. Verner (ed.), *British Rifleman*, pp. 137-52 *passim*.
282. Ludovici (ed.), *On the Road with Wellington*, pp. 290-1.
283. Anon., *Memoirs of a Sergeant late in the Forty-Third Light Infantry Regiment*, p. 114.
284. Donaldson, *Recollections*, p. 104.
285. Costello, *Adventures of a Soldier*, pp. 111-12.
286. Haley (ed.), *The Soldier who Walked Away*, pp. 78-9.
287. Verner (ed.), *British Rifleman*, p. 127.
288. J. Dobbs, *Recollections of an Old Fifty-Second Man*, ed. I. Fletcher (Staplehurst, 2000), pp. 18-19.
289. Bourachot (ed.), *Souvenirs militaires du Captaine Jean-Baptiste Lemonnier-Delafosse*, pp. 75-6.
290. Brindle (ed.), *With Napoleon's Guns*, p. 118.
291. Leslie, *Military Journal*, p. 218.
292. *Ibid.*, pp. 219-20.
293. *Ibid.*, p. 220.
294. C. Oman (ed.), 'A prisoner of Albuera: the journal of Major William Brooke from 16 May to 28 September 1811', in C. Oman, *Studies in the Napoleonic Wars* (Oxford, 1929), pp. 178-9.
295. Leslie, *Military Journal*, pp. 220-1.
296. *Ibid.*, p. 221.
297. Sherer, *Recollections of the Peninsula*, p. 159.
298. Cooper, *Rough Notes*, pp. 59-61.
299. Leslie, *Military Journal*, p. 222.
300. *Cit.* Cooper, *Rough Notes*, pp. 61-2.
301. G. Gleig, *The Light Dragoon* (London, 1855), p. 33.
302. Oman, 'A prisoner of Albuera', pp. 180-1.
303. Donaldson, *Recollections*, pp. 123-4.
304. Hibbert, *A Soldier of the Seventy-First*, pp. 60-1.
305. J. Tomkinson (ed.), *The Diary of a Cavalry Officer in the Peninsular and Waterloo Campaigns* (London, 1894), pp. 100-1.
306. B.H. Liddell Hart (ed.), *The Letters of Private Wheeler, 1809-1828* (1951), pp. 55-6.
307. Costello, *Adventures of a Soldier*, pp. 122-3.
308. Dobbs, *Recollections*, p. 25.

309. Kincaid, *Adventures in the Rifle Brigade*, pp. 75-6.
310. B.T. Jones (ed.), *Military Memoirs of Charles Parquin* (London, 1987), pp. 134-5.
311. Grattan, *Adventures*, I, pp. 97-8.
312. Ludovici (ed.), *On the Road with Wellington*, p. 303.
313. Grattan, *Adventures*, I, pp. 127-31.
314. Liddell Hart (ed.), *Letters of Private Wheeler*, p. 61.
315. Ludovici (ed.), *On the Road with Wellington*, pp. 311-13.
316. Gleig, *The Light Dragoon*, pp. 45-9.
317. Oman, 'A Prisoner of Albuera', pp. 185-6.
318. Blayney, *Narrative of a Forced Journey*, I, pp. 35-8.
319. Oman, 'A Prisoner of Albuera', pp. 193-6.
320. J. Catalina García (ed.), *Diario de un patriota complutense en la Guerra de la Independencia* (Alcalá de Henares, 1894), p. 19.
321. Sarasa, *Vida y hechos*, pp. 13-14.
322. Gille, *Prisonniers de Cabrera*, pp. 236-40.
323. Gleig, *The Light Dragoon*, pp. 94-5.
324. F. Hall, 'Recollections in Portugal and Spain during 1811 and 1812', *Journal of the Royal United Services Institution*, LVI, no. 11 (November 1912), p. 1537.
325. B.T. Jones (ed.), *Napoleon's Army: Military Memoirs of Charles Parquin* (London, 1987), pp. 114-16.
326. Gleig, *The Light Dragoon*, pp. 95-6.
327. Brindle (ed.), *With Napoleon's Guns*, p. 122.
328. P. Haythornthwaite (ed.), *Life in Napoleon's Army: the Memoirs of Captain Elzéar Blaze* (London, 1995), pp. 52-5.
329. Bourachot (ed.), *Souvenirs militaires du Capitaine Jean-Baptiste Lemonnier-Delafosse*, pp. 85-8.
330. Haythornthwaite (ed.), *Life in Napoleon's Army*, pp. 95-101.
331. North (ed.), *In the Legions of Napoleon*, pp. 166-7.
332. Fée, *Souvenirs*, pp. 110-11.
333. North (ed.), *In the Legions of Napoleon*, p. 87.
334. Jones, *Napoleon's Army*, pp. 113-14, 121.
335. *Ibid.*, p. 135.
336. Blaze, *Mémoires*, II, pp. 282-3.
337. Fée, *Souvenirs*, pp. 66-9, 80.
338. Brindle (ed.), *With Napoleon's Guns*, p. 137.
339. *Ibid.*, p. 125.
340. Blayney, *Narrative of a Forced Journey*, I, pp. 57-8.
341. Catalina García (ed.), *Diario de un patriota complutense*, pp. 34-9 *passim*.
342. Tomkinson (ed.), *Diary of a Cavalry Officer*, pp. 128-9.
343. I. Fletcher (ed.), *For King and Country: the Letters and Diaries of John Mills, Coldstream Guards, 1811-14* (Staplehurst, 1995), pp. 58, 63.
344. *Cit.* Warre (ed.), *Letters from the Peninsula*, p. 249.
345. Ludovici (ed.), *On the Road with Wellington*, p. 325.
346. A. Perich y Viader, 'Narració de los sis anys y quatre mesos que los franceses han estat en Catalunya, contant de los primers de febrer de 1808, fins al primers junys de 1814', ed. J. Pella y Forgas, *Boletín de la Real Academía de Buenas Letras de Barcelona*, no. 49, 495.
347. F. Casamayor, 'Años políticos y históricos de las cosas mas particulares ocurridas en la imperial, augusta y siempre heróica ciudad de Zaragoza', XXIX, f. 22, Biblióteca de la Universidad de Zaragoza, MS.135.
348. Ludovici (ed.), *On the Road with Wellington*, p. 355.
349. Carnicero Torribio, *Historia razonada*, III, pp. 94-9.
350. *Ibid.*, pp. 100-1, 112, 121-2.
351. *Cit.* C. Almuina Fernández (ed.), *Valladolid: diarios curiosos, 1807-1841* (Valladolid, 1989), pp. 300-1.
352. Catalina García (ed.), *Diario de un patriota complutense*, pp. 53-65 *passim*.
353. Grattan, *Adventures*, I, pp. 166-8.
354. Ludovici (ed.), *On the Road with Wellington*, p. 317.
355. R.N. Buckley (ed.), *The Napoleonic War Journal of Captain Thomas Henry Browne, 1807-1816* (London, 1987), pp. 155-6.
356. Grattan, *Adventures*, I, pp. 164-7.

357. S. Monick (ed.), *The Iberian and Waterloo Campaigns: the Letters of Lieutenant James Hope, 92nd (Highland)*
   Regiment, 1811-1815 (Heathfield, 2000), pp. 38-40.
358. Liddell Hart (ed.), *Letters of Private Wheeler*, pp. 73-4.
359. Donaldson, *Recollections*, pp. 148-9.
360. Hamilton, *Hamilton's Campaign*, p. 111.
361. Costello, *Adventures of a Soldier*, pp. 14-17.
362. Donaldson, *Recollections*, pp. 150-1.
363. F. Whinyates (ed.), *Diary of Campaigns in the Peninsula for the Years 1811, 12 and 13 by Captain William
   Swabey, an Officer of E Troop (present E Battery), Royal Horse Artillery* (London, 1895), pp. 70-1.
364. Grattan, *Adventures*, I, pp. 207-8.
365. Kincaid, *Adventures in the Rifle Brigade*, pp. 115-16.
366. Catley (ed.), *Journal of James Hale*, p. 67.
367. Kincaid, *Adventures in the Rifle Brigade*, pp. 117-18.
368. C. Boutflower, *The Journal of an Army Surgeon during the Peninsular War* (Manchester, 1912), pp. 125-6.
369. J.C. Stepney, *Leaves from the Diary of an Officer of the Guards* (London, 1854), pp. 269-72.
370. Hamilton, *Hamilton's Campaign*, pp. 117-18.
371. J. MacCarthy, *Recollections of the Storming of the Castle of Badajoz by the Third Division under the Command
   of Lieut. Gen. Sir Thomas Picton, GCB, on the Sixth of April 1812* (London, 1836), pp. 15-29.
372. Bankes (ed.), *Autobiography of Sergeant William Lawrence*, pp. 112-13.
373. Hamilton, *Hamilton's Campaign*, pp. 122-3.
374. Verner (ed.), *British Rifleman*, p. 229.
375. Anon., *Memoirs of a Sergeant late in the Forty-Third Light Infantry Regiment*, pp. 168-9.
376. Donaldson, *Recollections*, pp. 156-7.
377. Sturgis (ed.), *Boy in the Peninsular War*, pp. 273-4.
378. Patterson, *Adventures*, p. 190.
379. Costello, *Adventures of a Soldier*, pp. 177-9.
380. P. Haythornthwaite (ed.), *The Autobiography of Sir Harry Smith, 1787-1819* (London, 1999), pp. 68-73.
381. *Cit.* R. Gómez Villafranca, *Extremadura en la Guerra de la Independencia* (Badajoz, 1908), p. 259.
382. MacCarthy, *Recollections*, pp. 58-63.
383. Anon., *Memoirs of a Sergeant late in the Forty-Third Light Infantry Regiment*, pp. 170-3.
384. Donaldson, *Recollections*, pp. 164-5.
385. Dobbs, *Recollections*, p. 38.
386. Bankes (ed.), *Autobiography of Sergeant William Lawrence*, p. 122.
387. Anon., *Personal Narrative of a Private Soldier who served in the Forty-Second Highland*ers, p. 121.
388. Tomkinson (ed.), *Diary of a Cavalry Officer*, p. 162.
389. Fletcher (ed.), *For King and Country*, p. 169.
390. *Ibid.*, p. 161.
391. Donaldson, *Recollections*, pp. 167-8.
392. *Cit.* McGuffie, *Peninsular Cavalry General*, pp. 199, 202.
393. Fletcher (ed.), *For King and Country*, pp. 178-9.
394. Morley, *Memoirs of a Sergeant*, pp. 114-15.
395. Donaldson, *Recollections*, pp. 169-70.
396. Monick (ed.), *Douglas's Tale*, pp. 43-4.
397. *Cit.* S. Cassells (ed.), *Peninsular Portrait, 1811-1814: the Letters of William Bragge, Third (King's Own)
   Dragoons* (London, 1963), pp. 63-4.
398. Jones, *Napoleon's Army*, pp. 148-9.
399. *cit.* G. Wrottesley (ed.), *The Life and Correspondence of Field Marshal Sir John Burgoyne* (London, 1873), I,
   p. 204.
400. J. Wardell (ed.), *With the 'Thirty-Second' in the Peninsula and other Campaigns: a New Edition of 'The Life
   of a Soldier'* (London, 1904), pp. 184-5.
401. Bourachot (ed.), *Souvenirs militaires du Capitaine Jean-Baptiste Lemonnier-Delafosse*, pp. 94-5.
402. Fletcher (ed.), *For King and Country*, p. 184.
403. Liddell Hart (ed.), *Letters of Private Wheeler*, pp. 87-8.
404. *Cit.* Warre (ed.), *Letters from the Peninsula*, pp. 293-4.
405. Thompson (ed.), *Ensign in the Peninsular War*, p. 177.
406. Sherer, *Recollections of the Peninsula*, pp. 190-1.

407. Boutflower, *Journal of an Army Surgeon*, p. 143.
408. Tomkinson (ed.), *Diary of a Cavalry Officer*, pp. 196-8. Tomkinson here falls into an amusing error of which 'El Príncipe Borbón' (lit. 'the Prince of Bourbon') seems to have made no attempt to disabuse him. Thus, the real name of the guerrilla chieftain concerned was Tomás Príncipe, while the latter acquired the nickname 'Borbón' because in 1808 he had been a private soldier in the infantry regiment of that name. Understandable though it is, Tomkinson's mistake is a good example of the manner in which even British officers contributed to the myth of the guerrillas.
409. *Cit.* Fletcher (ed.), *For King and Country*, pp. 139, 223.
410. Leach, *Rough Sketches*, p. 73.
411. B. Stuart (ed.), *Soldiers' Glory, being 'Rough Notes of an Old Soldier' by Major-General Sir George Bell* (London, 1956) pp. 33-4.
412. Grattan, *Adventures*, II, pp. 88-90.
413. Carnicero Torribio, *Historia razonada*, III, pp. 153-6.
414. Fletcher (ed.), *For King and Country*, pp. 199, 205-6.
415. Catalina García (ed.), *Diario de un patriota complutense*, pp. 82-3.
416. Boutflower, *Journal of an Army Surgeon*, p. 157.
417. Grattan, *Adventures*, II, pp. 93-4.
418. Donaldson, *Recollections*, pp. 173-7.
419. Boutflower, *Journal of an Army Surgeon*, pp. 159-61.
420. Grattan, *Adventures*, II, pp. 95-6.
421. M. Glover (ed.), *A Gentleman-Volunteer: the Letters of George Hennell from the Peninsular War* (London, 1979), p. 52.
422. Patterson, *Adventures*, pp. 248, 252.
423. Fée, *Souvenirs*, pp. 140-2.
424. *Cit.*, C. Viñes Millet, *Granada ante la invasión francesa* (Granada, 2004), pp. 84-5.
425. Fletcher (ed.), *For King and Country*, p. 223.
426. Thompson (ed.), *Ensign in the Peninsular War*, p. 201.
427. Anon., *Personal Narrative of a Private Soldier*, pp. 141-2.
428. Fletcher (ed.), *For King and Country*, p. 229.
429. Green, J., *The Vicissitudes of a Soldier's Life, or a Series of Occurrences from 1806 to 1815* (Louth, 1827), p.114.
430. Anon., *Personal Narrative of a Private Soldier*, pp. 144-5, 152-3.
431. Fletcher (ed.), *For King and Country*, p. 243. The officer whose death Mills describes was Ensign Wentworth Burgess.
432. Anon., *Personal Narrative of a Private Soldier*, pp. 159-61.
433. *Cit.* W. Hay, *Reminiscences under Wellington, 1808-15*, ed. S. Wood (London, 1901), pp. 76-7.
434. Boutflower, *Journal of an Army Surgeon*, pp. 164-6.
435. Donaldson, *Recollections*, pp. 178-9.
436. Whinyates (ed.), *Diary of Campaigns in the Peninsula*, p. 138.
437. Carnicero Torribio, *Historia razonada*, pp. 189-91.
438. Catalina García (ed.), *Diario de un patriota complutense*, p. 90.
439. Donaldson, *Recollections*, pp. 178-81.
440. Grattan, *Adventures*, II, pp. 132-5.
441. Green, *Vicissitudes of a Soldier's Life*, pp. 125-30.
442. Anon., *Personal Narrative of a Private Soldier*, pp. 164-5.
443. Fée, *Souvenirs*, pp. 175-7.
444. Liddell Hart (ed.), *Letters of Private Wheeler*, pp. 110-11.
445. *Cit.* Almuina Fernández (ed.), *Valladolid: diarios curiosos*, pp. 346-7.
446. I. Fletcher (ed.), *In the Service of the King: the Letters of William Thornton Keep at Home, Walcheren and the Peninsula, 1808-1814* (Staplehurst, 1997), pp. 143-4.
447. Kincaid, *Adventures in the Rifle Brigade*, p. 208.
448. Tomkinson (ed.), *Diary of a Cavalry Officer*, pp. 239-40.
449. Whinyates (ed.), *Diary of Campaigns in the Peninsula*, p. 182.
450. Costello, *Adventures of a Soldier*, pp. 220-1.
451. Liddell Hart (ed.), *Letters of Private Wheeler*, pp. 115-17.
452. Hibbert, *A Soldier of the Seventy-First*, pp. 86-7.
453. Stuart (ed.), *Soldiers' Glory*, p. 69.
454. Sherer, *Recollections of the Peninsula*, pp. 237-8.

455. Glover (ed.), *Letters of George Hennell*, p. 90.
456. Kincaid, *Adventures in the Rifle Brigade*, pp. 217-18.
457. Wood, *The Subaltern Officer*, pp. 183-4.
458. Bankes (ed.), *Autobiography of Sergeant William Lawrence*, pp. 134-5.
459. Green, *Vicissitudes of a Soldier's Life*, pp. 163-4.
460. Whinyates (ed.), *Diary of Campaigns in the Peninsula*, p. 187.
461. Monick (ed.), *Douglas's Tale*, pp. 73-4.
462. Hay, *Reminiscences under Wellington*, p. 113.
463. Tomkinson (ed.), *Diary of a Cavalry Officer*, pp. 250-1.
464. Buckley (ed.), *Napoleonic War Journal of Captain Thomas Henry Browne*, p. 214.
465. Miot de Melito, *Mémoires*, III, pp. 278-81.
466. Fée, *Souvenirs*, pp. 247-9.
467. Blaze, *Mémoires*, II, pp. 363-4.
468. Stuart (ed.), *Soldiers' Glory*, pp. 72-3.
469. Wood, *The Subaltern Officer*, pp. 185-8.
470. Kincaid, *Adventures in the Rifle Brigade*, p. 225.
471. *Cit.* Glover (ed.), *Letters of George Hennell*, pp. 95-6.
472. Cadell, *Narrative*, pp. 158-9.
473. Green, *Vicissitudes of a Soldier's Life*, p. 169.
474. Glover (ed.), *Letters of George Hennell*, pp. 133-4.
475. Ludovici (ed.), *On the Road with Wellington*, p. 385.
476. *Cit.* L. Woodford (ed.), *A Young Surgeon in Wellington's Army* (Old Woking, 1976), pp. 38-9.
477. Monick (ed.), *Douglas's Tale*, p. 77.
478. *Ibid.*, pp. 79-80.
479. Catley (ed.), *Journal of James Hale*, p. 102
480. *Cit.* Woodford (ed.), *A Young Surgeon*, p. 39.
481. Sherer, *Recollections of the Peninsula*, pp. 257-8.
482. Stuart (ed.), *Soldiers' Glory*, p. 83.
483. Monick, *Letters of Lieutenant James Hope*, pp. 167-8.
484. Fletcher (ed.), *In the Service of the King*, pp. 160-1.
485. Wood, *The Subaltern Officer*, pp. 201-3.
486. Cooper, *Rough Notes*, p. 91.
487. Buckley (ed.), *Napoleonic War Journal of Captain Thomas Henry Browne*, pp. 229-30.
488. Bankes (ed.), *Autobiography of Sergeant William Lawrence*, pp. 147-9.
489. Cooper, *Rough Notes*, pp. 93-5.
490. Liddell Hart (ed.), *Letters of Private Wheeler*, p. 122.
491. Wood, *The Subaltern Officer*, pp. 207-8.
492. E. Sabine (ed.), *Letters of Colonel Sir Augustus Frazer, KCB, commanding the Royal Horse Artillery in the Army under the Duke of Wellington in the Peninsula written during the Peninsular and Waterloo Campaigns* (London, 1859), pp. 233-4.
493. Catley (ed.), *Journal of James Hale*, pp. 103-4.
494. Monick (ed.), *Douglas's Tale*, pp. 82-3.
495. G. Gleig, *The Subaltern* (London, 1826), p. 56.
496. Sabine (ed.), *Letters of Colonel Sir Augustus Frazer*, pp. 243-4.
497. Liddell Hart (ed.), *Letters of Private Wheeler*, pp. 125-6.
498. Green, *Vicissitudes of a Soldier's Life*, pp. 187-90.
499. N. Bentley (ed.), *Selections from the Recollections of Captain Gronow* (London, 1977), p. 13.
500. Leach, *Rough Sketches*, pp. 341-2.
501. Kincaid, *Adventures in the Rifle Brigade*, pp. 261-2.
502. Monick, *Letters of James Hope*, p. 190.
503. *Cit.* Thompson (ed.), *Ensign in the Peninsular War*, p. 268.
504. *Ibid.*, pp. 187-8.
505. Sturgis (ed.), *Boy in the Peninsula War*, pp. 315-19.
506. Liddell Hart (ed.), *Letters of Private Wheeler*, pp. 136-8.
507. Donaldson, *Recollections*, pp. 214-15.
508. Wood, *The Subaltern Officer*, pp. 222-4.
509. Ludovici (ed.), *On the Road with Wellington*, pp. 395-6.

Bibliography

Alcaide Ibieca, A., *Historia de los dos sitios que pusieron a Zaragoza en los años de 1808 y 1809 las tropas de Napoleón* (Madrid, 1830).

Alcalá Galiano, A. (ed.), *Memorias de Don Antonio Alcalá Galiano* (Madrid, 1886).

Almuina Fernández, C. (ed.), *Valladolid: diarios curiosos, 1807-1841* (Valladolid, 1989).

Anon., *Memoirs of a Sergeant late in the Forty-Third Light Infantry Regiment previously to and during the Peninsular War* (London, 1835).

Anon., *The Personal Narrative of a Private Soldier who served in the Forty-Second Highlanders for Twelve Years during the Late War* (London, 1821).

Anon., *Témoignages sur les campagnes d'Espagne et de Portugal: extraits du 'Carnets de la Sabretache', années 1899, 1902, 1908, 1920* (Paris, 1999).

Babst., G. (ed.), *Souvenirs d'un canonnier de l'Armée d'Espagne, 1808-1814* (Paris, 1892).

Bankes, G.N. (ed.), *The Autobiography of Sergeant William Lawrence, a Hero of the Peninsular and Waterloo Campaigns* (London, 1886).

Barrès, M. (ed.), *Memoirs of a French Napoleonic Officer: Jean-Baptiste Barrès* (London, 1925).

Bentley, N. (ed.), *Selections from the Recollections of Captain Gronow* (London, 1977).

Berazaluce, A. (ed.), *Recuerdos de la vida de Don Pedro Agustín Girón* (Pamplona, 1978).

Bigarré, A., *Mémoires du Général Bigarré, aide-de-camp du Roi Joseph, 1775-1813* (Paris, 1903).

Blanco White, J. *Letters from Spain* (London, 1828).

Blayney, A., *Narrative of a Forced Journey through Spain and France as a Prisoner of War in the Years 1810 to 1814* (London, 1814).

Blaze, S., *Mémoires d'un apothecaire sur le guerre d'Espagne pendant les années 1808 à 1814* (Paris, 1828).

Bourachot, C. (ed.), *Souvenirs Militaires du Captaine Jean-Baptiste Lemonnier-Delafosse* (Paris, n.d.).

Boutflower, C., *The Journal of an Army Surgeon during the Peninsular War* (Manchester, 1912).

Brindle, R. (ed.), *With Napoleon's Guns: the Military Memoirs of an Officer of the First Empire* (London, 2005).

Buckley, R.N. (ed.), *The Napoleonic War Journal of Captain Thomas Henry Browne, 1807-1816* (London, 1987).

Bunbury, T., *Reminiscences of a Veteran, being Personal and Military Adventures in Portugal, Spain, France, Malta, New South Wales, Norfolk Island, New Zealand, the Andaman Islands and India* (London, 1861).

Cadell, C., *Narrative of the Campaigns of the Twenty-Eighth Regiment since their Return from Egypt in 1802* (London, 1835).

Carnicero Torribio, J.C., *Historia razonada de los principales sucesos de la gloriosa revolución de España* (Madrid, 1814).

Casamayor, F., *Diario de los sitios de Zaragoza, 1808-1809*, ed. H. Lafoz Rabaza (Zaragoza, 2000).

Casse, A. du (ed.), *Mémoires et correspondance politique et militaire du Roi Joseph* (Paris, 1854).

Cassells, S. (ed.), *Peninsular Portrait, 1811-1814: the Letters of William Bragge, Third (King's Own) Dragoons* (London, 1963).

Castaños, F.J. de, *Reales Ordenes de la Junta Suprema Central de Gobierno del Reino y representaciones de la Sevilla y del General Castaños acerca de su separación del mando del Ejército de Operaciones del Centro* (Seville, 1809).

Catalina García, J. (ed.), *Diario de un patriota complutense en la Guerra de la Independencia* (Alcalá de Henares, 1894).

Catley, P. (ed.), *The Journal of James Hale, late Sergeant in the Ninth Regiment of Foot* (Windsor, 1997).

Clermont-Tonnerre, G. de, *L'expedition d'Espagne, 1808-1810* (Paris, 1983).

Cooper, J.S., *Rough Notes of Seven Campaigns in Portugal, Spain, France and America during the Years 1809-10-11-12-13-14-15* (London, 1869).

Costello, E., *Adventures of a Soldier, or Memoirs of Edward Costello, KSF, formerly a Non-Commissioned Officer in the Rifle Brigade and Late Captain in the British Legion comprising Narratives of the Campaigns in the Peninsular War under the Duke of Wellington and the recent Civil Wars in Spain* (London, 1841).

Dacombe, M. and Rowe, B. (eds.), *The Adventures of Sergeant Benjamin Miller while serving in the Fourth Battalion of the Royal Regiment of Artillery, 1796-1815* (London, 1999).

Dellard, J., *Mémoires militaires du Général Baron Dellard* (Paris, n.d.).

D'Espinchal, H., *Souvenirs militaires, 1792-1814*, ed. F. Masson and E. Boyer (Paris, 1901).

Dobbs, J., *Recollections of an Old Fifty-Second Man*, ed. I. Fletcher (Staplehurst, 2000).

Donaldson, J., *Recollections of the Eventful Life of a Soldier* (Edinburgh, 1852).

Douglas, R. (ed.), *From Valmy to Waterloo: Extracts from the Diary of Captain Charles François, a Soldier of the Revolution and the Empire* (London, 1906).

Fée, A.L.A., *Souvenirs de la Guerre d'Espagne, dite de l'Independance, 1809-1813* (Paris, 1856).

Fernyhough, R., *Military Memoirs of Four Brothers (Natives of Staffordshire) engaged in the Service of their Country, as well in the New World and Africa as on the Continent of Europe* (London, 1829).

Fletcher, I. (ed.), *In the Service of the King: the Letters of William Thornton Keep at Home, Walcheren and the Peninsula, 1808-1814* (Staplehurst, 1997).

Fortescue, J. (ed.), *The Notebooks of Captain Coignet* (London, 1989).

Fouché, J., *Memoirs of Joseph Fouché, Duke of Otranto, Minister of the General Police of France* (London, 1892).

Gachot. E. (ed.), *Mémoires du Colonel Delagrave sur la campagne de Portugal, 1810-1811* (Paris, 1902).

García de la Cuesta, G., *Manifiesto que presenta a la Europa el Capitán General de los Reales Ejércitos, Don Gregorio García de la Cuesta sobre susoperaciones militares y políticas desde el mes de junio de 1808 hasta el 12 de agosto de 1809 en que dejó el mando del Ejército de Extremadura* (Valencia, 1811).

García de León y Pizarro, J., *Memorias de la Vida del Excmo. Sr. D. José García de León y Pizarro escritas por el mismo*, ed. A. Alonso Castrillo (Madrid, 1894).

Gille, L.F., *Les prisonniers de Cabrera: mémoires d'un conscript de 1808*, ed. P. Gille (Paris, 1892).

Gleig, G., *The Subaltern* (London, 1826).

Gleig, G., *The Light Dragoon* (London, 1855).

Glover, M. (ed.), *A Gentleman-Volunteer: the Letters of George Hennell from the Peninsular War* (London, 1979).

Gonneville, A. de, *Recollections of Colonel de Gonneville*, ed. C. Yonge (London, 1875).

Gotteri, N. (ed.), *La mission de Lagarde, policier de l'empereur, pendant la Guerre d'Espagne, 1809-1811* (Paris, 1991).

Grattan, W., *Adventures of the Connaught Rangers from 1808 to 1814* (London, 1847).

Green, J., *The Vicissitudes of a Soldier's Life, or a Series of Occurrences from 1806 to 1815* (Louth, 1827).

Grivel, J., *Mémoires du Vice-Amiral Baron Grivel*, ed. M.G. Lacour-Gayet (Paris, 1914).

Guimbaud, L. (ed.), *Mémoires du Général Hugo* (Paris, 1934).

Haley, A. (ed.), *The Soldier who Walked Away: Autobiography of Andrew Pearson, a Peninsular War Veteran* (Liverpool, n.d.).

Hall, B., *Corcubión*, ed. J. Alberich (Exeter, 1976).

Hall, F., *Recollections in Portugal and Spain during 1811 and 1812* (Cambridge, 2003).

Hamilton, A., *Hamilton's Campaign with Moore and Wellington during the Peninsular War* (Troy, New York, 1847).

Haro Malpensa, J. de (ed.), *Guerra de la Independencia: La Mancha, 1808 – Diarios, Memorias y Cartas* (Alcazar de San Juan, 2000).

Hawker, P., *Journal of a Regimental Officer during the Recent Campaigns in Portugal and Spain under Viscount Wellesley* (London, 1810).

Hay, W., *Reminiscences under Wellington, 1808-15*, ed. S. Wood (London, 1901).

Haythornthwaite, P. (ed.), *Life in Napoleon's Army: the Memoirs of Captain Elzéar Blaze* (London, 1995).

Haythornthwaite, P. (ed.), *The Autobiography of Sir Harry Smith, 1787-1819* (London, 1999).

Haytor, A. (ed.), *The Backbone: Diaries of a Military Family in the Napoleonic Wars* (Bishop Auckland, 1993).

Herr, R. (ed.), *Memorias del cura liberal Don Juan Antonio Posse con su discurso sobre la Constución de 1812* (Madrid, 1984).

Hibbert, C., *The Recollections of Rifleman Harris as told to Henry Curling* (London, 1970).

Hibbert, C. (ed.), *A Soldier of the Seventy-First: the Journal of a Soldier in the Peninsular War* (London, 1975).

Horward, D.D., *The French Campaign in Portugal, 1810-1811: an account by Jean-Jacques Pelet* (Minneapolis, 1973).

Hulot, J.L., *Souvenirs militaires du Baron Hulot, général d'artillerie, 1773-1843* (Paris, 1886).

Ideville, H. d' (ed.), *Memoirs of Colonel Bugeaud from his Private Correspondence and Original Documents* (London, 1884).

Infantado, Duque de, *Manifiesto de las operaciones del Ejército del Centro* (Seville, 1809).

Iscar-Peyra, F. (ed.), *Ecos de la francesada: las memorias de Zahonero y Alegría* (Salamanca, 1927).

Jackson, Lady (ed.), *The Diaries and Letters of Sir George Jackson, KCH, from the Peace of Amiens to the Battle of Talavera* (London, 1872).

Jacob, W., *Travels in the South of Spain in Letters Written A.D. 1809 and 1810* (London, 1811).

Jones, B.T. (ed.), *Military Memoirs of Charles Parquin* (London, 1987).

Junot, L., *Mémoires de Madame la Duchesse d'Abrantes, ou souvenirs historiques sur Napoléon, la Révolution, le Directoire, le Consulat, l'Empire et la Révolution* (Brussels 1837).

Kincaid, J., *Adventures in the Rifle Brigade in the Peninsula, France and the Netherlands from 1809 to 1815* (London, 1830).

Lagneau, L., *Journal d'un chirugien de la Grande Armée, 1803-1815*, ed. C. Bourachot (Paris, 2000).

Lavaux, F., *Mémoires de campagne, 1793-1814*, ed. C. Bourachot (Paris, 2004).

Leach, J., *Rough Sketches of the Life of an Old Soldier during a Service in the East Indies, at the Siege of Copenhagen in 1807, in the Peninsula and the South of France in the Campaigns from 1808 to 1814 with the Light Division, in the Netherlands in 1815, including the Battles of Quatre Bras and Waterloo, with a Slight Sketch of the Three Years passed by the Army of Occupation in France* (London, 1831).

Lecestre, L. (ed.), *Lettres inédites de Napoléon 1e, an VIII – 1815* (Paris, 1897).

Lejeune, *Memoirs of Baron Lejeune, aide-de-camp to Marshals Berthier, Davout and Oudinot*, ed. A. Bell (London, 1897).

Leslie, C., *Military Journal of Colonel Leslie, KH, of Balquhain, while serving with the Twenty-Ninth Regiment in the Peninsula and the Sixtieth Rifles in Canada, 1807-1832* (Aberdeen, 1887).

Liddell Hart, B.H. (ed.), *The Letters of Private Wheeler, 1809-1828* (London, 1951).

Lowry Cole, M. and Gwynn, S. (eds.), *Memoirs of Sir Lowry Cole* (London, 1934).

Ludovici, A. (ed.), *On the Road with Wellington: the Diary of a War Commissary in the Peninsular Campaigns* (New York, 1925).

MacCarthy, J., *Recollections of the Storming of the Castle of Badajoz by the Third Division under the Command of Lieut. Gen. Sir Thomas Picton, GCB, on the Sixth of April 1812* (London, 1836).

McGuffie, T. (ed.), *Peninsular Cavalry General, 1811-13: the Life and Correspondence of Robert Ballard Long* (London, 1951).

Mackinnon, H., *A Diary of the Campaign in Portugal and Spain containing Remarks on the Inhabitants, Customs, Trade and Cultivation of these Countries from the Year 1809 to 1812* (Bath, 1812).

Marbot, M. de, *The Memoirs of Baron Marbot, late Lieutenant-General in the French Army*, ed. A.J. Butler (London, 1892).

Miot de Melito, A., *Mémoires du Comte Miot de Melito, ancien ministre, ambassadeur, conseilleur d'état et membre de l'institut* (Paris, 1858).

Monick, S. (ed.), *The Iberian and Waterloo Campaigns: the Letters of Lieutenant James Hope, 92nd (Highland) Regiment, 1811-1815* (Heathfield, 2000).

Moore, J.C., *A Narrative of the Campaign of the British Army in Spain commanded by His Excellency, Sir John Moore* (London, 1809).

Morley, S., *Memoirs of a Sergeant of the Fifth Regiment of Foot containing an Account of his Service in Hanover, South America and the Peninsula* (London, 1842).

Muir, R. (ed.), *At Wellington's Right Hand: the Letters of Lieutenant-Colonel Sir Alexander Gordon, 1808-1815* (London, 2003).

Naylies, J.J. de, *Mémoires sur la guerre d'Espagne pendant les années 1808, 1809, 1810 et 1811* (Paris, 1817)

Neale, A., *Letters from Portugal and Spain comprising an Account of the Operations of the Armies under their Excellencies Sir Arthur Wellesley and Sir John Moore from the Landing of the Troops in Mondego Bay to the Battle of Corunna* (London, 1809).

Noble, P.M. le, *Mémoires sur les opérations militaires des français en Galice, Portugal et la vallée du Tage en 1809 sous le commandement du Maréchal Soult* (Paris, 1821).

North, J. (ed.), *In the Legions of Napoleon: the Memoirs of a Polish Officer in Spain and Russia, 1808-1823* (London, 1999).

Oman, C. (ed.), 'A prisoner of Albuera: the journal of Major William Brooke from 16 May to 28 September 1811', in C. Oman, *Studies in the Napoleonic Wars* (Oxford, 1929), pp. 175-206.

Ormsby, J., *An Account of the Operations of the British Army and of the State and Sentiments of the People of Portugal and Spain during the Campaigns of the Years 1808 and 1809* (London, 1809).

Page, J. (ed.), *Intelligence Officer in the Peninsula: Letters and Diaries of Major the Honourable Edward Charles Cocks, 1786-1812* (Tunbridge Wells, 1986).

Perich y Viader, A., 'Narració de los sis anys y quatre mesos que los francesos han estat en Catalunya, contant de los primers de febrer de 1808, fins al primers junys de 1814', ed. J. Pella y Forgas, *Boletín de la Real Academía de Buenas Letras de Barcelona*, no. 49, 490-6.

Porter, R.K., *Letters from Portugal and Spain written during the March of the British Troops under Sir John Moore* (London, 1809).

Presa González, F., Bak, G., Matyjaszczyk Grenda, A. and Monforte Dupret, R. (eds), *Soldados polacos en España durante la Guerra de la Independencia Española, 1808-1814* (Madrid, 2004).

Rocca, A. de, *Memoirs of the War of the French in Spain*, ed. P. Haythornthwaite (London, 1990).

Rousseau, I. (ed.), *The Peninsular Journal of Major General Sir Benjamin Urban, 1808-1817* (London, 1930).

Sabine, E. (ed.), *Letters of Colonel Sir Augustus Frazer, KCB, commanding the Royal Horse Artillery in the Army under the Duke of Wellington in the Peninsula written during the Peninsular and Waterloo Campaigns* (London, 1859).

Sarasa, J.M., *Vida y hechos militares del Mariscal del Campo, Don Juan Manuel Sarasa, narrados por el mismo*, ed. J. del Burgo (Pamplona, 1952).

Schepeler, A. von, *Histoire de la révolution d'Espagne et de Portugal ainsi que de la guerre qui en resulta* (Liège, 1829).

Semple, R., *A Second Journey in Spain in the Spring of 1809 from Lisbon through the Western Skirts of the Sierra Morena to Sevilla, Córdoba, Granada, Málaga and Gibraltar, and thence to Tetuan and Tangiers* (London, 1809).

Sherer, J., *Recollections of the Peninsula* (London, 1823).

Shore, H. (ed.), *An Engineer Officer under Wellington in the Peninsula: the Diary and Correspondence of Lieut. Rice Jones, RE, during 1808-09-10-11-12* (Cambridge, 1986).

Simmons, T. (ed.), *Memoirs of a Polish Lancer: the Pamietniki of Dezydery Chlapowski* (Chicago, 1992).

Spurrier, A. (ed.), 'Letters of a Peninsular War commanding officer: the letters of Lieutenant Colonel, later General, Sir Andrew Barnard, GCB', *Journal of the Society of Army Historical Research* (XLVII, Autumn 1969), no. 191, 131-48.

Stanhope, Earl of, *Notes of Conversations with the Duke of Wellington, 1831-1851* (London, 1889).

Stepney, J.C., *Leaves from the Diary of an Officer of the Guards* (London, 1854).

Stothert, W., *A Narrative of the Principal Events of the Campaigns of 1809, 1810 and 1811 in Spain and Portugal interspersed with Remarks on the Local Scenery and Manners* (London, 1812).

Stuart, B. (ed.), *Soldiers' Glory, being 'Rough Notes of an Old Soldier' by Major-General Sir George Bell* (London, 1956).

Sturgis, J. (ed.), *A Boy in the Peninsular War: the Services, Adventures and Experiences of Robert Blakeney, Subaltern in the Twenty-Eighth Regiment* (London, 1899).

Thompson, W. (ed.), *An Ensign in the Peninsular War: the Letters of John Aitchison* (London, 1981).

Tomkinson, J. (ed.), *The Diary of a Cavalry Officer in the Peninsular and Waterloo Campaigns* (London, 1894).

Vaughan, C.R., *Narrative of the Siege of Zaragoza* (London, 1809).

Verner, W. (ed.), *A British Rifleman: Journals and Correspondence during the Peninsular War and the Campaign of Waterloo* (London, 1899).

Villaba, L. de, *Zaragoza en su segundo sitio* (Palma de Mallorca, 1811).

Wardell, J. (ed.), *With the 'Thirty-Second' in the Peninsula and other Campaigns: a New Edition of 'The Life of a Soldier'* (London, 1904).

Warre, E. (ed.), *Letters from the Peninsula, 1808-1812 by Lieutenant General Sir William Warre* (London, 1909).

Weigall, R. (ed.), *Correspondence of Lord Burghersh, afterwards Eleventh Earl of Westmorland, 1808-1840* (London, 1912).

Whinyates, F. (ed.), *Diary of Campaigns in the Peninsula for the Years 1811, 12 and 13 by Captain William Swabey, an Officer of E Troop (present E Battery), Royal Horse Artillery* (London, 1895).

Whittingham, F. (ed.)., *A Memoir of the Services of Lieutenant-General Sir Samuel Ford Whittingham* (London, 1868).

Wood, G., *The Subaltern Officer: a Narrative* (London, 1826).

Woodford, L. (ed.), *A Young Surgeon in Wellington's Army* (Old Woking, 1976).

Wrottesley, G. (ed.), *The Life and Correspondence of Field Marshal Sir John Burgoyne* (London, 1873).

Wylly, H. (ed.), *A Cavalry Officer in the Corunna Campaign: the Journal of Captain Gordon of the Fifteenth Hussars* (London, 1913).

Index